AN AMERICAN ILIAD

AN AMERICAN ILIAD

THE STORY OF THE CIVIL WAR

❖

Charles P. Roland

THE UNIVERSITY PRESS OF KENTUCKY

AN AMERICAN ILIAD
The Story of the Civil War

Published 1991 by The University Press of Kentucky.
Scholarly publisher for the Commonwealth, serving Bellarmine College,
Berea College, Centre College of Kentucky, Eastern Kentucky University,
The Filson Club, Georgetown College, Kentucky Historical Society,
Kentucky State University, Morehead State University, Murray State
University, Northern Kentucky University, Transylvania University,
University of Kentucky, University of Louisville, and Western Kentucky
University.

Editorial and Sales Offices: Lexington, Kentucky 40508–4008

This book was set in Palatino by the College Composition Unit
in cooperation with Ruttle Shaw & Wetherill, Inc.
The editors were David Follmer and Tom Holton;
the production supervisor was Kathryn Porzio.
The cover was designed by John Hite.
R. R. Donnelley & Sons Company was printer and binder.

Library of Congress Cataloging-in-Publication Data

Roland, Charles Pierce, 1918–
      An American Iliad : the story of the Civil War / Charles P.
   Roland.
         p.   cm.
   Includes bibliographical references and index.
   ISBN 0-8131-1737-2
      1. United States—History—Civil War, 1861–1865.   I. Title.
E468.R76   1991b   90-38392
973.7—dc20

About the Author

❖

C harles P. Roland is an Alumni Professor, Emeritus, at the University of Kentucky. A native of Tennessee, he holds a B.A. degree from Vander-bilt University and a Ph.D. from Louisiana State University. He has served on the faculties of Louisiana State University, Tulane University, and the University of Kentucky. He is the author of numerous books and articles on the South and on the Civil War. These include a history of the Confederacy and a biography of Confederate General Albert Sidney Johnston.

Professor Roland's career in American military history has been unusual, if not unique. He fought as an infantry officer in Europe during World War II. He has served as assistant to the chief historian of the United States Army, as the Harold Keith Johnson Visiting Professor of Military History at the United States Army Military History Institute and Army War College, as the Visiting Profes-sor of Military History at the United States Military Academy, and as chairman of the Department of the Army Historical Advisory Committee.

Professor Roland has been president of the Louisiana Historical Association and the Southern Historical Association.

To the memory of Bell Irvin Wiley

Contents

—— ❖ ——

	PREFACE	XI
I	A PARTING OF THE WAYS	1
II	THE RESORT TO ARMS	25
III	MOBILIZATION AND EARLY CAMPAIGNS	39
IV	EMERGING GENERALS AND ESCALATING COMBAT	67
V	UNION GOVERNMENT, ADMINISTRATION, AND EMANCIPATION	88
VI	CONFEDERATE GOVERNMENT AND ADMINISTRATION	103
VII	THE STRATEGIC BALANCE	118
VIII	THE TURN OF THE TIDE OF BATTLE	135
IX	THE CONTEST FOR EUROPEAN FAVOR	159
X	MILITARY SUCCESS AND POLITICAL VICTORY	172
XI	THE RESURGENT NORTH	197
XII	THE BELEAGUERED SOUTH	215
XIII	THE UNION TRIUMPHANT	238
XIV	REFLECTIONS ON MEN AND MEASURES	256
	SOURCES	264
	INDEX	272

PHOTOGRAPHS

Jefferson Davis   28
Abraham Lincoln   31
Ulysses S. Grant   60
David G. Farragut   65
Robert E. Lee   71
Confederate Dead Near the Shell-Marked Dunker Church   82
Dead of the First Minnesota Infantry   143
Raphael Semmes   168
Frederick Douglass   203
Ruins of Richmond   252

MAPS

Slave and Free Territories According to the Compromise of 1850   7
Principal Military Campaigns of the Civil War   50
The First Battle of Bull Run, July 21, 1861   53
The Battle of Shiloh, April 6–7, 1862   62
Jackson's Shenandoah Valley Campaign, May–June 1862   71
The Seven Days Battles, June 25–July 1, 1862   73
The Campaign of Second Bull Run, August 1862   77
The Battle of Antietam, September 17, 1862   82
Chancellorsville, May 2–6, 1863   127
The Vicksburg Campaign, Dec. 1862–May 1863   132
Gettysburg, July 1–3, 1863   141
Murfreesboro to Chickamauga, 1863   150
The Battles for Chattanooga, November 24–25, 1863   157
The Wilderness and Spotsylvania, May 5–12, 1864   178
Petersburg, 1864   184
The Campaign for Atlanta, May–July 1864   187

Preface

❖

Almost three thousand years ago an epic poem, the *Iliad*, by the legendary Greek poet Homer, told the story of the great war between the people of Greece and those of the city of Troy in Asia Minor. It was a story of heroism and sacrifice marred by cruelty and horror. The victory of the Greeks forever changed the course of Western history, and thereby of world history. More than a century ago the American people engaged in a great sectional conflict that reenacted all of the heroism and sacrifice, all of the cruelty and horror, of the Greco-Trojan war. The Union victory in the American Civil War forever changed the course of American history, and thereby of world history.

An American Iliad is a concise but comprehensive history, in narrative form, of the Civil War. The book reflects a synthesis of the major writings on the war, reinforced by my own research and focused through my interpretation. It is not primarily an analytical study of trends, causes and effects, or lessons learned. Instead, as the subtitle indicates, it tells the story of the war. The main emphasis is on the military action, that element which distinguishes war from all other human activities. Accounts of the major political, economic, diplomatic, social, and cultural developments of the epoch are adequately explained, but they are woven into the central narrative in a manner designed to show their role in the war effort itself.

Blended into the narrative are brief biographical and character sketches of the leading civilian and military figures of the war, with stress on the contrast between President Abraham Lincoln of the Union and President Jefferson Davis of the Confederacy, and between such generals as Grant and Sherman of the Union and Lee and Jackson of the Confederacy. The book holds that both political leaders and both sets of generals demonstrated remarkable determination and resourcefulness.

But Lincoln ultimately emerged as a superior war leader. This came about through his tenacity of purpose in holding to the goal of preserving the Union while remaining flexible in accepting the emancipation of the slaves as a war aim and in dealing with countless other controversial issues; through his wisdom in appointing a general in chief to provide unity of military command and concert of military action; and through his masterful use of the English language to communicate his goals and methods to the people. Also, despite the unsurpassed boldness and skill displayed by the Confederate generals, the Union authorities eventually were able to develop out of their greater numbers and material resources, and out of the superior organizational and managerial qualities of the northern society and economy, a more comprehensive and more effectual military strategy.

This study takes particular cognizance of the human and the fortuitous elements in war. It shows both the valor and selflessness and the cowardice and fecklessness of the soldiers. It shows both the brilliance and audacity and the stupidity and indecisiveness of the generals and their subordinate officers. It records the play of chance, uncertainty, and unmanageability in war, those ever-present factors to which the renowned German war philosopher Clausewitz paid special attention. It reveals the civilian side of war, the courage and steadfastness and the weariness, grief, and defeatism of the people at home; how the social and cultural resources of the North and South, as well as their political, economic, and military resources, were mobilized to support their war efforts. It describes the jubilation, struggles, and suffering of the freed blacks in the vicissitudes of early emancipation. It portrays the ugly backwash of war in the wake of invasion, destruction, and disruption in the South.

Finally, the book brings into sharp relief the overarching results of the war. These were the preservation of the Union, the eradication of American chattel slavery, and the conception of the nation as it exists today, a nation dedicated, though haltingly and imperfectly, to the ideals of liberty, equality, and democratic government expressed by Lincoln in his most famous utterance, the Gettysburg Address. The story of the Civil War is the epic story of the American people. It is their Iliad.

I am indebted to many persons for their assistance in the preparation of the present book. I especially wish to thank V. Jacque Voegeli and Carol Reardon for their painstaking reading of the manuscript and their many suggestions for improving it; Paul A. Willis, director of libraries at the University of Kentucky, and the entire library staff, for providing me with the space and services for accomplishing the research and writing; the McGraw-Hill College Division editors and the following outside readers who made numerous corrections and helpful recommendations: Merton L. Dillon, Ohio State University; William E. Gienapp, Harvard University; Daniel E. Sutherland, University of Arkansas–Fayetteville; and Hubert H. Wubben, Oregon State University; Thomas H. Appelton, Jr., for his invaluable help in correcting the page proofs; and Robert C. Hodges for his excellent work in preparing the index. I am forever grateful to my wife, Allie Lee Roland, for her constructive criticism of the manuscript, her patience and unwavering confidence in me, and her constant support of my endeavors.

Charles P. Roland

AN AMERICAN ILIAD

I

A Parting of the Ways

❖

scene of intense drama was opening in the United States Senate. The date was January 29, 1850; the venerable Whig Senator Henry Clay of Kentucky was on his feet; the chamber and galleries were hushed with anticipation. Renowned as a master of the art of political compromise, Clay had lately come back to the Senate out of retirement in the hope of achieving a settlement that would allay the long-festering passions between the North and the South and keep the country at peace. Thin and pallid from age and illness, but moved by an earnest spirit of patriotism and a keen sense of showmanship, flourishing in his hand a set of resolutions that he trusted would accomplish his object, he spoke.

The sectional impasse had grown out of political, economic, cultural, and social differences that reached back to the very origin of the nation and beyond. Disagreements over interpretations of the Constitution and over the legality of a bank of the United States, federal expenditures for internal improvements, and a protective tariff had created threatening stress lines between the North and the South. But the most persistent and most ominous of the stress lines was that over slavery, an institution that shaped and contributed to all of the sources of tension and added a burning moral and emotional element of its own.

The first great political compromise on this issue, following the adoption of the Constitution—the Missouri Compromise—occurred in 1820 after fierce debate in Congress. Besides admitting Missouri as a slave state and Maine as a free state to keep the balance, the compromise divided the immense unorganized and largely unsettled region of the Louisiana Purchase along the 36° 30′ line, with slavery prohibited in federal territories north of the line—areas in which governments preliminary to statehood were established but were still under direct federal authority—and allowed in federal territories south of the line.

The forensic clash over the compromise kindled deep fears in certain of the nation's statesmen. From his retirement at Monticello, former President Thomas Jefferson of Virginia wrote, "This momentous question, like a fire bell in the night, awakened and filled me with terror. I considered it at once the knell

1

of the Union"; and he explained, "A geographical line, coinciding with a marked principle, moral and political, once held up to the angry passions of men, will never be obliterated; and every new irritation will mark it deeper and deeper." He went so far as to hint at the possibility that the South would some day be obliged to resort to separation and war in self-defense.

Jefferson was not alone in his apocalyptic vision. With a radically different end in view, Secretary of State and future President John Quincy Adams of Massachusetts confided to his diary that he believed it would be noble to die for the cause of the emancipation of the slaves. Weighing the cost of civil war and servile insurrection against the prospect of a nation free of slavery, he wrote, "So glorious would be its final issue, that, as God shall judge me, I dare not say that it is not to be desired."

During the three decades following the adoption of the Missouri Compromise, the North and the South drew ever farther apart. The South became the "Cotton Kingdom," producing most of the world's supply of the snowy fiber as well as a great variety of other crops and of animals. The bulk of the commercial crops was grown on plantations that were worked by some 3.2 million black slaves representing a capital investment of about $1.5 billion. The large planters were the economic, social, and political elite of the region. Southern cities, small by northern standards, were the home of a class of affluent, slave-owning merchants, bankers, and professionals who were allied socially and politically with the large planters. Also populating the cities were numerous shopkeepers, skilled craftsmen, and common laborers. But the overwhelming majority of the southern whites were independent farmers and herdsmen.

Although three-fourths of the southern white population owned no slaves, the whites generally supported slavery. This attitude sprang, in part, out of ambition to become planters and slave owners. But it grew mainly from a pervasive conviction of white racial superiority accompanied by the fear that emancipation would bring violence and social degradation. Jacksonian political democracy was as influential in most southern states as it was elsewhere in establishing universal white adult male suffrage. Recent scholarship strongly challenges the once-popular view that the masses of southern whites were controlled by the wealthy slave-owning planters. But all were agreed in their approval of black slavery and white domination. Ironically, most of the white population equated democracy for whites with slavery for blacks.

The North expanded as a versatile and dynamic community featuring manufacturing, commerce, banking, farming, free labor, and the rapid growth of cities. The dominant economic and social class comprised merchants, manufacturers, bankers, and professionals. Less than half the population were farmers; the remainder were shopkeepers, tradesmen, mechanics, and factory laborers.

Slavery had been abolished in those northern states where it had once been practiced, and, for a variety of reasons, the northern population generally opposed the institution. First, the opposition came from a moral conviction that slavery was inherently wrong, a belief that stretched back to the very earliest colonial days, when it was especially firm among the Quaker community. By the mid-nineteenth century the conviction had spread to the great majority of the northern people. There was also a significant economic dimension in the northern antislavery sentiment, the fear of competition from slave labor and the awareness that work itself was degraded by slavery. Finally and paradoxically, a racial factor contributed to the northern attitude. Antipathy against slavery often went hand in hand with a racism that was similar in essence, if not in pervasiveness or intensity, to the southern racial feeling. Many northerners objected to the presence of slavery in their midst, in part, because they objected to the presence of blacks there.

Throughout the 1830s and 1840s the North witnessed a ferment of social reform in its religious and intellectual life. This included movements devoted to temperance, feminism, and pacifism, to improvements in the treatment of insane asylum inmates, and to the general uplift of society through education and a religious emphasis on ameliorating the circumstances of the earthly life. But the most revolutionary of these movements was the crusade against slavery, with William Lloyd Garrison of Boston its most uncompromising spokesman. The crusade grew out of the moral and cultural sensibilities and the social and economic interests of the region.

The South rejected most of the reforms, stigmatizing them as isms, and turned increasingly conservative in its thinking. The region particularly repudiated the abolitionist movement and began to look upon slavery as a "positive good" instead of a "necessary evil." Orthodox religion, adhering to a biblical justification of slavery, became the "mighty fortress" of the southern culture. Ominously, the two largest American churches, the Baptist and Methodist, split into northern and southern branches; the Presbyterian church divided into two schools of sharply differing theological and social beliefs.

Slavery was the most emotional and visible issue in the church separations, but the split actually symbolized a widening breach in the entire mythology or outlook of the two regions. The Reverend James H. Thornwell, foremost theologian and intellectual of the Old South, contrasted the two sectional points of view in terms of a social, cultural, and spiritual Armageddon: "The parties in this conflict are not merely abolitionists and slaveholders. They are atheists, socialists, communists, red republican jacobins on the one side, and the friends of order

and regulated freedom on the other. In one word, the world is the battleground, Christianity and atheism the combatants; and the progress
of humanity at stake."

In 1850, as Clay addressed the Senate, the spirit of sectional controversy was dangerously inflamed over the question of the spread of
slavery into the Mexican cession, a vast, politically unorganized area
recently acquired in the war with Mexico (1846–1848), and which ultimately would become all or parts of six states of the American Southwest. Members of the Senate were divided into four conflicting attitudes
on the question. The extreme northern attitude was that expressed in
the Wilmot Proviso, a measure proposed but defeated during the war
that would have prohibited slavery anywhere in lands annexed as a result of the hostilities. Whig Senator William H. Seward of New York
was the most prominent advocate of this school of thought. The extreme southern attitude insisted on the principle enunciated by Democratic Senator John C. Calhoun of South Carolina, chief author of the
doctrine of state rights, which demanded federal protection of slave
owners and their property in all territories.

Two groups held the intervening ground in the controversy. The
believers in what soon would be known as "popular sovereignty," led
by Democratic Senator Stephen A. Douglas of Illinois, chairman of the
Senate Committee on Territories, called for noninterference by Congress in order that the settlers in a territory might decide for themselves
the legality of slavery locally. Finally, there were those who wished to
extend the line of the Missouri Compromise to the Pacific Ocean. Democratic Senator Jefferson Davis of Mississippi was the leading supporter
of this proposition.

No American doubted the gravity of the moment. The previous
year Calhoun had drafted a manifesto urging the slave states to unite
politically in their opposition to the antislavery forces that were rising in
the North. At his behest, a convention of delegates from the slave states
was being formed to meet during the summer in Nashville. Without an
acceptable compromise on the issue of slavery in the Mexican territory,
there was the implied threat that the Nashville Convention would
adopt the ultimate measure of state rights as expounded by Calhoun,
that of secession.

In his proposals Clay offered something to all sides in the controversy. He called for the admission of California as a free state because
the population there, swollen by the 1849 gold rush, was large enough
for immediate statehood and had already approved a constitution excluding slavery; the organization of the remainder of the Mexican cession into the territories of Utah and New Mexico without "any restric-
tion or condition on the subject of slavery" (in other words, according
to the principle of popular sovereignty); the settlement of a Texas–New
Mexico boundary dispute in favor of New Mexico, but with compensa-

tion to Texas by federal redemption of the bonds that constituted the state's public debt; the abolition of interstate slave trading, but not slavery itself, within the District of Columbia; and a strong fugitive slave law that would compel state and local authorities to assist federal marshals in the arrest and return of runaways anywhere in the nation.

Clay drew fully upon his great powers of persuasion in this historic valedictory. Near the end of his address he grasped a fragment said to be from the coffin of George Washington, and holding it aloft like a relic of the True Cross, he exhorted his colleagues to take the necessary measures for preserving the republic that Washington had done so much to create.

On February 5 and 6 Clay again occupied the Senate floor to deliver a prolonged emotional appeal in support of the proposals he had submitted earlier. He pleaded earnestly for a spirit of charity and compromise on all sides. He expressed the sentiments of many Americans in arguing that slavery could not thrive in the Southwest because the soil and climate there were not suited for plantation agriculture. He accurately predicted that any attempt at disunion would bring on a bloody civil war, and he closed with a ringing adjuration that the senators "solemnly pause...at the edge of the precipice, before the fearful and disastrous leap is taken into the yawning abyss below."

The most memorable political rhetoric and philosophy of the great debate were expressed by Clay and the two other elder statesmen of the American forum—Calhoun and Whig Senator Daniel Webster of Massachusetts. Of these, the next to command the floor was Calhoun. An ardent nationalist in his early career, but now for more than two decades the foremost champion of southern sectionalism, he was a man of formidable intellect and an intractable sense of purpose. He had long sought to reconcile southern and national interests by blending the regional political, economic, and racial creeds into a class theory of society that protected the South and its institution of slavery, and established the region as a national stabilizing force between capital and labor. Because of his class theory of society, he has been called by the historian Richard Hofstadter "the Marx of the master class."

Ravaged by tuberculosis, too sick to deliver his own address, Calhoun sat swathed in flannels, his eyes sunken but luminous, while a colleague, Senator James M. Mason of Virginia, read his prepared speech. In it Calhoun reviewed the history of the sectional antagonism and attributed it to the growing imbalance of strength between the majority North and the minority South, an imbalance which he laid to the unfair actions of the federal government. Like Clay, he forecast disunion unless, he argued, proper measures were adopted to redress the balance.

What Calhoun had in mind but did not say explicitly was the establishment of a "concurrent majority," which in his writings he described as a political device "to give the weaker section, in some form or another, a negative on the action of the government," specifically, he suggested, through the creation of a dual presidency, each executive to represent a section of the country and each to possess the veto power over acts of Congress. His address concluded that if the North was unwilling to cooperate in restoring the sectional equilibrium, "...let the States we both represent agree to separate and part in peace"; and, somberly, if the North was unwilling for the South to depart in peace, "...we shall know what to do, when you reduce the question to submission or resistance."

Three days later, on March 7, Webster took the floor. Like his peers in the historic congressional triumvirate, he too was almost at the end of his course, already showing signs of the illness that would soon take his life. Portly and dark of visage, powerful in phrase and magisterial in gesture, he was perhaps unmatched in America as an orator. Ironically, his career had crossed Calhoun's as Webster had moved from an early New England sectionalism into the position of supreme spokesman of federal authority over state rights. Just as Calhoun ultimately came to identify southern political, economic, and social well-being with sectionalism, Webster came to identify New England political, economic, and social well-being with nationalism.

Although Webster abominated slavery and had long opposed any expansion of it, he now adopted, out of fear for the Union, a remarkably conciliatory tone. Speaking, he said, "not as a Massachusetts man, nor as a Northern man, but as an American," he asked his northern colleagues to forbear in their efforts to enact the Wilmot Proviso. He too believed slavery had reached its geographic limits and declared, "I would not take pains uselessly to re-enact the will of God." But he warned his southern colleagues that peaceable disunion would be impossible, and he urged the entire body to accept the compromise proposals. This address is remembered as Webster's greatest.

Congress enacted the proposals, but not immediately or directly as a result of the implorings of Clay and Webster. Ultimately, the following autumn, through the astute management of Senator Douglas, the Senate approved the measures, and, with the support of the Democratic Speaker of the House of Representatives, Howell Cobb of Georgia, the lower chamber followed suit. In both instances the victory occurred through a coalition of congressmen from both Whig and Democratic parties and from both sections of the nation.

Nor were the legislators' motives entirely patriotic. There is reason to believe the congressional will was influenced by the holders of Texas bonds, which until redeemed by federal funds seemed worthless. Even the fates intervened in favor of the compromise. During the spring and summer two of its most powerful opponents died. One of these was President Zachary Taylor, a slave-owning but nationalistic southerner

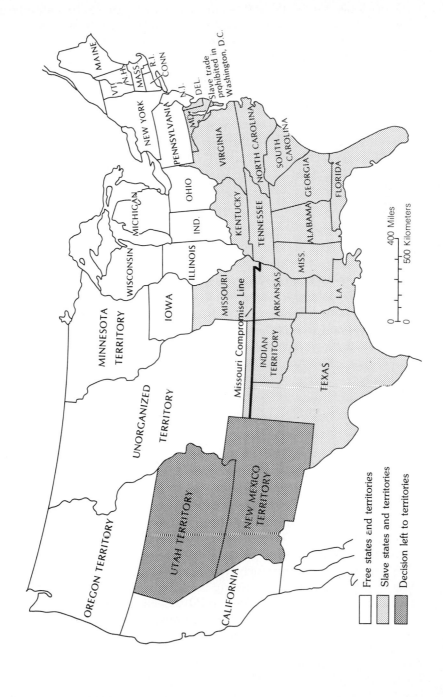

SLAVE AND FREE TERRITORIES ACCORDING TO THE COMPROMISE OF 1850.

who believed the question of slavery in the Mexican cession was a false issue and looked upon the entire controversy as representing a political maneuver. The other person to die was Calhoun, whose death preceded Taylor's and whose last words were reported to have been a cry of despair: "The South, the poor South."

With the passage of the Compromise of 1850 the nation breathed a sigh of relief over what seemed at the moment to be the end of the slavery dispute. President Millard Fillmore, Taylor's successor and a supporter of the compromise, called it a "final and irrevocable settlement" of the issue. The Nashville Convention failed to ignite the secessionist movement that such southern "fire-eaters" as Robert Barnwell Rhett of South Carolina hoped for. The southern states expressly approved the compromise in specially elected state conventions, but they warned grimly that a breakdown of the agreement would result in secession.

The presidential election of 1852 also seemed to put the nation's stamp of approval on the compromise. Although both major parties endorsed it, the Whigs with General Winfield Scott of Virginia as their candidate endorsed it only halfheartedly; their platform merely "acquiesced" to it. The Democrats firmly subscribed to the compromise, and by nominating Franklin Pierce of New Hampshire, a so-called doughface candidate (a northern term of derision for a northern man with southern ties and sympathies), they gave their party a strong southern flavor. The third participant in the contest was the Free Soil party, a group dedicated to prohibiting the further spread of slavery. Their platform explicitly denounced the compromise and condemned any expansion of slavery as a "sin against God and a crime against man." With the estrangement of many Whigs from their party, the Democrats were victorious.

But an ominous undercurrent of dissent flowed beneath the acceptance of the compromise. The preeminent congressional spokesmen for this mood were Senators William H. Seward and Jefferson Davis. Seward denounced political compromise in any form as being "inherently vicious and wrong," and he specifically attacked the Compromise of 1850 as a violation of the spirit of the Constitution. Then he added a statement that would one day return to haunt him, saying that even if the Constitution could be so construed as to sanction slavery, there was a "higher law" through which the practice must be banned from the western territories. Davis, in urging the extension of the Missouri Compromise line, argued that slavery could indeed flourish in the Mexican cession, and he condemned the Compromise of 1850 as representing a victory of a northern "aggressive majority" over the minority South. The North, he said, was following the path to division and war.

Countless northerners, particularly the New Englanders, never accepted the compromise in their hearts. The abolitionists condemned it openly. Webster chided the intransigence of his own people, saying,

"Massachusetts has conquered everybody's prejudices but her own. The question now is whether she will conquer her own prejudices." He branded as treason any violation of the agreement, and went so far as to say that if the northern states should willfully refuse to comply with it, and Congress fail to supply an adequate remedy, the southern states would "no longer be bound to observe the compact": apparently an oblique justification of secession itself. Long the idol of his region, he now became a target of scorn for many of its spokesmen, the "Ichabod" of John Greenleaf Whittier's verse:

> So Fallen! So lost! the light withdrawn
>   Which once he wore!
> The glory from his gray hairs gone
>   Forevermore!
>
> .   .   .   .
>
> Then, pay the reverence of old days
>   To his dead fame;
> Walk backward, with averted gaze,
>   And hide the shame!

Almost at once the "final and irrevocable settlement" began to crumble. Its most emotion-charged provision, the fugitive slave law, carried it directly home to many northerners. Whereas the question of slavery in the Mexican cession involved an area that to most Americans seemed as remote as Siberia, the enforcement of the fugitive slave law involved the seizure of runaways and alleged runaways in the streets of the North. A cry of outrage arose and mobs formed in city after city to prevent the return of the escapees. The most celebrated case of such action was that of the fugitive Anthony Burns in Boston (1854), where a multitude of aroused citizens attacked his guards, killing one of them, and looked on in fury as he was placed aboard a ship bound for Virginia. Such occurrences increased the heat of sectional hostility.

The novel *Uncle Tom's Cabin* by Harriet Beecher Stowe, published in 1852, helped feed the flame. Until its appearance, slavery was something of an abstract evil to most northerners, comparable perhaps to that of polygamy in faraway Utah. The fictional episode of the young slave woman Eliza with her child escaping from her pursuers in midwinter by leaping from one Ohio River ice floe to another, or that of the saintly Uncle Tom being beaten to death by order of the brutal Simon Legree, presented a flesh-and-blood portrait of slavery that gave an intimate, human, revolting dimension to the institution. As a serial, a bestselling book, and a stage play, the novel's message became ingrained in the national consciousness and conscience: in the North as an accurate description of an abhorrent institution; in the South as a gross libel of the regional character. President Abraham Lincoln is said later to have greeted the author as "the little lady who made this big war."

Another symptom of the fragility of sectional compromise could be seen in the political turmoil of the times. Calhoun, in his last speech to the Senate, had said that the national political parties, Democratic and Whig, were the only remaining cords binding North and South together, and that if these cords should break, the nation itself would divide. One of these cords, the Whig party, now broke. This came about as the result of a complex set of ethnocultural circumstances which, partly because of preoccupation with the slavery issue, neither of the major parties adequately addressed, but which were more immediately destructive to the Whigs. One of the most significant of these circumstances was the arrival beginning in the late 1840s of millions of European immigrants, the largest group being the Catholic Irish. A majority of the immigrants who were politically active became Democrats.

The appearance of great numbers of Roman Catholics within the previously largely Protestant population stirred deep fears of a threat to republican institutions and created a marked anti-immigrant and virulently anti-Catholic sentiment. As early as 1845 these feelings crystallized politically in the formation of the Native American party, whose members were called Know-Nothings because they practiced secrecy regarding their beliefs. Closely related to the anti-immigrant attitude was a strong temperance or prohibitionist movement that sought to achieve its goal through political action. The new party gained strength rapidly in response to the rising tide of immigration.

The party drew members from both sections of the nation and from both major parties, but the deepest inroads occurred in the northern wing of the Whig party because most of the newcomers settled in the North. Although the Know-Nothings did not put up a presidential candidate in 1852, within two years they would show remarkable strength in both state and congressional elections throughout the North.

Meanwhile, sectionalism began to challenge anti-Catholicism and other immigrant-related issues as a perceived threat to republican institutions. Many northerners at this time came to believe in the prevalence of a great Slave Power conspiracy to dominate the government, spread slavery throughout the country, destroy the northern system of free labor and open opportunity, and replace it with a closed, stagnant, and aristocratic mode of life. Although there is no evidence of such a conspiracy beyond the existence of an active southern economic and political interest group, the belief was not new. It now received a potent boost in the form of an act of Congress that opened again the debate over slavery in federal territories, thus rekindling the incendiary controversy that was supposed to have been resolved by the historic agreements, the Missouri Compromise and the Compromise of 1850.

The renewed controversy involved the remaining unorganized portion of the Louisiana Purchase, an area stretching from the western edges of Missouri and Iowa to the crest of the Rocky Mountains. Believed earlier to be unsuited to white habitation, a "Great American Desert," it had been overpassed in the trek of settlers to Oregon and California. Lying north of the Missouri Compromise line, the area was closed to slavery.

Southern leaders, alarmed by the sectional imbalance created by the admission of California and the probable coming admission of other free states, sought vigorously to correct it by increasing the number of slave states. One means of doing this was to annex additional lands that were considered fit for plantation agriculture. Some southerners therefore supported diplomatic efforts and armed invasions for the purpose of acquiring Cuba or parts of Central America. Far more menacing to national harmony, southern leaders also looked for ways to extend slavery into the proscribed part of the Louisiana Purchase.

In 1854 they found an opportunity to accomplish their purpose when Senator Douglas of Illinois, as chairman of the Committee on Territories, entertained a bill to organize the area into the Nebraska Territory, primarily in order to promote the construction of a railroad along a northern route to the Pacific. Only with southern support could he pass the bill through the Senate; only by repealing the Missouri Compromise line and making other concessions could he obtain southern support. Reluctantly, he added the repeal to his bill along with a provision to establish two new territories—Kansas and Nebraska—instead of one. This was interpreted by southerners as a trade-off, the southernmost territory, Kansas, to become a slave state and Nebraska a free state. Endorsed by a majority of the southern congressmen, the bill received the votes of enough northern Democrats to pass. Urged by Secretary of War Jefferson Davis, President Pierce signed it into law.

Douglas anticipated that the Kansas-Nebraska Act would "raise a hell of a storm." He underestimated. It provoked the formation of a new, potentially powerful, northern political party, the Republican party, whose central aim was to prevent the further spread of slavery. The principal elements in the party at first were "Anti Nebraska" Whigs, "Anti-Nebraska" Democrats, and former Free Soilers. A group of anti-Nebraska congressmen promptly issued an address, drafted mainly by Free Soil Senator Salmon P. Chase of Ohio, which expressed in ringing phrases the emotions of all who opposed the act. It was, he said, "a gross violation of a sacred pledge," "a criminal betrayal of precious rights," part of an "atrocious plot" to convert all the federal territories into a region of slavery and despotism.

The Republicans alone did not immediately have the strength to win in the northern states. Recent research indicates that at first the Know-Nothings were stronger. In the 1854 congressional elections the voters split into a variety of factions, including the Democratic, Whig, Native American, Republican, Union, and People's parties. But under whatever name, most northern voters firmly opposed the Kansas-Nebraska Act, and they were strong enough to elect a majority of anti-Nebraskans to the national House of Representatives.

The Whig party was the major immediate victim of the massive shifts occurring in the voting patterns in both the North and South. With large numbers of northern Whigs defecting to the Republicans and large numbers of southern Whigs defecting to the Democrats, and with many Whigs both northern and southern defecting to the Know-Nothings, the Whig party was at the point of extinction. Unforeseen at the moment, the Native American party also was destined soon to disappear after serving in the North as an important conduit from the other parties into the Republican party. The sectional issue of slavery in the western territories was about to eclipse nativism, anti-Catholicism, and temperance in the appeal to northern voters; the Republicans, as the chief proprietors of the sectional issue, were about to emerge as the main opponents of the Democrats in the North, and hence in the nation.

The situation in the Kansas Territory enhanced the Republican prospects. Douglas's doctrine of popular sovereignty was being tested there as non-slave-owning farmers began to pour in from the midwestern states and a few slave owners with their chattels arrived from Missouri and elsewhere. In the contest for local political control, illegal voters from outside the territory arrived on election days to support both sides, but the vast majority were proslavery "border ruffians" from nearby Missouri, many of them armed. Proslavery and antislavery groups elsewhere recruited settlers and provided them with financial support and other supplies. One of the more noteworthy of the antislavery groups, the New England Emigrant Aid Company, was alleged to have sent quantities of "Beecher's Bibles," rifles in boxes marked "Bibles" and named after the famed New York preacher Henry Ward Beecher, brother of the author of *Uncle Tom's Cabin*.

Kansas was in social and political disarray. Proslavery voters, a majority of them fraudulent, elected a proslavery territorial legislature, which quickly legalized the institution in Kansas. Antislavery settlers responded by electing delegates who assembled in Topeka and adopted a constitution outlawing slavery. The antislavery voters then elected a governor and legislature and petitioned Congress for statehood as a free state. President Pierce denounced the free-state movement as being illegal and threw his support behind the proslavery territorial legislature.

Inevitably, violence broke out between the rival groups. In the spring of 1855 a band of several hundred proslavery men, acting as a posse comitatus, seized and sacked the antislavery stronghold of Law-

rence, but apparently wihout killing any residents. Retaliation soon followed. When John Brown, a settler from Ohio and a fanatical abolitionist, learned of the assault on Lawrence, he and a small band including
four of his sons took vengeance by killing five proslavery settlers along
Pottawatomie Creek. A civil war seemed imminent.

"Bleeding Kansas" became a cause célèbre in the national press, especially after the occurrence in May 1856 of a violent affair on the floor
of the United States Senate involving the territory. Massachusetts Republican Senator Charles Sumner, in a vehement antislavery speech on
the Kansas issue, referred to Senator Andrew P. Butler of South Carolina as a Don Quixote who had chosen as his mistress "the harlot, slavery." South Carolina Congressman Preston Brooks, a relative of Senator
Butler, interpreting the remark as an insult to his kinsman, promptly
avenged it by attacking Sumner with a heavy walking cane and beating
him unconscious at his desk. Brooks became an instant hero in the
South, received new canes bearing inscriptions urging that he put them
to similar use, and was unanimously reelected when he resigned from
Congress. Sumner took three years to travel and recover his health.
Meanwhile, Massachusetts left his Senate seat vacant as a silent testi-
monial to the presumed debasing effects of slavery.

The presidential election of 1856 reflected the swift rise of the Republican party. The party candidate was John C. Frémont, a flamboyant
former military officer known as "the Pathfinder" because of his earlier
activities in western explorations. The marvelously catchy party slogan
said "Free Soil, Free Labor, Free Men, Frémont"; the platform denounced slavery along with polygamy as being a relic of barbarism.
Also prominent in the party newspapers and speeches was another
kind of Republican slogan: the appeal to ethnic sensibilities, which said
the western territories were to be "white man's country"; that they
were to be reserved "for free, white men." Freedom and racism were
the opposite yet complementary poles of Republican attraction.

The Republicans failed to capture the presidency in 1856. They
could count only on northern votes against the Democrats, and these
had to be shared with the residual Whigs and Know-Nothings, both of
whose conventions nominated former President Fillmore. Know-
Nothing strength was on the wane, especially after conservatives in the
party blocked an effort to repudiate the Kansas-Nebraska Act. Yet
Fillmore attracted enough votes away from Frémont to cost him a plu-
rality in a number of northern states.

The Democrats were again successful in their strategy of nominating a northerner who was friendly to the South, this time James
Buchanan of Pennsylvania. Southern Whigs and Know-Nothings cast a
substantial popular vote, but Buchanan was victorious in every slave
state except Maryland, which went to Fillmore, plus enough northern
states to win an electoral majority. Significantly, he was a minority vic-

tor in the popular vote of the nation as a whole (45 percent), and he lost heavily in the popular vote of the North. The Republicans could look with high hopes to the presidential election of 1860. Buchanan's election was a fleeting southern triumph; its effect was to widen the breach between the sections.

Buchanan was scarcely in the White House when the United States Supreme Court rendered a decision that further widened the breach. The Dred Scott case involved a slave who before the repeal of the Missouri Compromise line had been taken by his owner, an army officer, into the free state of Illinois and later into the Wisconsin Territory, which lay in that part of the Louisiana Purchase where slavery was prohibited. Scott was then brought back to the slave state of Missouri, where he subsequently sued for his freedom on the argument that he had become free as a result of residence in a free state and a free federal territory. The state courts rejected this argument, and eventually the case reached the Supreme Court on appeal.

Hoping to settle the slavery issue by judicial fiat, and encouraged by President-elect Buchanan to do so, the Court in March 1857, by a seven-to-two majority, denied Scott his freedom on the grounds that a temporary sojourn in a free state or territory did not bestow freedom. Chief Justice Roger Taney's ruling went much further to say that neither slaves nor free blacks were United States citizens under the protection of the Constitution. More unsettling at the time, Taney ruled, with the assent of five other justices, that the Missouri Compromise line was unconstitutional because the act of Congress establishing the line violated the due process clause by depriving slave owners of their property in slaves. According to this reasoning, Congress had no constitutional authority to ban slavery anywhere in federal territories. Significantly, the decision, by extension, prohibited territorial legislatures, because they were still under the direct supervision of Congress, from banning slavery.

That portion of the decision applying to the territories repudiated the fundamental tenet of the Republican party and aroused all citizens, regardless of party, who opposed the spread of slavery. Taney and four other members of the majority were from slave states, and the ruling was fiercely denounced in the North as a partisan, proslavery dictum. A rapidly rising Illinois political figure, Abraham Lincoln, predicted the Court would next rule that even a state could not outlaw slavery within its own borders. On the other hand, most southerners hailed the decision as a victory of law and justice over abolitionist fanaticism and sectional politics. In the end, the ruling had exactly the opposite effect from what its supporters had hoped. It turned out to be another step on the road to secession and war.

The situation in Kansas moved in the same direction. It would remain unresolved through the administrations of six territorial governors. Embracing the Dred Scott decision, President Buchanan used his influence in an effort to gain the admission of Kansas as a slave state, though clearly most of the inhabitants there opposed slavery.

In 1857 a convention of proslavery delegates met in the town of Lecompton and drafted a constitution that through devious wording allowed slavery regardless of whether it was approved by the voters. Although the constitution was ultimately rejected by a large majority, Buchanan urged Congress to approve it. The lawmakers refused to do so. He then supported a compromise measure, the English bill, that provided for another Kansas popular vote on the Lecompton constitution and offered the territory a generous grant of federal land in return for approval. The voters refused the bait and again rejected the constitution.

Kansas would not become a state until 1861, after many southern members had withdrawn from Congress. Then the territory would be admitted as a free state. In the mind of antislavery advocates, the entire Kansas imbroglio provided further evidence of the existence of an immense Slave Power conspiracy.

Against the backdrop of furious controversy over the Dred Scott decision and dissension over the status of Kansas came the most famous political debates of American history. The renowned Democratic Senator Douglas of Illinois was up for reelection. His opponent was Abraham Lincoln.

Lincoln was born into a Kentucky farm family and taken as a youth to Indiana and as a young man to Illinois, which became his permanent home. Reared with little formal schooling but with much practical experience in farming and performing odd jobs, he had largely educated himself and had risen to become one of his state's outstanding lawyers and a political figure of moderate attainments. He was exceptionally tall (six feet, four inches) and angular; his features were homely but craggily strong. He had a reputation for wit and wisdom, and for an Aesopian ability to blend the two in homespun fables. His closest friends were Kentuckians and ex-Kentuckians who, like his own family, now lived in Illinois; his wife, the former Mary Todd, was from a prosperous, slave-owning family of Lexington in the heart of the Kentucky bluegrass; his political model was Henry Clay.

Lincoln was imbued with the spirit of frontier democracy and nationalism. Though never a church member, he was deeply influenced by religion, and especially by his own reading of the Bible. These were the sources of a conviction in him that slavery was both a sin and a political and social curse. He had served two terms as a Whig in the Illinois state legislature and one term in the United States House of Representatives where he is best remembered for his opposition to the nation's participation in the Mexican War, which he believed was being waged for the purpose of gaining additional slave lands. Having moved early into the newly founded Republican party, he now challenged Douglas to a series of debates on the outstanding issues of the day, particularly that of slavery in the federal territories. Douglas accepted, and throughout the late summer and fall of 1858 the two men covered the state, speaking repeatedly before large and enthusiastic audiences. The entire nation, as well as the state of Illinois, listened.

Douglas had the advantage of superior experience and prestige. He was the "Little Giant" of Illinois politics. Also, he was the chief spokesman for the "moderate" position on the main issue; he held to the belief in popular sovereignty, notwithstanding that the Dred Scott decision was generally interpreted to have killed this option by rendering unconstitutional any laws prohibiting slavery in federal territories. He indicted Lincoln with intending to tamper with slavery in the South, for promoting a war between the sections, and for advocating political and social equality of the races, a proposition that was contrary to the laws of Illinois as well as the feelings of most of the citizens. Under Lincoln's program, said Douglas, the state would be overrun with freed blacks from Missouri and elsewhere.

Lincoln had a moderate position of his own to place before the voters. He was not an abolitionist, nor, by his own words, was he a believer in political or social equality for the blacks. Pressed by his opponent, he said he as much as any other man wished to see the white race remain dominant in the American society. He would leave slavery untouched where it already was legal. But he unalterably opposed the further spread of the institution and on an earlier occasion had uttered the memorable words: "'A house divided against itself cannot stand.' I believe this government cannot endure, permanently half slave and half free." He offered his supporters the hope that restricting slavery to the area it then occupied would place it on the path to "ultimate extinction, in God's good time."

Perhaps the most historic episode in the series of encounters occurred at the town of Freeport. There Lincoln asked Douglas a question that was designed to place him in a dilemma. "Can the people of a United States Territory in any lawful way...exclude slavery from its limits prior to the formation of a State Constitution?" If Douglas answered yes, he would be repudiating the Dred Scott decision and would alienate many voters in Illinois and most citizens of the South. If he answered no, he would alienate many other voters in Illinois and most citizens elsewhere in the North. He was too agile to be trapped by the question, which actually had already been asked and answered on less memorable occasions. He replied that because slavery could exist only with local laws to support and protect it, the people of a federal territory could exclude it, if a majority so desired, by enacting no laws at all concerning it. His "Freeport Doctrine" satisfied his Illinois supporters; he won reelection to the United States Senate. But Lincoln's arguments helped make him president of the United States two years later.

Efforts by some southerners in the late 1850s to reopen the African slave trade aggravated the sectional friction. William L. Yancey of Alabama, one of the most influential of the proslavery spokesmen, argued that without a fresh supply of slaves at reduced prices the Kansas-Nebraska Act and Dred Scott decision were hollow victories for the South. A southern commercial convention held in Vicksburg, Mississippi, voted overwhelmingly in favor of a resolution for the repeal of the federal law prohibiting the importation of slaves. A prominent editor, J. D. B. De Bow of New Orleans, became president of an organization that was devoted to the repeal of the statute. In the end nothing came of these moves, and they probably did not represent the wishes of a majority of southerners, but they served to confirm in the northern mind the fear that southern slave owners were determined to spread slavery throughout the territories.

The heat of the sectional controversy rose steadily throughout the decade. Beginning in 1854 with the violent episode involved in the return of the runaway Anthony Burns and the passage of the Kansas-Nebraska Act, many northern states passed new and more stringent personal liberty laws designed to nullify the fugitive slave law of the Compromise of 1850. The supreme court of Wisconsin declared the congressional law unconstitutional, whereupon the United States Supreme Court in 1859 overruled the Wisconsin tribunal. The nation witnessed the spectacle of the state-rights South appealing to federal authority in behalf of its "peculiar institution," while the nationalistic North appealed to state rights to attack it.

Modern scholarship reveals that because of the slowness, costliness, and uncertainty of retrieving runaways through the operation of the fugitive slave law, only a handful of slave owners made the attempt. The efforts of northerners to abort the law inflamed the sectional animosity: in northern minds as a token of righteous wrath against a monstrous evil, in southern minds as a symbol of the North's duplicity in refusing to live up to the sacred commitment of the Great Compromise.

Sectional denunciation passed all restraint. Every aspect of southern society felt the sting of the antislavery attack. Southern politics was described as an exercise in oligarchy and conspiracy, southern religion a blasphemy, southern education a mockery, southern family life a debauchery, southern character a morass of human depravity. Ralph Waldo Emerson of Massachusetts, perhaps the most renowned American writer and lecturer of his day, said: "I do not see how a barbarous community and a civilized community can constitute a state. I think that we must get rid of slavery or we must get rid of freedom. Life has no parity of value in the free state and in the slave state. In one it is

adorned with education, with skillful labor, with arts, with long pro-
spective interests, with sacred family ties, with honor and justice. In the
other, life is a fever; man is an animal, given to pleasure, frivolous,
irritable...." Senator William H. Seward made an address in which he
spoke of an "irrepressible conflict" between the forces of freedom and
slavery.

Southern spokesmen replied in kind. They scored the northern
population with being steeped in atheism, fanaticism, and hypocrisy;
with subjecting their "wage slaves" to privations and indignities beneath the condition of chattels; with practicing avarice and guile worthy
of a nation of Shylocks. George Fitzhugh, a Virginia author who wrote
a book arguing that all laborers everywhere ought to be made slaves,
expressed the prevailing mood of his region when he stigmatized the
free society of the North as a "monstrous abortion." The rhetoric of
malice set the mood for the violence to come.

An earnest of this violence occurred in October 1859. Grim John
Brown of recent Kansas memory reappeared on the national scene. Determined to strike a blow for liberty, he led a small band of dedicated
followers in an effort to kindle a general insurrection by seizing the
United States arsenal at Harpers Ferry, Virginia, and issuing arms and a
call for action to the slaves. Not a slave responded, and Brown and his
men were quickly overcome and taken by a detail of United States Ma-
rines under the command of Army Colonel Robert E. Lee. Brown was
promptly convicted and hanged for treason against the state of Virginia,
but not before he accurately predicted that the slavery issue would one
day purge the land with blood.

The South greeted the Harpers Ferry raid with alarm and rage. Although the vast majority of the northern population condemned
Brown's actions, southern fears and indignation spread as many prominent northerners applauded his motives if not his methods. Emerson
said Brown was a "new saint awaiting his martyrdom, and who, if he
shall suffer, will make the gallows glorious like the cross." Emerson's
friend, the poet and essayist Henry David Thoreau, called Brown "an
angel of light." Less discreet spokesmen approved Brown's methods
as well as his aims. Wendell Phillips of Massachusetts, a passionate
abolitionist, announced: "[Virginia] is a pirate ship, and John Brown
sails the sea a Lord High Admiral of the Almighty with his commission
to sink every pirate he meets on God's ocean of the nineteenth century." In death Brown became infinitely greater than in life; his body
"amouldering in the grave" would help to inspire the most fervent crusade of the nation's history.

Perhaps no other event weighed so heavily as Harpers Ferry in pre-
cipitating secession. In southern eyes Brown's act of incitement to servile bloodshed and the sympathy he received in the North were a
shocking foretaste of Seward's "irrepressible conflict." The captured

pikes which Brown had intended for arming the slaves were distributed
to the southern state governments by a dedicated fire-eater, Edmund
Ruffin of Virginia. Displayed on the walls of the state capitols, they
served as warnings of the ghastly end awaiting southerners if the abolitionists should have their way.

The emotions generated by Harpers Ferry were sharpened by the
political and economic tensions and contests of the times. Repeatedly
the United States House of Representatives enacted measures that appealed primarily to northern constituents, measures that included a tariff increase, a "homestead" bill to provide farms without charge to settlers on federal lands, subsidies for the construction of a northern
transcontinental railroad, and land grants for the support of agricultural
colleges. Repeatedly these measures died through southern opposition
in the Senate or vetoes at the hands of the "doughface" president. Finally, beginning in December 1859 the northern and southern congressmen, frequently bearing arms in the chamber, snarled and raged at one
another for two months over the election of a Speaker of the House.

In the thickening atmosphere of sectional discord the momentous
presidential election of 1860 took place. The Republican convention,
meeting in Chicago, astutely passed over the party's more extreme
spokesmen and selected a moderate as its contender. Seward's earlier
radical oratory hurt his cause, as did his outspoken sympathy for immigrants and Catholicism. The abolitionist Salmon P. Chase of Ohio
was also considered too dangerous on the slavery issue. Edward Bates
of Missouri lost out because his Know-Nothing associations were
thought to be a liability among immigrant voters, especially the substantial German-American element. It was Lincoln, with his pragmatic
outlook and carefully worded speeches, especially one delivered in February 1860 at the Cooper Union in New York, whose name now came to
the fore, and on the third ballot he received the nomination. Hannibal
Hamlin of Maine, a rather obscure former Democrat, was the nominee
for vice president.

Aware that their party possessed no strength at all in the South, the
Republicans adopted a platform designed to garner every possible vote
in the states of the North and West. Although it recognized the right of
any state to manage its "own domestic institutions"—in other words, to
practice slavery—it denied the authority of Congress, a territorial legislature, or any individual (presumably the president or the Supreme
Court) "to give legal existence to slavery in any territory of the United
States." The platform also called for those economic measures that were
attractive to northern and western constituents, but which in the past
had been systematically defeated by southerners.

The moment of truth had come for the Democratic party. Since 1853
it had held the presidency through a tenuous sectional alliance which
was no longer feasible. The Democratic convention met in April in

Charleston, South Carolina, a hotbed of southern emotions. Most of the southern delegates were intractably committed to a platform proposed by the Alabama fire-eater William L. Yancey, a platform that demanded federal protection of slavery in the territories.

The nonsouthern delegates, comprising a majority of the whole, supported Stephen A. Douglas for president and a platform that on the slavery issue pledged only abidance by the decisions of the Supreme Court, a vaguely worded endorsement of the Dred Scott decision. In many ways Douglas was an excellent party choice. He had a wide following; he was one of the most able and influential of all the nation's politicians; he held strong ties with the South. But his Freeport Doctrine, which suggested a legal way of evading the effect of the Dred Scott decision, and his opposition to the admission of Kansas on the Lecompton constitution made him unacceptable to the southern delegates.

The convention majority rejected the Yancey platform in favor of the Douglas platform, whereupon the headstrong Alabamian promptly led most of the delegates from the seven states of the lower South, plus Arkansas, out of the meeting. Lacking the two-thirds majority required by party rules, the convention adjourned to reassemble two months later in Baltimore. Efforts there to mend the split were futile. The remaining delegates then nominated Douglas for president along with a southern moderate, Herschel V. Johnson of Georgia, for vice president. The southern bolters, some of whom had first met in Richmond, then assembled in Baltimore, adopted the Yancey platform, and nominated Vice President John C. Breckinridge of Kentucky for president and Senator Joseph Lane of Oregon for vice president. Democratic unity had finally succumbed to sectional rancor; the last of the cords that, in Calhoun's view, held the nation together had now snapped.

Many ex-Whigs of the upper South joined with a remnant of the Know-Nothings to form a new party, which they named the Constitutional Union party. Meeting in Baltimore, they wrote a platform that avoided the most burning issue of the day, the question of slavery in the federal territories, and simply endorsed an adherence to the Constitution, the Union, and the enforcement of the laws. Like a paean to God, flag, and mother, the platform expressed noble sentiments of universal appeal, but it had no chance at the polls. The Constitutional Unionists nominated the conservative Senator John Bell of Tennessee for president and the orator and former Senator Edward Everett of Massachusetts for vice president.

In the North and West the presidential contest was chiefly between Lincoln and Douglas. In the South it was chiefly between Breckinridge and Bell. Although the Republicans attempted to mute their antislavery statements, their sectional rhetoric was unmistakable; southern anti-Republican rhetoric was unrestrained. Each side pictured the other as a menace to the national destiny. In the North and West Douglas was accused of being a doughface and Breckinridge a disunionist; in the South Lincoln was portrayed as a "black" abolitionist whose election would visit havoc upon the region.

Republican leaders did little to assuage the southern fears about Lincoln. Charles Sumner declared that the Constitution offered no protection to slavery. Seward erroneously asserted that Lincoln had avowed himself an advocate of the "higher law" and the "irrepressible conflict." Lincoln remained astutely silent, refusing to attempt a refutation of the false statements being made about him, because, he said, "...bad men...North and South" would distort anything he might say.

The Republican appeal to northern and western voters won the election for Lincoln. Although he was a minority victor in the popular voting—39.9 percent of the total—he gained a comfortable majority of the electoral votes, 180 against 123 for the three other candidates together. He was able to do this by winning a majority in most of the populous states of the North and West (54 percent of the popular vote of the area as a whole), thereby gaining virtually all of their electoral votes, with none in the South. The Republican victory in the North represented to a large extent a coalescence of former Frémont Republican elements with the former Fillmore Know-Nothing elements, plus substantial support from the Protestant immigrant groups, especially the German-American Protestants, and a disproportionate number of young native-born voters.

Breckinridge carried all the slave states except Virginia, Kentucky, and Tennessee, which voted for Bell; but he was a minority victor in the South just as Lincoln was in the nation. Breckinridge won the states of the lower South plus North Carolina, Maryland, and Delaware by capturing pluralities; he received fewer votes there than Bell and Douglas combined. Douglas won heavy minority votes in the North and West and demonstrated surprising strength—better than 12 percent of the total—in the South, where he campaigned courageously and vigorously. But he carried only Missouri plus three of New Jersey's seven electoral votes.

The election itself provided no drastic mandate on the issues of slavery or secession. It actually repudiated both the northern abolitionists and the southern fire-eaters. But the outcome kindled deep apprehension in the South because it placed in executive power a man and a party who represented principally the aspirations of the North and West, and who were outspoken enemies of the South's most sacrosanct economic and social institution.

The changing editorials of the heretofore unionist southern newspapers clearly indicated the effects of Lincoln's triumph on the southern mind. The *New Orleans Bee* offers an excellent example. It supported

Douglas during the campaign, and shortly before the election issued a remarkable expression of unionism, saying: "... whether the Presidential election terminates in the choice of Bell, or Douglas, or Lincoln or Breckinridge; whether the next Congress is Black Republican or Conservative; whether Seward counsels irrepressible conflict, or [Robert Barnwell] Rhett strives to muster an armed force to prevent Lincoln's inauguration; whether John Brown is canonized in New England, or solemn sanhedrins of Secessionists devote the Union to the infernal Gods. The real Union men have not the slightest idea of breaking up the Confederacy [the editor's archaic name for the United States of America]."

But immediately after the election the *Bee* wrote: "The result proved astounding. It showed the tremendous power and popularity of Black Republicanism.... What could be alleged against such convincing and irrefragable proof of Northern unsoundness? With what shadow of reason could Southern men be advised to submit and await the possible events of the future when abolitionism had swept every Northern Commonwealth, and had even displayed unexpected and growing power in some of the slaveholding States themselves?"

The fire-eaters moved quickly to take advantage of the inflamed southern attitude. Robert Barnwell Rhett had failed at the Nashville Convention ten years before in his effort to persuade the southern states to secede in a group. He and other southern extremists were now ready to resort to what he called the "desperate alternative" of secession by separate state action. The South Carolina legislature, still in session since the choosing of presidential electors, at once voted a call for a state convention to decide the momentous issue. The governors of other states of the lower South said their states would follow the lead of South Carolina.

By now the secessionist sentiment in the Palmetto State was almost unanimous. The sentiment in the state convention—meeting in Charleston, a city decked with state flags and secessionist bunting, a city that breathed the very air of secession—was unanimous. On December 20 the 169 delegates voted without a single dissent to sever the state from the Union. News of the action turned Charleston wild. Businesses closed, church bells pealed, artillery roared, militia companies paraded, old men ran shouting into the streets. One may imagine that John C. Calhoun from his shaded sepulcher in the St. Philip's churchyard looked on with a bittersweet satisfaction.

The withdrawal of South Carolina and the breakdown, to be discussed later, of efforts in the United States Congress to establish a new sectional compromise set off a powder-train of secession across the lower South. Mississippi acted on January 9, 1861. Except for South Carolina, it was perhaps the fiercest state in its sectional emotions; a modern scholar has called it a "storm center of secession." The day after Mississippi departed, Florida did so. The next day Alabama followed.

Secession was not quite so quick or predictable in the three other states of the lower South. Although the vast majority of their citizens believed in the right of secession as an ultimate act of self-preservation, and most were of the opinion that the present circumstances justified the step, many questioned the wisdom of immediate separation and especially immediate separation by a single state. Some advocated waiting to see what the Lincoln administration would actually do about slavery; others advocated withdrawing only by group action of the slave states. These opponents of immediate secession by individual state action called themselves "cooperationists." The advocates of immediate secession by individual state action contemptuously called them "submissionists."

The action of Georgia was critical. The decision of the legislature to call a convention came only after serious debate. Former Congressman Alexander Stephens, a revered political leader in the state, opposed the action, saying, "This government of our fathers, with all its defects, comes nearer the objects of all good government than any other on the face of the earth." Unionists Herschel V. Johnson and Benjamin H. Hill were of like mind with Stephens.

But the most powerful Georgia voices had a different ring. United States Senator Robert Toombs and Secretary of the Treasury Howell Cobb, both of whom had previously been unionists, now despaired of justice for the South under a Republican administration. Toombs spoke in Homeric terms, imploring the legislators to "...throw the bloody spear into this den of incendiaries!...Withdraw yourselves from such a confederacy....Make another war of independence...fight its battles over again; reconquer liberty and independence." And again, "Secession by the 4th of March next should be thundered from the ballot box by the unanimous vote of Georgia." Cobb wrote, "Each hour [after Lincoln's inauguration] that Georgia...remains a member of the Union will be an hour of degradation, to be followed by certain and speedy ruin." Aroused by such appeals, the legislature authorized a convention and the die was cast. On January 19, after overriding a strong cooperationist effort to delay the action, the convention voted 218 to 89 for immediate secession.

Secession in Louisiana was perhaps more doubtful than in Georgia. The state's sugar planters depended for their prosperity on a protective tariff, which was likely to disappear in a southern republic dominated by the cotton interests. The New Orleans merchants had powerful financial ties with northern bankers. Forty percent of the city's population were European immigrants, many of whom had little if any sentimental commitment to southern independence. Nevertheless, the secessionists controlled the legislature and voted a call for a convention.

Following the collapse of the congressional compromise efforts, the recently unionist *New Orleans Bee* said: "The North and South are heterogeneous and are better apart....We are doomed if we proclaim not our political independence."

A majority of the delegates elected to the Louisiana state convention were pledged to immediate secession. All moves by cooperationists to delay hasty action were defeated, and on January 26 the convention chose secession by a vote of 113 to 17. At least some of the secessionist delegates were aware of the radical nature of their action. In opposing a vain resolution that the convention's decision be submitted to a popular referendum, one of them said, "We are in times of revolution. We were sent here to act, and matters of form must sink into insignificance."

Texas was the only state of the lower South in which the government itself was divided on the issue of secession. A majority of the members of the state legislature favored secession and authorized the election of delegates to a convention. This action alone virtually assured secession, and on February 1 the convention voted for it 166 to 8. But Governor Sam Houston, hero of the Texas revolution and an unflinching Jacksonian nationalist, opposed secession and ultimately was removed from office for refusing to take an oath of allegiance to the Confederate States of America. Texas was also the only state of the original seceders in which the convention's decision was submitted to a popular vote. Coming in the wake of the convention's action, the referendum confirmed the ordinance of secession by a three-to-one majority.

By early February 1861 the seven states of the lower South were out of the Union, swept out by the doctrine of state rights and a great surge of regional fear and emotion. The critical question now: What would be the response of the rest of the nation?

II

The Resort to Arms

❖

The nation's response to secession was at first extremely uncertain. President Buchanan, who would remain in office until Lincoln's inauguration on March 4, 1861, was by nature a conciliatory man. He also had strong sympathies for the South, and the makeup and attitude of his cabinet reflected this persuasion. Southerners held a number of positions in the cabinet: Howell Cobb as secretary of the treasury, Jacob Thompson of Mississippi as secretary of the interior, and John Floyd of Virginia as secretary of war. Outside the cabinet, such prominent southern political leaders as Senator John Slidell of Louisiana and Senator Jefferson Davis of Mississippi were among Buchanan's closest confidants. Unquestionably, these men influenced his behavior.

The president's own political thinking was murky. A literal reading of his 1860 annual message to Congress indicates incompatible views on the relationship between the nation and its constituent parts. He declared secession to be illegal, but that the federal government had no right to coerce a state to remain in the Union. Seward parodied the address as saying it meant that "no state has the right to secede unless it wishes to" and that "it is the President's duty to enforce the laws, unless somebody opposes him."

Buchanan can legitimately be faulted for indecision and a weakness of will. Certainly his behavior in the national crisis is unimpressive when compared with that of an Andrew Jackson or an Abraham Lincoln. But Buchanan feared, possibly rightly, that a coercive move or threat at that point by the federal government would scatter rather than extinguish the sparks of secession.

He gave his annual address with its opinions on secession in early December 1860 before any state had actually withdrawn. His forbearance did not, of course, prevent secession by the seven states of the lower South. Possibly his views encouraged the states to withdraw; but, more likely, they would have done so in any event, and his tolerance may very well have helped prevent secession at that time by the eight remaining slave states. Indirectly it may have helped prevent secession altogether by some of them. With at least a trace of reason he could believe he might by caution be able to contain the secessionist fire. In the last weeks of his term, after secession was a fait accompli and the southern members gone from his cabinet, he strengthened his hand by appointing staunch unionists in their stead.

Reinforcing Buchanan's insistence on caution was his hope for the adoption of yet another great political compromise that would prevent or limit secession. Both houses of Congress appointed committees to study the feasibility of such a move, and the likeliest of the proposals was submitted to the Senate committee on December 18 by Senator John J. Crittenden of Kentucky, who now held the seat once occupied by Henry Clay and who saw himself to be Clay's heir as the architect of political accommodation. The most important article in the Crittenden Compromise called for amending the Constitution so as to restore the Missouri Compromise line and extend it to the border of California, with slavery to be prohibited in federal territories north of the line but recognized and protected south of it.

Led by Senator Jefferson Davis, southerners on the committee expressed a willingness to accept the compromise if the Republicans would do so. This the Republicans refused to do, in part on the advice of President-elect Lincoln, who said privately he was ready to support a guarantee of slavery in the states where it already existed, but advised, "...entertain no proposition for a compromise in regard to the extension of slavery.... The instant you do, they have us under again; all our labor is lost, and sooner or later must be done over.... The tug has to come and better now than later." Thus the most promising of the compromise efforts failed. That in the long run it would have averted or curbed secession is problematical, but at the moment the rejection of the Crittenden Compromise played a significant part in causing such states as Georgia, Louisiana, and Texas to move for immediate withdrawal.

Compromise efforts attempted outside of the federal government also failed. The most notable of these was made by the Washington Peace Convention, which met in February in the national capital on the invitation of the Virginia state legislature. With ex-President John Tyler in the chair, delegates from twenty-one states—none from the seceded states—drew up a set of proposals quite similar to the Crittenden Compromise, but containing certain articles designed to overcome Republican objections, especially a criticism by Lincoln that the Crittenden proposal would encourage southerners to seek the annexation of new slave lands south of the border. The Washington Convention would provide a sectional veto—a form of Calhoun's concurrent majority—in the creation of new federal territories by requiring majority votes of both the free-state and slave-state members of Congress. These proposals were unacceptable to both the Republican leaders and the delegates from the slave states of the upper South; hence, they also came to naught.

While the Buchanan administration agonized over the progress of secession, the seceded states moved decisively with their own plans.

On February 4, delegates from six states met—joined later by those from Texas—in the senate chamber of the Alabama statehouse and began the work of forming a new southern nation. Among the group of fifty were many of the leading politicians, slave owners, and lawyers of the South. With Howell Cobb in the chair, they hurriedly drafted and adopted a provisional constitution for an interim government for a new political entity, which they named the Confederate States of America. The assembly itself became the congress of the provisional government, the college of electors for a provisional president and vice president, and the constitutional convention for the drafting of a permanent instrument of government. The provisional constitution provided that within one year a permanent government be elected and the permanent constitution be ratified by the states.

The most urgent task before the assembly was the election of a provisional president and vice president. Swiftly and, in light of subsequent Confederate history, with remarkably little political or personal jousting, the assembly unanimously chose Jefferson Davis as the provisional president and Alexander Stephens as provisional vice president. In selecting these men the delegates rejected the southern fire-eaters, one of the most prominent of whom, Rhett, was a member of the assembly, and another, Yancey, was conspicuously present in the city. Fire-eaters were too volatile and dangerous; the situation called for moderates who could bring stability out of revolution, for a Washington and a John Adams instead of a Patrick Henry and a Samuel Adams.

Davis was a southern moderate who embraced secession only after his own state had withdrawn from the Union. He, like Lincoln, had been born into a Kentucky farm family. But Davis was reared in Mississippi where his family migrated when he was an infant, and where the Davises rose to become affluent cotton planters and slave owners. Although he had previously been moved by a powerful sense of American patriotism, he was imbued with the spirit of the plantation aristocracy and the state-rights political doctrines of Thomas Jefferson and John C. Calhoun.

Davis was educated in the classical tradition at Transylvania University in Lexington, Kentucky, and in the martial tradition at the United States Military Academy, class of 1828. After the tragic death in 1835 of his bride of only six weeks—Zachary Taylor's daughter—Davis resigned his commission and spent ten years in semi-seclusion as a planter and a student of history and government. Then he met and married a vivacious young woman, Varina Howell, of Natchez. Marriage energized him. Almost immediately he entered politics and was elected to the United States House of Representatives. Resigning his position there to rejoin the Army in the Mexican War, he commanded a Mississippi volunteer regiment with such valor and skill that he emerged from the conflict the most illustrious military hero in the state's history.

In 1847 Davis went to the United States Senate where he became perhaps the most articulate champion of the southern cause. Four years later he left that body to enter a contest for the governorship of his state. But he lost because of his adverse views toward the Compromise of 1850. Rescued from political eclipse when his friend President Franklin Pierce appointed him secretary of war, Davis rendered outstanding service in this position. In 1857 he was again elected to the United States Senate. He resigned from the Senate upon the secession of Mississippi and accepted command of the state's military forces.

Davis was tall, erect, and slender, his bearing unmistakably military; though his features were too sharp to be called truly handsome, they were distinguished; southerners considered them genteel. When on February 15 he arrived in Montgomery to take up his duties as provisional president of the Confederacy, he was introduced to an admiring crowd by the eloquent Yancey, who said, "The man and the hour have met." Few persons in the Confederacy would then have disagreed.

JEFFERSON DAVIS
(Library of Congress)

Vice President Stephens was a man of diminutive and sickly body and wizened countenance, but with a keen and comprehensive mind. A gifted politician, he served Georgia in the United States Congress from 1843 until he retired in 1859 to resume the practice of law. As a compelling Whig orator in the House of Representatives, he impressed his party and congressional colleague and friend Abraham Lincoln, who after listening to one of the Georgian's presentations in Congress said it was the best speech of an hour's length that he had ever heard. Both men opposed the Mexican War; this created a special bond between them.

Stephens was an enigma in the Confederate administration. He held both the Union and the federal Constitution in great affection; he had supported Douglas in the recent presidential election; he had opposed the secession of Georgia. Yet he was an ardent advocate of state rights, and he saw no inconsistency in his thinking. Ultimately, he would turn the doctrine of state rights against the government of the supreme creature of those rights—the Confederate States of America. He was also an ardent believer in southern slavery; he identified the institution as the foundation upon which the southern republic rested.

The permanent Confederate constitution drafted by the convention and promptly ratified by the states was strikingly similar to the United States Constitution. The Confederate document differed primarily in certain phrases and provisions that in the past had led to sectional controversy. It made explicit the recognition of state rights and the legality and permanence of slavery. The preamble contained no general welfare clause and declared the constitution to be the work of the people of the Confederate States of America, "...each State acting in its sovereign and independent character." It forbade any Confederate law impairing the right to own slaves in Confederate states or territories. But the importation of slaves, except from the United States, was prohibited. The constitution outlawed protective tariffs on imports and general appropriations for internal improvements. On the other hand, it reversed the United States Constitution in permitting a tax on exports, this being designed to favor the South in its domination of the world's supply of cotton.

The Confederate organic law also differed from that of the United States in establishing a single, six-year term for the president, empowering him to veto selected parts of appropriations bills without killing the entire bill, and allowing cabinet members, when authorized by the congress, to sit in that body for the discussion of measures pertaining to their departments. The constitution was silent on the right of secession, though such a right was implicit in its affirmation of state sovereignty in the formation of the Confederate government.

Davis set about at once to form an administration and, together with the convention acting as a congress, to begin the formidable task

of breathing life into the new nation. He quickly appointed a cabinet
with Robert Toombs as secretary of state, Christopher G. Memminger
of South Carolina as secretary of the treasury, Leroy P. Walker of Alabama as secretary of war, Stephen R. Mallory of Florida as secretary of
the navy, Judah P. Benjamin of Louisiana as attorney general, and John
H. Reagan of Texas as postmaster general. The group included some of
the South's foremost public figures, especially in Toombs and Benjamin
(former United States Senators), and it gave adequate representation to
the various states of the Confederacy. Southerners said the right men
were in the right places.

By retaining the main features of the United States laws, changing
them only where they did not conform to the Confederate constitution,
and preserving the federal administrative machinery and services—
postal employees and mail delivery, for example—the Confederate government eased its transition into being. Significantly, one of its very
first acts was to create a Confederate army by calling on the various
states to provide quotas of troops and arms. Coming events would soon
make this a decision of vast import. One of Davis's first acts was the
dispatch of Confederate commissioners to Washington in a vain effort
to arrange an amicable settlement there.

Meanwhile, the most sensitive issue facing both President
Buchanan and the provisional Confederate leaders was the possession
of federal properties—military posts, forts, arsenals, customs houses,
post offices—within the seceded states. As the states withdrew from
the Union they demanded, in accord with their affirmed sovereignty
and independence, the surrender of all federal installations inside
them; in most instances the local officials, many of them southerners,
acceded. A few, however, refused to do so. One of these was Lieutenant Adam J. Slemmer, the commanding officer at Fort Pickens, a re-
doubt guarding the entrance to Pensacola harbor. Another officer who
refused to surrender was Major Robert Anderson, a Kentuckian of
southern sympathies fated to be located at perhaps the most explosive
spot on earth—the birthplace of secession, Charleston.

Anderson stood by his sense of honor in declining to give up Fort
Sumter, a masonry works that lay in the harbor and both protected and
threatened the city. President Buchanan rejected the demands for the
fort's surrender made by South Carolina commissioners in Washington,
and later by Confederate commissioners, and instead dispatched an un-
armed ship, *Star of the West,* with provisions and reinforcements. When
on January 9, 1861, the vessel was driven off by fire from the South
Carolina shore batteries, the president chose not to retaliate or regard
the incident as an act of war.

On March 4 Lincoln became president and inherited the secession
crisis. He had no specific program for meeting it, but in his inaugural he
set forth certain broad principles by which he would be guided. From a
windswept platform in front of the Capitol with its dome still under

ABRAHAM LINCOLN
(Library of Congress)

construction, and before taking the oath of office from Chief Justice
Taney, whose Dred Scott decision he had vehemently denounced, Lincoln asserted his conviction that the Union is permanent, secession anarchy, and violence in the cause of secession insurrection. He said he
intended to execute the laws of the Union in all the states, and to "hold,
occupy, and possess" the federal properties.

But he again reassured the South that he would not interfere with
slavery where it was already legal, and he appealed to the citizens of
the seceded states by promising not to assail them and saying there
would be no conflict unless they began it. Then, earnestly and elo-
quently, "While you have no oath registered in Heaven to destroy the
government, I shall have the most solemn one to 'preserve, protect,
and defend' it. . . . We must not be enemies. Though passion may have
strained, it must not break our bonds of affection. The mystic chords of
memory, stretching from every battlefield, and patriot grave, to every
living heart and hearthstone, all over this broad land, will yet swell the
chorus of the Union, when again touched, as surely they will be, by the
better angels of our nature."

In view of the situation at the Pensacola and Charleston forts, the
most ominous words in Lincoln's address were his declaration of resolve to "hold, occupy, and possess" the federal properties. How this
was to be done, whether by force or diplomacy, and whether he intended to include those establishments already in the hands of the seceded states, he did not say. Coming events would supply the answers.

He was scarcely in office when he learned the Fort Sumter garrison was almost out of provisions and Anderson would be obliged to surrender unless soon resupplied. Lincoln found himself beset with messages from throughout the North urging strong action and with criticisms over his lack of a plan for dealing with the crisis. But the nation's top military officer, elderly General Winfield Scott, hero of the Mexican War, said the fort could not be reinforced, and he suggested that both it and Fort Pickens be surrendered in order to conciliate the slave states of the upper South and prevent them from withdrawing. Lincoln was tempted to give up Fort Sumter if by doing so he could avert the secession of Virginia. He is said to have remarked that a fort for a state would not be a bad business. His newly appointed cabinet was seriously divided on the question.

The cabinet represented all sections of the nation comprising the states loyal to the Union. It also contained some former Democrats as well as men holding a variety of points of view within the Republican party. William H. Seward was the secretary of state. Former governor of New York, recently United States Senator from that state, also recently considered the foremost Republican contender for the presidency itself, he was, to many citizens both North and South, including himself, "Mr. Republican." Salmon P. Chase of Ohio, another aspirant to the presidency, an ardent abolitionist, was secretary of the treasury. Simon Cameron of Pennsylvania, Republican boss in his state, was secretary of war. Gideon Welles of Connecticut, conservative, secretive, honest beneath his wig and behind his luxuriant whiskers, the forthcoming diarist who would supply future historians with much of what they know about the inner workings of the Lincoln administration, was secretary of the navy. Caleb Smith of Indiana was secretary of the interior; Edward Bates of Missouri attorney general; and Montgomery Blair, formerly of Missouri and now of Maryland, postmaster general.

Seward played a slippery game in the Fort Sumter affair. With a sublime spirit of condescension he assumed the role of mentor to the presumably naive and bumbling Lincoln. Behind the President's back, Seward gave the Confederate commissioners in Washington what they interpreted as assurances the fort would be surrendered, and on April 1 he sent a memorandum to Lincoln saying, "We are at the end of a month's administration, and yet without a policy either domestic or foreign."

Seward advocated abandoning Fort Sumter but strengthening Fort Pickens, and at the same time he presented another recommendation that must have left Lincoln breathless. Seward suggested a plan for reuniting the nation by issuing ultimatums designed to start a war between the United States and a number of the leading countries of Europe. He believed the spirit of American patriotism aroused by a foreign war would bring the errant southern states back into the Union. He patronizingly offered to shoulder the responsibility for such a policy. Lincoln rejected the recommendation and quietly but firmly rebuked Seward by saying that he, Lincoln, must make the decisions and bear the responsibility.

In the end Lincoln decided, with the support of most of the cabinet, to attempt to resupply Fort Sumter with necessities only and to send a flotilla of warships along with the relief expedition in the event the Confederates opposed the move. He issued instructions for this to be done. But in a bizarre cross-up of communications he signed conflicting orders for the strongest of the warships, the *Powhatan*; consequently, it sailed for Pensacola, thus rendering the Fort Sumter relief escort impotent. At the same time Lincoln notified the governor of South Carolina of the coming attempt and promised that no troops, arms, or ammunition would be sent into the fort if the relief effort was not resisted.

Word of the expedition brought the Confederate authorities to a fateful decision. By now the possession of Fort Sumter meant far more than merely assuring access to the Charleston harbor; it had become an important symbol of Confederate independence itself. If the fort was to be taken, now was the time to do it, before the garrison was strengthened by any form of relief.

On April 9 Davis assembled his cabinet and received a unanimous, or perhaps almost unanimous, recommendation in favor of aggressive action. The one person alleged to have objected was the unlikeliest of the group to have done so, the impulsive Toombs, who, according to one source said, "It is suicide, it is murder, and will lose us every friend at the North. You will wantonly strike a hornets' nest which extends from mountains to ocean; and legions, now quiet, will swarm out to sting us to death. . . . It is unnecessary, it puts us in the wrong. It is fatal." Whatever was said, Davis made the decision to act and had his secretary of war telegraph the Confederate commander at Charleston, General P. G. T. Beauregard, to demand the immediate surrender of the fort, and attack and take it if the demand was rejected.

At dawn on April 12, after receiving what he deemed an unsatisfactory reply to the surrender demand, Beauregard opened fire on the fort. The old Virginia fire-eater Edmund Ruffin, now a member of a South Carolina militia unit, was allowed the honor of pulling the lanyard for at least one of the historic opening shots. The bombardment went on for almost forty hours while the citizens of Charleston, many of them from the rooftops of the mansions along the waterfront, watched in excitement and awe. Meanwhile, the weakened federal relief expedition lay helpless outside the harbor, making no attempt to come to the fort's assistance. Anderson and his little garrison returned the fire gallantly but ineffectually. Finally, with the fort reduced to rubble, but, incredibly, without a single human casualty from the Confederates' fire, Anderson raised the flag of surrender.

Scholars have long debated who was responsible for the event that precipitated the war. Did Lincoln play a Machiavellian game in which he deliberately provoked the Confederates to open fire in order to place upon them the onus of aggression and unite the northern population behind a hitherto faltering administration? Did Davis calculatingly begin the war in a move to kindle a spirit of Confederate patriotism, develop support for an inchoate administration, and attempt to induce the remaining slave states to secede and join the Confederacy? There is some evidence for answering yes to both questions.

Davis explicitly mentioned the idea of provoking a hostile enemy action in connection with an effort to end the standoff at Pensacola. On April 3 he wrote the Confederate military commander there, Major General Braxton Bragg, saying, "There would be to us an advantage in so placing [the federals] that an attack by them would be a necessity, but when we are ready to relieve our territory and jurisdiction of the presence of a foreign garrison that advantage is overbalanced by other considerations." These considerations now justified seizing Fort Pickens by force, said Davis, and he ordered that it be attempted if the risk was not excessive. Only after being informed the risk was too high did he discard the plan. His thinking on this occasion anticipated and made virtually certain his decision a few days later to attack Fort Sumter.

After the bombardment of Fort Sumter, Lincoln expressed satisfaction over the outcome and said to the commander of the unsuccessful relief expedition, "You and I both anticipated that the cause of the country would be advanced by making the attempt to provision Fort-Sumpter [sic], even if it should fail; and it is no small consolation now to feel that our anticipation is justified by the result." A few weeks later Lincoln told his Illinois friend Orville H. Browning, "The [relief] plan succeeded. They attacked Sumter—it fell, and thus, did more service than it otherwise could." The *New York Times* described the relief expedition plainly as a feint and boasted that its object was to place upon the Confederates the blame for beginning the war.

Certainly both Lincoln and Davis gave serious thought to the advantages in having the other fire the first shot if it came to that. Understandably, both would have preferred having possession of the fort without being obliged to fight either to hold it or gain it. But both were willing to fight, if necessary, in order to possess the fort, and both hoped the other would begin the fighting if it should occur. Davis was at the disadvantage of being required to attack the fort in order to attain his goal. Lincoln could hold it indefinitely, if not attacked, by simply resupplying it occasionally; if attacked, he would be a defender and not an aggressor. Given the attitudes of both men, each correct according to his own premises, hostilities were inevitable.

The intentions and motives that led to Fort Sumter are arguable, the results beyond question. Toombs's warning, if uttered, now proved remarkably accurate. In the North the attack upon the flag stirred a tidal wave of patriotic wrath and determination to avenge the act and punish its perpetrators. "It was," said a northern newspaper, "an audacious and insulting aggression upon the authority of the Republic, without provocation or excuse." Another journal interpreted the event as "precisely the stimulus which...a good Providence sends to arouse the latent patriotism of a people."

The day after the fort's surrender, Lincoln issued a ringing proclamation identifying the attack as insurrection and calling upon the several states for their militia to the aggregate of 75,000 troops to be used to suppress "combinations...too powerful to be suppressed by the ordinary course of judicial proceedings." He also summoned Congress to meet in a special session beginning July 4. Four days later he proclaimed a blockade of the ports of the seceded states.

The North's response was not confined to the Republican party. Although northern Democrats pursued throughout the secession crisis a more conciliatory course toward the South than did Republicans, the Democrats now came to Lincoln's support in his determination to put down insurrection. In a gesture of personal good will and national unity, the leading northern Democrat, Douglas, stood by and held Lincoln's hat during the inaugural address. The day before Lincoln issued his call for troops, Douglas visited him and pledged assistance in the cause of preserving the Union. Before Douglas's untimely death a few months later he declared, "There can be no neutrals in war; only patriots—or traitors."

The southern response to Fort Sumter, and especially to Lincoln's proclamation, was similar in vigor to the northern response. It came in a great outpouring of spirit and determination to resist coercion. Governor Francis Pickens of South Carolina spoke for his people when he said, "Thank God the war is open...we will conquer or perish." Rhett welcomed the coming of hostilities as a spur to southern unity and dedication. Davis in his inaugural address as provisional president had expressed the hope for amicable relations between the Confederacy and the Union. "But," he said, "if this be denied to us, and the integrity of our territory and jurisdiction assailed, it will but remain for us, with firm resolve, to appeal to arms and invoke the blessings of Providence on a just cause." He now replied to Lincoln's proclamation with one of his own, calling upon the Confederate states to muster 100,000 troops and inviting shipowners to apply for commissions as privateers to constitute a "militia of the sea."

Obliged to decide between participating in a war to coerce the seceded states or withdrawing and joining them, the four states of the upper South cast their lot with the Confederacy. Their ties of blood and culture with the South proved stronger than their political ties with the Union. In many respects the decision of Virginia was the most poignant and the most crucial. The Virginians held a strong spirit of American nationalism, priding themselves as being offspring of the very Founding Fathers of the Republic. In the beginning they were cool toward the idea of secession. Governor John Letcher was sharply critical of South Carolina's hasty action; and though the Virginia legislature authorized a special convention to consider the state's course in the crisis, the body was required to submit its decision to the people for approval. On April 4 it rejected secession by a vote of 88 to 45. Meanwhile, Virginia urgently sought ways for a compromise to save the Union.

Lincoln's proclamation changed the picture at once. Governor Letcher bitterly refused the call for Virginia militia. On April 17 the convention, still sitting to await the result of the Fort Sumter affair, voted 88 to 55 in favor of secession, and set May 23 as the date for the referendum. By this time the state was in effect out of the Union, having already ratified the Confederate constitution, been admitted to the Confederacy, and received regiments of Confederate troops, all contingent in theory upon the outcome of the popular vote. Not surprisingly, the outcome was a substantial majority in favor of what in fact had already occurred—secession.

The secession of Virginia from the Union touched off a secessionist movement within Virginia itself. The counties of the Alleghenies and westward, where slavery and plantation agriculture were only shallowly rooted, opposed the withdrawal of the state, and when it took place their representatives began a move that culminated in the formation of the state of West Virginia, which in 1863 would be recognized by and admitted to the Union. Here was a paradox within a paradox: that Confederate Virginia, the product of secession, would fiercely condemn the withdrawal of its western counties, while the federal government, sworn enemy of secession, would applaud and abet it within a state.

Like Virginia, the three other states of the upper South had at first considered secession, then turned it down. All now rejected Lincoln's call for troops. Governor Henry M. Rector of Arkansas declared that the people of his state would defend it against northern "mendacity and usurpation," and on May 6 the state convention voted to secede. Governor John M. Ellis of North Carolina said the state would have no part in a war upon the liberties of a free people, seized the federal properties in North Carolina, and began to call up volunteers for state defense. On May 1 the state convention unanimously adopted secession.

Governor Isham G. Harris of Tennessee said his state would furnish 50,000 troops, not to Lincoln, but for the defense of Tennessee and other southern states. During early May, Harris and the legislature entered into a military alliance with the Confederacy, declared Tennessee independent, and ratified the Confederate constitution, these actions to be dependent upon approval in a referendum set for June 8. The Tennessee referendum, like that of Virginia earlier, went heavily in favor of what was already accomplished—the withdrawal of the state from the Union.

By gaining the four states of the upper South the Confederacy added sufficient strength to enable it to make a powerful bid for success in a war for independence. The addition of this area increased the white population of the southern republic by almost 80 percent and the industrial output comparably. Virginia was the most important state to join the Confederacy, not only because of its large population and relatively heavy manufacturing capacity, but also because of its historic political stature and prestige. Confederate authorities paid homage to the Old Dominion by making Richmond their permanent capital.

The border slave states were fated not to secede, though all of them harbored strong Confederate sympathies. The refusal of the Delaware legislature to authorize a convention settled the issue there. Maryland was more sharply divided. Governor Thomas H. Hicks vainly sought to keep the state neutral, and the legislature, despite the presence of many secessionist members, refused to call a convention. Geographically the state was pivotal. Its withdrawal would isolate Washington from the Union, with consequences that were made vividly apparent when on April 19 a formation of Massachusetts troops in answering Lincoln's summons was attacked in the streets of Baltimore by a prosouthern mob. Lincoln quickly suspended the writ of habeas corpus and permitted the military authorities to arrest many southern sympathizers, including legislators, and to seize a number of strategically important positions in the state. These measures prompted the writing by James Ryder Randall of the stirring song "Maryland, My Maryland," with its outraged line, "The despot's heel is on thy shore." But Lincoln's move forestalled any formal attempt at secession by the state.

Determined and partially successful efforts to secede occurred in both Kentucky and Missouri. Governor Beriah Magoffin of Kentucky and Governor Claiborne F. Jackson of Missouri were secessionists who rejected Lincoln's call for troops. But both legislatures refused to authorize conventions to consider separation. Kentucky for some time attempted to remain neutral, but was soon invaded by Confederate troops and then by Union troops. Missouri quickly became a scene of civil strife between secessionists and unionists. Eventually, acts of secession were adopted and Confederate governments set up by delegations representing sections of both states; both were admitted into the Confederacy, and both sent representatives to the Confederate congress; both had stars in the Confederate flag. But the Confederate governments of Kentucky and Missouri reflected the will of minorities only, and military events would soon make them merely "governments in exile."

By holding the border slave states the Union may have retained the balance of power for deciding the outcome of the Civil War. The population of the region, counting West Virginia, was more than 40 percent of that of the Confederacy, and the strategic location of the area was of paramount value. Lincoln was said to have remarked he hoped God was on the side of the Union, but that it must have Kentucky. He is known to have said: "I think to lose Kentucky is nearly the same as to lose the whole game. [With] Kentucky gone, we cannot hold Missouri, nor, I think, Maryland. [With] These all against us...the job on our hands is too large for us. We would as well consent to separation at once, including the surrender of this capital."

The Confederacy also nurtured the long-held southern ambition to expand into the American Southwest. Two areas in particular were objects of Confederate design there. Treaties of alliance with the five "civilized Indian nations" of Indian Territory—the Cherokees, Choctaws, Chickasaws, Creeks, and Seminoles, in the present state of Oklahoma—accepted an Indian nonvoting delegate to the Confederate congress and provided for the future admission of an Indian state. Indian units served in the Confederate army, but with a single notable exception, most Confederate Indian troop activity was confined to Indian Territory. Confederate sympathizers in the southern part of the New Mexico Territory organized themselves into the Confederate Territory of Arizona, sent a delegate to the Confederate congress, and received territorial recognition. Military defeat early in the war dashed Confederate hopes in the area.

By summer 1861 secession was an accomplished fact. Both North and South were preparing in dead earnest for the conflict that so long had been in the making. When Confederate President Jefferson Davis proclaimed June 13 as a day of prayer for victory, a semiliterate Louisiana plantation overseer scrawled into his journal this dread malediction: "...My prayer Sincerely to God is that Every Black Republican in the Hole combined whorl Either man women o chile that is opposed to negro slavery as it existed in the Southern confederacy shal be trubled with pestilences & calamitys of all kinds & drag out the Balance of there existence in misry & degradation with Scarsely food & rayment enughf to keep sole & body to geather and O God I pray the to Direct a bullet or a bayonet to pirce the hart of every northern Soldier that invades southern Soil & after the Body has Rendered up its Traterish Sole gave it a trators reward a birth in the Lake of fires & Brimstone My honest convicksion is that Every man women & chile that has gave aid to the abolishionist are fit Subjects for Hell I all so ask the to aid the Southern confedercy in mantaining ower rites & establishing the confederate Government Believing in this case the prares from the wicked will prevailith much—Amen—."

The editor of the *New York Daily Tribune* wrote with more polish but no less venom: "...we mean to conquer [the southern people]—not merely to defeat, but to conquer, to SUBJUGATE them—and we shall do this the most mercifully, the more speedily we do it. But when the rebellious traitors are overwhelmed in the field, and scattered like leaves before an angry wind, it must not be to return to peaceful and contented homes. They must find poverty at their firesides, and see privation in the anxious eyes of mothers and the rags of children." The black funnel of war loomed on the horizon.

III

Mobilization
and Early Campaigns

❖

The outcome of war depends upon the means, both material and imma-
terial, available to the contestants. In numbers and physical resources
the Union vastly overmatched the Confederacy. The twenty-three Union
states contained a population of almost 23 million. The eleven Confederate
states counted slightly above 9 million, including 3.5 million slaves and 132,760
free blacks who would not be used in the armed forces, leaving a white population of approximately 5.5 million from which the Confederacy drew its fighting men. According to the bare census figures, the Union enjoyed a numerical
military advantage of more than four to one.

These figures must be modified in weighing the actual advantages and disadvantages of the two sides. The Union slave states and areas settled by
southerners in such states as Ohio, Indiana, and Illinois provided the Confederacy with many thousands of troops, while areas of Confederate disaffection
within the South provided the Union with comparable numbers. Unionist East
Tennessee particularly gave the Union a salient of civilian support within the
Confederate lines, and the many other islands of unionist sentiment throughout the South enhanced this advantage.

As laborers, the southern blacks furnished an immense amount of support
to the Confederacy and freed hundreds of thousands of white men to fight.
Hence, in calculating the statistics on the opponents, a number equal to that of
the slaves and free blacks ought to be subtracted from the northern population.
Against this must be numbered approximately 134,000 former southern slaves
who eventually were enrolled in the Union armies and the greater numbers of
former slaves who served them as workers when they pressed into the interior
of the Confederacy. Finally, the North was able to recruit significant numbers of
soldiers among immigrants from Europe arriving during the conflict, while the
Confederacy obtained relatively few troops from this source.

These various factors obviously make impossible the establishment of a precise ratio of numerical strength between the North and South. Nor is it possible to arrive at a precise theoretical ratio for success in war. Using the Napoleonic war as a guide, the renowned nineteenth-century German military philosopher Karl von Clausewitz wrote: "All else equal, numbers will determine victory in combat.... In ordinary cases an important superiority of numbers, but which need not be over two to one, will be sufficient to ensure victory, however disadvantageous other circumstances may be." He reckoned that with a numerical superiority of 2.5 to 1 a western European alliance would be able to conquer France.

Clausewitz's opening words quoted above—"All else equal"—introduce an infinite number of other considerations. Never in war is all else equal; in the Civil War it was exceptionally unequal. Significantly, the most glaring inequality in the martial capabilities of the North and South lay in a field that was relatively ignored by Clausewitz, that of the material necessities for waging war.

The Civil War was forerunner to the wars of the twentieth century in that it pitted industry against industry and economy against economy as well as armies against armies. The most striking disparity in resources lay in the industrial superiority of the Union. The northern factories in 1860 produced by value more than 90 percent of the nation's manufactured goods. In the kinds of production that were most important to military power the inequality was far greater. For example, the North produced 17 times as much cotton and woolen textiles, 30 times as many boots and shoes, 20 times as much pig iron, 13 times as much bar, sheet, and railroad iron, 24 times as many locomotives, 32 times as many firearms, and 11 times as many ships and boats. The Confederacy had no factories for producing munitions, steel, car wheels, or sewing machines, and it possessed none of the "parent industries," none of the machine tools to create the machinery for manufacturing the implements of war. The United States census taker immediately after the war wrote perceptively, "It was mainly for the want of these [resources], and not for lack of courage, will, or skill, that the revolt failed."

Recognizing the industrial weakness of their region, southern leaders depended heavily upon its great agricultural production to supply the means for procuring the sinews of war. But the South's peacetime economy rested primarily on the sale of its famed commercial crops, especially on the cotton which fed the mills of Europe and New England. In war, the European trade would be subject to a northern blockade, and the New England market would be closed. Indeed, the diversified northern agriculture would prove to be as important a wartime asset to the Union as southern agriculture to the Confederacy. As producers of food in the form of grain, vegetables, fruits, and animals, the northern farms combined with the northern factories to give the Union a balanced and effective economy of great wartime strength.

In the critical resource of transportation the North was also immensely superior. The Civil War has been called the first complete railroad war; one study of the conflict bears the striking and significant title *Victory Rode the Rails*. Northern railways in 1860 amounted to approximately 20,000 miles; southern rail mileage in an area of comparable size was only half that figure. Northern railroads were far more effectively linked into systems of trunk lines that covered the entire region. Northerners owned most of the nation's ships and boats, and the North was much better supplied with wagons, draft animals, and roads. The longer the war lasted, the more pronounced would become all these northern advantages because of the inability of Confederate industry to replace losses and maintain existing facilities.

The foregoing discussion makes clear that the outcome of the Civil War would have been inevitable if it had depended entirely on numbers and material resources. But important as these factors unquestionably are, they alone do not assure victory or defeat. History offers many examples to the contrary. In the beginning the Confederate leaders and most of the southern population believed the Confederacy had a strong prospect of success; many scholars today endorse this view. Numbers, arms, equipment, supplies, and transportation account for only part of the calculus of victory. The intangibles of war, such as the nature of the war aims, the spirit of the population and the soldiers, and the boldness, originality, skill, and inspirational qualities of the military and civilian leaders also make vital contributions to the result. Here the Confederacy at first held the upper hand.

The Confederate war aim, which was to establish southern independence, was less difficult in the purely military sense than the Union war aim, which was to prevent the establishment of southern independence. The Confederacy could achieve its aim simply by protecting itself sufficiently to remain in existence. The Union could achieve its aim only by destroying the will of the southern population through invasion and conquest. The Confederate aim was the more concrete and visible; it evoked a defense of hearth and home that appealed to a great majority of white southerners regardless of class or condition, or of one's views on slavery or secession. The Union aim was an abstraction in that it called for prodigious effort, hardship, and sacrifice for no immediate or obvious gain, but only because of a sense of national patriotism to preserve the Union.

Strategically and tactically, at least in theory, the nature of the respective war aims also favored the Confederacy. More troops, arms, and supplies would be required for the offensive operations of the Union than for the defensive operations of the Confederacy. As Union forces penetrated the South their lines of communication would become progressively longer, more tenuous, and more vulnerable, making necessary the assignment of large numbers of men to serve and guard them.

In waging a defensive war the Confederacy would enjoy the advantage of "interior," and therefore shorter, lines of communication, which ordinarily would make possible a more rapid concentration of forces at points of engagement. The weaponry of the times, especially the rifled musket with its increased range and accuracy, strengthened the defense of a fixed position by elevating the costliness of the attack. Confederate General P. G. T. Beauregard, in justifying his own ideas of how the Confederacy ought to have fought the war, said later that no other people had ever undertaken a struggle for independence with more relative advantages.

Once at war the immediate task of both the Union and Confederate governments was that of raising, equipping, and training the huge armies required to carry out their purposes. Both governments went about this business in a similar fashion, but with some significant differences. At the outbreak of the conflict the United States regular army, the bulk of which was dispersed along the western frontier, contained only 16,402 soldiers of all grades and ranks. Most of the enlisted men chose to remain with the Union, but 313 of the officers, almost a third of the whole number, resigned their United States commissions and joined the Confederacy. This group included a number of the highest-ranking and most distinguished officers of the "Old Army." The Union generally kept units of its small regular army, including the officers, virtually intact, but those officers who left the Union were scattered throughout the Confederate army, thus forming a trained and experienced cadre to leaven the entire mass.

President Lincoln's original call for state militia specified a term of only three months' service, but when Congress met in special session opening July 4 he asked for authority to call up at least 400,000 more volunteers, and Congress responded by authorizing 500,000 for a period of three years. The states were assigned troop quotas according to population, and the volunteer regiments were raised by state action. The usual method was for a prominent citizen to announce he was forming a regiment and call for volunteers. The volunteers elected their officers of company grade (lieutenants and captains) and these officers then elected the field grade officers (majors, lieutenant colonels, and colonels). The president appointed the officers of the rank of general, although the state governors often exercised influence in these appointments also. After a brief period of elementary drill and instruction the regiment was mustered into federal service.

The Confederacy raised its army in pretty much the same way. One significant difference was that the 100,000 troops originally called up by

Davis were enlisted for a twelve-month period. In May the Confederate Congress authorized an additional 400,000 troops. States were called upon to raise and equip militia and volunteer regiments, which were then mustered into Confederate service, and individual volunteers were accepted directly into the Confederate army although they were then assigned to state units. A bewildering series of congressional acts allowed differing terms of service, including that for the duration of the war, for three years, for one year, for six months, or for an unspecified length of time. Belatedly, in January 1862, the term of service of all state militia troops or volunteers coming in thereafter was set at three years or the duration of the war. Confederate troops elected not only their company grade officers but in many states their field grade officers also.

In a frenzied effort to provide the incoming thousands of soldiers with arms and equipment, both national governments and their various state governments placed orders with private firms and sent agents overseas to make purchases there. The Union also placed unprecedented orders with its own armories, one of the most important being that at Springfield, Massachusetts, which supplied 1,600,000 muskets during the struggle. The Confederacy in the beginning, with no armories or private armaments factories, was obliged to rely more heavily on overseas purchases and on the seizure of arms in federal arsenals in the South. Confederate volunteers were at times accepted with their own arms, thus creating a troublesome variety of weapons in some regiments. Also, Confederate cavalrymen and artillerists supplied their own horses.

During the spring and early summer of 1861 while their forces were being mobilized, the opposing leaders sorted out as best they could the many confusing and often contradictory elements in the situation and made the fundamental strategic decisions that would set the course of the war. Lincoln decided to mount an offensive against the Confederacy. When the aged General Winfield Scott, with deep insight into the nature of war, recommended a massive invasion on numerous fronts by an army of 300,000 to be accompanied by a prolonged naval blockade, critics scorned the proposal and nicknamed it the "anaconda plan," a plan to squeeze the Confederacy to death as the great constrictor snake squeezes its prey.

Lincoln rejected Scott's plan as being too cumbersome and too slow, especially in view of the impending expiration of the volunteers' terms of service. Ironically, Scott more accurately than anyone else at the time gauged the dimensions of the job that had to be done, though his plan was woefully short of the need. Lincoln was probably obliged to turn down any such plan at the moment because of the popular clamor in the North for a quick campaign and a cheap victory, but he shared the hope of such a possibility.

Davis rejected recommendations for a quick invasion of the North and decided instead to wage a defensive war, or, as he later put it, an "offensive-defensive" war. He meant by this expression that the general Confederate strategy would be that of the defensive, to repel invasion by Union forces, but that counteroffensives would at times be employed to carry out this strategy. For this decision he was severely criticized by many prominent Confederates, including Governor Henry A. Wise of Virginia and Robert Barnwell Rhett, who railed implacably against Davis for failing to carry the war to the enemy.

A number of modern students of the war have endorsed such criticism of Confederate defensive strategy by arguing that in a prolonged struggle the inferior resources of the South doomed it to defeat. T. Harry Williams held this point of view. E. Merton Coulter wrote that the defensive was "disastrous and soul-killing" to the impulsive southern population. But the consensus among scholars of military affairs would probably support Davis's decision. Clausewitz said, "Defense is the stronger form of war," and an outstanding modern English critic of Confederate leadership, General J. F. C. Fuller, conceded that the defensive was the soundest strategy for the Confederacy. Grady McWhiney and Perry D. Jamieson argue that the wisest strategy for the Confederacy would have been that of employing exclusively defensive tactics which would have taken advantage of the increased range and accuracy of the recently issued rifled musket.

Davis initially adopted a policy of territorial defense by dividing the Confederacy into eight departments, each with its own troops and each to be defended against invasion, with no ground to be voluntarily yielded to the enemy. This strategy is open to criticism because it required a dispersal of Confederate troops, thus violating the hallowed strategic principles of unity of command and concentration of force. Davis was cognizant of these principles, but he was also aware that the nature of the southern mind, its emphasis on localism and state rights, and of the southern economic and social structure, the presence of millions of slaves, demanded local protection. He reasoned that a military policy of concentration, though usually advisable, was not appropriate to the peculiar circumstances facing the Confederacy.

Davis was obliged to alter his strategic policy as the war progressed. In February 1862 he explained the Confederates' loss of Forts Henry and Donelson in Tennessee and of Roanoke Island on the Atlantic, to be discussed later, as being the result of efforts to protect the entire area of the Confederacy. Gradually he moved to a policy of concentrating the bulk of Confederate forces within major armies, but he retained the departmental administrative organization and never completely gave up the principle of territorial defense.

Both sides would rely heavily on the strategic and tactical theories taught at the United States Military Academy and on practical lessons learned in the recent Mexican War. The ranking officers of both sides were graduates of the academy and veterans of the war. All had been exposed at West Point and afterward to the doctrines of Baron Antoine Henri Jomini, one of Napoleon's staff officers, who had sought to derive rational, mathematical rules of warfare from his famed commander's operations. Jomini's favorite principles included those of command of key terrain, maneuver, concentration of force, and use of interior lines of communication.

Although apparently none of the Civil War officers were students of Clausewitz, he is looked upon today as one of the most profound of thinkers on the nature of war, and his writings are often used in evaluating the strategy and tactics of the Civil War. He fought against Napoleon but drew many of his ideas from reflecting upon Napoleon's campaigns. Clausewitz defined war as an extension of politics by other, that is, military, means. He said the key to victory lay in attacking the enemy's "center of gravity," which might be accomplished in a variety of ways, including the capture of the head of state, or the capital city, or a vital piece of territory, or by exacting a toll in casualties or resources beyond the point of toleration. The ultimate means of achieving victory, however, was through the destruction of the enemy's armed forces.

Clausewitz minimized the significance of Jomini's rules and emphasized the violence, irrationality, chance and uncertainty, and the "friction" or unmanageability of war. He stressed the importance of intuition, boldness, initiative, innovativeness, will, and character in the leader. "What genius does," he wrote, "must be the best of all rules, and theory cannot do better than to show how and why it is so." The Civil War offered ample and vivid demonstrations of the principles identified by both Jomini and Clausewitz. The war also developed a body of tactical and strategic precepts of its own.

As the preparation for war went on, the Confederacy moved to establish itself as a permanent political entity. The permanent constitution was adopted in March 1861 by the Montgomery convention and was promptly ratified by the seceded states; elections occurred in November for members of Congress and for the presidential and vice presidential electors. In the absence of political parties and opposing candidates, Davis and Stephens were unanimously elected for six-year terms as permanent president and vice president. Meanwhile, to honor a pledge made in urging Virginia to secede, the Confederates in July shifted their capital from Montgomery to Richmond.

The major features of Confederate policy emerged while the Confederate government itself was still provisional. Although Davis and the convention members had been state rightists in their prewar roles as political spokesmen for the South, they now promoted southern nationalism in fashioning a defense for the Confederacy. This may have been, in part, because Davis and the other more prominent figures were from the new Southwest where sectional solidarity was stronger than state allegiance. Or, it may have been the result, as suggested by Professors Herman Hattaway and Archer Jones, of Davis's past military experience with the United States Army.

Davis was keenly aware that the sense of southern nationalism was inchoate and not pervasive in the southern population, and that it must be developed in the war itself. "The recollections of this great contest," he said in an early address, "with all its common traditions of glory, of sacrifice and blood, will be the bond of harmony and enduring affection amongst the people, producing unity in policy, fraternity in sentiment, and just effort in war." He reconciled southern nationalism with state rights by disavowing any authority of the Confederate government to coerce a state. Southern unity, he said, must grow out of a "homogeneity of interest, policy, and feeling."

The first concrete product of the policy based on southern nationalism was the Confederate army. Davis greatly strengthened the national character of the army by his directions to Secretary of War Walker, who called upon the states to raise, organize, and equip assigned quotas of volunteers, but then to turn them over to the Confederate authorities for training, deployment, and operations; also, Walker authorized the acceptance of privately raised volunteer units and of individual enlistees directly into the Confederate army. Walker commissioned purchasing agents to obtain arms and equipment from private sources in Europe and the North. In the excitement of the early months, before the realities of war came home to them, southern youths were eager to enlist. Walker said in July 1861 that he was obliged to turn away 200,000 for lack of arms and supplies. Even so, the Confederate army was 200,000 strong, and increasing daily.

By this time the opposing armies were taking shape and the hundreds of thousands of recruits were under military instruction in hastily constructed and often makeshift camps of tents or log huts scattered across the borders of the North and South. The conditions of camp life in both forces quickly soured the initial enthusiasm of the recruits. These conditions were primitive: the sanitary facilities hopelessly inadequate, the rations coarse and poorly cooked, and the diet unbalanced and nutritionally deficient. A shortage of money and supplies in the Confederacy combined with the more rural nature and lack of education among the southern soldiery to exaggerate these problems in the Confederate camps.

Army regulations concerning camp life were to a great extent unenforced, perhaps unenforceable, by the untrained junior officers, whose authority was weakened by the necessity of gaining their rank through popular election. An inspection late in 1861 of two hundred Union regimental camps disclosed that more than one-fourth of them were filthy with garbage, open latrine trenches, and heaps of manure and offal. Infestations of lice, fleas, and rodents were common. The basic diet of salt pork, bread, and coffee was supposed to be supplemented with "desiccated" (dried) vegetables, which most soldiers rejected as inedible, or with fresh vegetables, which were difficult to procure. Soldiers were able to purchase sweets, tobacco, and a limited variety of other foods and supplies from camp sutlers, civilian merchants who serviced the armies.

The conditions of camp life made disease a major problem; diarrhea and common colds were universal among the solders, and dysentery, influenza, and pneumonia took many lives. The medical services were appallingly short of trained doctors and up-to-date medicines and equipment. Deadly epidemics swept through the camps. These sieges included typhoid and smallpox and the great endemic southern disease of malaria. During one later eighteen-month period the Confederate army suffered 17,000 deaths from typhoid alone. Also among the illnesses lethal to Civil War soldiers were such so-called childhood diseases as chicken pox, mumps, whooping cough, and measles, to which many of the rural men had never been exposed and therefore had little natural resistance. The medical science of that day was virtually helpless against these illnesses. Disease in the Civil War was a far grimmer reaper than weapons.

The military training itself was, in many instances, as primitive as the living conditions of camp life. Although both armies included a small number of experienced officers at the company and regimental level, most of the leaders were as green as their men. Many of the officers literally studied the training manual, Winfield Scott's *Infantry Tactics* or William J. Hardee's *Rifle and Light Infantry Tactics*, the night before in order to be able to drill their troops the following day. Often the drill commands and the drill itself were unorthodox. One Confederate wrote, "Every amateur officer had his own pet system of tactics"; a Union soldier said, "Mistakes are corrected by making still worse mistakes. The men in ranks grin, giggle and snicker, and now and then break out into a coarse, country hee-haw." But drill they did; according to one Union recruit, "The first thing in the morning is drill, then drill, then drill again....Then drill, and lastly drill. Between drills, we drill and sometimes stop to eat a little and have roll-call."

The most important item of training was that of employing the weapons. The weapon used by the great majority of the soldiers throughout the war was the rifled musket, either the .577 caliber Enfield, which was manufactured in England, or the .58 caliber Springfield, which was manufactured at an armory in Massachusetts. These weapons fired a conical leaden bullet known as the Minié ball (pronounced "minnie" in both armies); the rifling in the barrel of the musket imparted a spin to the projectile that multiplied its range and accuracy. An expert marksman could hit a man at 400 yards; the bullet would kill at more than twice this distance. The Springfield was the favorite of the soldiers of both armies, though the Confederates usually had to capture these muskets in order to get possession of them. Confederate factories eventually turned out great quantities of a musket similar to the Springfield. All of these weapons had to be loaded from the muzzle, a complicated and awkward exercise requiring nine separate steps. A skilled musketeer could get off no more than three aimed shots per minute.

Although most Civil War soldiers were accustomed in civilian life to using small firearms, the handling of cannon was a new experience for those who were assigned to the artillery. The basic artillery piece in both armies was the Napoleon twelve-pounder howitzer, which, like most of the other Civil War cannon, was muzzle-loaded. It was served by a crew consisting of a sergeant and eight gunners who, after mastering the elaborate drill of sponging the barrel, loading, priming, sighting, and firing, could shoot two rounds per minute.

The soldiers were often unruly, and discipline was difficult to maintain. Americans generally opposed regimentation of any kind and were notoriously disrespectful of arbitrary authority and disdainful of any behavior they considered pompous. Some officers were unable to keep order. On occasion, unpopular officers were mobbed and beaten by their troops. A more subtle form of soldier protest was that of ridicule, such as shaving the tail and mane of the officer's horse.

Many of the forms of discipline were harsh. Soldiers who were guilty of violating orders or going absent without leave might be ridden on a wooden horse or "bucked and gagged," a humiliating and extremely painful experience in which a gag was placed in the culprit's mouth and he was forced to sit for hours with his knees drawn up sharply and held in place by a piece of wood tied behind them and with his hands securely bound in front. Deserters might be flogged and branded with the letter *D* before being dismissed from service and imprisoned. Deserters might also receive capital punishment. James I. Robertson, Jr., has written that more executions, some five hundred, occurred in the two armies during the Civil War than in all other American wars combined. Almost two-thirds were for desertion.

The rigors of training combined with loneliness, homesickness, lovesickness, and boredom to make camp life utterly miserable to most of the recruits. Many of them countered the misery by deserting or going absent without leave. But the majority countered it by turning to diversions of one kind or another. They sought female companionship at every opportunity by attending dances and parties in nearby towns and on surrounding farms. Many sought companionship of a more questionable form by consorting with female camp followers, often euphemistically called laundresses, and by visiting the brothels that sprang up within reach of every camp. As a result, venereal diseases soon took their place on the list of debilitating camp maladies.

Many soldiers sought comfort in alcohol. The Union army issued periodic rations of whiskey on the debatable theory that availability in controlled amounts would curb excessive appetite. The Confederate army did not follow this practice. But whiskey was easily obtainable to the men of both armies; it was among the sutlers' commodities, and there were accessible sources outside the camps. The quality of much of the purchased alcohol is suggested in such nicknames as "Old Red Eye," "Rot Gut," "Spider Juice," or "Bust Skull." Drunkenness at times became a serious evil in both armies. Major General George B. McClellan said in 1862 that total abstinence would be worth an additional 50,000 troops to the Union cause.

Profanity and gambling, two of the most common features of soldier life throughout the ages, were also common features during the Civil War. Oaths and curses punctuated the speech of what was probably a majority of the troops both northern and southern. Gambling took place on a wide range of activities, including horse races, cockfights, athletic contests, and spontaneous fistfights. Even louse races were staged for wagering. Card and dice games went on continuously when the men were not occupied at drill or in other military activities. One of the more captivating vignettes of camp life in the army of Confederate General Thomas J. "Stonewall" Jackson is that of the rude soldiers hastily concealing their cards and winnings under blankets as the stern Puritan commander strode by on his way to a prayer meeting.

Prayer meetings were plentiful. A majority of the soldiers were from homes where simple religious faith still prevailed, and the men brought a large measure of this sensibility into the armies with them. All of the major religious denominations provided chaplains; regular services were a part of the camp routine. The more devout soldiers spent time individually in reading the Bible and in prayer; groups of them held informal devotionals on frequent occasions. Even those soldiers who were indifferent to religious exercises and were accustomed to violating the religious sanctions of the day would later throw away their cards or dice, "passports to sin," they called them, before going into battle. Robertson has concluded that faith in God was the strongest ingredient in sustaining the morale of the soldiers both blue and gray.

In spite of the shortcomings of camp life and training, and of the hardships and delinquencies of the men, events were moving rapidly toward a showdown. The war was about to begin in earnest.

The initial engagements in the war occurred in efforts to hold or take the important border slave region. In Missouri in May a young Union army officer, Captain Nathaniel Lyon, urged and aided by Con-

PRINCIPAL MILITARY CAMPAIGNS OF THE CIVIL WAR

gressman Francis P. Blair, Jr., nephew of the postmaster general, surrounded and captured an encampment of Governor Claiborne Jackson's pro-Confederate militia near St. Louis. Reinforced and promoted to the rank of brigadier general, Lyon then defeated a small Confederate force under Brigadier General Sterling Price and drove it, accompanied by Governor Jackson, into the southwestern corner of the state near Springfield where it received additional troops from other parts of the Confederacy. By late June most of Missouri was in Union hands.

Western Virginia was the scene of similar operations. From Ohio in June a force of 20,000 Union troops under Major General George B. McClellan moved into the state, retook Harpers Ferry, and by July, after small engagements at Rich Mountain and Carrick's Ford, had regained control of Virginia west of the Alleghenies. The Confederacy was never able to recover this area even though its premier general, Robert E. Lee, later was temporarily placed in command there. This Union success led to an important political success by securing the movement that was under way for the establishment of the state of West Virginia. In addition, the military victory placed a Union force in position to threaten the Shenandoah Valley and the flank of the main Confederate army, which occupied Virginia east of the mountains.

While these events were taking place in Missouri and western Virginia, the stage was being prepared for the first major Union offensive to end the war. This was to be accomplished, it was hoped and believed, by a single campaign to defeat the Confederate army in Virginia and capture the capital, Richmond, a tempting prize that lay only one hundred miles south of Washington. There was strong popular approval of such a stroke. Northern newspapers demanded action and coined the slogan "Forward to Richmond." After a Union setback on June 10 at Big Bethel Church near Yorktown on the peninsula formed by the York and James rivers, the pressure on Lincoln became irresistible, if any pressure was required. He now ordered Brigadier General Irvin McDowell, commanding the largest Union field army, to make the move.

McDowell commanded a force of about 35,000 troops encamped across the Potomac River from Washington. Aware of their lack of proper training, he pleaded for more time, but the president refused with the remark that the Confederates were just as green. Confronting McDowell twenty-five miles to the south was Confederate General Beauregard of Fort Sumter memory, who commanded 22,000 troops disposed behind a small stream named Bull Run and covering an important rail center at Manassas Junction. A Union force of about 18,000 under the command of Major General Robert Patterson was located near Harpers Ferry at the mouth of the Shenandoah Valley; near Winchester twenty-five miles to the south was a Confederate force of about 12,000 under the command of General Joseph E. Johnston.

McDowell's plan called for a Union movement that would "turn," or pass around, the main Confederate position and seize its line of communications along the Orange and Alexandria Railroad. Meanwhile, informed of the Union intentions by a Confederate intelligence agent— Mrs. Rose O'Neal Greenhow, a prominent Washington social figure— Davis ordered General Johnston to reinforce Beauregard with his army from the Shenandoah Valley. Skillfully screening his move with cavalry, Johnston slipped away from Patterson, who was supposed to keep him occupied, and executed the first Civil War tactical movement of its kind by boarding most of his troops on the Manassas Gap railroad and bringing them quickly to Manassas Junction to join the Confederate main body. By July 20 the Confederate force of about 35,000 was concentrated in a defensive position behind Bull Run. Although Johnston was the senior of the Confederate generals, he deferred to Beauregard who actually would command the army in the coming engagement.

Before dawn on July 21 the Union attack began with a demonstration against the center of the Confederate line and a wheeling movement of two divisions around the Confederate left flank. After successfully crossing Bull Run at Sudley Ford, the Union troops found themselves hotly engaged by a Confederate brigade under Colonel Nathan G. Evans, who had been apprised of the Union move by Beauregard's brilliant young signal officer, Captain E. Porter Alexander, and had moved his unit to a strong defensive position on the Confederate flank.

Beauregard and Johnston, riding to the sound of the fighting, found Evans's troops being pressed back on Henry House Hill south of the Warrenton Turnpike. There in midafternoon the Union advance was halted by the fierce resistance that had been strengthened through the shifting of Confederate units from other parts of the line that were under less pressure. Probably the most dramatic action was that of Brigadier General Thomas J. Jackson's brigade. Certainly it inspired the most dramatic rhetoric when Brigadier General Barnard E. Bee of South Carolina exclaimed, "There stands Jackson like a stone wall!" thus coining an immortal sobriquet.

Late in the afternoon, as the Union attack faltered, and after Beauregard had received the last reinforcements from the Valley, he launched a counterattack. The Union soldiers, exhausted and dispirited, had little fight left in them. Their line broke before a wave of charging Confederates uttering a dread, high-pitched shout that was to become famous as the "rebel yell." McDowell's army soon became a mass of demoralized men, and mixed with the supply train and groups of Washington picknickers who had come out to watch the fun, all trudging back along the pike. A chance hit on a wagon by a Confederate shell temporarily blocked the road and added panic to the dejection and fatigue. A regular army reserve unit of about 2,000 men at Centre-

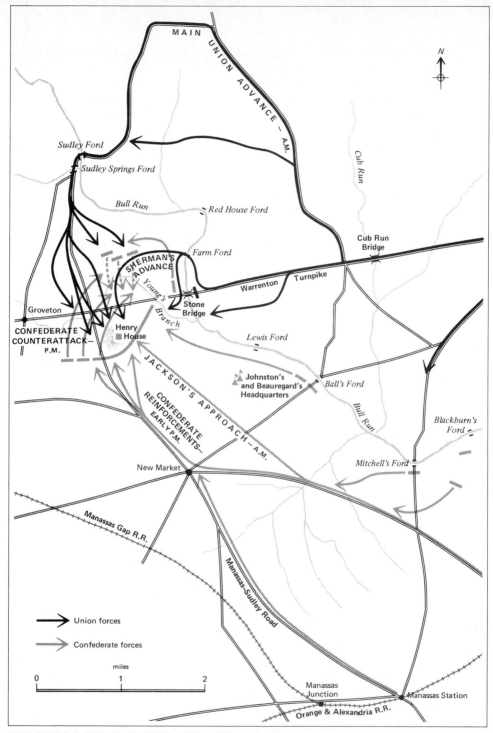

THE FIRST BATTLE OF BULL RUN, JULY 21, 1861

ville was the only organized force that stood between the victorious southerners and Washington.

Washington did not fall. Perhaps the Confederates could not have taken it if they had tried. They did not try. Davis arrived on the battlefield during the afternoon and urged his generals forward; Jackson was quoted as saying that with 5,000 fresh troops he could gain the city. The condition posed by Jackson—5,000 fresh troops—is probably the key to the outcome, for there were no fresh troops. Every Confederate unit had been thrown into the fray. Johnston later justified his own caution by explaining that the raw and weary southerners were as disorganized by victory as the northerners by defeat.

A bitter and enduring controversy soon arose between Davis and the generals as to who was responsible for the alleged failure to exploit the victory. The battle of Manassas as the Confederates called it, or Bull Run as the Federals called it, was a Confederate victory, a complete tactical victory, though the losses were severe on both sides: 481 Union dead, 1,011 wounded, 1,216 missing (mostly captured); 387 Confederate dead, 1,582 wounded, 13 missing.

Hard after the battle of Bull Run the Confederacy won another tactical victory at Wilson's Creek in southwestern Missouri. On August 10 Union General Lyon impetuously led his force of only 5,400 in a fierce surprise assault on Price's army, now enlarged to 12,000 by the arrival of Brigadier General Ben McCulloch with additional troops from Arkansas. Lyon conducted the main attack while Brigadier General Franz Sigel made an encirclement to strike the Confederates from the rear. At the height of the battle, with victory seemingly at hand, Lyon was killed and the attack was repulsed with heavy casualties on both sides, 1,235 Union and 2,084 Confederate. Price now hoped to retrieve the state for the Confederacy.

The early Confederate successes on far-flung battlefields kindled a flame of enthusiasm and overconfidence in the southern mind. Southerners had long believed they possessed exceptional military prowess, that one of them was a match for several Yankees. This assumption seemed now to have been vindicated; perhaps the war would soon be over. The effect on the northern mind was extremely sobering. Gone were the illusions of a quick and easy victory. Were the rebels, after all, actually superior fighters? Some Union officers by their behavior appear to have thought so. But to the northern population at large these defeats were a challenge as well as a humiliation. Northerners braced themselves to the task of waging a long, hard war. Badly shaken but grimly determined, Lincoln sought a general who could reverse the current of defeat.

McClellan seemed to be that general. He was the one Union officer who had beaten the Confederates in the field. In late July Lincoln summoned him to Washington, placed him in command of the main Union army, now named the Army of the Potomac, and told him it was up to him to save the country. Brimming with self-confidence, McClellan began drilling the disorganized and demoralized regiments into a cohesive fighting force.

The new commander was a United States Military Academy graduate with an exemplary record as a cadet. His military career in the Old Army included service in the Mexican War as a member of General Scott's staff, that remarkable school of tactics and generalship for so many young officers who would play important roles in the Civil War. Disillusioned with peacetime army life, McClellan in 1857 resigned his commission to enter the rapidly expanding railroad business, in which he quickly demonstrated outstanding ability. By the time of the outbreak of the war he was president of the Ohio and Mississippi Railroad.

McClellan was handsome and articulate, a superb organizer and trainer, and immediately a favorite of his soldiers, who affectionately named him "Little Mac." A Napoleonic pose in an 1862 photograph, right hand thrust into his blouse over the abdomen, accurately conveys his view of himself. But he turned out to be as diffident in action as he was vigorous in training. Confederate General Richard Taylor said after the war that in this respect McClellan resembled King Frederick William of Prussia, who regarded his giant and magnificently drilled grenadiers as being too precious for gunpowder.

Although Lincoln elevated McClellan to the position of general in chief upon General Scott's retirement in November, the president soon became impatient with the delay in mounting an offensive. With a bittersweet humor he commented that McClellan was suffering from "the slows," and on one occasion Lincoln said if McClellan did not intend to use the Army of the Potomac, he (Lincoln) would like to borrow it for a few days to see what he could do with it.

There also appeared between Lincoln and his general a source of friction deeper than disagreement over timing or tactics. McClellan was a Democrat in his political preference, and he strongly opposed any move to tamper with slavery or with the southern social system. He believed the war ought to be waged in such a way as to restore the Union precisely as it had been before secession. He became openly contemptuous of Lincoln and on one occasion ostentatiously snubbed him when he visited the army in the field. Lincoln swallowed McClellan's insults and once said he would hold the general's horse if only he would bring success.

McClellan's procrastination and political attitudes drew the fire of those Republicans in Congress who wished to make emancipation a major war aim and were therefore known as Radicals. Emotions boiled over when in October a strong Union reconnaissance force, acting under McClellan's order, was defeated with severe losses at Ball's Bluff on the south bank of the Potomac about thirty miles above Washington.

The most celebrated casualty was the commander of the expedition, Colonel Edward Baker, who was also a Republican senator from Oregon and a personal friend of Lincoln. This affair helped lead to the formation of the joint congressional Committee on the Conduct of the War, a Radical-dominated group whose purpose was to promote its war aim as well as a more energetic prosecution of the war.

Irritated at McClellan and sensitive to the Radical criticism, Lincoln on January 27, 1862, issued an order for all Union armies to advance on February 22, Washington's birthday. Instead of planning an advance directly upon the Confederates to his front, as Lincoln apparently intended, McClellan countered with a proposal to turn their position by moving his army, now more than 100,000 strong, on transports down the Potomac and into the Chesapeake Bay to the lower Rappahannock River, thus to make a roundabout approach to Richmond. While this plan was still being studied, the war suddenly took a dramatic turn west of the Alleghenies.

Commanding the Confederate Department of the West was General Albert Sidney Johnston, a native of Kentucky, a West Point graduate, and a Texan by adoption. He had been one of the most distinguished officers of the Old Army and was an especially close personal friend of Jefferson Davis. When in September Johnston was appointed to his command, he established his headquarters in Nashville, Tennessee, but his chief concern was the situation in Kentucky. A month earlier Confederate Major General Leonidas Polk had seized the Mississippi River bluffs at Columbus, Kentucky, thus violating the state's attempted neutrality, and Union forces had promptly moved into Louisville and other points.

In an effort to hold Kentucky for the Confederacy, Johnston immediately sent the main body of his army from Nashville to Bowling Green, where he established his headquarters and the Confederate state capital. He deployed almost half his entire force of 45,000 at Bowling Green under the direct command of Major General William J. Hardee, 12,000 at Columbus under Polk, with a detachment at Belmont, Missouri, across the Mississippi from Columbus, and 5,000 at Mill Springs on the upper Cumberland River in eastern Kentucky under Brigadier General Felix K. Zollicoffer. The mission of Zollicoffer's force was to guard the approaches from eastern Kentucky into eastern Tennessee. Smaller forces held fortified works designed to guard the points at which the Tennessee and Cumberland rivers penetrated the western segment of the Confederate line: Fort Henry on the Tennessee and Fort Donelson on the Cumberland, both in the state of Tennessee immediately below the Kentucky border.

The Union command in the West was divided. Major General John C. Frémont, former Republican standard-bearer, with headquarters at St. Louis, was now in command of the Department of the West, a sprawling area that stretched from the Cumberland River in western Kentucky through southern Illinois and across the Mississippi all the way to the Rocky Mountains. Major General Robert Anderson, promoted for his defense of Fort Sumter, commanded the Department of the Cumberland, which included central and eastern Kentucky and theoretically eastern Tennessee. When in October Anderson fell ill, he was replaced by Brigadier General William Tecumseh Sherman, who had led a brigade with skill and boldness in the battle of Bull Run.

Subordinate to Frémont, commanding the district of southern Illinois and southeastern Missouri, was an obscure officer named Ulysses S. Grant. A native of Ohio, undistinguished graduate of West Point, and veteran of the Mexican War, Grant in 1854 resigned his commission under a cloud because of alleged excessive drinking, and at the outbreak of the Civil War was making a modest living as a merchant in Illinois. He responded to the call for men, and, because of his previous military training and experience, and possibly through the influence of an Illinois congressman, received a commission as colonel of an Illinois regiment.

From these unpromising beginnings Grant would rise to become the supreme military leader of the Union in the war. He quickly demonstrated an aptness for command and was promoted to brigadier general. Grant later summed up the philosophy of generalship which he was about to put into practice, saying: "Find out where your enemy is. Get at him as soon as you can. Strike at him as soon as you can and as often as you can, and keep moving on."

Aware of the obvious strategic importance of the three major rivers that transected the western lines—the Mississippi, Tennessee, and Cumberland—Grant made his headquarters at Cairo, Illinois, where the Ohio joins the Mississippi, and when Polk's Confederates seized Columbus, Kentucky, Grant at once seized Paducah and Smithland where the Tennessee and Cumberland join the Ohio. By these moves he gained possession of pivot points from which he could easily transport and support troops by water to threaten or strike a number of important military objectives on the three rivers.

The opening engagements of what would become the campaign for Kentucky and Tennessee occurred at the extremities of the Confederate line. On November 7 Grant with a force of about 3,000 attacked Polk's garrison at Belmont, but withdrew after an indecisive affair in which both sides claimed victory.

In early November, Lincoln removed Frémont from command of the Department of the West. The general had proved inept in his military operations, lax in supervising army contracts, and, to be discussed later, premature in his attitudes and actions concerning emancipation. Major General Henry Halleck replaced him. Halleck was a West Pointer who was known throughout the army as "Old Brains" because he was a productive author whose works included a heralded treatise on military operations. At the same time, Major General Don Carlos Buell replaced Sherman, who seemed on the brink of a nervous collapse under the problems of command in central and eastern Kentucky.

In January 1862 an attempted invasion of eastern Tennessee by Buell's subordinate, Brigadier General George H. Thomas, a Virginian who had remained in the Union service, bogged down in the winter mud. This failure was turned into a victory when the Confederates under Zollicoffer crossed the Cumberland River and on January 19, by order of his recently assigned superior, Brigadier General George Crittenden, attacked Thomas in the battle of Logan's Crossroads, or, as known by the Confederates, the battle of Mill Springs. The Confederates were defeated. The battle was a small affair; the outcome did not alter the strategic balance in the western theater, but it was a harbinger of events to come elsewhere along this line.

The Confederate position in the West was extremely weak. Johnston now commanded a total of about 72,000 troops, more than a fourth of them west of the Mississippi; Halleck and Buell together had well over twice this number. Moreover, the Confederates were deployed in a "cordon" or line defense, subject to a concentrated Union attack at any particular point of choice. Aware of these weaknesses, Johnston had intended and attempted to enlist enough additional troops within his department to create an adequate reserve force to be located at Nashville. All efforts to do this had failed. Johnston said that after the initial fever of enthusiasm among the people of the threatened states, they had become listless; they were "not up to the revolutionary point."

The most vulnerable spots in the Confederate line lay where the Tennessee and Cumberland rivers flowed through it, a situation quickly grasped by Johnston's opponents. Grant proposed to attack Fort Henry on the Tennessee in concert with an assault by a gunboat flotilla under Flag Officer Andrew Foote. Halleck approved the proposal, and on February 3 the expedition got under way from Cairo. Grant's force of 17,000 was landed from transports below the fort, and early in the afternoon of the sixth Foote began shelling it. The Confederate commander, Brigadier General Lloyd Tilghman, finding himself completely outgunned and being aware of Grant's deployment, sent most of his 2,500 men out to Fort Donelson twelve miles away on the Cumberland. After two hours of unequal exchange of fire, Tilghman surrendered.

Johnston now made a momentous decision. With his lines of communication threatened by a Union movement by boat up the Tennessee River, and his Bowling Green position menaced by Buell's approach from below Louisville with an army of a total strength of approximately 73,000, Johnston decided to abandon the entire Kentucky–Tennessee line and concentrate his scattered forces in northern Mississippi for a possible counterstroke. He sent General Beauregard, who had recently been assigned as his second-in-command, to take charge of this operation while Johnston withdrew from Bowling Green through Nashville with the major element of his command.

Although Johnston had already decided that Fort Donelson could not be held, at the last minute he made the grave mistake of further dividing his forces by ordering an additional 12,000 troops to the defense of the fort, bringing the total there to about 17,000. The senior officer in command at the fort was Brigadier General John B. Floyd, the former secretary of war of the United States.

When Foote on February 14 attempted to repeat his earlier success by attacking Fort Donelson point-blank with his gunboats, he found it far more formidable than Fort Henry and was driven off with severe damage by the Confederate batteries. But Grant's army, at first delayed by flooding and now strengthened to 27,000, encircled the fort. The next day the Confederates attempted to break through Grant's line in order to join Johnston's withdrawing column in Nashville, which is what he had ordered done if the fort proved indefensible. Although the surprise Confederate assault was temporarily successful, the Confederates were unable to escape; the commander made no real effort to do so, and the Union line was soon closed around them.

That night, in a remarkable charade of irresponsibility, the Confederate command was passed down to hapless Brigadier General Simon Bolivar Buckner, who at once asked Grant's terms of capitulation. Grant's reply provided him with a nickname as lasting as Stonewall Jackson's: "Unconditional surrender." Buckner complied, the fort fell, roughly a third of Johnston's entire force was captured. The only significant body of troops not taken were those of a then-unknown cavalry colonel named Nathan Bedford Forrest, who led his men to escape through the icy backwaters. The fall of the Tennessee forts laid the western theater of the Confederacy open to immediate Union penetration.

Lincoln responded to the electrifying news of these western victories by attempting to remedy the divided command situation there. On March 11 he appointed Halleck to the command of the entire theater. Halleck, still in St. Louis, sent Grant, who inexplicably had been momentarily removed from command because of an alleged violation of orders, to take command of the Army of the Tennessee, some 40,000 troops that had been transported one hundred miles up the Tennessee River from Fort Henry and were now encamped around Pittsburg Landing, a steamboat landing near the Tennessee–Mississippi state line. Halleck ordered Buell, at Nashville with the Army of the Cumberland, to join Grant at Pittsburg Landing. Grant, now promoted to major general,

ULYSSES S. GRANT
(Library of Congress)

would exercise command until the arrival of Halleck to take over the combined force. Meanwhile, Grant was to avoid a general engagement unless attacked.

In theory Halleck's plans were sound enough. He was carrying out Jomini's tactical dictum to concentrate one's own force against a fraction of the opposing force. But the Confederate leaders had also studied Jomini, and they were straining every nerve to concentrate their forces first. Beauregard established his headquarters at the little town of Corinth in northeastern Mississippi, where two of the most important railroads of the Confederacy, the Memphis and Charleston and the Mobile and Ohio, crossed. This town was to the Confederates what Cairo had been to the Federals, with railroads being to Corinth what rivers were to Cairo. Beauregard brought the Columbus troops to Corinth by the Mobile and Ohio Railroad; Johnston brought the Bowling Green troops there by foot to northern Alabama and then by the Memphis and Charleston Railroad. Corinth was only one day's march from Grant's camp at Pittsburg Landing.

The Confederate authorities in Richmond strengthened the concentration at Corinth by sending an additional 15,000 troops by rail and river from Pensacola and New Orleans. By late March Johnston held a slight numerical advantage over Grant's army at Pittsburg Landing. These moves represented a remarkable pioneer strategic use of railroads. Both Davis and his military adviser, General Robert E. Lee, wrote Johnston urging him to attack Grant before Buell's arrival. This is exactly what Johnston had in mind and what he did.

Unfortunately for the Confederates, the concentration of their forces in the West was not absolute. In northwestern Arkansas Major General Earl Van Dorn, successor to Price, commanded some 20,000 troops. On March 8 Van Dorn attacked the opposing Union army, now under Brigadier General Samuel R. Curtis, in the battle of Pea Ridge (or Elkhorn Tavern). The Confederates were defeated, thus dashing their hopes for another attempt to gain Missouri. The Texas hero Ben McCulloch was killed in the battle. Eventually Van Dorn was ordered by Johnston to join the Confederate forces gathering in Corinth, but he arrived too late for the great test of arms that occurred nearby.

Grant wished to advance upon Corinth before the junction of Confederate forces there but was restrained by Halleck's orders. Grant's heedless aggressiveness now betrayed him. Although he was aware of the Confederate buildup at Corinth, he completely misinterpreted its significance. He believed the Confederates were too demoralized by recent defeats to be able to mount a counteroffensive, and he told the commander of Buell's advance division, "There will be no fight at Pittsburg Landing; we will have to go to Corinth where the Rebels are fortifying." Even as Grant spoke those words, Johnston's army was deploying into its attack formation a few hundred yards from the Union camp line.

The battle of Pittsburg Landing—or Shiloh as the Confederates named it, after Shiloh Methodist Church near which the fighting began—was the first really great battle of the Civil War. When Beauregard on the eve of the operation lost his nerve and wanted to call it off, Johnston redeemed his earlier indecisiveness by overruling his shaken subordinate and ordering the attack. Here was a classic case of a commander overcoming Clausewitz's "friction of war" by strength of will and superior insight into the intentions of his opponent.

The Confederate army of approximately 40,000, striking at dawn on April 6, achieved complete strategic surprise and almost complete tactical surprise and at first drove the disorganized Union troops before it. But the Union army of about 35,000 on the field soon rallied and fought tenaciously. Both Johnston and Grant, after Grant's arrival at about 9:00 A.M. from his Savannah, Tennessee, headquarters, conducted themselves with exemplary steadiness and coolness. By noon the ferocity of the combat reached a pitch perhaps never exceeded dur-

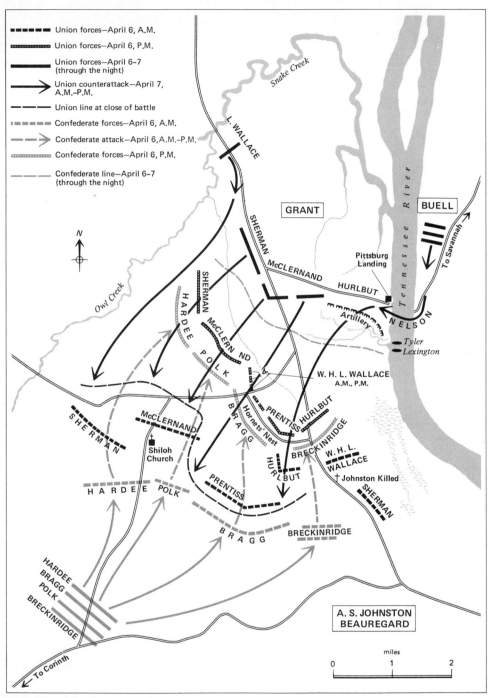

THE BATTLE OF SHILOH, APRIL 6–7, 1862

ing the war. Appropriately, the hottest portion of the line, on the Union left, became forever known as the "hornets' nest."

Early in the afternoon Johnston fell while attempting to turn or envelop the hornets' nest in order to cut the Union army away from its base on the river. Beauregard took command and, after what Sherman called "a perceptible lull" of about two hours in the fighting, continued the Confederate assault throughout the afternoon until his army was in possession of the entire battlefield except for a final Union defensive perimeter around the bluff above the steamboat landing. Shortly before dark Beauregard halted the attack to rest his exhausted men and because he had received false information that Buell's column was headed elsewhere. He ordered the attack renewed at dawn.

Perhaps the Confederates could not have destroyed Grant's army even if their attack had not been halted. By late afternoon the Union line, shortened and tightened, was supported by a massive battery of artillery. It also had now been joined by one of Grant's divisions commanded by Brigadier General Lew Wallace, which had been stationed a few miles down the river and had become lost for several hours in the woods while marching to the battle. Beauregard's decision was nevertheless a grave mistake; either he should have continued the battle the first day on the chance of consummating a victory or he should have withdrawn altogether. During the night Buell's column of 20,000 joined Grant, and when the battle resumed the following day, the Confederates who were on the field, outnumbered roughly two to one, faced destruction.

Grant promptly counterattacked and drove the southerners back across the ground they had won at heavy cost the day before. Early in the afternoon, sensing that his army was at the point of collapse, Beauregard broke off the engagement and began a weary and dispirited withdrawal to Corinth. Fortunately for the Confederates, Grant made little effort to pursue. When Sherman's forces made a tentative effort to do so, they were blocked by a determined Confederate rearguard composed of the cavalry of Forrest and Colonel John Hunt Morgan. "Bloody Shiloh" was over, leaving 1,754 Union and 1,723 Confederate dead, 8,508 Union and 8,012 Confederate wounded, and 2,885 Union and 959 Confederate missing, mostly as prisoners. It was a narrow Union tactical victory, but a strategic victory of major proportions because it left a Union army lodged deep in the western sector of the Confederacy and paved the way for a renewal of the Union advance there.

Shiloh gave a foretaste of all the other major engagements of the Civil War. It exemplified the heat and fury and the chance and uncertainty of combat. It demonstrated the brilliance and boldness as well as the indecisiveness and shortsightedness of the generals and their subordinates, and the courage and steadfastness as well as the cowardice and panic of the soldiers. It tallied the awful cost of battle and taught both sides what tremendous effort and sacrifice would be required for victory.

Shiloh's customarily serene woods and fields were littered with the dead, dying, and wounded. Its improvised hospitals were centers of feverish activity as the gore-daubed surgeons, overwhelmed by multitudes of casualties, cut and sawed and ligatured, creating ghastly mounds of severed arms and legs. Confederate nurse Kate Cumming left a searing description of one of Corinth's military hospitals, previously the Tishomingo Hotel, where she found the disabled soldiers, "mutilated in every imaginable way," lying so close together on the bloody floors that it was difficult to avoid stepping on the men as she did her work. Amputation went on continuously, followed in most instances by death. Union transports and supply boats were jammed with battle victims, "men wounded and mangled in every conceivable way," wrote one of them, "the dead and dying lying in masses, some with arms, legs, and even their jaws shot off, bleeding to death, and no one to wait upon them or dress their wounds." Brigadier General James A. Garfield of Ohio, future president of the United States, pictured Shiloh after the fighting as a scene of "unutterable horrors."

In addition to Shiloh, military actions farther west favored the Union. In February 1862 Confederate Brigadier General Henry H. Sibley led a force of about 4,000 Texans into New Mexico with the hope of securing Arizona Territory and possibly of seizing California. He succeeded in taking Albuquerque and Santa Fe, but on April 15 was defeated at Glorieta Pass near Santa Fe by a Union force under Colonel Edward R. S. Canby. The remnant of Sibley's army fell back all the way into Texas, ending the brief Confederate threat to the far Southwest.

While the battles of Shiloh and Glorieta Pass were being fought, Union campaigns of equal importance were in progress to open the Mississippi River, vital artery of the American continent. As Grant's army moved up the Tennessee to concentrate at Pittsburg Landing, a force of some 23,000 of Halleck's troops, led by Brigadier General John Pope, moved down the west bank of the Mississippi. The Confederates abandoned the fortified but exposed town of New Madrid, Missouri, located just above the southwestern tip of Kentucky, and concentrated on the heavily fortified Island No. 10 in the Mississippi.

Flag Officer Andrew Foote ran his gunboats past the island and ferried Pope's troops across the river below it. This isolated the Confederates by cutting their line of communications, and the day after Shiloh the garrison of 7,000 surrendered. A weak Confederate works named Fort Pillow on the Chickasaw Bluffs of the Mississippi above Memphis was now deemed indefensible and abandoned. On June 5 Foote's reinforced flotilla destroyed a makeshift Confederate fleet in the river at Memphis and took the city.

As the Union army and river fleet moved down the Mississippi, a dramatic campaign was launched from the southern extremity of the stream. In early October 1861 Confederate Flag Officer George N. Hollins unsuccessfully attacked the blockading Federal fleet at the mouth of the river. Shortly after, Union Flag Officer David Glasgow Farragut, a native Tennessean and a renowned veteran of some fifty years' service, assembled a fleet of seventeen warships at Ship Island off the Mississippi Gulf Coast and moved against Forts Jackson and St. Philip, Confederate works on the Mississippi seventy-five miles below New Orleans. During the night of April 23–24, 1862, after a blazing gun battle with the forts and a Confederate flotilla that included the dreaded ironclad rams *Manassas* and the unfinished *Louisiana*, the dauntless Farragut successfully ran past the forts and headed for New Orleans.

The Union fleet reached New Orleans on the twenty-fifth to find it undefended. Most of the troops originally assigned for that purpose had been sent to reinforce the Confederate attack at Shiloh. Consequently, Confederate Brigadier General Mansfield Lovell, in command at New Orleans, abandoned the city without a fight. Forts Jackson and St. Philip, besieged by a northern army of 15,000 under the command of Major General Benjamin F. Butler that had followed the fleet on transports, surrendered on the twenty-seventh. On May 1 Butler's force landed in New Orleans to begin a historic occupation there.

DAVID G. FARRAGUT
(Culver Pictures)

The tightening Union grip on the Mississippi was paralleled by successful operations along the Atlantic coast of the Confederacy. In order to strengthen the blockade, which in the beginning was largely ineffectual, the Union navy began a program of seizing bases along the seaboard. In late August 1861 an amphibious expedition commanded by Flag Officer Silas H. Stringham took the Confederate positions guarding the Hatteras Inlet, North Carolina, in an effort to cut off the blockade runners' and privateers' haven in Pamlico Sound. In January 1862 another amphibious force captured the Confederate position on Roanoke Island, which dominated the channel between Pamlico and Albemarle sounds. These captures rendered useless all the North Carolina ports except Wilmington on the Cape Fear River, which flows into the Atlantic below the sounds.

The most important of the coastal operations was the seizure in October 1861 of Port Royal Sound, South Carolina, an excellent harbor located between Charleston and Savannah. Flag Officer Samuel F. Du Pont commanded the fleet and the expedition, with Brigadier General Thomas W. Sherman leading an army of 17,000 to occupy and hold the position. The inability of Confederate fortifications to withstand the naval gunfire caused General Robert E. Lee, who had been placed temporarily in command of the Confederacy's lower Atlantic coastal defenses, to give up most of the fortifications there, withdraw the troops and guns, obstruct the rivers, and establish a line of earthworks farther inland, beyond the reach of the Union warships. This line guarded the stretch between Charleston and Savannah, including the railroad that linked them, leaving only the two cities to be defended by outer rings of heavily reinforced forts. The defense worked remarkably well throughout the remainder of the war. The cities eventually would fall, but only to a Union army from the interior.

The Union successes in the spring of 1862 lifted northern hearts and depressed southern hearts. But Shiloh's multitude of casualties sickened both populations; New Orleans never laughed again during the war, said the city's novelist George Washington Cable. Lincoln also was shocked by the carnage, yet he began to see the way toward a victorious end of the struggle. Importuned to dismiss General Grant for alleged drunkenness at Shiloh, Lincoln was quoted as saying, "Tell me what brand of whiskey he drinks. I want to send some of it to all my generals." What he actually said was, "I can't spare that man. He fights."

IV

Emerging Generals and Escalating Combat

❖

Although the Union victories of the winter, spring, and early summer 1862 in the West and along the Atlantic were sweet to the northern palate, Lincoln's statement that he could not spare a general who fights was prompted by his displeasure over McClellan's failure to launch a direct attack on the strongest of the Confederate armies. General Joseph E. Johnston's Confederate force of 60,000 was still intact and in position to guard Richmond and threaten Washington.

When in early March 1862 McClellan seemed on the point of attempting his turning maneuver around the Confederate right flank, Johnston nullified it by withdrawing some thirty miles to the south bank of the Rappahannock River. McClellan now proposed a grander turning maneuver that called for transporting his army farther down the Chesapeake Bay in order to seize the Confederate capital by approaching it along the Virginia Peninsula formed by the York and James rivers. Lincoln accepted the plan, but he did so reluctantly because it left Washington exposed.

McClellan's plan also faced another obstacle. At Norfolk, Virginia, just across Hampton Roads from the mouth of the James River, lay the Confederate ironclad warship *Virginia*, formerly the United States wooden ship *Merrimack*. On March 8 the *Virginia* attacked and almost shattered the blockading Union fleet of wooden vessels in Hampton Roads. McClellan insisted that the *Virginia* be put out of commission before he began operations. Secretary of War Edwin M. Stanton, Cameron's successor, feared the Confederate ship might even steam up the Potomac and bombard Washington.

The Union had its own ironclad, the *Monitor*, a ship of radical design, like a round cheesebox on a raft, with guns mounted in a revolving turret, invented by a resourceful Swedish-American marine engineer, John Ericsson. The day after the *Virginia*'s rampage the *Monitor* arrived in Hampton Roads and challenged the Confederate vessel. After an indecisive engagement of four hours the *Virginia* limped back into Norfolk harbor, leaving the *Monitor* in control of the bay. The crippled *Virginia* was never to venture forth again. Eventually it was demolished by its crew to avoid losing it to the invading Union army. Besides indicating that the wooden navies of the world were fast becoming obsolete, the battle of the ironclads in Hampton Roads cleared the way for McClellan's advance.

In late March McClellan began his move to Fortress Monroe on the tip of the Virginia Peninsula and soon had concentrated more than 100,000 troops there. Although Lincoln urged him to "strike a blow," he laid deliberate siege to Yorktown and allowed Confederate Brigadier General John B. Magruder with only 17,000 men stretched across the lower Peninsula to delay the advance for almost a month, ample time for Johnston to interpose the bulk of his army between McClellan and Richmond. McClellan exaggerated the Confederate numbers reported to him by his chief intelligence agent, the detective Allan Pinkerton, and avoided a decisive engagement.

Meanwhile, General Lee, now assigned under the direction of President Davis to the "control of [Confederate] military operations," took steps to strengthen Johnston's hand against the Federal threat. From relatively secure points along the lower Atlantic, Lee drew reinforcements piecemeal to Virginia. But his most important action was designed to weaken McClellan by keeping the Union forces divided. Lincoln had held one corps of the army, McDowell's, in the Fredericksburg area but intended to release it to McClellan when satisfied that the capital was in no immediate danger.

Lee sought to deny Lincoln this satisfaction. The only Confederate army still in position to threaten Washington at all was a force of some 17,000 commanded by Stonewall Jackson in the Shenandoah Valley. On April 21 Lee wrote Jackson suggesting that he attack the Federals there and, if possible, move down the Valley, north, that is, in such a way as to create the impression he intended to cross the Potomac into Maryland. "I have hoped," said Lee, "in the present divided condition of the enemy's forces that a successful blow may be dealt them by a rapid combination of our troops before they can be strengthened themselves either in position or by re-enforcements."

Jackson's execution of Lee's suggestion exceeded all hopes and gave the world an unforgettable demonstration of the leadership of intuition, audacity, and will, those qualities most valued by Clausewitz, and of the employment of terrain, interior lines, mobility, surprise, and concentration of force against divided opponents, those tactical principles most prized by Jomini. Jackson's command was surrounded by more than three times as many Union troops. But the Federals were divided into three forces under Major General Nathaniel Banks at the mouth of the Valley; Frémont, restored to a smaller command, in the Alleghenies west of the Valley; and Brigadier General James Shields on the eastern side of the Valley, thus allowing Jackson to strike each separately in turn.

He did so with unsurpassed boldness and skill, sweeping up and down the Valley, using the Massanutten Mountain along the Valley's trough as a shield, and darting through the mountain's gap and around its extremities to take his opponents repeatedly unawares. Between May 8 and June 9 he marched his men almost four hundred miles, fought five battles, and captured as many Federal soldiers as he had in his entire force, in addition to taking large quantities of arms and supplies.

Great as these tactical accomplishments were, the strategic accomplishment was greater. As Lee anticipated, Jackson's campaign not only tied down some 60,000 Union troops in the Valley; it also induced Lincoln to withhold McDowell's entire corps from McClellan in an effort to trap Jackson and protect Washington at the same time, thus preventing the Union forces in Virginia from concentrating against Johnston's army on the Peninsula.

As the Valley campaign drew to a close, the major armies on the Peninsula came to battle only five miles from Richmond and in view of the city's church spires. In approaching the city McClellan disposed his army astride the rain-swollen and seemingly impassable Chickahominy River, with three of his five corps north of the stream in order to cover his base on the York River and be in position for McDowell's corps, still expected from northern Virginia, to link up. On May 31 Johnston threw the bulk of his army against the two Union corps south of the Chickahominy in the battle of Seven Pines or Fair Oaks. Johnston's plan was good, to engage a portion of the enemy with the mass of his own army, but the execution was faulty. The attack was tardy and the coordination weak. McClellan was able with great difficulty to bring reinforcements from north of the river and halt the Confederate advance. Late in the afternoon Johnston was severely wounded in attempting to get the elements of his army to attack in unison. The next day Davis named Lee to command the army.

Robert E. Lee was the incarnation of the cavalier tradition so dear to the southern heart. He was descended from two of the most venerated families of Virginia, the Lees and Carters, and was the son of "Lighthorse Harry" Lee, one of the most illustrious soldiers of the American Revolution. Lee was an exemplary cadet at West Point (class of 1829) and a celebrated hero of the Mexican War. Of his role there Winfield Scott, the war's most brilliant general, said, "American success in Mexico was largely due to the skill, valor, and undaunted energy of Robert E. Lee.... He was the very best soldier I ever saw in the field." In ad-

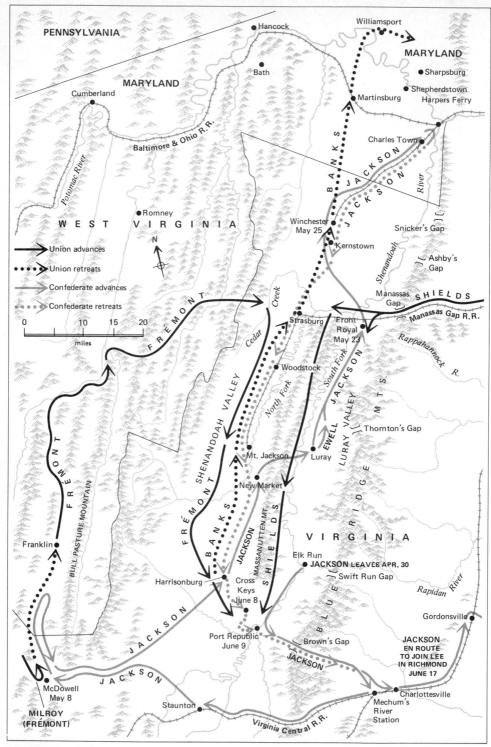

PENNSYLVANIA

MARYLAND

Hancock

Williamsport

MARYLAND

Bath

Sharpsburg

Shepherdstown
Harpers Ferry

Cumberland

Martinsburg

Baltimore & Ohio R.R.

Potomac River

Charles Town

WEST VIRGINIA

Romney

BANKS

JACKSON

JACKSON

Jackson River

Snicker's Gap

Winchester
May 25

Kernstown

Ashby's
Gap

N

Union advances

Union retreats

Confederate advances

Confederate retreats

Shenandoah

Manassas
Gap

SHIELDS

Manassas Gap R.R.

FRÉMONT

Cedar Creek

Strasburg

Front
Royal
May 23

Rappahannock R.

0   10   15   20
miles

FRÉMONT

SHENANDOAH VALLEY

Cedar

Woodstock

North Fork

South Fork

JACKSON

LURAY VALLEY

EWELL

Thornton's Gap

FRÉMONT

Mt. Jackson

Luray

BANKS

New Market

MASSANUTTEN MT.

SHIELDS

BLUE RIDGE MTS.

VIRGINIA

Franklin

BULL PASTURE MOUNTAIN

Elk Run
JACKSON LEAVES APR. 30

Swift Run Gap

Rapidan River

Harrisonburg

Cross
Keys
June 8

Gordonsville

JACKSON

Port Republic
June 9

Brown's Gap

JACKSON
EN ROUTE
TO JOIN LEE
IN RICHMOND
JUNE 17

JACKSON

McDowell
May 8

JACKSON

Staunton

Charlottesville

Mechum's
River
Station

MILROY
(FRÉMONT)

Virginia Central R.R.

JACKSON'S SHENANDOAH VALLEY CAMPAIGN, MAY–JUNE 1862

ROBERT E. LEE   (Valentine
Museum, Richmond, Virginia)

dition to all this, Lee was a devout Episcopalian and a strikingly handsome man of Jovelike bearing. He had been Lincoln's first choice to
command the Union army in the war.

Lee's allegiance to the Confederacy presents contradictions. He had
opposed both slavery and secession, and he was noted in the United
States Army for his breadth of mind and nationalistic outlook. But he
cast his lot with Virginia when the state seceded, saying he could not
draw his sword against his own people. After the war, in a letter to the
British historian Lord Acton, Lee would explain his decision by saying
he believed that the maintenance of the rights and authority reserved
by the Constitution to the states was the safeguard to the preservation
of a free government. "I consider it as the chief source of stability to our
political system, whereas the consolidation of the states into one vast
republic, sure to be aggressive abroad and despotic at home, will be the
certain precursor of that ruin which has overwhelmed all those that

have preceded it." In this passage he identified the dilemma and the danger in the rise of great powers.

Whether Davis was right to make Lee an army commander is prob-lematical. Lee's inspired leadership of the principal Confederate army, which he at once named the Army of Northern Virginia, would win many brilliant victories and place him among the great field command-ers of all history. But the appointment deprived the Confederacy of his strategic guidance at the seat of the government. Hattaway and Jones have concluded that his position in Richmond resembled that of a present-day chief of staff of the United States Army, and they approv-ingly quote biographer Douglas Southall Freeman's statement that there were few, if any, periods of Lee's service "during which he con-tributed more to sustain the Confederate cause." Possibly he ought to have been left where he was.

Lee quickly decided to renew the attack against McClellan, but to concentrate the Confederate army on the single Union corps, Brigadier General Fitz John Porter's Fifth Corps, that now remained north of the Chickahominy. From a dazzling cavalry ride conducted by Brigadier General J. E. B. "Jeb" Stuart around McClellan's entire army, Lee learned that the Union right flank was "in the air"; that it was neither anchored on a strong terrain feature such as a river or swamp, nor was it "refused," curved back to form a defensive perimeter. To strengthen his blow, Lee ordered Jackson to bring his force by rail via the Virginia Central Railroad to Ashland Station north of Richmond and join the at-tack by turning Porter's open flank and striking him from the rear.

On June 26 Lee opened his counteroffensive in what would become known as the Seven Days' battles by attacking Porter's line at Mechan-icsville. But Lee now experienced the same kind of difficulties that had beset Johnston, difficulties of the "friction of war." Things began to go wrong and abort Lee's plan. The worst thing to go wrong was Jackson's uncharacteristic tardiness and lethargy throughout the entire operation, apparently the effect of fatigue from his earlier exertions. Porter held off the attacks of three Confederate divisions, those of Brigadier General A. P. Hill, Major General D. H. Hill, and Major General James Long-street, and upon learning of Jackson's presence, Porter withdrew to Gaines' Mill where on the 27th Lee renewed his attack. Though driven from his position, Porter was able to withdraw south of the Chickahominy to Savage Station, where on the 29th Lee again assailed him, but without decisive results.

All the while McClellan held most of his army idle south of the Chickahominy. Deceived by artful Confederate demonstrations there, he continued to exaggerate his opponents' strength and persisted in be-lieving the main Confederate attack would fall south of the river. On the 27th, increasingly nervous, he decided to change his base from the York River to Harrison's Landing on the James River where it could be

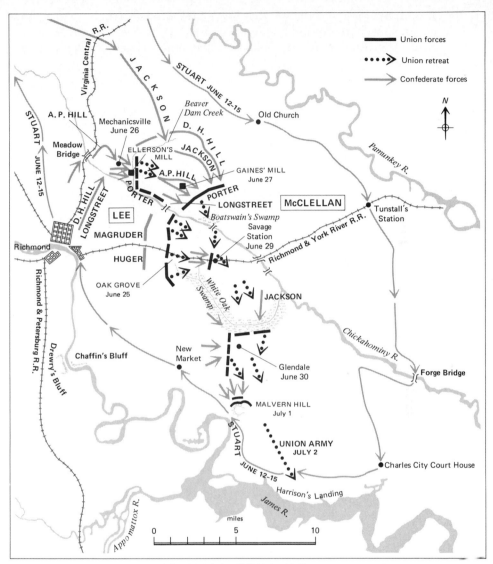

THE SEVEN DAYS' BATTLES, JUNE 25–JULY 1, 1862

supported by the navy, and he ordered his entire army there. This was a retreat if not an abandonment of the campaign for Richmond.

Demoralized and furious at Lincoln for withholding McDowell's corps, McClellan dictated to Stanton a report which included one of the most insubordinate messages ever composed by a general to his superiors. It said, "I have lost this battle because my force was too small....This Government has not sustained this army....If I save this army now, I tell you plainly that I owe no thanks to you or to any other persons in Washington. You have done your best to sacrifice this army." Fortunately for McClellan, a subordinate deleted this part of the telegram.

Lee sensed that McClellan was headed for the James River and attempted to strike the Union army a crippling blow while it was on the move. But the Confederates were unable to penetrate the Union covering force in the battle of Glendale (June 30), and McClellan successfully established his army in a strong position on the face of Malvern Hill. On the afternoon of July 1, believing the Union army was continuing its retreat, Lee attacked Malvern Hill only to be repulsed bloodily; especially punishing was the massed Union artillery fire. Nevertheless, the following day McClellan withdrew to Harrison's Landing and the Peninsula campaign was over.

In all but the final results the Seven Days' battles were a series of indecisive engagements capped by a Union victory in which together the Confederates suffered far more casualties than the Federals, over 20,000 to fewer than 16,000. But Lee's boldness aborted the Union offensive and saved the capital of the Confederacy. These accomplishments, coming in the wake of stunning Confederate losses at Shiloh and New Orleans, immensely boosted the morale and will of the southern population. Thus the Seven Days' battles were a Confederate strategic victory of incalculable dimensions.

Sorely disappointed, Lincoln visited McClellan at his base in an effort to learn his plans and spur him into effectual action. Instead of submitting specific plans, McClellan handed the departing president a letter lecturing him on the proper political objects of the war, urging that the southern economy and society, and especially slavery, remain untouched. Only in this way, he said, could Lincoln save "our poor country." McClellan, and Lincoln, were under mounting fire from the Radicals because of these already-known views, which, together with McClellan's failures in the field, brought a wave of despondency throughout the North. Lincoln himself was despondent, but he refused to give in to the feeling. Instead, he declared, "I expect to maintain this contest until successful, or till I die, or am conquered, or my term expires, or Congress or the country forsakes me." Also, he now moved to adopt new measures in the hope of ending the military impasse.

What Lincoln did was to combine the scattered Union forces in northern Virginia into a single army and place General Pope, captor of Island No. 10, in command. Lincoln also brought Halleck to Washington as general in chief. The president was soon to become disappointed in Halleck for failing to give genuine direction and energy to the Union armies: in other words, failing to carry out his assignment. Lincoln was to say of him that he was of little more use than a "first-rate clerk." But Halleck did free the president of many administrative details, and eventually Halleck would become an important cog in the Union military machine, though not as general in chief.

Worn out with McClellan's delays, Lincoln began withdrawing his army from the Peninsula in early August in a move to join it to Pope's command on the Rapidan River, thus creating a force of 150,000. Lee did not wait for the Union armies to combine against his 70,000. Before he discerned his opponent's intention he started Jackson's corps north by rail to deploy near Gordonsville as a screen against Pope. Jackson hoped to repeat his earlier spectacular successes by attacking an isolated unit of the enemy. Instead, on August 9 Banks led his corps in a sharp assault on Jackson at Cedar Mountain that temporarily broke the Confederate line. Eventually Jackson got his reserves up and forced Banks to withdraw; Lee was now fully alert to the threat from the north.

When on August 13 Lee learned of the reduced Union strength on the Peninsula, he sensed that Pope was to be reinforced from there and began at once to move the bulk of his army to join Jackson, leaving a small force to guard Richmond. Lee hoped to swing across the Rapidan River east of Pope and strike his base at Brandy Station on the railroad. Pope, however, prevented this move by retreating behind the Rappahannock. Lee, now aware of the approach of Union troops withdrawn from the Peninsula, planned an attack on Pope before their arrival. While Longstreet's corps occupied Pope on the Rappahannock, Jackson with the other corps would turn the Union position by marching north through Thoroughfare Gap in the Bull Run Mountains, then east to fall upon Pope's base at Manassas Junction on the railroad. Lee and Longstreet would follow a day later and join forces with Jackson for a massed assault on the disorganized foe.

Lee's plan exemplified his tactical theory. He had made this theory explicit a few days earlier in an explanatory message to Jackson which said, "...to save you the abundance of hard fighting...I ventured to suggest for your consideration not to attack the enemy's strong points, but to turn his position...so as to draw him out of them." Lee's tactics in the Second Bull Run campaign were daringly unorthodox. By dividing his army, he temporarily exposed each segment to defeat separately, a decision he defended by saying simply, "The disparity of numbers between the contending forces rendered the risk unavoidable." He later amplified this statement by saying he preferred the risk of action to the certain loss of inaction: a dictum that might stand as the very essence of his theory of generalship.

Marching almost sixty miles in two days (August 25–26), Jackson's column captured, plundered, and burned the Union depot at Manassas. When Pope attempted to turn on the isolated Confederate corps it disappeared into a woods near Groveton on the Warrenton Turnpike, where Pope was unable to discover it for an entire day. On the 28th

Jackson emerged to attack an isolated Union division that approached along the turnpike; then at dark he withdrew into an abandoned railway cut west of the turnpike. All the following day the Federals unsuccessfully assaulted Jackson's position.

In the late afternoon Pope ordered Porter to attack Jackson's right flank, but Porter refused to do so because his scouts now reported the presence of Longstreet's corps moving into position on his own left flank. On August 30, as the Union army continued to concentrate its efforts on Jackson, Lee delivered a powerful counterattack with Longstreet's corps against the exposed Union flank, Porter's corps, and drove it back to the very Henry House hill where Jackson had gained his nickname the year before. During the night Pope began a withdrawal of his demoralized army to Centreville.

The following day Lee, hoping to deliver a coup de grâce to his defeated foe, again sent Jackson in an arc to the north and east to cut off the retreating Union column. But Jackson's troops were exhausted from their previous efforts, and he was halted by the Union rear guard in hard fighting at Chantilly. Lee, aware of the arrival of heavy Union reinforcements from the Peninsula, now called off his attack and began to ponder a new strategic move, one to be launched into the North itself.

Union defeat at Second Bull Run, or Manassas to the Confederates, stirred bitter recrimination within the army and the government. As always, casualties were heavy: 16,000 Union and more than 9,000 Confederate. McClellan blamed the defeat on Pope. Pope blamed it on Porter, McClellan's friend and protégé, brought court-martial charges of negligence and disobedience against Porter, and ousted from the service the soldier whose corps had borne the brunt of the fighting on the Peninsula and had been chiefly responsible for repelling the Confederate assault on Malvern Hill. Years after the war Porter would be exonerated and reinstated to his regular army rank of colonel.

Again Lincoln was in despair. One observer believed he was almost ready to hang himself. Riding out to the Soldiers' Home on the outskirts of Washington where he often sought quiet and relief, Lincoln said, "We may as well stop fighting." But he did not stop fighting. Instead, over the earnest protests of most of his cabinet, especially Stanton and Chase, he restored McClellan to the command of all the troops in northern Virginia, now combined into an enlarged Army of the Potomac.

The decision was taken at grave political risk. In addition to the general disappointment with McClellan over the failure of the Peninsula campaign, he was, as already noted, despised by the Radicals because of his political views. Secretary of the Navy Welles recorded the opinion that if McClellan should fail this time, "...the wrath and indignation against [Lincoln] and the Administration will be great and unrestrained." Lincoln scolded the vain and temperamental McClellan

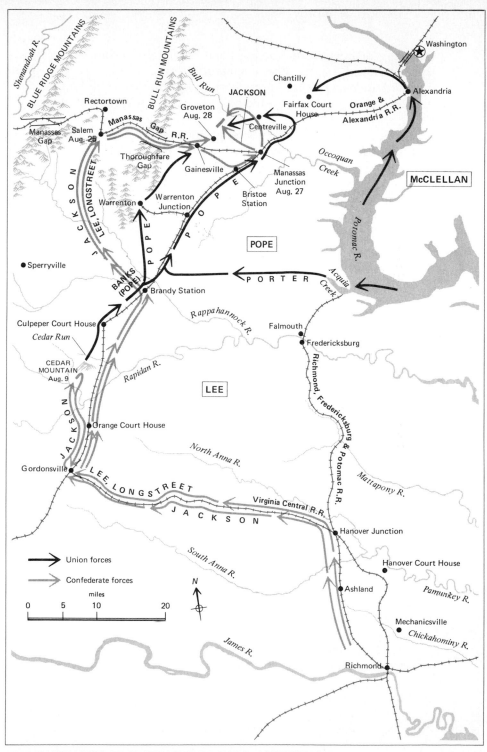

THE CAMPAIGN OF SECOND BULL RUN, AUGUST 1862

for being dilatory in reinforcing Pope before the recent battle, but he was convinced that no other commander could so effectually bring the defeated and demoralized army back to fighting trim. "If he can't fight himself," explained the president, "he excels in making others ready to fight."

At summer's end, largely through the spectacular operations of Lee and his lieutenants, Confederate fortunes were on the rise. The southern army in Virginia, seemingly invincible, was on the offensive. Also, despite the Union's western victories the preceding spring, the Union effort in the West was now at a deadlock. Having arrived at Pittsburg Landing soon after the battle there, Halleck took more than a month of marching and entrenching to move the army twenty miles to Corinth, only to find the Confederates gone when he got there. They had withdrawn to Tupelo, located on the Mobile and Ohio Railroad forty miles south of Corinth.

Halleck, instead of keeping his force, now above 100,000, concentrated for a decisive campaign down the Mississippi River to join the Union force at New Orleans, sent Buell east with the Army of the Ohio to take Chattanooga, and spread the Army of the Tennessee along the lines from Corinth to Memphis and back to Cairo. When on July 11 Halleck was called to Washington as general in chief, Grant was left in command of the Army of the Tennessee, with headquarters at Jackson, Tennessee, on the Mobile and Ohio Railroad fifty miles north of Corinth. Buell was not under his command, and Grant took no immediate action to concentrate his own forces in order to keep pressure on the Confederates in his direct front.

Thus Confederate victories in the East and Union inertia and dispersal in the West gave the southern leaders an opportunity to mount a great strategic triple counteroffensive in the fall of 1862. Lee would invade Maryland to supply his hungry troops, attempt to bring the state into the Confederacy, and possibly obtain foreign recognition of Confederate independence, for which, to be explained later, the time appeared to be ripe. Braxton Bragg, now a full general and in command of the main Confederate army in the West, would invade Kentucky with similar objects in mind. Van Dorn, in command of the remaining Confederate forces in Mississippi, would attempt to recapture the important rail center at Corinth and invade western Tennessee.

The Maryland campaign may be viewed as the main Confederate effort because it involved the largest Confederate army in a strike at the very nerve center of the Union. With Stuart's cavalry screening the march, Lee moved rapidly northwest around the Union army and on September 5, with bands playing "Maryland, My Maryland," began crossing the Potomac near the town of Frederick some forty miles above Washington. He at once issued a proclamation inviting the people of the state to bring it into the Confederacy, and at the same time he suggested to President Davis that he make a peace proposal to the Union government, a move that Lee hoped would increase the peace party in the North.

Lee was quickly disappointed at the cool reception given his proclamation by the citizens of western Maryland, and Davis considered the peace proposal untimely. Thus the outcome of the campaign would rest entirely on the shoulders of Lee and his ragged and hungry army.

Lee intended to strike for Harrisburg, capital of Pennsylvania, and an important communications center lying at the point where the Pennsylvania Railroad crossed the Susquehanna River. He would shield his march behind South Mountain, a prolongation of the Blue Ridge running almost to Harrisburg. Capture of this city would sever the direct line connecting Washington and the eastern seaboard to the states of the northwest. It would also place at Lee's disposal the rich farmland of western Maryland and Pennsylvania, and would threaten such major eastern cities as Washington, Baltimore, and Philadelphia.

To secure his line of communication through the Shenandoah Valley to his base in northern Virginia, Lee needed to hold Harpers Ferry at the mouth of the Valley, and on September 9 he sent Jackson with 15,000 troops to seize that strategic spot from the 10,000-man garrison guarding it. Once it was taken, Jackson was to rejoin the main body of the army on the march into Pennsylvania. Lee was willing to take such a risk because he believed he understood his opponent's timidity, as he explained to an anxious subordinate: "[McClellan's army] will not be prepared for offensive operations—or he will not think it so—for three or four weeks. Before that time I hope to be on the Susquehanna."

Ordinarily Lee's appraisal of McClellan's attitude would have been accurate. But the Union commander, urged by Lincoln, now moved with greater than usual vigor to keep his army between Lee and Washington. By September 13 the Army of the Potomac was north of the river and concentrated around Frederick. Then and there something happened that offers a remarkable illustration of Clausewitz's contention that chance and uncertainty are two of the most common and most important elements in warfare. A Union soldier in bivouac spied on the ground a small bundle that, upon investigation, turned out to be three cigars wrapped in a sheet of paper. The paper was a copy of Lee's campaign order which had been dropped by some unknown officer. The order quickly reached McClellan and cleared his mind of the "fog of war," a condition shared by all commanders but which seems especially to have plagued him. When he became aware of what had befallen him he is said to have exclaimed, "Here is a piece of paper with which if I cannot whip 'Bobby Lee,' I will be willing to go home."

Knowing that Lee's army was divided, with Jackson's corps still south of the Potomac, McClellan ought to have been able to win a truly decisive victory. Or so most students of the campaign have concluded.

His tactical plan was sound: to move his army through the passes in South Mountain—Turner's Gap, Fox's Gap, and Crampton's Gap—place it between the segments of the Confederate army, and, in McClellan's words, "cut the enemy in two and beat him in detail." But the execution of the plan was slow and faulty. Not until the following morning, September 14, did McClellan get his columns moving; not until noon did they reach the South Mountain passes. By then Lee had detected the Union move and disposed forces to plug the gaps. By late evening, after hard fighting, the Union army was in possession of them, but Lee was now withdrawing to recross the river into Virginia. McClellan had lost a golden opportunity to deal the Confederacy a perhaps mortal blow.

Lee now offered him another opportunity. Upon receiving word from Jackson that the defenders of Harpers Ferry had capitulated, Lee decided to make a stand at Sharpsburg north of the Potomac and ordered Jackson to join him there. This decision is difficult to explain except in the light of Lee's understanding of his opponent's character. Lee's chief biographer, Douglas Southall Freeman, suggests he may have believed also that a tactical victory here would enable him to resume the original campaign plan.

Lee never shrank from risk, and this may have been his most daring judgment. At the moment, he had fewer than 20,000 troops at Sharpsburg. McClellan with more than twice that number was closer to Lee than Jackson was and might have been capable of smashing him before Jackson's arrival. Again McClellan moved with caution and deliberation, and though his army was in position on the afternoon of the 16th he did not attack until the following morning. Jackson by then was on the field with a portion of his troops, after marching the twelve miles from Harpers Ferry during the night. McClellan's second grand opportunity was slipping away.

Even now, at least in theory, the Army of the Potomac should have destroyed its opponent. Lee still had fewer than 30,000 men in line, and, because of unusual straggling by the barefoot and bleeding soldiers on the rocky Maryland roads, would have hardly more than 40,000 when all reserves had arrived from Harpers Ferry. McClellan's total force was more than twice that number. Lee's back was to the Potomac; a defeat here would mean the destruction of his army.

McClellan failed to accomplish this feat. His tactical plan called for a main effort of three corps—those of Brigadier General Joseph Hooker, Major General Edwin V. Sumner, and Brigadier General Joseph K. F. Mansfield—against Lee's left flank to sever it from the river while another corps, Burnside's, occupied the rest of the Confederate force by attacking the right flank at its anchor on Antietam Creek, a tributary of the Potomac. McClellan planned at the critical moment to commit his reserves for the fatal stroke at the center of the line.

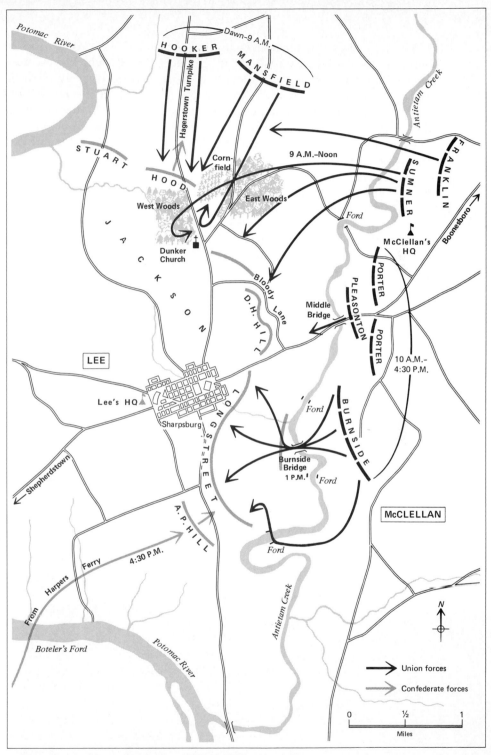

THE BATTLE OF ANTIETAM, SEPTEMBER 17, 1862

The fatal stroke never fell. Beginning at dawn the Union army delivered a powerful attack against the Confederate left, which was held by Jackson's corps. The southerners had no earthworks but fought from behind rocks and fences and used whatever protection the terrain afforded. Coordination among the three attacking Union corps was slack, and though Hooker temporarily penetrated Jackson's line at the Dunker Church on the Hagerstown Turnpike, Lee sealed the breach by shifting troops from Longstreet's corps on the right.

At the extreme right of the Confederate line Burnside's Union corps attacked at midafternoon. After repeated charges it was able to take the Stone Bridge, afterward known as the Burnside Bridge, across Antietam Creek and the high ground beyond, only to be repulsed at the end of the day by A. P. Hill's division, the last of Jackson's corps to arrive, clad in captured blue jackets, after a grueling march from Harpers Ferry during which Hill was reported to have urged his soldiers on by prodding laggards with the point of his sword. The battle of Antietam—Sharpsburg, to the Confederates—closed at dark after what is remembered as the bloodiest day of the Civil War, with more than 12,000 Union casualties and almost 14,000 Confederate.

The Federal effort came within an inch of success. Throughout most of the battle the Army of Northern Virginia hung on the edge of disaster. Hill's arrival at the last possible moment saved the day for the

CONFEDERATE DEAD NEAR THE SHELL-MARKED DUNKER CHURCH

southerners. Lee's deathbed words uttered five years after the war—
"Tell Hill he must come up"—were possibly an unconscious return of
the mind to that desperate field. During the night and the following day
the two armies faced each other in their positions, too wounded and
weary to resume the fighting. In remaining north of the Potomac Lee
again exhibited a breathtaking audacity, for his resources were almost
spent. McClellan failed to renew the assault, which, had he done so
with all the troops at his command, might have destroyed the crippled
Confederate army.

Throughout the campaign McClellan had yielded to caution, vastly
overestimating the Confederate strength and refusing to take the risk of
full commitment. His greatest tactical mistake during the actual battle
was to withhold some 20,000 troops from the corps of Fitz John Porter
and Major General William B. Franklin and the cavalry commanded
by Brigadier General Alfred Pleasonton as a reserve against a feared
counterattack by a Confederate reserve that existed only in his imagination. Thus he violated the military principle of "economy of force,"
and failed to employ all available troops. During the night of September
18 the Confederates recrossed the Potomac into Virginia, leaving
McClellan to issue pronouncements of a victory that "saved the
Union," but provoking Lincoln to expressions of disgust over the escape of Lee's army.

The battle of Antietam was a tactical draw, though the Confederates
counted it a victory because the Union attack was repelled. Yet, notwithstanding Lincoln's displeasure, the entire campaign amounted to
an important strategic victory for the Union because Lee failed to accomplish any of the objects of his northern advance. Moreover, two
crucial nonmilitary results, to be more completely explained later,
emerged from the Confederate failure: the British government, which
had been thinking seriously of offering formal recognition of Confederate independence, now decided to wait; and President Lincoln, who
had been planning to issue an emancipation proclamation but believed
it ought to be done in the glow of a victory, now decided he had
enough of one to go ahead with his announcement.

While Lee's operations in Virginia and Maryland during the sum-
mer were unfolding, General Bragg undertook his campaign against the
Union forces in the West. His main opponent was General Buell, whose
army was in northern Alabama making its way east toward its goal,
Chattanooga, with advance elements within twenty miles of the city.
Deliberate and tentative by nature, similar in this respect to McClellan,
Buell found himself hampered by the daring and destructive Confederate cavalry raids in Tennessee and Kentucky led by Brigadier General
Nathan Bedford Forrest and Colonel John Hunt Morgan. Buell's slug-
gishness and the failure, first of Halleck and then Grant, to keep pressure on Bragg permitted him to carry out an almost incredible strategic

use of the railroads in which the Confederates half-circled the Union army by hauling a force of 30,000 from Tupelo, Mississippi, roundabout by way of Mobile and Atlanta to Chattanooga, a movement of some 776 miles.

Bragg originally intended to cut Buell's line of communications by moving from Chattanooga to seize Nashville. Meeting in Chattanooga in late July with Major General Edmund Kirby Smith, the Confederate commander in eastern Tennessee, Bragg believed he had persuaded Kirby Smith to join him in this operation. But Kirby Smith had a different idea. Influenced by Morgan, whose home was in Lexington, Kentucky, Kirby Smith believed Kentucky was ripe for Confederate possession; on August 15, preceded by Morgan's cavalry, Kirby Smith led his army of 20,000, not toward a junction with Bragg, but directly into eastern Kentucky with Lexington as his immediate objective. Defeating a small Union force at Richmond thirty miles south of Lexington, he occupied Lexington on September 2.

Although Bragg was Kirby Smith's senior in rank, he now felt obliged to alter his plan and make Kentucky his objective. Marching his army from Chattanooga across the Cumberland highlands of central Tennessee, he arrived on September 14 at Glasgow, Kentucky, where he issued a proclamation inviting not only Kentucky but the entire Northwest to join the Confederacy. Like Lee's invitation to Maryland, Bragg's overture fell on deaf ears. The next day Bragg's advance reached Munfordville, where it confronted a Union force of some 4,000 under Colonel John T. Wilder. After a highly unorthodox episode in which Wilder was permitted to visit the Confederate lines and satisfy himself that resistance would be futile and capitulation honorable, he surrendered the garrison.

Bragg had indicated that Louisville and possibly Cincinnati were his objectives. Although the Federal War Department frantically rushed troops to protect the two cities, the Confederates probably could have taken Louisville if they had marched directly upon it from Munfordville. Buell was on the move by way of Nashville to challenge them, but Bragg was between Buell and Louisville and Kirby Smith was closer to Louisville than Buell was. Bragg, however, now turned east in the direction of Lexington, hoping to facilitate a junction with Kirby Smith, and scattering his divisions widely throughout the countryside to forage and recruit additional soldiers. With the road to Louisville now open, Buell promptly marched there.

Lincoln was dismayed at the failure to stalk and engage the Confederate army in Kentucky, and he ordered Buell replaced by General George H. Thomas but changed his mind when Thomas protested against the shift in command. A chastened Buell with a force increased to 60,000 now moved to the offensive.

Bragg was not prepared for a pitched battle. Although the total Confederate strength in Kentucky was now almost equal to the Union strength, the Confederates were badly dispersed. Recruitment efforts were disappointing; many Kentuckians were pro-Confederate but wary of risking open support. Kirby Smith explained the situation pithily and bitterly: "Their hearts are evidently with us, but their blue-grass and fat grass [cattle] are against us." Another cause for the lack of Confederate concentration was the violation of the important military principle of unity of command. Kirby Smith exercised an independent command; Davis had turned down Bragg's recommendation that he, Bragg, the senior officer, be placed in sole command of the expedition. Kirby Smith, erroneously believing Lexington to be threatened by a Union column from Cincinnati, remained in the Lexington area and resisted Bragg's efforts to combine the two forces.

Bragg attempted to solve these problems through both political and military measures. First, he sought to establish the refugee Confederate government of Kentucky through which he hoped to apply Confederate laws, especially conscription. Second, unable to command Kirby Smith, Bragg tried to negotiate a concerted movement of the two Confederate armies. Under the impression Buell was heading for the state capital, Frankfort, Bragg and Kirby Smith, meeting October 1 in Lexington, agreed to converge upon the Union army before it reached its destination. Meeting with the two generals was the Confederate gubernatorial claimant, Richard Hawes, successor to the original Confederate claimant, George W. Johnson, who had been killed fighting in the southern army at Shiloh.

On October 4, under Confederate military auspices and with Bragg and Kirby Smith in attendance, Hawes was inaugurated governor in Frankfort. But by now the appearance of the military situation was radically changed. Buell's objective was not Frankfort; at Lincoln's prodding, the objective was Bragg's army, still dispersed, with Kirby Smith's force now at Frankfort and Bragg's troops scattered from Bardstown to Danville forty miles south of Frankfort. Desperately, Bragg attempted to concentrate all of the Confederate troops at Harrodsburg thirty miles south of Frankfort. Before he could do so, elements of the opposing armies came together at Perryville ten miles southwest of the planned concentration point. Though neither commander had planned a battle here, the urgent need of both armies for water from Doctor's Creek precipitated the fighting.

The battle of Perryville (October 8, 1862) was of medium size in the numbers of men engaged, but it was large in fury and in ultimate consequences. Only about a third of Bragg's army, some 15,000 troops from Leonidas Polk's and William J. Hardee's two corps, were at Perryville. Approximately two-thirds of Buell's force, more than double the Confederate strength, were present. Nevertheless, under Bragg's personal command the Confederates attacked the Union left. At first successful, the assault was eventually repulsed though only half of Buell's troops ever got into the fight. Because of atmospheric conditions that muffled the sound of the firing, Buell and the rest of his army apparently remained unaware that a battle was raging only a short distance away. At the end of a day of hard fighting, with approximately 3,700 Federal casualties and over 3,000 Confederate casualties, both lines were still intact. During the night, before Buell could bring his entire strength to bear, Bragg withdrew the Confederates to Harrodsburg.

All the Confederate troops were now close enough together to achieve a quick concentration which would have given them sufficient strength, though still outnumbered, to challenge the Federals. But Bragg, discouraged by the low yields both in recruiting and foraging, and by news of Confederate defeat in Mississippi, to be discussed below, and advised by his corps commanders Polk and Hardee, decided to abandon Kentucky. While the army marched by way of the Cumberland Gap back into Tennessee, he traveled to the Confederate capital to explain the campaign in person. Although Davis was aware that Bragg's corps commanders were critical of his conduct in Kentucky, Davis accepted his explanation and left him in command of the army. As the Confederates retreated into eastern Tennessee, the Federals moved back into middle Tennessee, assembling at Nashville. Bragg rejoined his army in Knoxville with orders to advance upon Buell.

In many ways the Kentucky campaign ended quite similarly to Lee's Maryland campaign. Temporarily the Confederate march into Kentucky had turned the Union position in the West and redressed the balance there; Perryville, like Antietam, was viewed by the Confederates as a narrow tactical victory for the South. Yet the campaign as a whole was a strategic victory for the Union because it failed either to gain Kentucky for the Confederacy or to cripple the northern army in the West.

As Lee's army recuperated in northern Virginia after the ordeal of Antietam and Bragg's army converged toward Harrodsburg prior to Perryville, the Confederates in northern Mississippi, commanded by Van Dorn, undertook the third operation of the southern counteroffensive—the effort to regain Corinth. Grant anticipated and attempted to prevent the Confederate move by ordering an attack on one wing of the Confederates, which was commanded by General Sterling Price and located at Iuka, a town on the Memphis and Charleston Railroad twenty miles east of Corinth. Two Federal forces were supposed to converge on Price, one led by Brigadier General William S. Rosecrans, who had replaced Pope when that general was ordered to Virginia, the other led by Brigadier General Edward Ord. Price escaped by striking Rosecrans on September 19, before the Union forces made junction, slipping away during the night and marching his troops south of Corinth to join Van Dorn's column twenty miles west of the town. This brought the united Confederate force up to about 22,000. Rosecrans retired into prepared works at Corinth.

On October 3 Van Dorn struck Rosecrans's entrenched army of approximately equal strength in the battle of Corinth. After penetrating the outer Union line west of the town, the Confederates were stopped by secondary defenses. Halting the attack at dark, Van Dorn regrouped and renewed the battle the following morning. Repeated frontal assaults were bloodily defeated, especially at Battery Robinett, a key Union position on high ground a mile west of the town, and in the early afternoon the Confederates retired, eventually to Holly Springs approximately fifty miles southwest of Corinth and equally distant southeast of Memphis. Union casualties at Corinth were 2,520; Confederate casualties, 3,433. Thus the Confederate effort to retake this important rail junction and strike back into western Tennessee ended in utter failure tactically as well as strategically.

Together the three Confederate reverses in the fall of 1862 were an important turning point in the war. Never again would the South be able to mount so nearly coordinated a series of operations. There would be later Confederate tactical victories, but they would yield no comparable strategic opportunity. Perhaps no one on either side then saw the full significance of these events. Lincoln was profoundly displeased with the performance of both McClellan and Buell. When McClellan, tactically idle a month after Antietam, complained that his horses were too tired for aggressive action, Lincoln replied sarcastically, "Will you pardon me for asking what the horses of your army have done since the battle of Antietam that would fatigue anything?"

His patience spent, Lincoln in late October relieved Buell of command and replaced him with Rosecrans, the victor of Corinth. Less than two weeks later the president removed McClellan and replaced him with Burnside. Neither McClellan nor Buell would get another command. Rosecrans remained so long in Nashville collecting supplies that Lincoln was at the point of dropping him before he ever fought another battle. Burnside began at once moving the Army of the Potomac toward Fredericksburg on the Rappahannock and an appointment with catastrophe.

V

Union Government, Administration, and Emancipation

❖

The initial impression in office made by Lincoln on the American public was not promising. To many easterners he was a "hayseed," a western prairie politician with uncouth speech and manners. He was caricatured as a gangling, rustic Ichabod of a man who cultivated popularity among the masses with his salty comments and anecdotes. Many citizens feared his lack of experience in administration would severely handicap him in running the affairs of state.

He seemed especially unqualified to be a war leader. His only military experience had been as the elected captain of an Illinois militia company in the Black Hawk Indian war of the early 1830s. He parodied this experience by recounting how he had led attacks on fields of wild onions. A story was told how he managed to get his company through a narrow gate in a fence. Unable to put the troops in proper formation, he halted them, ordered them to "fall out," then ordered them to "fall in" on the other side of the fence: an inelegant but eminently practical solution to the problem. Perhaps it gave a glimpse of the pragmatic, effectual war leader he was to become.

Some persons agreed with the early views of Secretary of State Seward that Lincoln would be a mere figurehead and Seward the power behind the throne. Lincoln's seeming indecision during the early weeks of the Fort Sumter crisis gave additional ammunition to his critics and little if any to his supporters.

Seward was not the only strong-willed man in Lincoln's cabinet. Rivaling Seward in ability and ambition was Secretary of the Treasury Salmon P. Chase of Ohio; like Seward, he was an aspirant for the presidency.

Lincoln soon demonstrated that he was president in fact as well as in name. His decisions and actions in the culmination of the Fort Sumter episode proved that he, and not a cabinet strongman, was in control of that situation. His response to the Confederate attack gave further indication of his self-confidence and determination. By delaying the opening of the special session of Congress until July 4, he gave himself almost three months in which to deal with the crisis as president and commander in chief of the armed forces, without being obliged to answer immediately to the lawmakers.

His measures during this period reflected a conviction that the president held broad discretionary powers to meet such an emergency. The measures demonstrated also that he possessed the strength of will to exercise these powers. In addition to his call for troops and establishment of a blockade, he increased the size of the regular army, directed Secretary of the Treasury Chase to advance federal funds for military purposes, and authorized restricted suspensions of the privilege of habeas corpus.

In his message to Congress when it assembled, Lincoln explained that "whether strictly legal or not," these actions were in accord with popular demand and were a public necessity, and that he trusted Congress would readily ratify them. Presented with a fait accompli, and because most of the members doubtless approved of the actions, Congress did so. Eventually, after the war, the Supreme Court validated the actions. Lincoln also expressed the broader view that a violation of parts of the Constitution might sometimes be necessary in order to save the whole. He once explained this view by saying, "Often a limb must be amputated to save a life; but a life is never wisely given to save a limb."

Temporarily, Lincoln and a majority in Congress were agreed on a single war aim, preservation of the Union. In July, influenced by the Union military defeat at Bull Run, Congress enacted an explicit resolution to this effect, including a declaration that the rights of the several states (in other words, slavery) also would be preserved. Inevitably, this simple, doubtless simplistic, war aim would multiply as the war lengthened, expanded, and grew in intensity. From the beginning, the Radical Republican congressmen believed emancipation ought to be linked with the preservation of the Union. Led by Representative Thaddeus Stevens of Pennsylvania and Senator Charles Sumner of Massachusetts, and including Representative George W. Julian of Indiana and Senators Benjamin F. Wade of Ohio and Zachariah Chandler of Michigan, this group worked indefatigably in pursuit of its goal.

The Radicals also worked to shape the nature of the Union war effort itself. They were able to dominate the special congressional joint Committee on the Conduct of the War. Through its investigative function, the committee exposed fraud in military contracts and purchasing, and inefficiency in strategic and tactical operations. In some ways it mimicked the activities of the commissioners of the French revolutionary armies; it attempted to promote Republican generals of Radical persuasion, and it censured and badgered Democratic generals known or suspected to believe in a limited war aim.

General McClellan and other officers who supported him were prime targets of the committee. After the Union defeat at Ball's Bluff, the committee found a scapegoat in General Charles P. Stone and harassed him out of service. The committee's views and activities created strong tension between the Radicals and both Republican moderates and Democrats in Congress, and between the Radicals and the president. The chief links between the congressional Radicals and the Lincoln administration were Secretary of the Treasury Chase and Secretary of War Stanton, who in January 1862 replaced Simon Cameron after revelations of corruption and incompetence in his department. Stanton played a strong supporting role in the persecution of General Stone and in McClellan's fall from grace as a general, though probably most students of the war would say McClellan himself played the lead role in his own decline.

The Radicals argued that fighting a war caused by slavery made no sense without the abolition of slavery as a war aim. More practically, they pointed out that slaves were being used in large numbers by the Confederates to support their war effort and that emancipation was therefore a legitimate Union war measure. Influenced by this reasoning, Congress in August 1861 passed an ineffectual act providing for the seizure of all property being used to support the rebellion. Almost a year later, on July 17, 1862, with the scope and fury of the war vastly increased, Congress enacted the Second Confiscation Act, a sweeping measure providing for the confiscation of all property belonging to persons in rebellion against the United States, and explicitly for the emancipation of their slaves.

Although Lincoln signed these acts, he believed the second act was unconstitutional. He also disapproved of it on political grounds, because he was aware that at that point a large portion of the northern population, especially the Democrats, rejected emancipation as a war aim. He and his attorney general did little to enforce the acts. When certain of the Union generals, Frémont in Missouri in August 1861 and David Hunter in the department comprising the coastal region of Georgia, South Carolina, and Florida in May 1862, issued emancipation orders, Lincoln overruled them. By both words and actions he made clear that he intended to control the pace of progress on the explosive question of emancipation.

The Lincoln administration and Congress were involved in other measures of long-range importance to the future of the country. With the southern representatives gone from the Capitol, Congress now moved to enact a number of measures that the South had persistently and successfully opposed, including a strong protective tariff on many manufactured items, generous land grants as subsidies for the building of a transcontinental railroad along a northern route, a homestead act giving settlers 160-acre tracts of land from the national domain, and the Morrill Act for supporting with federal land grants the establishment of state agricultural and mechanical colleges. Thus the nation was not only to be reunited; it was to be reshaped according to northern economic, social, and cultural designs.

Meanwhile, the war mounted in violence, and Lincoln sought measures that would ensure victory in the shortest time and at the least cost. Frequently, he bypassed Congress and the courts in the urgency of his search. This was particularly so in his dealings with the Copperheads, persons in the North accused of committing acts of assistance to the Confederacy or disloyalty to the Union. There were many northern citizens of southern birth, ties, or sympathy, especially in such states as Ohio, Indiana, and Illinois; the Confederate army contained thousands of soldiers from their midst. Racial antipathies were strong throughout the North, particularly among those northerners of southern origin; many citizens everywhere resented what they looked upon as a war for the purpose of abolishing slavery. Also, many of the farmers of the Midwest were hostile toward the Republican economic program because they believed it pandered to the business and industrial interests of the Northeast at the expense of the farmers' welfare.

Out of this discontent, and with the encouragement and cooperation of Confederate agents, arose the secret organizations calling themselves the Knights of the Golden Circle, or Order of American Knights, or Sons of Liberty. Their immediate aims, like those of the many midwestern Democrats who were not members, were to win control of the northern state governments and to end the war. The more extreme among the disaffected northerners would do this by granting independence to the Confederacy, but a great majority believed peace could be achieved through some sort of negotiation that would restore the Union by allowing slavery to continue. Opposition to the Lincoln war measures ranged from discouraging enlistment, and later combating the draft, to such acts as assisting Confederate raiders and plotting to free Confederate prisoners of war and burn northern cities.

Lincoln dealt summarily with persons accused of such deeds or plots. Refusing, in many instances, to go through the tedious and time-consuming process of bringing formal accusations of treason into the courts, he preferred to suspend by executive action the privilege of habeas corpus and permit suspects to be arrested and held without trial. In September 1862 he issued a proclamation that for the duration of the insurrection all persons discouraging enlistment or otherwise engaged in disloyal practices would be subject to arrest and trial by a military court or commission.

More than 13,000 persons are known to have been arrested and held in this way, and there were other arbitrary arrests and detentions both by federal agencies and the states. One doubtless exaggerated estimate places the total at 38,000. Also, a few alleged Copperhead newspapers were suppressed for varying periods of time or denied mailing privileges through the United States postal service. These included such northern papers as the *New York World*, the *New York Journal of Commerce*, and the *Philadelphia Evening Journal*. Recent research indicates that most of the arrests, detentions, and newspaper suppressions occurred in the border slave states or portions of the Confederate states under Union control, areas where conditions were unsettled by conflicting loyalties. But enough of the controversial government actions took place elsewhere to suggest that Lincoln was willing to apply extraordinary methods wherever he felt them required to win the war.

These actions aroused fierce animosity among many northern citizens, though the majority considered them necessary. The actions were challenged ineffectually in the courts. When in May 1861 a Maryland secessionist named John Merryman was placed under military arrest, Chief Justice Taney attempted by a writ of habeas corpus to have him brought before a civilian court. The commanding officer of the district refused to do so; Lincoln upheld the officer, citing the Constitutional provision for the suspension of habeas corpus in cases of rebellion or invasion. Taney then issued an opinion (*ex parte Merryman*) that Congress alone had this authority, but he was powerless to enforce his view. Lincoln continued the practice of resorting to martial law by executive proclamation. In open letters he defended this as being justified by the desperate nature of the situation. To a group of protesters he said: "Must I shoot a simple-minded soldier boy who deserts, while I must not touch a hair of a wiley [sic] agitator who induces him to desert?"

The most famous instance of a military arrest and conviction, and of its resolution both out of court and in court, was that of the Ohio congressman Clement L. Vallandigham, who was arrested in May 1863 for violating an order of General Burnside, then commanding general of the Department of Ohio. The order prohibited public statements of sympathy for the enemy. Vallandigham was tried by a military commission, found guilty, and sentenced to prison for the duration of the war. Aware of the danger of arousing widespread popular disapproval, Lincoln shrewdly changed the sentence to that of banishment to the Confederacy. When Vallandigham later in the war returned by way of Canada to the Union and even entered conspicuously into northern politics, Lincoln wisely ignored him.

The question of military jurisdiction over civilians in wartime was not settled until after the Civil War. The United States Supreme Court in 1866, in the case *ex parte Milligan,* repudiated the military trial of several persons in Indiana who during the last year of the war had been convicted and sentenced to death for plotting the release of Confederate prisoners of war. The high court ruled that martial law is legal only in situations in which insurrection or invasion has actually closed the civil courts and deposed the civil administration. This ruling may have saved the lives of the convicted individuals, but, coming when it did, it obviously had no effect on the exercise of martial law during the war.

Aside from the actual fighting, the major task in waging the war was in raising, maintaining, and administering an immense national military establishment. The largest force, the Union army, came from a variety of sources, including the regular army, the state militia organizations, state volunteer units, and conscription. The vast majority of the troops were three-year state volunteers, but the waning of enthusiasm that followed the bloody Union failures in Virginia during the summer of 1862 obliged the administration to resort to the so-called militia draft, a call for 300,000 additional state militia for nine months of service. In some instances these troops had to be raised by state conscription.

Finally, in March 1863, as volunteering again lagged alarmingly, Congress passed an Enrollment Act making all able-bodied male citizens between twenty and forty-five subject to a national draft. Actually designed to stimulate volunteering because of the shame then associated with conscription, the act assigned recruit quotas by congressional district, subtracting from the quota the number of men who volunteered or had already served. If this number fell below the quota, the deficiency would be made up by conscription. The act also provided ways for avoiding service by hiring a substitute or paying a "commutation" fee of $300 for this purpose. Conscription was extremely unpopular and met with considerable resistance and occasional violence. In early July 1863 the New York City draft riots were serious enough that they had to be quelled by federal troops diverted from Gettysburg. Some 46,000 men were actually drafted, and 118,000 substitutes enlisted: together these amounted to only approximately 6 percent of the armed forces of the Union.

The chief inducement to volunteer, aside from patriotism, was the payment of a $300 bounty, to which many state and local governments added supplements. Countless abuses arose under these overlapping measures, which encouraged "bounty jumping": enlisting, deserting, and reenlisting in another district. Some individuals accumulated thousands of dollars in this manner; one man confessed to jumping bounty thirty-two times. The enlistment policies also spawned a group of operators known as "bounty brokers," men who devised schemes for attracting recruits and charged a commission on their bounties.

The manner of recruiting and organizing the volunteer units demonstrated the residual strength of the political doctrine of state rights in the North, though this doctrine did not pose the problem for the Union government that it did for the Confederate government, to be discussed later, and though the doctrine was not always called by its name in the North. It resulted in the organization of the Union army into units that were identified by their state of origin—95th New York Infantry Regiment, for example—and commanded by officers appointed by the state governors. Early in the war the principle of state rights prompted the governors to commission state purchasing agents to supply their units with arms and other equipment, for which the states were later compensated by Congress. Throughout the war, the state governments, especially the governors, gave zealous support to the welfare of their own troops and played key roles in the entire war effort. Among the more dedicated and energetic of the governors were John Andrew of Massachusetts, Andrew Gregg Curtin of Pennsylvania, Richard Yates of Illinois, and Oliver Morton of Indiana, all Republicans.

Yet many northern adherents of state rights opposed certain of Lincoln's measures for waging the war, particularly the curtailment of habeas corpus, military arrests and trials, and the draft. Democratic Governor Horatio Seymour of New York, a supporter of the war effort who worked hard in raising troops to meet the state's quotas, was a staunch critic of Lincoln's practices; Seymour was perhaps as hostile to conscription as any Confederate governor. Had the North, like the South, been subject to the threat of invasion and to actual invasion with its accompanying hardships and dislocations, friction between northern state and federal authorities doubtless would have grown much fiercer, though probably not to the extent that it did in the Confederacy. Under the existing circumstances, Lincoln was able to call upon the deep spirit of nationalism in the North, the determination to preserve the Union, to override any contrary impulses generated by northern state rights, and convert them into a source of Union strength.

Eventually the Union army recorded over 2.9 million individual enlistments. Because of the multiple enlistments of many individuals, the actual number of soldiers who served is problematical; estimates range from 1.5 million to more than 2 million. The army reached a peak strength in the spring of 1865 of about 1 million. The critical figure in the maintenance and administration of this huge army was Secretary of War Stanton. A lawyer by profession, a former Democrat and vitriolic critic of Lincoln, Stanton was a man of bedrock integrity, inexhaustible energy, and dictatorial methods; ultimately his efficiency and ruthlessness would make him to the Civil War what Lazare Carnot was to the French Revolutionary Wars, the "Organizer of Victory."

Stanton brought together the virtually autonomous heads of the army bureaus (the adjutant general, quartermaster general, chief of ordnance, chief of engineers, and commissary general) into a war board directly under his supervision, and he persuaded the civilian boards of trade of the northern cities to appoint advisory committees to assist in the job of supplying the army. Thus Stanton drew support for the Union war effort from the superior organizational, managerial, technical, and mechanical knowledge and skills present in the modern commercial and industrial society of the North.

Nowhere was this support more visible or more critical than in the work of Quartermaster General Montgomery C. Meigs. Builder of the District of Columbia aqueduct and the arched bridge over the Potomac at Washington—the longest construction of its kind in the world—and of the newly erected wings of the national Capitol, Meigs was highly experienced in dealing with private suppliers and contractors. He developed and oversaw the Union army supply system that procured the uniforms, tents, wagons, horses, and myriad other goods directly from the nation's private manufacturers, contractors, and marketers. He also used his position to induce the various northern railroad companies to adopt a uniform gauge, thus greatly enhancing the efficiency of northern transportation.

Professor Russell Weigley says of Meigs, "[He] was a man of the new day, of the materialistic, mechanically and scientifically inclined America born in the second half of the century of industrialization, urbanization, and technological change." In the words of Hattaway and Jones, Meigs eventually made the Union soldier the "best-provided-for fighting man in all history."

The work of the other departments was comparable to that of the quartermaster department, if less spectacular. Notwithstanding the troops' complaints about desiccated vegetables and "embalmed beef," Hattaway and Jones conclude that the Union soldiers enjoyed twice the amount of food available to Napoleon's men of a half-century earlier. In other words, the Union soldiers were probably also the best-fed fighting men in all history. Tragically, this was an inadequate measure of the soldiers' well-being; even the best of provisions and care of that day fell far short of the needs. More than twice as many Union soldiers died of malnutrition, exposure, and inadequate medical care (250,000) than of battle wounds (110,000); this amounted to almost 12 percent of the strength of the army according to the larger estimates of Union numbers, or approximately 16.6 percent according to the smaller estimates of Union numbers.

All the goods and services sustaining the Union war effort rested on a base of finance. The person directly responsible for organizing this base was Secretary of the Treasury Chase. Like the other members of the administration, nothing in his career had prepared him for a task of such immensity. Ultimately, the federal government would find it necessary to raise nearly $4 billion to prosecute the war, a staggering sum for those times. Almost immediately Chase was obliged to turn to borrowing money through the sale of long-term, interest-bearing bonds (usually 6 percent), which would become the primary source of Union financial support. Repeatedly he asked for, and Congress created, bond issues and issues of interest-bearing, short-term Treasury notes running to hundreds of millions of dollars. Together, they amounted to almost $2.7 billion during the course of the war: 66 percent of the monetary cost of the Union effort.

When in the summer of 1862 the purchase of bonds lagged because of the discouraging military prospect, Chase turned to an astute Philadelphia broker, Jay Cooke, to market them. Reaping a handsome commission for his services, Cooke mounted a newspaper and door-to-door campaign that blended nationalism with the profit motive. He was said to have made the bonds "stare in the face of the people in every household from Maine to California." Although most of the bonds actually were bought by banks and wealthy individuals as promising investments, Cooke's methods attracted hundreds of thousands of purchasers among the ordinary citizens, thus giving them a financial as well as a patriotic stake in a Union victory. Chase was criticized for approving a system that allowed a private agent to represent the government and profit heavily from it, but the system did work; like Robert Morris, who is remembered as the "financier of the American Revolution," Cooke is remembered as the "financier of the Civil War."

Another measure recommended by Chase, the creation of the national banks, was designed to stimulate the sale of bonds as well as to provide a source of stable currency. Legislation passed by Congress in February 1863 and June 1864 established a system whereby constituent banks were required to invest at least one-third of their capital in government bonds and were in turn permitted to issue "national banknotes" redeemable in gold in amounts up to 90 percent of the value of the bonds. When it became apparent that many state banks preferred to remain independent and continue issuing their own notes, Congress in March 1865 placed a tax on these notes, thereby obliging most of the state banks to enter the national system.

The sale of bonds was not sufficient to prevent a financial crisis early in the war when public confidence sagged because of the fear that England might intervene over the seizure by the federal navy of a British ship, the *Trent*, which was known to be carrying Confederate diplomats. When in December 1861 funds in the Treasury dropped so low that it, and all the banks, suspended specie payment, the redemption of notes in gold or silver, Congress, with Chase's reluctant approval, authorized the issue of $150 million in non-interest-bearing Treasury notes that were not redeemable in gold or silver, but were declared "legal tender" and receivable in payment of taxes and public and private debts.

Fiercely opposed by most Democrats and some Republicans as being illegal and immoral, these Treasury notes were disparagingly called "greenbacks." Although they circulated in the economy at a discount, fluctuating according to Union military prospects, at one time a greenback dollar dipping almost to one-third of the value of a gold dollar, they served the urgent purpose of enabling the government to pay its bills in emergencies. Eventually a total of $447 million in this kind of paper would be created.

The third way in which the government raised money for the war effort was by imposing special taxes. These included a direct tax on the states by quota according to population, a graduated individual income tax that reached a maximum of 10 percent on incomes exceeding $10,000 a year, and a series of excise taxes and licenses that drew revenue from virtually every product and occupation. Taxes provided $667 million, 21 percent of the money spent by the Union in fighting the war. These relatively stiff levies also had the important secondary effect of supporting the value of the greenbacks and curbing what otherwise might have been severe inflation.

Together the Union financial measures were successful in financing the war effort without rationing or price controls, crippling shortages and hoarding, or ruinous inflation. The diversified northern economy of industry and agriculture along with a sophisticated establishment in commerce and banking, directed generally by prudent and provident government war policies, demonstrated that it was equal to the task it was called upon to perform. In the words of James M. McPherson, "To a remarkable degree, [it] was able to produce both guns and butter."

The most radical and most dramatic action of the Lincoln administration was the emancipation of the slaves. It strengthened the war effort and forever altered the social and economic fabric of the South, and, to an extent, that of the entire nation. Yet for a number of reasons, emancipation was not at first a part of Lincoln's war aim. He was sensitive to the popular aversion against abolitionism and the accusation that it was the cause of the war; he recognized this feeling as a political liability for Republicans in the forthcoming congressional elections.

To a degree, Lincoln shared the aversion to abolition by the federal government. He believed there was no constitutional warrant for such action. The United States had, in fact, previously held that the emancipation of slaves exceeded belligerent rights under the laws of war; ironically, the most explicit statement to this effect had been made by Secretary of State John Quincy Adams, who later became an advocate of military emancipation under certain conditions. Lincoln also was aware that the adoption of emancipation as a war aim would tend to harden southern resistance. He wished, he said, to avoid turning the war into "a violent and remorseless revolutionary struggle." He intended instead "to keep the integrity of the Union prominent as the primary object of the contest."

As the war ground on and Congress began to move toward forced emancipation, Lincoln reflected on ways of dealing with the problem and produced a plan that met his constitutional objections to federal intervention. His proposal sought to induce the loyal slave states to adopt their own programs of gradual emancipation by offering federal compensation and voluntary relocation of the blacks in Central America or the Caribbean. In March 1862 he persuaded Congress to enact a measure offering compensation to states undertaking this step. He told delegates from the loyal slave states that slavery was doomed by the "friction and abrasion" of the war, and he urged them repeatedly to avoid Radical emancipation by accepting his plan. These overtures met with a disappointingly cool reception.

The issue of emancipation in all the loyal slave states would not be resolved until the war was over, and then by the adoption of the Thirteenth Amendment to the Constitution, which abolished slavery everywhere in the United States. Meanwhile, the issue was resolved in the Confederate states as an incident of the war itself. By the summer of 1862 Lincoln was won over to the argument that emancipation in the states in rebellion was a feasible and justifiable war measure. He later explained: "I felt that measures, otherwise unconstitutional, might become lawful, by becoming indispensable to the preservation of the constitution, through the preservation of the nation."

He also believed that the mood of northern voters had shifted enough to make the political risk acceptable. Yet he felt the time for the move had not quite come. To declare slavery abolished in areas beyond his control, he said, would be recognized by the whole world as a futile gesture, "like the Pope's bull against the comet."

When in August the prominent abolitionist editor of the New York Tribune, Horace Greeley, published a plea for emancipation, Lincoln replied in a published letter: "My paramount object in this struggle is to save the Union, and is not either to save or to destroy slavery. If I could save the Union without freeing any slave I would do it, and if I could save it by freeing all the slaves I would do it; and if I could save it by freeing some and leaving others alone, I would also do that." Lincoln then added that his statement represented official policy and did not modify his personal wish that all men everywhere could be free.

Although there is no reason to question the sincerity of Lincoln's reply to Greeley, he actually had already made up his mind that a proclamation of emancipation of slaves in the areas in rebellion was expedient, if not essential, to the salvation of the Union. The proclamation was already written and lay in his desk drawer; but, persuaded, perhaps by Seward, that it ought not be announced amid the Confederate victories of the summer, "our last shriek on the retreat," Lincoln anxiously awaited a turn in the tide of the war.

The turn came in September on the red fields of Antietam, enough of a turn, at least, to convince Lincoln that the time was propitious for his announcement. On September 22 he issued a preliminary emancipation proclamation declaring that the slaves in states in rebellion on January 1, 1863, would be "forever free." Hoping to curb popular disapproval as much as possible, he explained the step as a measure of military necessity, endorsed voluntary colonization of the ex-slaves, and again called upon the loyal slave states to adopt gradual emancipation.

In the fall congressional elections the Democrats made effective use of the proclamation to help win back from the Republicans thirty-two seats in the House of Representatives, plus the governorships of New York and New Jersey and control of the legislatures in Illinois and Indiana. Possibly because of these Democratic gains, Lincoln on December 1 recommended to Congress a constitutional amendment providing for compensated, gradual emancipation in all states where slavery existed, and for voluntary colonization of the freedmen outside the United States. Presumably this included any Confederate states that might lay down their arms and reestablish their loyalty to the Union prior to the date that emancipation was to occur.

Also, in his December address to Congress, Lincoln sought to allay the fears of many northerners that they were about to be submerged in a flood of ex-slaves. He pointed out that most of the freed persons probably would remain in the South once slavery was gone, that even if all of them were equally distributed throughout the country they would constitute only one black to seven whites, and, finally, that the North itself could decide whether to receive them. The last assurance apparently alluded to a policy that was already in effect in the black exclusion laws of a number of northern states, including his own state of Illinois.

But Lincoln made clear that he had no intention of delaying the effects of the proclamation. On January 1, 1863, he issued the definitive proclamation emancipating all slaves in those parts of the Confederacy that were still in rebellion. Again, he justified the move on "military necessity." Hoping to encourage a revival of loyal unionism in those portions of the Confederacy that were under more or less firm Union military control, the state of Tennessee and extensive areas in northern Virginia and southern Louisiana, he exempted them from the effects of the proclamation. To counter the accusation that he was attempting to incite a servile insurrection, Lincoln told those freed by the proclamation to abstain from violence except in self-defense.

As several persons, including Seward, pointed out at the time, the proclamation had no immediate effect on slavery itself. It liberated no slaves in areas where Lincoln had the power to liberate them, and, as Lincoln had said, it was like the pope's bull in that it liberated none in areas where Lincoln lacked the power to do so. It did, however, have an important immediate effect on the minds and hearts of the northern population.

By adding emancipation to his war aim, Lincoln partly defused the Radicals' criticism of his program and gained a significant measure of unity within his administration. He, of course, further alienated many northerners, mostly Democrats; but, on balance, he may have strength-ened his support among the general population, though this is debat-able, and the question of emancipation would remain to plague him later. Despite his justification of the action on military grounds alone, he also added indirectly a moral dimension to the Union war aim, a di-mension that transcended the political goal of preserving the Union and helped rekindle the flagging zeal of an indeterminable number of north-ern soldiers and civilians. Finally, Lincoln's move eventually liberated millions of slaves as the Union armies completed their conquest of the South.

Emancipation and the employment of blacks as soldiers went hand in hand. Small numbers of them were enrolled by Union generals here and there early in the war, and in August 1862 Stanton approved the enlisting of 5,000 black troops in South Carolina. But this practice, like emancipation itself, was heartily opposed by many citizens and their political spokesmen; Lincoln at one time said he believed "it would be productive of more evil than good." As the national mood on this ques-tion shifted, his mood shifted, and by 1863 he had become an unqual-ified supporter of the idea; in March he wrote with enthusiasm but ex-aggeration, "The bare sight of 50,000 armed and drilled black soldiers on the banks of the Mississippi would end the rebellion at once."

The final emancipation proclamation and the resort to conscription removed all limits on the number of black soldiers. The enlistment of blacks, including former slaves, now became widespread, stimulated by the belief that their use would relieve a comparable number of whites from military service, keep the freed blacks in the South, and help win the war all at the same time. Most of the ex-slaves who enlisted did so willingly, but the army recruiting squads could be ruthless in their methods of persuasion. They often seized and pressed into service freedmen inhabiting the runaway camps or at work in the fields, some-times without allowing the blacks an opportunity for as much as a good-bye to wives or children. Eventually, approximately 179,000 blacks, a majority of them former slaves, served in the Union army, and almost 20,000 in the navy.

The black servicemen experienced severe discrimination, including lower pay than whites, and, as a rule, relegation to the more menial jobs. White soldiers at first held them in utter contempt, but many of the whites came to respect them as fighting men. If captured by the Confederates, the black soldiers were not considered prisoners of war; instead they were designated as "slaves captured in arms" and thus liable to execution, but the Confederate authorities backed away from carrying out this policy on the threat that a like number of Confederate prisoners would be put to death. The Confederacy refused until the war was almost over to exchange black prisoners of war.

Black troops were sent into heavy combat in a number of operations, most notably the siege of Port Hudson, Louisiana, the attack on the Charleston defenses, and, late in the war, an assault on the Confederate siege lines at Petersburg, Virginia, and the Union onslaught in the battle of Nashville. The fear of capture, as well as the hope of freedom, may at times have inspired the blacks to fight with unusual fury and tenacity. After an early episode of black troops under fire, at Milliken's Bend above Vicksburg, Mississippi, a plantation girl wrote in her diary, "It is said the Negro regiments fought there like mad demons, but we cannot believe that." Yet General Grant said that the blacks "behaved well" in this engagement. Perhaps the most celebrated episode of blacks in battle was that of the gallant but futile and costly assault in July 1863 by the Fifty-fourth Massachusetts Volunteer Infantry Regiment on Battery Wagner at Charleston.

The presence of black troops seems also to have fired the Confederates to fight with extraordinary fury and tenacity. Confederate and black soldiers were found at Milliken's Bend lying dead side by side, each impaled on the other's bayonet. Infuriated by the employment of black ex-slaves against them, and seized by the frenzy of combat, Confederate soldiers in the field often refused to allow black soldiers to surrender, or killed them afterward. These episodes seem mainly to have represented spontaneous outpourings of rage on the part of the common Confederate soldiers, similar to outpourings of rage against Japanese troops attempting to surrender in World War II.

The most notorious of these killings occurred in April 1864 in the capture of Fort Pillow, Tennessee, by Forrest's cavalry. Almost two hundred blacks were slain there, many of them begging for mercy. Smaller numbers were dispatched in a similar fashion at the siege of Petersburg. Both times the killings were stopped by the personal intervention of the officers in command, although Forrest was accused of having initially ordered those at Fort Pillow carried out.

Black soldiers and sailors, whether as combat or service troops, made heavy sacrifices, suffering more than 20 percent of their numbers in fatal casualties, some from wounds but most from disease. The performance of the blacks in uniform, like that of the whites, varied from occasion to occasion. What Brigadier General Charles Francis Adams, Jr., said of the blacks in the Petersburg action may be endorsed for their overall record: "They seem to have behaved just as well or as badly as the rest, and they suffered more severely." Black fighting men rendered a significant contribution to the Union war effort, and thus to the liberation of their people from slavery.

In its war measures, the Lincoln administration worked largely by pragmatism and common sense, by trial and error. The nation had never experienced such stress as that of the Civil War; there were few established procedures or precedents for meeting its demands. It generated situations covered only in broad theoretical terms by the United States Constitution; it challenged many of the most sacrosanct principles of republican government; it created dilemmas in which either choice left serious problems in its wake. It necessitated both authoritarian decisions and delicate compromises. Lincoln's near-mystical reverence for the Union and his determination to preserve it, which was shared by most if not all of the northern population, Democrats and Republicans alike, combined with his personal qualities of leadership to develop a program that ultimately forged the superior Union resources into a sword of victory.

VI

Confederate Government and Administration

❖

From the beginning the Davis administration found itself immersed in the demands of war. The problems of raising, supplying, training, and employing military forces of unprecedented size, meeting the needs of a civilian population caught up in the travail of an immense war, and carrying on the day-to-day functions of civil government in a nation struggling to be born were overwhelming. Ultimately, Davis and his associates failed to measure up to the task they had set for themselves. But they devoted to it every ounce of their energy, determination, and ingenuity; so sweeping were their initiatives that Emory Thomas has aptly called the Confederate war effort "a revolutionary experience."

The most urgent task was that of maintaining the strength of the armies. Military reverses during the winter of 1861 and the spring of 1862, especially the bloody battle of Shiloh, combined with the severity of life in camp and field and the hardships of families left at home to dampen the zeal for volunteering. It was not appreciably rekindled by the offer of a $50 bounty and sixty-day furlough to those who would reenlist for three years or the duration of the war.

Urged by Lee and other generals, Davis recommended and the Confederate Congress in mid-April enacted the first national conscription measure in the history of the English-speaking peoples. All able-bodied men between eighteen and thirty-five, with certain specified exceptions, were to be conscripted into the Confederate army to serve for three years unless the war should end sooner. More immediately important than conscription itself, the act also extended for like periods the one-year terms of men already in uniform. Eventually, the age limits would be widened to seventeen and fifty, with men under eighteen and over forty-five to constitute state reserves. Conscripts or their substitutes would make up some 20 percent of the soldiers of the Confederacy.

The Confederate conscription acts were radical and sweeping measures. Containing no provisions for exemption because of dependents, the acts visited extreme hardship upon countless families. Because the acts ran counter to long-established precedents and overrode time-honored state prerogatives, many southerners, including some of the most prominent public figures, opposed them. Conscription was denounced as being both illegal and intrinsically unsound. Governor Joseph E. Brown of Georgia said of it: "I cannot consent to commit the state to a policy which is in my judgment subversive of her sovereignty and at war with all the principles for the support of which Georgia entered this revolution." To Vice President Stephens he wrote, "[The acts are a] bold and dangerous usurpation of the rights of the states." Stephens questioned both their constitutionality and their merit, saying, "Conscripts will go into battle as a horse goes from home; volunteers as a horse towards home: you may drive the latter hard and it does not hurt him."

Emotions were inflamed also by the numerous ways in which the conscription acts permitted individuals to avoid military service by hiring substitutes, or by holding civilian occupations deemed essential to Confederate or state governmental administration or to the war effort. The most criticized exemption of all was that of one white man for every plantation of as many as twenty slaves. Though doubtless this policy was expedient for maintaining discipline and production on the plantations, to many non-slave owners it represented class favoritism; they said the "twenty-nigger law" converted the struggle into a "rich man's war and a poor man's fight." The Confederate Congress attempted later to meet these objections by disallowing substitution, curtailing exemption, and, to placate the smaller slave owners, reducing from twenty to fifteen the number of slaves required for an owner to remain at home.

Volunteering and conscription together mobilized most of the available southern manpower. From a white population of about 5.5 million, the Confederacy mustered from 800,000 to 1 million men into service during the four years of the war. The Confederate army at its peak stood between 400,000 and a half million. Nearly four out of five of the white men of military age were brought to the colors, an exceptionally high proportion made possible because slavery provided much of the necessary labor to support the economy. A like proportion of the American population today would reach 36 to 43 million. Possibly the Confederacy overmobilized its manpower; a smaller army and a larger number of men left on the farms and in other essential jobs might have yielded greater overall strength and resilience.

Finance was as serious a problem for the Confederacy, if not more serious, as manpower and supplies. Upon the shoulders of Secretary of the Treasury Memminger fell the staggering task of raising from a predominantly agricultural and debtor society the vast sums of money required for total war. A hard-money advocate prior to the war, he hoped to raise most of the funds by taxation; at his urging, the Congress in

August 1861 enacted a direct tax on the states which yielded only about $17.5 million and was largely met by the issue of state treasury notes— paper money. Popular opposition to taxation among the rural, conservative society soon obliged Memminger to turn to borrowing through the sale of interest-bearing bonds. Because the planters were chronically short of cash he permitted them to purchase the bonds on credit by pledging their forthcoming crops, thus giving rise to the expression "produce loans." He hoped to use the cotton acquired in this way as security for larger cash loans by European bankers.

Strenuous efforts in taxation and borrowing were continued throughout the war by the Confederate government. In April 1863 the Congress enacted an ambitious law imposing an 8 percent excise tax on a lengthy list of products, a variable license tax on virtually all occupations except farming, and a graduated income tax that reached 15 percent on incomes above $10,000. The law also included an ingenious but impossible-to-collect "tax-in-kind," requiring of the farmers and planters one tenth of their produce. Numerous bond issues were authorized, and imaginative efforts made to market them, both in the Confederacy and in Europe. The most notorious of the European bond sales was carried out with a French financier named Emile Erlanger, who sold $25 million in cotton-secured bonds, but exacted a 23 percent discount for his services.

Tax revenues and loans fell woefully short of Confederate needs. It has been estimated that only 1 percent of the Confederate revenue was raised in taxes and 39 percent through the sale of bonds. For the other 60 percent, Memminger was left with one alternative: the issuing of treasury notes. Beginning in 1861 with an issue of $119 million in what was supposed to be a temporary expedient, he repeatedly recommended and the Congress repeatedly authorized increasing amounts of this form of money.

Eventually the total of Confederate treasury notes exceeded $1.5 billion. Added to this flood of paper were great amounts of state treasury notes, plus promissory notes issued by banks and insurance and railroad companies. Congress refused to make the treasury notes legal tender, which probably would have done no good anyway. The combination of the existence of vast sums in unredeemable paper money and the desperate shortage of commodities in the South inevitably brought ruinous inflation. In June 1864 Memminger resigned in despair, and Davis appointed George Trenholm, a renowned Charleston banker, to the position. Trenholm attempted heroic measures of taxation, called for and received great donations in all kinds of valuables, and made heavy personal sacrifices in his efforts to cure the evil of inflation. All were futile. By early 1865 a Confederate paper dollar was worth less than two cents in gold; soon it would become a mere souvenir of a lost cause.

In creating and distributing military supplies the Davis administration demonstrated both resourcefulness and shortsightedness. The resourcefulness lay in what Raimondo Luraghi has hailed as an impressive experiment in state socialism: the establishment within the largely nonindustrial South of an extensive chain of government-owned or subsidized factories for producing naval vessels, weapons, ammunition, uniforms and boots, and the various accouterments of war.

The most important organizer of this enterprise in government-owned factories was the chief of ordnance, General Josiah Gorgas, a Pennsylvania-born graduate of the United States Military Academy and an industrial wizard who because of his marriage to an Alabama woman cast his lot with the South. During the last two years of the war his factories poured out a steady stream of arms and munitions. As the struggle reached its climax he would boast: "Where three years ago we were not making a gun, a pistol nor a sabre, no shot nor shell (except at the Tredegar Works)—a pound of powder—we now make all these in quantities to meet the demands of our large armies." Professor Frank E. Vandiver has written of this accomplishment: "The world has hardly seen such a miraculous transformation of ploughshares into swords."

The other hero of Confederate military industrial production was General Joseph R. Anderson, proprietor of the Tredegar Iron Works in Richmond. With government financial subsidies and laborers assigned from the army, and with the employment of hundreds of slaves and equal numbers of convicts from the state penal institutions, Anderson made his works the mother arsenal of the Confederacy. He developed iron mines for the needed ore, bartered nails, spikes, and bar iron for food to feed his workers, constructed and operated a tannery and shoe factory, and purchased blockade runners to sail with cotton and return with other necessities. The Tredegar Works produced cannon, iron plating for naval vessels, machinery for other factories, a submarine, and torpedoes for use against federal warships. Not until the capture of Richmond by Union forces did Anderson's furnaces go cool. One of the reasons the Confederacy fought so stubbornly to hold the city was to hold the Tredegar Works.

Davis was far less fortunate in his choice of administrators other than Gorgas. Confederate Quartermaster General Abraham C. Myers attempted a program comparable to the one Gorgas carried out brilliantly. Myers relied on government-constructed factories for the soldiers' uniforms and shoes, and he purchased the needed horses and mules from civilian breeders and suppliers. Partly because Myers was a weak administrator, allowing himself to be submerged in bureaucratic details, and partly because of unavoidable shortages in the southern economy, he was less successful than Gorgas. The armies were chronically short of clothing, especially of shoes, and the foot soldiers complained bitterly about those issued with wooden soles and canvas uppers. After the Union occupation of Kentucky and Tennessee, a major horse- and mule-breeding area, Myers was never able to provide the armies adequately with these essential animals. By 1864 this problem was almost as acute for the Confederacy as the shortage of men.

Confederate Commissary General Lucius B. Northrop was even less successful than Myers in meeting the needs of the armies. Confederate soldiers were almost constantly hungry; during the final year of the war they were famished and emaciated, and sometimes wracked with scurvy. Modern studies of soldier behavior have indicated that malnourishment reduces not only a soldier's physical energy, but also his determination and morale, including even his personal courage. Unquestionably, the soldiers of the Confederacy suffered this kind of debilitation, especially late in the war. Confederate livestock were even more severely underfed than the men. In the spring of 1863 a Union soldier described Lee's supply trains as having the appearance of all the "crippled Chicago emigrant trains that had ever escaped off the desert." If this soldier had the opportunity to observe Lee's trains two years later, he must have been struck by how fit they had looked at the time he wrote his original observation.

Northrop appears to have been inefficient. Even the patient Lee criticized him sharply. Northrop also had the reputation of being officious and contentious; he aroused the ire of the farmers by the insolent and abrasive manner in which his agents impressed—seized—supplies and paid for them with virtually worthless certificates of indebtedness. Northrop was a prewar friend of Davis's, and the president kept him in office until the final weeks of the conflict: in the eyes of many southerners, a case of blatant cronyism.

Although Northrop was in part responsible for his problems, they also were caused by conditions beyond his control. Confederate diarist Mary Boykin Chesnut wrote sympathetically: "If I were to pick out the best-abused man in Richmond...I should say Mr. Commissary General Northrop was the most cursed and vilified. He is held accountable for everything that goes wrong in the army." Confederate soldiers were not hungry because of a lack of food in the region generally. Southern plantations and farms beyond the reach of the Union armies produced good crops throughout the war. Urged by presidential proclamation and congressional resolutions, the landowners turned away from the production of such commercial crops as cotton, tobacco, and sugar and grew instead great quantities of corn, wheat, and vegetables.

But Northrop was obliged to depend heavily on Confederate transport facilities because the countryside in which the armies operated could not alone supply the immense amount of food required. Much of it had to be brought from other parts of the South. The railroads were the major carriers, and though they managed to sustain the Confederacy for four years of prodigious effort, they fell far short of its true needs. Southern industry was unable to replace locomotives and rails as they wore out under an extraordinary volume of traffic; the available engines and cars became increasingly feeble as they crept laboriously over the outworn tracks. Frequently the gauges of the two-score of independent lines did not match; seldom did the tracks of the different lines actually make contact with one another in a given city, and time-consuming transfers of freight had to be made by carts at every station.

Perhaps the most serious Confederate rail problem was the lack of coordination among the many lines. Recognizing the vital role of the railways and the danger from the lack of coordination, Davis attempted to cure the evil by promoting voluntary agreements among the companies. He appointed skilled coordinators, first, William Wadley, later, Captain Frederick W. Sims, who worked out excellent plans for pooling engines and cars, establishing priorities for military needs, adjusting schedules, and setting rates.

When the voluntary agreements failed to work, the Confederate Congress in May 1863 enacted a measure empowering the president to seize uncooperating lines and take the necessary steps. Curiously, Davis shrank from enforcing the act, perhaps because he feared that to do so would provide additional evidence for those who were already calling him a dictator. Professor Robert C. Black says he appeared to be "smitten by a fatal hesitation." Finally, in February 1865 the Congress passed a sweeping measure that in effect brought into the army the officials and employees of all lines of military significance. But by now, says Black, "even the prerogatives of an Egyptian Pharaoh could not have saved the Confederacy...."

As a result of the countless inefficiencies in transportation, the depots and warehouses of the Confederacy were often piled with provisions while the troops and animals in the field went hungry. The shortages of Confederate supplies and services of all kinds and from all causes took a dreadful toll; more than 60 percent of the Confederate fatalities, which amounted to 16 percent of the total strength of the army, or more than 20 percent if the lower estimate of total strength is accepted, were from nonbattle sources.

One of the most controversial episodes of the war is that of the treatment of the multitudes of prisoners of war: 195,000 Union soldiers, 215,000 Confederates, excluding those paroled at the time of capture. Alleged deliberate southern cruelty to Union prisoners created in the North an enduring atrocity legend that has not completely disappeared in the late twentieth century. The one person later executed as a war criminal was the commandant of the most notorious of the southern stockades, Major Henry Wirz of Andersonville prison in Georgia. After the war the Georgia chapter of the United Daughters of the Confederacy erected a statue of him at the town of Andersonville. Inscribed on it are these words by Jefferson Davis: "When time shall have softened passion and prejudice, when Reason shall have stripped the mask from misrepresentation, then Justice, holding evenly her scales, will require much of past censure and praise to change places."

Conditions at Andersonville may have been worse than at any other Civil War prison. The stockade was established late in the war when the Confederacy was being ripped open by invasion, was desperately short of troops, supplies, and transportation, and was straining every fiber to survive. The customary exchange of prisoners had been suspended by General Grant, then in command of all Union armies, for a number of reasons, including accusations that paroled Confederates had rejoined their units before being properly exchanged, which doubtless was true; the refusal for a long while of Confederate authorities to exchange black soldiers; and the hard but practical reasoning that an equal number of soldiers exchanged helped the Confederates proportionately much more than it did the Federals.

Designed for 10,000 prisoners, Andersonville at its peak held about 33,000 inmates, most of them brought from prisons elsewhere that were threatened by the oncoming Union forces. Andersonville contained a total of 49,485 men during the thirteen months it was in existence. An appalling number of them, 13,700, or more than 27 percent, died of disease and previously inflicted wounds, both aggravated by overcrowding, filth, malnutrition, and inadequate medical care.

The Union treatment of Confederate prisoners, considering all the North's advantages, was equally questionable. Elmira Barracks in northern New York, though it held far fewer inmates than Andersonville, probably matched the Georgia prison in the inadequacy of its quarters, especially for the bitter winter cold, and in the filth of its sanitation facilities. Of the 12,147 Confederates confined there, 2,980 died: almost 25 percent. Overall statistics on prisoner fatalities are instructive: 15.5 percent of the inmates in Confederate prisons died; 12.1 percent of those in Union prisons died.

Professor Edward Channing concluded more than half a century ago that each side cared for its prisoners about as well as it cared for its own soldiers. Comparative wartime fatality statistics suggest that each side may have cared for the prisoners better than for its own soldiers. Death rates among the prisoners both North and South were markedly lower than the death rates from nonbattle causes in the Confederate army; death rates among both sets of prisoners were also lower than the nonbattle death rates in the Union army if the smaller estimate on the size of the army—1.5 million—is accepted. Shocking as the suffering and loss of life among the prisoners unquestionably were, no objective Civil War scholar today believes that either group of authorities was guilty of following a policy of deliberate cruelty toward them.

The problems of Confederate administration, both civil and military, with the resources available and in the midst of a conflict of such proportions as the Civil War were probably insuperable. It cannot be demonstrated that any other set of men could have done a better job than Davis and his associates did. Yet there were weaknesses and mistakes at the highest levels which the Confederacy could not afford. The number of turnovers in the Davis cabinet, ten in all, indicates an unusual degree of instability. Although the appointees were prominent men, a number of the most able public figures of the South were not in the group. The most distinguished member in the original Confederate cabinet, Toombs, soon left to become a general. Another southerner of comparable experience and vigor, Howell Cobb, was already in uniform and never became a member of the administration. Most of the outstanding men of the region, including Davis himself, preferred armed service to civil service. Ironically, the South's military-mindedness was in this respect a liability to its war effort.

Davis needed the strength of a Joshua and the patience of a Job. He had great strength but little patience. Although he was a man of high intelligence, immense determination, and unshakable courage, his personality made him extremely difficult to work with. He was by nature imperious, opinionated, reserved, and humorless. All these qualities had been sensed with remarkable perceptiveness by his wife Varina upon their initial meeting when she was only seventeen years old. She wrote her mother at that time, "[Davis] has a way of taking for granted that everybody agrees with him when he expresses an opinion....The fact is, he is the kind of person I should expect to rescue one from a mad dog at any risk, but to insist upon a stoical indifference to the fright afterward."

Davis's most disagreeable characteristics were exaggerated by the stress of his wartime duties. Secretary of the Navy Mallory, an acute observer and a supporter and friend of Davis, wrote a critical but balanced evaluation, saying: "Few men could be more chillingly, freezingly cold." Mallory noted that Davis made no attempt to "cultivate the good will of [opposition] congressmen....It was not in his nature and his restless, manly, open, and turbulent spirit turned from what to him [was] the faintest approach to seeking popularity, and he scorned to believe it necessary to coax men to do their duty in the then condition of the country." These traits were amplified also by the precarious condition of Davis's health. He became physically fragile—dyspeptic and partially blind—infirmities that were aggravated by the accidental death of his five-year-old son, Joe, in April 1864, a tragic occurrence imparting an eerie similarity to the wartime personal lives of Davis and Lincoln.

Davis tended increasingly to be secretive, to withdraw from contact with the world, and to devote his energies to details at the expense of policy. This was especially true of his relations with the War Department, in which understandably he considered himself to be an expert. A perceptive official in the department once wrote with exaggeration, but with a measure of truth: "All the revolutionary vigor is with the enemy.... With us timidity—hair splitting." Partly as a result, the office of secretary of war was occupied by five persons in succession. The office of secretary of state had three different incumbents; that of attorney general had four; and that of secretary of the treasury, two. Davis ought not be held responsible for all the shortcomings of the administration, but he unquestionably contributed to them.

Stability in the War Department was particularly crucial for an administration in the toils of war. In the summer of 1861 Davis moved Judah P. Benjamin of Louisiana from the position of attorney general to that of secretary of war to succeed Walker; in March 1862, after Benjamin had come to cross-purposes with some of the generals, particularly Jackson, Davis shifted him to the State Department and appointed George W. Randolph of Virginia secretary of war. In November 1862, when Davis overrode Randolph's order for transferring troops from west of the Mississippi to east of the river, Randolph quit in resentment because he believed he was being treated like a mere clerk. Davis then appointed to the position James A. Seddon of Virginia, a perceptive and hard-working but physically frail man who resigned in exhaustion near the end of the war. John C. Breckinridge of Kentucky, former vice president of the United States and then a Confederate general, held the office during the final weeks of the war and worked to prepare the South for defeat.

Benjamin as secretary of state became the most influential member of the cabinet. Appointed to succeed R. M. T. Hunter of Virginia, who had followed Toombs, Benjamin would remain in the office until the end of the war. He was intelligent and capable; he became Davis's chief adviser and confidant; he has been called the "brains of the administration." Partly because of envy, but also because Benjamin was annoyingly suave, bland, and imperturbable, and doubtless because he was a Jew, he was the most disliked and distrusted member of the cabinet. In the position of attorney general, Benjamin was succeeded by Thomas Bragg who was followed by George Davis, both North Carolinians. Only Secretary of the Navy Mallory and Postmaster General Reagan remained in their jobs from beginning to end.

In addition to the friction within the inner circles of the administration, Davis's policies and practices ran afoul of certain deep-seated southern social and personal attitudes. His own individualism and strong-headedness collided with that of many of the other southern spokesmen, and with that of a number of his generals. He was fiercely denounced for his alleged obstinacy, arbitrariness, conceit, and incompetence. In a book entitled *The First Year of the War*, published in 1862, one of the most prominent southern journalists, Edward A. Pollard of the *Richmond Examiner*, voiced the opinion of the opposition when he wrote that Davis was losing the war because he ignored "the wisdom of the people" and "desired to signalize the infallibility of his own intellect in every measure of the revolution, and to identify, from motives of vanity, his own personal genius with every event and detail...."

Davis and some of the most prominent Confederate generals were at loggerheads almost throughout the entire war. At the very beginning he and Joseph E. Johnston quarreled over the order of Johnston's rank, and Davis never had any faith in the general's ability. Davis had a similar unfortunate relationship with Beauregard, originating after the first battle of Bull Run, when Davis implied that the Creole general was remiss in failing to pursue the defeated Federals.

Possibly the most damaging quarrel between Davis and a general occurred with Toombs, who attributed to West Point favoritism Davis's veto of a promotion. The impetuous Georgian, who was also one of the region's most influential political figures, resigned his Confederate commission in a rage and spent the rest of the war denouncing Davis's leadership. Professor Frank L. Owsley wrote perceptively, "The Confederacy really wasn't big enough for both Jeff Davis and Bob Toombs." Some scholars have speculated that the institution of slavery, in which the master's authority was absolute, had rendered these southerners incapable of subordinating their individual wills to the common welfare.

If Davis quarreled with certain of his generals, he was exceptionally firm in his support of others. Early in the war when a popular demand arose to dismiss Albert Sidney Johnston because of the loss of Forts Henry and Donelson, Davis refused and said, "If Johnston is not a general we don't have one." When Lee offered to step down after Gettysburg, Davis would not hear of it. In the public mind the conduct of Johnston and Lee subsequently justified Davis's trust in them. But his loyalty to some of his other generals was viewed quite differently. He was accused of keeping the unpopular Northrop in the job of commissary general merely because of a favor Northrop had done for him years before the war.

The loudest protests of this sort were over Davis's loyalty to General Bragg, who by 1863 had become the most criticized army commander in the Confederacy. Jokes about Bragg's incompetence and indecisiveness circulated: for example, that he died and went to heaven, but when invited by Saint Peter to enter, he insisted first on falling back to reorganize. When after the loss of Chattanooga in the fall of that year, Davis placed Bragg at least nominally in supervision of all Confederate military operations, the denunciation reached a fortissimo. Pollard expressed in the *Examiner* the indignant sarcasm felt by a multitude of southerners when he wrote, "From Lookout Mountain, a step to the highest honor and power is natural and inevitable."

The Davis administration suffered also because many of his policies and measures ran counter to the deepest political, social, and economic characteristics of the South. A conflict on the scale of the Civil War required the administrative machinery and programs of a modern industrial, centralized, and bureaucratic state. In attempting to create this kind of machinery and carry out these kinds of programs in a rural, agricultural region that was committed to decentralization and individual liberty for its citizens, the Confederate government inevitably aroused strong opposition.

One of the sources of this opposition was the doctrine of state rights, the political principle upon which the Confederacy was founded. Davis near the end of the war addressed this point when he wrote that the extreme advocates of state rights had materially increased the difficulty of defending the South against invasion. He accused them of "hindering the action of this Government, obstructing the execution of its laws, denouncing its necessary policy, impairing its hold upon the confidence of the people, and dealing with it rather as if it were the public enemy than the Government which they themselves had established for the common defense and which was their only hope for safety from the untold horrors of Yankee despotism." Certain students of the war, the foremost being Professor Owsley, have attributed Confederate defeat largely, if not altogether, to state rights. He wrote that in this principle the seeds of death were sown at the birth of the Confederacy, whose epitaph, he said, ought to bear the inscription: "Died of State Rights."

On this question, as on all other Civil War questions, there is disagreement. Another distinguished student of the history of the Confederacy, Professor E. Merton Coulter, argued that since state rights was the fundamental southern political principle, the Confederacy ought to have grounded its policies on this doctrine.

Recent scholarship has tended to deemphasize state rights as a cause for the Confederate downfall, and statistics have been presented to indicate that the states whose officials have been most pointedly accused of obstructing Confederate policy in the name of state rights provided their full share of men and supplies. Some students of the conflict have suggested that the wartime appeal to state rights was more the result than the cause of Confederate failure. Some contend that state rights actually strengthened the Confederate effort. This thinking is summed up by Beringer, Hattaway, Jones, and Still: "State rights was not a decisive factor in the Confederate defeat and even had the positive effect of assisting the war effort by using abilities and resources at the state and local levels to supplement the work of the central government."

Whatever effect the practice of state rights may have had, there can be no doubt the principle ran counter to that of southern national control and worked against the concentration of Confederate military resources. The early Confederate strategy of territorial defense, attempting to protect all areas from invasion, was dictated in part by the demands of the state governors that Confederate troops be stationed in their own states. Also, it is clear that many thousands of southern men under arms were enrolled in state military formations and standing idle at the time of crucial Civil War battles. Shiloh offered perhaps the most glaring example of this occurrence; there, according to Professor Kenneth Williams, an additional 5,000 Confederate reserves probably would have been sufficient to destroy Grant's army. This was fewer than the number of men being held in the military formations of any Confederate state.

The most vocal of the state-rights governors were Joseph E. Brown of Georgia and Zebulon Vance of North Carolina, who insisted on holding out substantial numbers of men and arms in the state militia and civil offices. As already indicated, Brown opposed and obstructed Confederate conscription with every device at his command; Vance was almost as strongly hostile to it. Late in the war, when Georgia was in the throes of invasion, Brown flirted with the idea of making a separate peace with the Federals.

Vance was intransigent in his determination that his state's resources be used primarily for its own soldiers. He opposed the activities of Confederate purchasing agents in North Carolina; he fiercely resisted a Confederate law demanding half the cargo space on blockade runners in which a state owned part interest, and wrote: "Is it possible that such an unblushing outrage is intended by the government?...I will fire the ships before I agree to it." He hoarded surplus clothing against the needs of the North Carolina troops; according to his own statement, Vance had on hand at the war's end 92,000 uniforms and great stores of leather and blankets, while his state's troops were comfortably clad. These were extra supplies that might have gone to threadbare soldiers from elsewhere.

Davis clashed angrily with Brown and Vance concerning the authority of the Confederate government over the men and material resources of their states. That the tension between southern nationalism and state rights dampened morale and severely handicapped the Confederate war effort seems beyond debate.

Almost every action of the Confederate government to mobilize southern resources and suppress disloyalty encountered fierce opposition on one ground or another. The anger and resistance aroused by the impressment of supplies has already been noted. There was another and more ironic form of resistance to impressment, the opposition of slave owners to the impressment of their slaves for labor in support of the war effort. In preparing for his attack at Shiloh, General Albert Sidney Johnston sought to increase his strength by replacing noncombatant soldiers with slaves. When the nearby planters rejected his appeal, he said ruefully, "These people have given their sons freely enough, but it is folly to talk to them about a negro or a mule."

The motives behind this opposition to the impressment of slaves were mixed. The owners resented the loss of the slaves' labor; they also feared that the value of the slaves might be reduced by sickness or injury; doubtless some of the owners, possibly many of them, were moved by a sincere concern over the welfare of slaves turned over to military or bureaucratic managers. Whatever the reasons, the slave owners resisted the practice, and often were able to prevent it.

Among the more vehemently censured characteristics of the Confederate government was that of the secrecy which both Davis and the Congress often followed in the interest of national security. Davis was extremely reluctant to take the people into his confidence, and the Congress frequently debated and enacted important legislation behind closed doors. Of the many southern spokesmen who denounced these actions, the most eloquent and convincing was the famed Alabama fire-eater William L. Yancey, a member of the Confederate senate and a supporter of the Davis administration, who made the remarkably modern argument that the better informed the people of the South were, the more enthusiastically they would respond to the demands of the war.

Nothing done by the Confederate administration aroused more resentment than the suspension of the writ of habeas corpus and the occasional declaration of martial law in threatened areas. In February 1862 after the fall of Fort Donelson the Congress authorized Davis to suspend the writ where he felt the military situation required it. He did so in New Orleans and later in portions of North and South Carolina. Though done sparingly, these suspensions brought an outburst of criticism. Even fiercer protests greeted the imposition of martial law by some of the generals in parts of Arkansas, Louisiana, Mississippi, and Georgia. Governor Brown condemned this along with most other administration measures as being subversive of the sovereignty of the state; Robert Toombs wrote of these suspensions: "Davis and his Janissaries—the regular army—conspire for the destruction of all who will not bend to them in their selfish and infamous schemes."

In the spring of 1863, better to enforce the conscription act, the Congress entertained a bill to grant Davis authority to suspend habeas corpus at his discretion. Many citizens opposed the bill out of fear of a violation of their constitutional rights. Also, because it was intended primarily to assist in enforcing the conscription act, opponents of conscription fought the bill relentlessly with lurid tales of the mistreatment of honest citizens by ruthless military commanders. The bill was defeated. The *Charleston Mercury* gloated over the result, but warned of the necessity of constant vigilance against still further attempts to deprive the people of their liberties.

For almost a year the writ of habeas corpus was freely used by those state judges who opposed conscription to release drafted men from the conscription officers, and deserters from the provost marshals. Superintendent of Conscription John S. Preston complained, "From one end of the Confederacy to the other every constituted authority, every officer, every man and woman is engaged in opposing the enrolling officer in the execution of his duties." Davis appealed to the Congress by warning that without the suspension of the writ, "desertion, already a frightful evil, will become the order of the day." In February 1864, after fierce debate, Congress granted him the authority for a period of one year. A year later he pleaded for a renewal of the authority, saying, "[It] is not simply expedient, but almost indispensable to the successful conduct of the war." This time the lawmakers refused. The Confederacy died with the rights of its citizens fully protected against Confederate "tyranny."

The Confederacy died with its freedom of the press also unimpaired, a press which often engaged in the most unrestrained censure of the Davis administration. Understandably, in light of the extraordinary southern opposition to any kind of government controls, Davis made no attempt to curb the press. Edward A. Pollard in the influential *Richmond Examiner* harped constantly on the incompetence of the administration. Robert Barnwell Rhett wrote in the *Charleston Mercury* accusing Davis of everything from being an advocate of "reconstruction," by which he meant reconciliation with the Union, to attempting to make himself a military despot. Such statements by these and other respected writers aroused popular suspicion and disaffection against the Confederate government. Thus, ironically, some of the staunchest advocates of secession played a significant role in its failure.

The duration and severity of the war, and the growing conviction that it could not be won, kindled a spirit of pacifism within many southern citizens and gave heart to the southern Unionists. Lincoln's plan of easy reconstruction, announced in December 1863, represented in part an appeal to these sentiments: an appeal similar to that of President Woodrow Wilson's Fourteen Points to the war-weary German population of World War I. The leading southern pacifist was none other than the vice president of the Confederacy, Alexander Stephens. Always of two minds about the move for southern independence, Stephens fatuously believed that some kind of a peace arrangement could be negotiated with the Lincoln administration in which each state would be permitted to retain its own sovereignty and decide its own destiny.

A North Carolina Unionist newspaper editor, William W. Holden of the *Raleigh Standard*, responded to Lincoln's plan by challenging Governor Vance with a peace platform in the 1864 governor's race. Holden lost, but he attracted enough votes to show that the peace urge ran strong in the state, as it did in many other parts of the South.

The Unionists and pacifists joined other critics in venting their wrath against the Davis administration. All the chief measures for supporting the war effort—conscription, impressment, taxation, and suspension of the writ of habeas corpus—were furiously condemned, with

Stephens leading the attack. Even many former friends of the administration now turned cool toward it.

The Confederacy lacked the time and opportunity to develop formal political parties. But this did not prevent the emergence of politics itself, politics in a form that may have been more destructive of unity and morale than a presidential election and partisan politics would have been. In the absence of parties, the Confederate Congress quickly split into pro- and anti-Davis factions. Senators Benjamin Hill of Georgia and Robert Barnwell of South Carolina were able Davis supporters in the upper house; Speaker of the House Thomas S. Bocock of Virginia and Representative Ethelbert Barksdale of Mississippi played a similar role in the lower house.

The most outspoken anti-Davis congressmen were Representative Henry Stuart Foote of Tennessee and Senator Louis T. Wigfall of Texas. As a bitter political foe of Davis in Mississippi politics before the war, Foote led the assault with "colicky" outbursts against the Davis war measures. Wigfall endorsed most of the measures, but as an admirer of General Joseph E. Johnston and an advocate of a strategy of western concentration, he scored the administration mercilessly for its alleged incompetence in the prosecution of the war.

There was no constitutional way short of impeachment to remove Davis from office, but the outcome of the congressional elections that took place in the fall of 1863 actually represented a vote of no confidence in his administration. In virtually every instance an anti-administration candidate won, turning the Congress into an almost solidly hostile body. Because the lawmakers could agree on no coherent program of their own, they were obliged to continue enacting most of the measures recommended by Davis. But the friction between the congressmen and the chief executive, revealed in unrestrained invective in the legislative halls and corridors, eroded to the vanishing point any spirit of cooperation within the Confederate government.

VII

The Strategic Balance

——— ❖ ———

A mbrose E. Burnside led his troops with apparent bravura. Physically impressive, even spectacular, with a luxuriant growth of cheek whiskers to which he bequeathed his name (later inverted to *sideburn*), he looked like a winner. Actually, he was nervous and unsure of himself, and in accepting command of the army had protested his unfitness for the job. Nevertheless, once in command he marched the Army of the Potomac swiftly to the north bank of the Rappahannock opposite Fredericksburg. His plan was to turn Lee's position by crossing the river and placing himself between Lee and Richmond before the Confederate general divined his intentions and concentrated against him.

At first all seemed to go well for Burnside. By November 20, 1862, the entire Union force of 120,000 was in place. If he had been able to cross the stream at once, his tactics might have succeeded because Fredericksburg was lightly held by the Confederates at that time. Lee's army was dispersed across the entire Virginia front, with Jackson's corps still in the Shenandoah Valley from the Antietam campaign. But Burnside's pontoons for bridging the river did not arrive until early December. By then it was too late to cross the river with assurance of success because the Army of Northern Virginia, 74,000 strong, was concentrated and firmly established along the ridge known as Marye's Heights that lay back of the town. Burnside nevertheless persisted in his plan and ordered the bridging to begin on December 11. The stage was set for a ghastly drama.

The Confederates occupied the forward slope of the ridge. Longstreet's corps held the left sector of the line with its left flank anchored on the Rappahannock above Fredericksburg and its center directly overlooking the town. Jackson's corps was concentrated on the right beyond a gorge formed by Deep Run Creek; Stuart's cavalry extended the Confederate right to the river below Fredericksburg. The position had formidable defensive strength, enhanced on Longstreet's front by field fortifications prepared at his order.

According to Burnside's order, the three "grand divisions" into which he had organized the Army of the Potomac were to advance with Sumner's grand division on the right opposite Fredericksburg, Hooker's grand division in the center, and William B. Franklin's grand division on the left. The Union artillery would support the movement from Stafford Heights, a commanding elevation less than a mile across the river from Fredericksburg. The infantry was to cross the river, deploy, and deliver a frontal assault.

Franklin's engineers had relatively little trouble in constructing their spans because their crossing sites were beyond the range of Jackson's guns. But the other engineers were exposed to the murderous fire of a detachment of Mississippians stationed by Longstreet in Fredericksburg. Not until Burnside's artillery battered the town and Union infantry crossed in boats to drive the marksmen from the rubble were the engineers able to complete their task on the Union right.

The assault began in the early morning of December 13. So poorly coordinated that Sumner's command did not move until 11:00 A.M. and much of Hooker's command not until 4:00 P.M., the operation was doomed from the beginning. Only once was there a flicker of hope for success. In the early afternoon Major General George Gordon Meade's division of Franklin's command briefly penetrated a section of Jackson's line only to be promptly driven back by a counterattack. Lee from his command post on Telegraph Hill, afterward known as Lee's Hill, observed the Confederate charge and listened to the exultant rebel yell, then turned to Longstreet and in a flash of self-revelation, said, "It is well that war is so terrible—we should grow too fond of it."

Hooker's attack was against Longstreet's position on Marye's Heights. Repeatedly and with sublime courage the blue-clad soldiers charged the thundering, smoking ridge only to see their formations cut to pieces by the musketry of the closely packed infantry supported by a crossfire of artillery. At dusk Hooker stopped the action. He later explained with profound bitterness, "Finding that I had lost as many men as my orders required me to lose, I suspended the attack." More than 12,000 Union soldiers lay dead or wounded on the bloody slopes; Confederate casualties amounted to somewhat more than 5,000. It was a tremendous Confederate victory won at relatively light cost.

Maddened by his failure, Burnside was set to renew the attack. He proposed personally to lead his old corps the next day in what would have amounted to a suicidal charge on the Confederate position. His subordinates wisely dissuaded him from the idea and prevailed on him to retire his army across the Rappahannock, which during the night of December 15 he successfully did. Lee may have missed an opportunity to destroy or further cripple the Army of the Potomac by failing to counterattack it while it was still south of the river. Possibly he could have done so while it was huddled for two days amid the Fredericksburg ruins. But when Jackson attempted a forward movement of his own troops at twilight of the first day he drew such heavy enemy artillery fire from Stafford Heights that he halted the action, and Lee ordered no assault.

While Burnside was engaged in the disastrous Virginia operations, Rosecrans and Bragg came together in a fierce but indecisive encounter in middle Tennessee. Rosecrans had long remained in Nashville collecting supplies and paralyzed by the forays of Bragg's cavalry led by Forrest and Morgan. Threatened early in December with removal from command because of his delays, Rosecrans responded tartly that if his superiors no longer had confidence in him, they ought at once to replace him. This did not occur, and when in late December he learned that Forrest was riding into western Tennessee and Morgan into Kentucky, he moved against the Confederate army at Murfreesboro only thirty miles to the southeast.

Bragg also was under pressure to take aggressive action. A month earlier Davis had placed General Joseph E. Johnston, idle since being wounded the preceding summer, in command of a department that embraced all Confederate troops in Tennessee and Mississippi. This made him Bragg's immediate superior, with the authority to take personal command of the Army of Tennessee if he should deem it advisable. Johnston chose not to do so, but the new command arrangement rendered it imperative that Bragg make a move.

The strategic situation in the West also dictated the move. Union forces were now menacing the only segment of the Mississippi River still in Confederate hands, that lying between the fortified towns of Vicksburg, Mississippi, and Port Hudson, Louisiana. Accordingly, Johnston attempted to create a mobile reserve that could be used either in Tennessee or Mississippi as required, while Forrest's cavalry harassed the Federal lines of communication to their forces in Mississippi. Bragg determined to strike a blow that would both redress the strategic situation and ensure the security of his own command. On the last day of the year he did so in a move that anticipated and frustrated Rosecrans's offensive plans.

Just after dawn on December 31 the armies of Bragg and Rosecrans, Bragg with 38,000 troops, Rosecrans with about 43,000, met in battle a mile north of Murfreesboro. Each general planned an attack in which the main effort would envelop or turn the other's right flank. Deployed for battle, both armies were astride the Nashville Turnpike and railroad from Nashville and also astride Stone's River, a stream some thirty yards in width that ran generally parallel to the pike and railroad. Bragg attacked first. With Hardee's corps, skillfully led, making the main effort on the Confederate left and Polk's corps supporting it, the Confederates drove back the Federal main body west of the river and by noon were threatening the turnpike, Rosecrans's line of supply and reinforcement. This line was also being fiercely harassed in the Federal rear by Brigadier General Joseph Wheeler's Confederate cavalry.

Bragg now ordered Breckinridge's division, which had been held east of the river to guard against a Federal attack there, to reinforce the assault west of the stream. The fiercest fighting of the afternoon occurred at the angle in the Federal line which was held by a brigade of Thomas's division in a dense, circular thicket of cedars known as the Round Forest, a position that covered both the railroad and the turnpike. The Federal line held, the Confederate attack lost its momentum, and Bragg lost the tactical initiative.

Both armies spent the next day resting, reorganizing, and preparing to reopen the struggle. On January 2 Bragg sent Breckinridge back east of the river to attack Union forces building up there, but the unsupported assault, launched in the late afternoon, broke down under heavy casualties inflicted by massed Union artillery fire from a commanding position west of the stream. The major fighting was over. Rosecrans was reinforced from Nashville the following day, while Bragg tried to make up his mind whether to renew the attack; that night Bragg began withdrawing along the line of the railroad to Tullahoma, Tennessee, thirty miles south and east of Murfreesboro.

Tactically the battle of Stone's River (Murfreesboro, to the Confederates) was a draw. Losses were heavy on both sides. The Federals suffered almost 13,000 dead, wounded, and missing; the Confederates almost 12,000. When Grant later heard the engagement referred to as a Union victory, he said dryly that a few more such victories would have lost the war. Although Bragg's decision to withdraw was approved by both of his corps commanders, both considered his conduct of the battle indecisive and irresolute. It provided yet another episode in the long history of Bragg's decline as an army commander, and of the decline of the Army of Tennessee itself.

In the broad view the battle of Stone's River was an important strategic victory for the Union because it left a powerful army poised to move against the key Confederate rail center of Chattanooga. It was important also in bolstering Union morale. Lincoln expressed his gratitude to Rosecrans by referring to the "hard-earned victory, which, had there been a defeat instead, the nation could scarcely have lived over." But during the weeks that followed, as both Rosecrans at Murfreesboro and Bragg at Tullahoma settled into winter quarters, the Union offensive in Tennessee appeared indefinitely stalled, with Bragg's force effectively denying all approaches to the primary Union objective, Chattanooga.

The Union effort to secure the remaining segment of the line of the Mississippi River also suffered reverses that brought it to a halt at the end of the year. During the late autumn Grant pressed a column by land toward Grenada, Mississippi, establishing his advance base at Holly Springs on the Mississippi Central Railroad leading to Jackson and New Orleans. In early December he sent an expedition under Sherman, now a major general, by river from Memphis. The overland expedition quickly fell victim to Confederate cavalry raids as Forrest cut the Union rail and telegraph communications in Tennessee and Van Dorn on December 20 swept around the Union positions in northern Mississippi to seize and destroy the base at Holly Springs.

Nine days later Sherman's attempt to take Vicksburg by moving his troops on transports up the Yazoo River north of the city and attacking from there met a bloody repulse at the Chickasaw Bluffs overlooking the stream's south bank. Grant now made a key decision, to shift his approach to the Mississippi River in spite of Sherman's failure there. While the long railroads were too vulnerable, the great river was an indestructible line of communication. But for the moment, and for many months to come, Vicksburg remained firmly in Confederate hands.

To Lincoln, December was a month of unremitting gloom. From all fronts the telegraph brought news of Union reverses, and Rosecrans's declaration of victory at Murfreesboro in early January was not sufficient to dispel the dark mood. Only a clear victory in Virginia could do that. Burnside now devised a plan for crossing the Rappahannock above Fredericksburg in order to turn Lee's impregnable position there. But the corps commanders of the Army of the Potomac, bereft of all traces of confidence in Burnside, protested directly to Lincoln, who turned wearily to Halleck for approval or disapproval of the plan. "Your military skill is useless to me, if you will not do this," he wrote plaintively.

When Halleck threatened to resign rather than give Burnside an explicit order based on an approval or disapproval of his plan, Lincoln left the matter in Burnside's hands. In late January the Army of the Potomac began an ill-starred movement up the Rappahannock. Torrential rains turned the Virginia roads into their usual winter quagmires; Burnside's notorious "Mud March" bogged down and ended with the troops in winter quarters at Aquia Creek on the Potomac. Dissension and recrimination now rent the army. The chief agitator was Hooker, who openly denounced Burnside as an incompetent and Lincoln an imbecile and declared that the nation needed a dictator to achieve victory. When Burnside attempted to relieve the insubordinate corps commander, Lincoln interceded and regretfully relieved Burnside instead. In his place, Lincoln made the fateful decision to appoint the splenetic and malcontent Hooker.

That Lincoln was keenly aware of the risks involved in the appointment is clear in his letter to Hooker at the time, certainly one of the most extraordinary communications ever sent from a head of state to a field commander. He told Hooker he had made the appointment for reasons he deemed sufficient. Among these were his belief that Hooker was a brave and skillful soldier, that he did not mix politics with soldiering, and that he was self-confident and ambitious, which, said Lincoln, "within reasonable bounds, does good rather than harm."

But Lincoln bluntly set forth what he knew of Hooker's shortcomings. He accused the general of allowing his ambition to undercut Burnside, in which, said Lincoln, he committed a great wrong both against the country and a brother officer. Lincoln let Hooker know he was aware of the general's views on the need for a dictator. "Of course," Lincoln said, "it was not for this, but in spite of it, that I have given you the command." Then, with exquisite irony, "Only those generals who gain success can set up dictators. What I now ask of you is military success, and I will risk the dictatorship."

Lincoln went on to say he feared that the spirit of criticism and obstruction which Hooker had fostered in the army would now turn against Hooker himself. Lincoln promised to assist in putting it down, because, he warned, "Neither you nor Napoleon, if he were alive again, could get any good out of an army while such a spirit prevails in it." Having delivered what should have been a thorough chastening, Lincoln urged Hooker to beware of rashness, but "with energy and sleepless vigilance go forward and give us victories."

Hooker entertained no doubts of his ability to gain victories. A West Point graduate and a man of large and powerful physique, he had served with distinction in the Mexican War but later had resigned his commission and settled in California. Appointed a brigadier general of volunteers early in the war, he received a promotion for his aggressive leadership in the opening battles in Virginia. As an effective corps commander he earned the nickname "Fighting Joe Hooker," though it seems to have been coined through a mistake of a newspaper typesetter who omitted the comma from a dispatch which actually read, "Fighting, Joe Hooker." Hooker now went to work with immense energy, and by spring 1863 the Army of the Potomac, 134,000 strong, was ready to move.

Hooker's campaign plan was similar to Burnside's abortive last plan, but more sophisticated. Hooker proposed to fix Lee's army at Fredericksburg by threatening it with two corps of the Army of the Potomac under Major General John Sedgwick while the Federal cavalry of 12,000 troopers, now concentrated for the first time under Major General George Stoneman, rode wide around the Confederate left and deep into its rear to cut or threaten the line of communication above Richmond. Meantime, Hooker would lead the bulk of his army, organized into five corps commanded by Major Generals Darius N. Couch, Meade, Henry W. Slocum, Oliver O. Howard, and Daniel E. Sickles, across the river above Fredericksburg and strike at Lee's line of communication directly behind the Confederates.

These operations, believed the Union general, would oblige Lee to abandon his unassailable position on Marye's Heights and either withdraw into the Richmond defenses or be destroyed in the open by a Federal attack in overwhelming strength. "I have the finest army the sun ever shone on," said Hooker. "My plans are perfect, and when I start to carry them out, may God have mercy on General Lee, for I will have none."

Lee was vulnerable. Anxious over a renewed Federal threat from the Virginia Peninsula, and desperately in need of supplies because his immediate area was stripped, Lee took advantage of the break in Federal pressure after Fredericksburg to send Longstreet with two divisions to secure Richmond and forage across the line in North Carolina. Lee intended to bring these troops back to the main body by rail in time to meet a general Federal advance, and he instructed Longstreet to be prepared for such a move.

The decision to separate the Confederate forces turned out to be a grave mistake; the plan for reconcentration went awry. Longstreet, finding himself opposed by a weak Federal corps under Burnside, laid siege to this force at Suffolk, south of Richmond. Hooker moved faster than Lee had anticipated, and Longstreet failed to disengage in time to rejoin the main body. Lee faced Hooker's onslaught with a seriously weakened Army of Northern Virginia, a force only slightly above 60,000.

Hooker's early moves, begun April 27, went well, and his intentions were temporarily concealed from Lee. With the Union cavalry on its grand sweep and Sedgwick crossing the Rappahannock on pontoons at Fredericksburg, the main body forded the river at a number of points above the town and marched rapidly along the country roads threading a densely wooded area known appropriately as the Wilderness. If the attacking force could move through this area unchecked and into the open country, it would be in the rear of Lee's army, and his position would be successfully turned.

It was not to be. While the Federal cavalry rode afar, Lee held most of his cavalry with him under Stuart, whose reconnaissances soon revealed the Federal operations. Lee responded quickly and boldly by ordering a single division, Major General Richard H. Anderson's from Longstreet's command, to march west along the Orange Turnpike and check the Federal advance by erecting and fighting from earthworks. Meanwhile, Lee started moving the rest of his army there, leaving only Major General Jubal A. Early with 10,000 men on Marye's Heights to contain Sedgwick.

Anderson established his line beyond the Tabernacle Church, situated six miles west of Fredericksburg, and stopped the advance of the Federal vanguard, Major General George Sykes's division of Meade's corps, at that point. As the troops of Jackson's corps moved into position Lee extended the Confederate line north and south but was unable to avoid leaving the flanks exposed. Hooker's general attack opened the morning of May 1. For a time it went extremely well. While the two corps of Couch and Slocum engaged the Confederates and held them in position, Meade's corps advanced virtually uncontested into the gap between the Confederate right flank and the river. Lee appeared to be trapped.

Then Hooker's nerve failed him. Operating blind because of the absence of his cavalry, he lost confidence in his plan. At 1:30 P.M., from his headquarters at Chancellorsville, a single house located at a road junction in the Wilderness some three miles behind the battle line, he issued an unequivocal order to his corps commanders to withdraw and dig in around Chancellorsville. The corps commanders protested but obeyed.

By evening a Federal defensive line was taking shape with its left flank anchored on the Rappahannock, its center at Chancellorsville, and its right flank sharply refused, drawn back deep into the Wilderness to the west so that one entire corps (Howard's) faced south. As the Federals pulled back and began throwing up earthworks, the shorter Confederate line advanced and concentrated opposite the Chancellorsville angle in the Federal line. Meanwhile, Confederate cavalry screened the Confederate flanks, tested the Union flanks, and discovered one of them highly vulnerable. Stuart reported to Lee that Howard's right flank, the right flank of the Army of the Potomac, was "in the air."

From Hooker's behavior in assuming the defensive, Lee sensed that he now held the initiative. That night he and Jackson designed one of the most audacious tactical moves in the history of modern warfare. Seated at a campfire in the woods and drawing diagrams on the ground, they planned an attack to be led by Jackson on Howard's open flank, while Lee and the remainder of his troops held the Federal army in position. When Jackson proposed to take his entire corps of 26,000 in the attack, leaving only 17,000 to face Hooker's 73,000, even Lee was taken aback. But, wrote Freeman, Lee's "fighting blood" was stirred. A moment's reflection, then quietly, "Very well. Go ahead."

Jackson and his troops marched at dawn on May 2. Guided along an obscure iron furnace trail through the woods, they emerged on the Brock Road and followed it to the Orange Turnpike near the Wilderness Tavern. Federal patrols reported the movement, but Hooker mistook it for a retreat and dispatched Sickles in a vain pursuit that was halted by Jackson's rear guard. Reconnoitering ahead of his column, Jackson planned an assault in three waves to sweep down the length of Howard's line. Naval tacticians would have said he was "crossing the T."

The blow fell late in the afternoon, preceded by the scurrying of deer and other wildlife flushed from their haunts. Struck by surprise in the flank, two entire Union divisions were driven down the turnpike past Hooker's headquarters at Chancellorsville. The Confederate charge threatened to sever the remainder of the Union line from the rear. But darkness, the steadfastness of the rallied Union troops, and the disorganization and exhaustion of the Confederates halted the attack well before midnight. Determined to regain the momentum and cut the Union army away from the river, and thus away from its line of reinforcement or retreat, Jackson rode forward to reconnoiter the situation.

It was his last tactical action. He and his escort, mistaken for Federal horsemen as they returned to the lines, received the fire of Confederate pickets and Jackson fell, severely wounded at the height of his most spectacular operation. His command devolved upon A. P. Hill, the senior division commander, and when Hill was wounded later the same night, it devolved upon Stuart. Sporadic fighting continued in the darkness and tangled woods; Stuart made plans to renew the attack at dawn.

Renew it the Confederates did. Stuart's lines pressed forward, occupying the important terrain at Hazel Grove, a slight knoll just south of the turnpike which had been abandoned by the Federals upon Hooker's orders. Confederate artillery at Hazel Grove now played effectively upon the Federal lines, and the position served as a keystone for the junction of Stuart's troops with the remainder of the Confederate army under Lee's direct command. At his Chancellorsville headquarters General Hooker grew increasingly apprehensive over the course of the battle as he perceived it.

An event at mid-morning shattered what remained of the Union general's morale. A Confederate cannonball fired from Hazel Grove struck the porch pillar against which he was leaning and left him dazed. Refusing to relinquish the command, he overruled the urging of his corps commanders and issued orders for the execution of a plan he had conceived the night before: the withdrawal of the army into a new defensive position to the rear of Chancellorsville.

At this point Lee's hopes for a decisive victory were upset by news from another front. Sedgwick, responding to Hooker's orders of the previous day, repeatedly attacked Early at Fredericksburg during the morning of May 3, drove the Confederates from their position, and threatened Lee's main force from the rear. A single division, that of Major General Lafayette McLaws of Longstreet's command, dispatched by Lee, managed to halt Sedgwick at Salem Church. Gambling that Hooker would remain passive with the bulk of the Union army, Lee now sought to take advantage of interior lines to strike his divided opponents by turns.

Leaving Stuart with only 25,000 men to contain Hooker and ordering Early to combine forces with McLaws, Lee joined them with Anderson's division for a concentrated assault the afternoon of May 4 on Sedgwick's isolated force. Lee's estimate of Hooker was accurate; the Union commander remained idle and squandered another opportunity

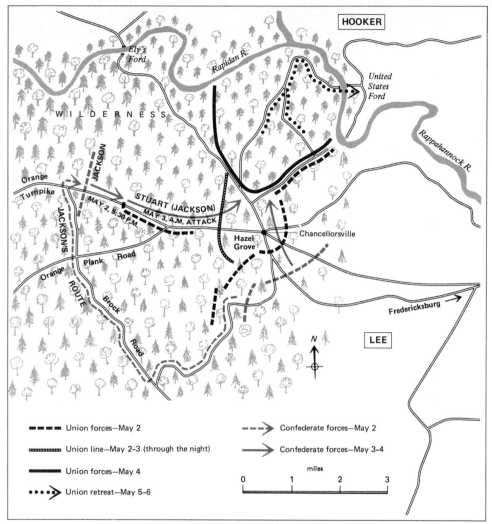

CHANCELLORSVILLE, MAY 2–6, 1863

for a possible victory. Lee's bold action removed the threat to his rear, but he was unable to achieve his aim of destroying Sedgwick, who fought a skillful delaying battle and escaped by withdrawing across the river during the night.

Lee now reconcentrated his army for what he hoped would be a decisive blow against Hooker. It was destined not to fall. During the night of May 5 Hooker again overruled his corps commanders, who wished to remain and fight, and ordered the Army of the Potomac to withdraw beyond the Rappahannock. When the Confederate skirmishers advanced on the morning of May 6 they found the Union lines abandoned. The great battle of Chancellorsville was over, leaving approximately 13,000 Confederate and 17,000 Union casualties.

Chancellorsville was unique. More than any other Civil War battle it represented a victory of generals, Lee and Jackson, over another general, Hooker. In the earlier battle of Fredericksburg the Army of the Potomac was stopped, defeated; at the end it no longer had the capability of attacking. At Chancellorsville the Army of the Potomac was not defeated as an army; at the end it was still capable and willing to continue the struggle. Theoretically, Hooker by bold action still could have won. Lee and Jackson's grasp of the situation, their audacity, willingness to seize the initiative when offered an opportunity, and presence of mind in the turmoil of combat all contrasted strikingly with Hooker's weakness and indecisiveness. As a corps commander Hooker had reached the level of his capacity. Elevated to the top command, he faltered at the most critical hour of his career.

Chancellorsville made Lee immortal in the minds of his men. On the second day of the battle, as the Federal line recoiled and Lee rode forward to preserve and direct the momentum of his army's advance, a great, spontaneous shout of adoration arose from the throats of the begrimed soldiers. A staff officer described the scene and said, "I thought it must have been from such scenes as this that men in ancient days ascended to the dignity of gods." But Lee was keenly aware of the heavy losses his army had suffered in the battle, losses that could not be replaced. The gravest loss was that of Jackson. When Lee learned of the amputation of one of Jackson's arms, he said, "He has lost his left arm, but I have lost my right." Privately he wrote, "Any victory would be dear at such a price. I know not how to replace him." Lee was right. Jackson died a few days later from pneumonia, and the Army of Northern Virginia was never the same again.

News of Chancellorsville brought a fresh agony to Lincoln. "My God!" he exclaimed. "What will the country say! What will the country say!" Accompanied by General Halleck, he visited Hooker's army, now encamped at Falmouth on the north bank of the Rappahannock just above Fredericksburg. Lincoln again faced the difficult decision whether to appoint a new commander. He decided to give Hooker another chance, but wrote him that he thought it best not to undertake to renew the offensive until the army was again restored to top condition. Yet, he said, if Hooker believed he could attack with a good prospect of success, Lincoln wished to place no restraint upon him. Pointedly, almost as if to say, "I told you so," he passed on to Hooker something else, something he had learned while inspecting the army. "I must tell you," he wrote, "I have some painful intimations that some of your corps and Division Commanders are not giving you their confidence."

Thrilling as Chancellorsville was to the Confederate authorities, it did not blind them to the disturbing realities of their military situation.

Their lines in Virginia held firm, but west of the Appalachians they were dangerously bent and vulnerable. Throughout the spring Davis and his advisers had considered plans for recouping the strategic balance. Most of these plans involved the shifting of troops from Lee's army to the Confederate armies in the West. General Joseph E. Johnston favored such a plan, and in early March Lee himself wrote Davis that for some time he had hoped the situation in Virginia would take a turn allowing him to send as much as an entire corps there.

The most persistent spokesman of the western strategy among Confederate officers was General Beauregard. Brilliant and resourceful but erratic and visionary, Beauregard since August 1862 had been in command of the Department of South Carolina and Georgia, with headquarters at Charleston. From this relatively idle position he wrote his friends both in the army and in Congress urging the western move, which he believed would bring a decisive Confederate victory over Rosecrans in Tennessee. This in turn would isolate Grant in Mississippi and force him either to withdraw or be destroyed by a concentration of the western Confederate forces upon him there. Within the Confederate cabinet, Secretary of War Seddon favored a transfer of troops to the West; within Lee's army his corps commander Longstreet advocated it.

Meanwhile, the situation on the Virginia front caused Lee to change his mind, if he ever had seriously entertained the idea of parting with a portion of his army. When on the eve of Chancellorsville Seddon attempted to put a form of the western strategy into effect by asking Lee to send a division to Tennessee, Lee demurred. He said the threat of Hooker's powerful army made such a move unwise. Let the Confederate armies in Tennessee and Mississippi be reinforced from less exposed points along the lower Atlantic coast, he said; the Confederacy could not match the Union in shifting troops from one major theater to another.

This was consistent with what Lee had said all along: the Confederacy must concentrate at the vital strategic locations; it could not "meet the enemy at all points of his choosing." Temporarily, Hooker's advance, and the battle of Chancellorsville which resulted, put an end to the question of sending troops away from Virginia, but conditions in the West would soon bring it up again.

The most urgent conditions there prevailed along the lower Mississippi River, where General Grant in early January 1863 moved his headquarters to Memphis as a preliminary to taking personal charge of the stalled campaign against Vicksburg. He found himself faced with a serious command problem. President Lincoln and Secretary of War Stanton earlier had promised the Vicksburg command to Major General John A. McClernand, a political appointee and Illinois volunteer general who had fought well at Shiloh and had recruited many of the troops in the Vicksburg expedition. McClernand now challenged Grant's authority and wrote him bluntly, "Two generals cannot command this army."

Grant needed no lecture on the importance of the principle of unity of command. He promptly joined the expedition at Milliken's Bend, its base on the west bank a few miles above Vicksburg, and issued orders as the army commander which designated McClernand as a corps commander. McClernand grudgingly acquiesced in the arrangement by obeying Grant's orders; Lincoln acquiesced by ignoring McClernand's letter of protest. It was a practical if not entirely satisfactory solution to the problem.

Grant then settled down to the task of finding a way to take the formidable city fortress confronting him. Months of travail and repeated exercises in trial and error were required to do it, but eventually, after devising an extraordinarily ingenious plan of operations, he succeeded. Quite early Grant perceived that the best approach to Vicksburg lay in avoiding the virtually impenetrable maze of swamps and bayous north of the city and the impregnable defenses along the Yazoo bluffs. He saw the wisdom of moving on Vicksburg from the south, where the land was firm and traversed by passable roads. But the Vicksburg defenses themselves rendered extremely hazardous, if not prohibitively costly, any effort to navigate downstream to a position below the city; Confederate fortifications at Port Hudson, Louisiana, on the east bank more than 100 miles below Vicksburg, blocked the river approach from New Orleans.

Grant experimented with a number of ways to accomplish the task. He undertook to bypass Vicksburg by having his troops dig canals, one designed to divert a portion of the Mississippi by cutting across the neck of the loop on which the city stood, the other to connect with bayous that joined the river below the city. He tried hard to find natural water routes that would enable his forces to bypass the city's defenses. He tested a route west of the Mississippi through Lake Providence, located in Louisiana some fifty miles north of Vicksburg, and linked with the Mississippi below Vicksburg via the Red River, but he was unable to overcome the problems of navigation. He launched an expedition east of the Mississippi through the Yazoo Pass, a cutoff from the Mississippi 150 miles north of Vicksburg, and another expedition through Steele's Bayou, which lay between Vicksburg and the Yazoo Pass. These efforts failed also because of the natural obstacles to navigation and the work of the Confederates in obstructing and defending the waterways.

All the while Grant meditated another plan and waited for the spring weather that would make it feasible. In mid-April he set it in motion. Acting Rear Admiral David D. Porter's gunboats, accompanied by transports loaded with supplies, successfully, though with heavy damage, ran past the Vicksburg batteries during the night and anchored at a point on the west bank forty miles below the city.

While Sherman's corps demonstrated against the Confederate defenses at Chickasaw Bluffs and a Union cavalry expedition under Colonel Benjamin H. Grierson created some damage and great alarm and confusion by staging a spectacular raid from the Tennessee border through central Mississippi to Baton Rouge, Louisiana, Grant sent the main body of his army, the two corps of McClernand and Major General James B. McPherson, down the west bank of the Mississippi to rendezvous with Porter's fleet. Sherman's corps then followed along the same route, and on the 30th Grant began ferrying his army across to the east bank. By May 6, the very day the Army of the Potomac was withdrawing across the Rappahannock after Chancellorsville, Grant completed the passage of the Mississippi.

The Confederate command system in the West was not equal to the crisis it now faced. It was, in a sense, a divided command. On May 1 General Johnston, the Department commander, whose headquarters were with Bragg's army at Tullahoma, Tennessee, wired Lieutenant General John C. Pemberton, now commander of Confederate troops in Mississippi and eastern Louisiana, "If Grant's army lands on [the east side] of the river, the safety of Mississippi depends on beating it. For that object you should unite your whole force." Grant was momentarily vulnerable to these tactics; by combining all available Confederate forces and attacking immediately, Pemberton would have enjoyed a numerical advantage of approximately 50,000 to 41,000. This was the option of boldness. But it was also the option of risk; it required the temporary abandonment of Vicksburg itself in order to concentrate against Grant.

President Davis on May 9 ordered Johnston to go to Mississippi and take personal charge of operations there. This was a wise move, but Davis wired Pemberton saying Grant would be compelled to stay in contact with his fleet, and Davis emphasized the importance of holding Vicksburg and Port Hudson in order to preserve the Confederate line of communications with the area beyond the Mississippi. Pemberton interpreted Davis's instructions to mean that Vicksburg itself ought not be abandoned, even temporarily. So, instead of obeying Johnston's order, Pemberton cautiously probed to the south, not to attack Grant, but with the purpose of severing or threatening his line of supply and at the same time keeping Vicksburg covered.

Pemberton's decision was based on Davis's premise that Grant must remain continuously in touch with his fleet, a premise that turned out to be false. Grant was already on the move inland, determined to abandon his base, forage for supplies, cut off the line of Confederate reinforcement, and take Vicksburg from the rear.

Moving rapidly on a broad front, Grant on May 12 drove a small Confederate force out of Raymond, fifteen miles west of Jackson, and the following day seized Clinton on the railroad between Vicksburg and

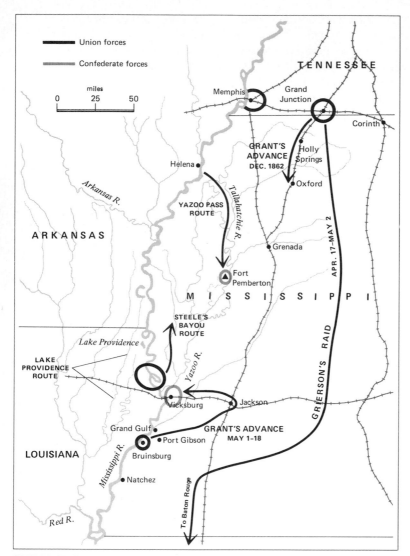

THE VICKSBURG CAMPAIGN, DEC. 1862–MAY 1863

Jackson. Johnston arrived at Jackson that same day and took personal command of the 6,000 Confederates gathered there. Upon learning that the Federals were between him and Pemberton, he sent orders for Pemberton to attack Grant from the rear, but he wired Richmond saying he himself had arrived too late. The next day Grant drove the Confederates out of Jackson. Johnston was not paralyzed by these reverses. With some 15,000 reinforcements on the way from Bragg's army and the Atlantic coast, Johnston continued to attempt a junction with Pemberton north of Jackson. All efforts to do so miscarried; the Confederate defense of Vicksburg was in complete disarray.

Beginning in April the siege of Port Hudson by the army of Major General Nathaniel P. Banks, commander of the Gulf Department with headquarters in New Orleans, accompanied Grant's operations against Vicksburg. In concentrating his forces at Port Hudson, Banks was obliged to thin his garrisons elsewhere. This prompted the Confederate commander in that portion of Louisiana west of the Mississippi, Major General Richard Taylor, to advance upon New Orleans in an effort to compel Banks to bring most of his troops back for the defense of the city.

Taylor's object was to enable the 7,500 Confederate troops defending Port Hudson, who also were under Pemberton's command, to break out and join the forces opposing Grant. Moving swiftly, Taylor soon recaptured much of southern Louisiana west of the river. But New Orleans, located on the east bank of the broad stream, actually was in little danger, and Banks refused to take thè bait. Holding tenaciously to his purpose, he succeeded in nailing the Port Hudson defenders in position.

The prospect of disaster in Mississippi coupled with Lee's victory at Chancellorsville brought to a head the strategic debate that for some time had been going on in the Confederacy. Secretary of War Seddon now applied again to Lee for a division of troops to be sent as reinforcements to Mississippi. General Longstreet urged that a detachment be sent to strengthen Bragg in Tennessee. Again Lee opposed such moves. Replying to Seddon, he repeated what he had said earlier: the distance to Mississippi was too great to indicate success in such a transfer. Significantly, he added also that the uncertainty as to how his troops would be used in the West made the venture inadvisable. Any weakening of the Army of Northern Virginia, he asserted, would oblige it to retire into the Richmond defenses where it would no longer be a strategic threat. "It becomes a question," he said, "between Virginia and the Mississippi."

The final strategic decision came in a meeting on May 14–17 of Lee and Davis and the Confederate cabinet. Lee argued convincingly in favor of a move into the North. He believed this would be the best way to relieve Federal pressure in the West. He also believed it would strengthen the peace party in the North and possibly bring an end to the war. Of the greatest immediate importance, it would allow him to feed his army on the rich northern countryside and give respite to the depleted barns and smokehouses of northern Virginia. In the face of such formidable opposition, Seddon withdrew his proposal; most, if not all, of the cabinet members agreed with Lee; and Davis approved his plan. Lee returned to his field headquarters and began to prepare the orders that would take his army on its fateful mission.

Lee has been severely criticized for his emphasis on the importance of the eastern theater and his resistance to the weakening of his own army. Some students of the Civil War see his behavior as representing a myopic if not selfish anxiety over the security of his beloved Virginia. Others believe he simply allowed his immediate cares to blind him to the strategic needs of the Confederacy as a whole. Hattaway and Jones endorse the latter explanation in saying Lee suffered temporarily from a measure of "cognitive dissonance" that caused him to minimize the danger in the West. If Lee at this time failed to recognize the importance of the West, his failure was indeed temporary. He had said a year earlier, "If the Mississippi Valley is lost, the Atlantic States would be ruined." Within a few months he would in fact send troops from his army to bolster the Confederates in Tennessee.

Whether a resort to the western strategy at this time would have succeeded will never be known. When it was attempted later, it failed. Certainly Lee's call for a decision between Virginia and the line of the Mississippi was not an irrational call; it addressed the imperative need for a focus to Confederate strategy. His insistence on the importance of the East grew out of a conviction that northern Virginia, as a buffer of protection to the Confederate capital and as a springboard of operations against Washington and the major northern cities and their transportation net, was the most valuable strategic area held by the Confederacy; that an intact Army of Northern Virginia was the most effective instrument of Confederate strategy.

In any event, the supreme commitments were now made and the machinery was in motion. During the late spring and early summer of 1863 the strategic situation stood at a delicate balance. Grant held the upper hand in Mississippi; Rosecrans and Bragg remained at a stalemate in middle Tennessee; Lee had the advantage of recent victory, high morale, and the seizure of the initiative in the East. The coming campaigns in these three localities would play major roles in determining the outcome of the war.

VIII

The Turn of the Tide of Battle

———— ❖ ————

On June 4, 1863, the advance units of the Army of Northern Virginia began their march to a point on the Potomac a few miles above Harpers Ferry and 100 miles above Washington. Lee's most urgent aim after crossing the river was to move through the narrow strip of western Maryland, and, behind the long escarpment of South Mountain, to press into the rich fields of southern Pennsylvania where his hungry troops could replenish their supplies.

His strategic goals were varied. His most immediate purpose was to draw the Union army out of Virginia; his secondary purpose was to cause the Union authorities to recall troops from Tennessee or Vicksburg, or both, and thus to relieve the pressure in those places. There is compelling evidence also that Lee had even larger aims in mind. His character, his theory of warfare, his previous conduct as a commander, and his behavior on this campaign argue that he hoped to strike a decisive blow of some kind if he could create the opportunity to do so. He wrote the secretary of war that he might be able to draw his opponent into a position where the Union force could "be assailed"; and Lee was quoted after the war by one of his subordinates as having said explicitly that he hoped to take the enemy force at a disadvantage, defeat and "virtually destroy" it, and perhaps end the war.

As he put his troops in motion, Lee asked Davis to strengthen his army by bringing up reinforcements from the relatively idle points in the Carolinas, Georgia, and Florida. He recommended also that Beauregard be brought to northern Virginia and placed in command of a force, if only an army "in effigy," to threaten Washington from the south and confuse the Union authorities.

Lee pointed out to Davis that in spite of recent victories the Confederacy was growing relatively weaker as the war continued. But he believed the northern population was demoralized by Chancellorsville and the military stalemate elsewhere, and he again advised a southern peace overture to encourage the northern peace party and bring pressure for an armistice. Although this recommendation greatly underestimated the determination of the North to preserve the Union, it indicated on Lee's part a clear understanding that the Confederacy lacked the capability of destroying the Union's armed forces; that the Confederacy could win only by destroying the will of the northern people to continue the war.

Davis, anxious over the security of Richmond and beset with other cares, did not respond to Lee's overtures. The Army of Northern Virginia, with Longstreet's command now rejoined, was embarked on its most critical campaign with approximately 76,000 troops. In an effort to compensate for Jackson's absence, Lee had reorganized it into three corps of infantry, with Longstreet in command of First Corps; Richard Ewell, recently promoted to lieutenant general, in command of Second Corps; and A. P. Hill, also a new lieutenant general, in command of Third Corps. Stuart remained in command of the cavalry corps with a strength of about 12,000.

Stuart's cavalry skillfully screened the opening movements of the operation. But on June 9 he allowed himself to be surprised and attacked near Brandy Station by a Union cavalry force of equal strength under command of Major General Alfred Pleasonton. After a drawn battle Pleasonton withdrew, leaving Stuart to claim victory. But an outbreak of criticism in the army, and an editorial in the *Richmond Examiner* accusing Stuart of arrogance, negligence, and bad management, sorely wounded the pride of the "bold dragoon," to borrow Emory Thomas's colorful title for him. Perhaps Stuart yearned to restore his image with a spectacular performance in the coming campaign.

Lee's plans were only temporarily upset by the action at Brandy Station. By mid-June the head of his column was across the Potomac; by the 28th the bulk of the lead corps (Ewell's) was in Carlisle, Pennsylvania, only twenty miles from Harrisburg. Notwithstanding Lee's lofty orders against pillaging, the Confederates were foraging luxuriously, paying for supplies with Confederate currency or receipts that were supposed to be redeemed by the Confederate government. Also, reprehensibly, without any tactical purpose, the Confederate cavalry and units of Longstreet's corps were arresting blacks, some of them free blacks, to be sent to Virginia as runaway slaves.

Everything seemed to be proceeding smoothly for Lee. But not all was well; one important element of his army, much of his cavalry and its brilliant but flamboyant commander, were out of place. Taking advantage of Lee's loosely worded, discretionary orders, Stuart with three of his five brigades was on another ride around the entire Army of the Potomac. He succeeded in encircling his opponent, sweeping all the way to Carlisle and capturing en route a Union wagon train of 125 vehicles. But in doing so he deprived Lee of his vital services of reconnaissance. At one point Lee said in exasperation, "I do not know what to do; I cannot hear from General Stuart, the eye of the army." When at noon on July 2, in the middle of the war's greatest battle, Stuart rode into army headquarters, Lee greeted him, "Well, General Stuart, you are here at last." From Lee, this was a stinging reprimand.

Meanwhile, Hooker, after a week of indecision, proposed to take advantage of the absence of the Confederates on his front by marching on Richmond. Lincoln vetoed this plan and restated what had now become his fixed strategy for victory: that Lee's army, and not Richmond, was the true objective of the Army of the Potomac. A few days later he used one of his homespun metaphors in urging Hooker to strike the Confederates while they were on the move. "If the head of Lee's army is at Martinsburg [located in the Valley] and the tail of it...between Fredericksburg and Chancellorsville, the animal must be very slim somewhere. Could you not break him?"

Actually, Lincoln's patience with Hooker was about played out. Under prodding, Hooker withdrew north of the Potomac and headed for Lee's line of march. But when his request for reinforcements from the Harpers Ferry garrison was rejected, he made the mistake of tendering his resignation, doubtless in the belief that it would be turned down. Lincoln promptly accepted it and on June 28 named Meade to the top command. Meade at once started the Army of the Potomac north to intercept the Confederate movement.

Not until the evening of the 28th did Lee learn from a Confederate agent, possibly an officer in civilian clothes, that the Union army was located in the vicinity of Frederick, Maryland, only thirty-five miles southeast of his own headquarters which was now at Chambersburg just east of the northern tip of South Mountain and forty-five miles from Harrisburg. The information was vague, but Lee, sensing danger and perhaps opportunity as well, immediately sent out orders for his army to concentrate in the vicinity of Cashtown some fifteen miles east of Chambersburg. By the evening of June 30 Longstreet's and Hill's two corps, some 43,000 troops, were gathered here. Ewell with two divisions from Carlisle and one from York was on his way.

The agent also informed Lee of Meade's appointment as the commanding general facing him. The two men were not strangers to each other; they were personal friends and had served together on General Scott's staff during the Mexican War. As always, Lee made a quick and astute appraisal of his new opponent, an appraisal that would turn out to be remarkably prophetic. "General Meade will commit no blunder in my front," he said, "and if I make one he will make haste to take advantage of it."

Ironically, the greatest battle of the Civil War was not planned in advance by either commander. It began as a chance skirmish the afternoon of June 30 when Brigadier General James Johnston Pettigrew's

Confederate brigade reached the outskirts of Gettysburg eight miles southeast of Cashtown. Pettigrew's division commander, Major General Henry Heth, said he had ordered the march to Gettysburg for the purpose of seizing a supply of Union army footwear said to be stored there, though it seems unlikely that such valuable equipment would have been left by Ewell's men, who had already been through the town. Receiving fire from Union cavalry as he approached Gettysburg, and under instructions to avoid a battle, Pettigrew returned to Cashtown. That night A. P. Hill, the corps commander, approved Heth's plan to employ his entire division the following morning to drive off the worrisome cavalry and secure the shoes.

What the Confederates did not know was that the Union cavalry at Gettysburg, two brigades commanded by Brigadier General John Buford, was the advance element of the entire Army of the Potomac. Moving cautiously but resolutely, Meade had planned a defensive position along Pipe Creek in Maryland just below the Pennsylvania line.

The events of July 1 drastically altered the plan. Fighting gallantly along McPherson's ridge west of Gettysburg, Buford's troopers temporarily stopped Heth's advance. In response to Buford's urgent call for reinforcements, Major General John Reynolds, commander of the lead corps (First Corps), rode ahead, joined Buford, evaluated the situation, and ordered his troops forward. Soon Reynolds lay dead of a Confederate bullet, leaving Brigadier General Abner Doubleday in command of the corps. By midmorning the Union infantry began to arrive on the line and the intensity of the battle increased steadily. Buford's action, followed by Reynolds's decision to reinforce him, changed the site of the forthcoming battle from Pipe Creek to Gettysburg.

Meanwhile, Ewell, on the march from Carlisle to Cashtown, but with the option from Lee to come to Gettysburg instead, now obeyed the axiom to move to the sound of the guns and diverted his columns to Gettysburg. Arriving from the north and northeast, he found himself in position to strike the right flank of the Union line, which he did without hesitation. By midafternoon two Union corps, First Corps and Eleventh Corps, with the entire force commanded by Major General Oliver O. Howard, commander of Eleventh Corps and senior Union officer on the field, were engaged against two divisions of Hill's corps and two divisions of Ewell's corps.

The Confederates had concentrated more quickly; the bulk of the Union army was still on the march in a column that stretched back for miles. The Union defenders at Gettysburg were at a numerical disadvantage of approximately three to four. Threatened with envelopment by Ewell's attack on the right flank, the Eleventh Corps now began to give way, and Howard ordered the Union line to fall back to a stronger position. During the withdrawal, and especially in the confusion of the Eleventh Corps in moving through Gettysburg, the Union force lost approximately 4,000 troops as prisoners.

Providently, Howard had chosen as the fallback position the key terrain feature of the immediate area, Cemetery Hill, just south of Gettysburg. So named because it was topped by the local burial ground, it was a modest elevation of gentle slopes that overlooked the town and dominated the roads entering from that direction. Howard had the foresight earlier in the day to place a division in reserve there, and it served as a rallying force for the battered and weary soldiers of the two forward corps as they arrived. They were greeted and steadied also by Major General Winfield Scott Hancock, a man of outstanding ability and reassuring presence. Commander of the Second Corps, he had been sent forward by Meade to take charge on the field and select a suitable defensive line.

Lee arrived on the scene in the early afternoon. Seeing at a glance the importance of Cemetery Hill, he sent word to Ewell to take the position, "if he found it practicable," but to avoid a general engagement until the arrival of the rest of the army. Given a discretionary order, Ewell, unlike Jackson, hesitated and finally decided the attempt was not practicable. Possibly he was right. An authority on the battle, Edwin B. Coddington, believes that unless the Confederates had launched a fresh attack within an hour after the Union line began to withdraw, an action which he says only a Jackson was likely to have accomplished, a limited attack would have had little chance of success, and Lee had charged Ewell not to bring on a general engagement.

Lee informed Longstreet that afternoon of his intention to renew the attack the following day. Longstreet protested. Because of his faith in a strategy of western concentration, he had opposed the move into Pennsylvania; he now objected to a continuation of the battle and urged Lee to disengage and move around the south flank of the Union army so as to interpose his force between it and Washington and oblige Meade to make an assault. But Lee's mind was made up. He hoped to defeat Meade before the Union army could be fully concentrated. "If Meade is there tomorrow I will attack him," he said.

Lee's original plan was for Ewell to make the main effort the following morning against the Union right flank on Cemetery Hill, and in the late afternoon of the first day Lee visited Ewell to order it. Ewell's response and the comments of his division commanders, Major Generals Jubal A. Early and Robert E. Rodes, were so lacking in confidence that Lee changed his mind and decided to make the main effort on the opposite end of the line with Longstreet's corps. It is ironic that the attack was to be led by the general with the strongest doubts about the entire operation. But Longstreet was the senior corps commander, and a leader of great tactical skill and indomitable spirit. Not for nothing was he known as "Lee's War Horse."

Lee misgauged the speed of the Union concentration. By the morning of July 2 six of the seven infantry corps of the Army of the Potomac were present and the seventh was in supporting distance, a total force of about 87,000. Meade himself had arrived about midnight and had approved Hancock's arrangements. The Union line at the northern end was now refused, curved back from its position on Cemetery Hill to occupy Culp's Hill also, which overlooked Cemetery Hill from the east. The line ran two miles south from Cemetery Hill along the low elevation known as Cemetery Ridge and the hill named Little Round Top that overlooked both Cemetery Ridge and Cemetery Hill from the south. South of Little Round Top lay a still larger hill known as Round Top, which was not occupied. The prevailing terrain features that shaped the Union line suggest the rough form of a fishhook, Cemetery Hill the hook, Culp's Hill the barb, Cemetery Ridge the shank, and Little Round Top the eye.

By the morning of July 2 Lee's army occupied a line in which Ewell's corps faced the northern sector of the Union position on Culp's Hill and the northern face of Cemetery Hill. Hill's corps occupied the high ground along the northern end of Seminary Ridge (so named because of a small Lutheran seminary located there), which lay west of Gettysburg. Seminary Ridge and Cemetery Ridge were generally parallel and approximately one mile apart. Lee's plan was to employ Longstreet's corps, which was not in the fighting of the first day and was not yet on line, in a main attack launched from Hill's right against the southern flank of the Union army. Hill and Ewell were to stage diversionary actions along their fronts.

But the Union southern flank was not where Lee believed it to be or Meade intended it to be. Again the Clausewitzian principle of friction is apparent. Lee, from information supplied by the reconnaissance of his engineers, was under the impression that Cemetery Ridge was only lightly held and the Union left flank in the air. According to his order, Longstreet was to attack up the Emmitsburg Road, which crossed the lower end of Seminary Ridge and ran diagonally through the interlying valley and over the west face of Cemetery Hill into Gettysburg. If the Union army had been deployed as he believed, his attack would have enveloped its position on Cemetery Hill.

Not until about 4:00 P.M. did Longstreet get his attack launched. Both he and Lee probably share the blame for this tardiness. Lee, though having the previous evening expressed an intention to attack the morning of July 2, did not actually issue his order until midmorning of that day. Longstreet, opposing the plan, executed it with reluctance, grumbling, and delays. The order required a circuitous march of more than five miles to avoid detection, and Longstreet's divisions were unable to deploy for action until after two o'clock.

The attack was further delayed because the commander of Longstreet's right flank division, Major General John Bell Hood, now reported a formidable Union force directly in his line of approach along the Emmitsburg Road. At least twice Hood asked permission to swing

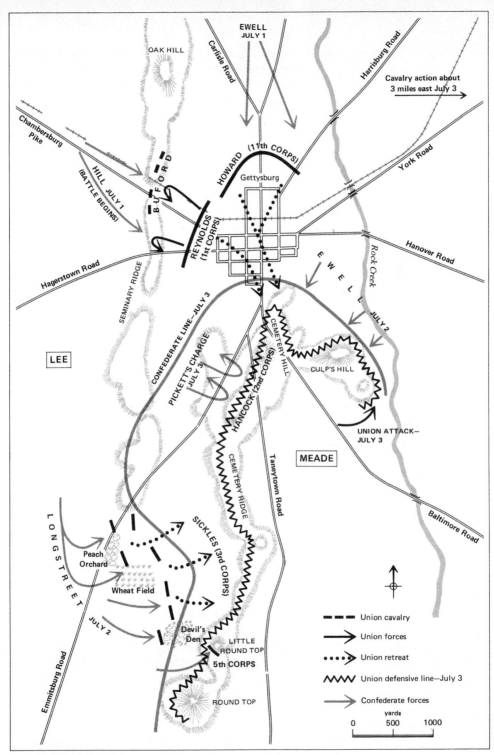

GETTYSBURG, JULY 1–3, 1863

141

south and east around Round Top in order to strike the Union line from the flank and rear, but Longstreet refused and chose not to provide Lee with Hood's information. Finally, Longstreet said peremptorily, "We must obey the orders of General Lee."

The troops that lay in Hood's path belonged to the Third Corps, commanded by Major General Daniel E. Sickles, an impulsive and strong-minded New Yorker. According to Meade's intentions, Sickles's troops were supposed to be anchoring the Union left flank on the lower end of Cemetery Ridge and Little Round Top, the key terrain feature of the southern portion of the battlefield. If they had been there, the Confederate approach to Cemetery Hill as ordered by Lee would have been made across much of the Union front, and the Confederate right flank would have been vulnerable to an enveloping counterattack with the Confederate ranks exposed to enfilading fire, a particularly deadly kind of fire that falls along the line of the target.

Early that morning, believing, as he later said, that Meade was equivocal as to exactly where his troops were to be situated, Sickles had advanced them to what he considered a stronger position almost a mile forward of the rest of the Union line: They now formed an angle with one division facing west along the Emmitsburg Road and the other facing south along the edge of a peach orchard and an adjacent wheat field, with the flank of the line at the Devil's Den, a rugged, boulder-strewn hill and ravine lying some four hundred yards west of Little Round Top.

Sickles's move left Little Round Top undefended, which is the condition Lee's scouts discovered and reported to him, and which influenced him in issuing his order to attack along the Emmitsburg Road. The location of Sickles's corps unintentionally but inevitably altered the direction of the Confederate attack after it began and entirely changed the course of the battle that afternoon. The location of the corps also destined it to bear the brunt of and be virtually destroyed by Longstreet's smashing assault. In some of the fiercest combat of the war, the Confederates took the peach orchard, wheat field, and Devil's Den, occupied Round Top, and thrust almost to the crest of Cemetery Ridge and Little Round Top.

Once the operation began, Longstreet threw himself into it with full vigor. He wrote later that the action of his corps was the "best three hours' fighting ever done by any troops on any battlefield," a boast tacitly endorsed by Harry W. Pfanz, the most thorough student of the operation, who adds that the performance of the more-numerous Union forces opposing the attack mirrored that of the Confederates, "but less brightly."

Fortunately for the Union cause, by the time the Confederates reached Little Round Top in the late afternoon it was strongly occupied by blue-clad soldiers. A short time earlier, Brigadier General Gouverneur

K. Warren, Meade's chief of engineers, had discovered the vulnerability of the position, diverted a column of troops to it, and prevailed upon Meade to send reinforcements there. The struggle for Little Round Top was bitter, but in the end it remained securely in Union hands.

The diversionary attacks by the corps of Hill and Ewell, though fierce in spots, were badly timed and ill coordinated. Two of Hill's divisions were scarcely engaged; only that of Major General Richard H. Anderson, covering Longstreet's left flank, saw heavy action. Ewell launched his attack two hours later, and though it succeeded in seizing portions of both Cemetery Hill and Culp's Hill, it was counterattacked and driven off Cemetery Hill immediately and repulsed at Culp's Hill except for occupying a line of trenches on the southeastern slope that had been left vacant earlier by troops sent to assist Sickles. Also, during the night a Federal counterattack seized Round Top from the Confederates holding it. The ineffectualness of the supporting Confederate actions had permitted Meade to reinforce critically threatened points by shifting troops back and forth on the interior, and hence shorter, lines within the "fishhook."

DEAD OF THE FIRST MINNESOTA INFANTRY   (Library of Congress)

Thus the second day of Gettysburg ended in Confederate failure. Yet the decision still hung in the balance; both armies had suffered grievously, but both were intact. Over the renewed objections of Longstreet, who again importuned Lee to maneuver around the south end of the Union position, Lee made the fateful choice to renew the attack the following day by concentrating against the center of the Union line on Cemetery Ridge, which he believed was weak because of the transfer of troops to defend the flanks.

That night Meade held a council of war with his principal commanders, and, supported by their recommendations, decided to remain in position and offer battle once more. As the officers filed out of the room he said to Brigadier General John Gibbon, commander of a division in Hancock's corps at the middle of the line: "If Lee attacks tomorrow, it will be in your front. He has made attacks on both our flanks and failed and if he concludes to try it again, it will be on our center." Seldom has a general made such an accurate prediction of his opponent's intention.

Again Lee placed Longstreet in command of the operation. The main effort was to be made by one of Longstreet's divisions, Major General George E. Pickett's, that had not been in the previous day's battle, reinforced by one division plus two additional brigades from Hill's corps. Lee estimated this force to be 15,000, but, because of Hill's casualties the preceding day, it probably was not more than 13,500, and possibly was even smaller. Hill was to stand by and be prepared to support the attack and exploit the anticipated breakthrough. Ewell was to renew his attack on Culp's Hill. Stuart, who had arrived the day before, was to lead his bedraggled troopers on a turning sweep around the Union right flank.

The entire Confederate operation was almost completely uncoordinated. Lee apparently intended for the attacks to begin simultaneously at dawn on July 3, and Ewell said he received explicit orders to this effect. But there was no written order, and either Lee never made his intentions clear to Longstreet or Longstreet failed to comprehend them. Longstreet spent the night of July 2 planning a move to envelop the Union left flank. His troops were not in position to launch the attack on the Union center at dawn, nor would they be in position to do so until several hours later.

Ewell launched his attack on Culp's Hill before dawn, but it was a piecemeal and futile effort. Most of his corps remained idle, and by now the Union forces there were strengthened by the return of the troops that had been sent to the other sector of the line the day before. A Federal counterattack stopped the assault and drove the Confederates back. Fighting went on throughout the morning; when it ended around noon Culp's Hill remained firmly in Union possession.

The main Confederate effort, Pickett's charge, began just before 3:00 P.M. on the bright, hot summer day. It was the most dramatic military action in American history. The attack was launched from Seminary Ridge and aimed at a point on Cemetery Ridge shortly south of Cemetery Hill, a location marked by a small copse of trees. The advance was preceded by a crashing artillery duel of an hour and a half between the massed batteries of both armies. As the guns fell silent, the assault began. At first it was a pageant of dressed lines and streaming battle colors. Then it became a pageant of never-to-be-forgotten valor; and of death, first as the more than two hundred pieces of the Union artillery opened again with explosive shells at long range, then as the gunners switched to canister and the Union infantry poured rifle fire into the approaching and thinning gray ranks. Still they marched, repeatedly filling in the gaps, firing a volley from the foot of the slope, and gathering into bunches as they pressed up toward their objective.

Incredibly, a handful of Confederates actually reached the objective, scaled the low stone wall at its front, and fought hand to hand with the defenders. But it was a doomed effort; the Confederate tide had reached its highwater mark. Union reinforcements rushed to the threatened point, and soon the surviving Confederates were in retreat, back down the slope strewn with the bodies of their comrades and across the valley to the sanctuary of Seminary Ridge. Stuart's sweep around the Union right flank ended in an indecisive encounter east of Gettysburg with Brigadier General David M. Gregg's division of Union cavalry.

Longstreet had said that no 15,000 troops on earth could carry out the mission assigned him that day. Pickett's charge was made by even fewer. Most of Hill's troops did no more than watch the grand and grim spectacle, and Longstreet attempted nothing with the battered remaining divisions of his corps. He was right in what he had said; no 15,000 troops on earth could have done what those dauntless soldiers were asked to do.

Gettysburg was the greatest battle of the war in the dramatic circumstances surrounding it and in the number of troops actually engaged. It was also the greatest battle in its harvest of dead and wounded: 23,000 Union casualties; 28,000 Confederate.

Many students of Lee's Gettysburg campaign have placed the principal blame for its failure on Ewell or Longstreet. But Lee was the commander and ultimately must bear the responsibility. He conducted the movement into Pennsylvania with his usual boldness and skill. With proper cavalry reconnaissance, he might have been able to maneuver and strike so as to gain a significant victory. Even as the battle actually occurred, on the first day he had a fair chance of victory; each succeeding day reduced that chance. By the third day, a Confederate victory probably would have required a miracle. Gettysburg was Lee's worst-fought battle. His orders during the engagement were tardy, fragmentary, and imprecise. His renowned biographer and most ardent admirer, Freeman, admits that during the second day of the engagement the Army of Northern Virginia was virtually without a commander.

Lee's decision to launch the fatal assault on the last day is subject to the severest criticism. It is equally subject to speculation. It violated his own expressed tactical doctrine of avoiding frontal assaults and executing turning movements instead. It was altogether inconsistent with his actual tactics in his greatest offensive victories, Second Bull Run and Chancellorsville. Lee's behavior at Gettysburg may simply have been the product of his natural combativeness and willingness to take the big risk, intensified now by his spectacular victory at Chancellorsville. Of his decision at Gettysburg he said, "I believed my men were invincible."

Lee's conduct at Gettysburg may also have been affected by exhaustion. For two years now he had been subject to unremitting physical, mental, and emotional stress. During the past year he had been engaged in five campaigns against forces that were capable of destroying his army at a blow. He was now fifty-six, with only seven years of life remaining; in March he had suffered the first of the heart attacks that eventually would take his life, and there is some evidence that during the battle he was plagued by diarrhea. Throughout the critical action of the second afternoon he sat on a stump near the Lutheran seminary without the slightest expression of anxiety on his face, sending only one message and receiving only one report. Possibly the novel *The Killer Angels* accurately depicts the Lee of Gettysburg, a man whose brain was numbed by campaign fatigue.

From the crest of Seminary Ridge Lee witnessed the great repulse of July 3. Riding among his stunned soldiers as they drifted back to their original position, he acknowledged responsibility for the failure and urged them to brace themselves for a Union counterattack. The counterattack did not come, though Lee invited it by keeping his army in place for another full day. Then he began a withdrawal to Virginia.

The Confederate withdrawal was carried out with consummate skill, but it was an exercise in extreme attrition and hardship, and a nightmare of agony for the thousands of wounded piled on wagons jolting over the rocky roads under torrents of rain. Finding the Potomac in flood and the pontoon bridges gone, the Army of Northern Virginia appeared doomed. It was not doomed. Meade proceeded cautiously, probed Lee's lines and found them ready, and launched no attack. Confederate engineers located a suitable ford and improvised a bridge, and the Army of Northern Virginia recrossed to fight again.

Why Meade neither attempted a counterattack immediately after the failure of the final Confederate assault nor made a determined effort to trap and destroy Lee's crippled army north of the Potomac have raised some of the most enduring questions and controversies about the Civil War. General Hancock, severely wounded in the battle, was said to have urged a counterattack before the defeated Confederates could be rallied. Historians have condemned Meade as being excessively wary, but Coddington defends Meade's decisions as being eminently prudent under the circumstances, and argues that an attack by Meade involved the grave risk of a Gettysburg in reverse. However wise, Meade's course of action forfeited his chances of gaining fame as a great general. Great generals usually take great risks.

Lincoln was bitterly disappointed. Convinced that Meade had squandered an opportunity to destroy Lee's army, Lincoln wrote him bluntly: "I do not believe you appreciate the magnitude of the misfortune involved in Lee's escape. He was within your easy grasp, and to have closed upon him would, in connection with our other late successes, have ended the war. As it is, the war will be prolonged indefinitely.... Your golden opportunity is gone, and I am distressed immeasurably because of it." Persuaded the letter would cause Meade to resign, Lincoln did not send it. He later resorted to his custom of venting his feelings through a wry comment, saying that Meade's pursuit of Lee reminded him of an old woman trying to shoo her geese across a creek. Meade was not the kind of general Lincoln wanted for the supreme command of his armies.

As the war in the East reached a climax at Gettysburg, the war in the West reached a climax at Vicksburg. Grant's capture on May 14 of Jackson, Mississippi, and the withdrawal of Joseph E. Johnston's limited force from that place set the stage for the final Union drive upon the river fortress. Leaving Sherman's corps at Jackson to destroy Confederate factories and supplies and keep an eye on Johnston, Grant led the main body of his force directly west toward Vicksburg.

Pemberton with some 22,000 troops occupied Champion's Hill midway to Grant's objective and blocked the railroad there. On May 16 Pemberton struck fiercely at an exposed wing of McClernand's corps, but Grant quickly brought up reinforcements and launched a turning movement around the Confederate south flank with the Big Black river crossing as his immediate objective. Pemberton, with his line of communication and retreat threatened, disengaged his army at Champion's Hill and withdrew into a strong defensive position on the east side of the Big Black, within a horseshoe bend of the stream.

In taking this action, Pemberton erred again. Still confused by Davis's emphasis on the importance of Vicksburg itself, he ignored Johnston's continued urging for him to abandon the city and join forces with Johnston north of the Union line of operations. Grant later acknowledged the soundness of Johnston's plan when he said Pemberton's decision to make a stand at the Big Black assured an ultimate Union victory because it rendered a Confederate concentration impossible. "Pemberton might have made a night march [from Champion's Hill] to the Big Black," wrote Grant, "crossed the bridge there and, by moving north on the west side, have eluded us and finally returned to Johnston. But this would have given us Vicksburg. It would have been his proper move, however, and the one Johnston would have made had he been in Pemberton's place. In fact it would have been in conformity with Johnston's orders to Pemberton."

Reinforced to 54,000, with the bulk of Sherman's corps recalled from Jackson and marching to turn the Confederate position by crossing the Big Black to the north, Grant gave Pemberton no opportunity to reconsider his decision. On May 17 a spirited attack by McPherson's corps expelled the Confederates from their position east of the river and sent them reeling in retreat into the Vicksburg entrenchments. That night Grant and Sherman sat on a log and watched by the light of pitch-pine bonfires as their troops marched on hastily improvised bridges across the Big Black, the last natural barrier to their long-sought and difficult objective.

The following day Grant's columns closed on the doomed fortress city, with Sherman on the right, McPherson in the center, and McClernand on the left. By extending his right flank to the Mississippi above Vicksburg, Grant secured a direct and invulnerable line of communication with his base at Memphis. He was now in position to starve the Confederates into surrender.

Warfare by siege was not to Grant's taste. Believing the Confederates demoralized by their recent setbacks, he hoped to take Vicksburg by storm before they had time to recover. On May 19 and again three days later Grant made direct assaults on the Vicksburg entrenchments, only to be repulsed with severe casualties. He now settled down to conventional siege operations which would last more than a month. Before the campaign ended he had an opportunity to do something he probably had wanted to do all along. When on May 30 McClernand issued a statement congratulating his corps in words that seemed to take most of the credit for the success of the entire campaign, Grant summarily relieved him of command. Again Lincoln was deaf to the politician-general's appeals.

The opposing lines at Vicksburg were developed into elaborate systems of dugouts and earthworks, with the Union lines inexorably pressed forward by approach trenches. Sappers on both sides ran tunnels under the other's position, and the explosion of a Union mine blew a temporary but inconsequential breach in the Confederate defenses. So close together were the entrenchments that soldiers tossed improvised hand grenades back and forth between them. Under almost constant bombardment by Grant's guns reinforced by the mortars of Porter's fleet, the citizens of the town moved into caves. Cut off from all supplies, both civilians and soldiers were slowly but surely reduced to the point of starvation.

Confederate efforts to relieve the siege were fruitless. Demonstrations staged by General Edmund Kirby Smith west of the Mississippi posed no real threat to Grant. Nor did Johnston's force, now some

30,000 strong, against Grant's army of 70,000 entrenched and well-supplied veterans, though Johnston continued to plan relief operations until the very end of the siege. The end came on July 4 in the formal surrender of Pemberton and his command, 29,511 officers and men. Five days later occurred the anticlimactic surrender of the encircled and now useless Port Hudson and its defenders.

Grant's superior generalship was the key to the Union victory. To find a practical approach to Vicksburg he devised the most comprehensive joint army-navy operation of the war. To feed his army once it was east of the Mississippi he was ingenious and bold enough to abandon temporarily his supply lines and resort to foraging. To prevent the divided Confederate forces from concentrating against him he performed a remarkable exercise in the seizing and exploiting of interior lines of communication. Finally, his actual siege of the city was conducted with the effectiveness, if not the elegance, of the fabled French engineer Vauban.

Grant's qualities did not go unnoticed in Washington. General Halleck compared the Vicksburg operations with those of one of Napoleon's most celebrated victories, the capture of Ulm. More significant for Grant's future, as the Union columns were closing in on their objective, Lincoln wrote describing the campaign as "one of the most brilliant in the world."

The capture of Vicksburg and Port Hudson opened the entire Mississippi River to Union gunboats and transports. In Lincoln's memorable words, "The Father of Waters again goes unvexed to the sea." The Confederacy was cut in half; so isolated was the Trans-Mississippi Department that Davis took the extraordinary step of authorizing General Kirby Smith to assume charge of civil as well as military affairs there. He was to follow as closely as possible the policies in effect east of the river. Davis explained to Congress that the obstruction of communications made this action necessary.

While the Gettysburg and Vicksburg campaigns were under way, the third great Union offensive of the year, that in Tennessee, appeared to be stuck indefinitely. Not until late June was Lincoln, through Halleck, able to prod Rosecrans into forward motion, though the president vainly urged the importance of keeping pressure on Bragg in order to prevent the transfer of reinforcements from Tennessee to Mississippi. Eventually, a peremptory telegram obliged the reluctant Rosecrans to undertake an advance from his comfortable base at Murfreesboro.

Lincoln and Halleck were right in believing that Bragg's force, depleted by transfers to Johnston, would not be able to withstand a determined Union offensive. Beginning his advance on June 23, Rosecrans staged one of the war's most successful campaigns of maneuver. By sending a column under Major General Gordon S. Granger to threaten a turning movement of the Confederate south flank, Rosecrans

MURFREESBORO TO CHICKAMAUGA, 1863

induced Bragg to shift much of his army southward, thus exposing the gaps in the Cumberland Plateau above his tactical base at Tullahoma. Rosecrans then directed the remainder of his army through the lightly defended gaps.

Bragg's will, eroded by the distrust and recrimination of his corps commanders Polk and Hardee, was not equal to the occasion. After a successful Union raid that seized the railroad behind the Confederate position at Tullahoma, Bragg ordered a general retreat on the evening of June 30. Momentarily, he considered making a stand at the Elk River, but two days later he changed his mind and began withdrawing his entire army to its main base, the city of Chattanooga.

Chattanooga aptly has been called the gateway to the lower Confederacy. Located at the Moccasin Point on the Tennessee River, so named because its shape resembles an Indian's shoe, and at the spot where the river cuts through the Cumberland mountain range, the city was one of the most important rail centers of the South. Here the region's major transverse railroad, the Memphis and Charleston, joined one line going south to Atlanta and ultimately Charleston and the other leading northeast to Richmond. Union possession of Chattanooga would open the door to Georgia with its vital fields and factories.

Lincoln was anxious for Rosecrans to move against Bragg before he had time to organize a defense. But Rosecrans insisted on moving cautiously and on repairing the railroad behind him in order to secure his line of supply from Nashville. He also preferred to wait for a planned supporting campaign that would threaten Bragg's position from behind. General Burnside was preparing to lead a column of 24,000, the newly constituted Army of the Ohio, from Lexington, Kentucky, to seize Knoxville, thus severing the Confederate rail line to Virginia and carrying out Lincoln's fond hope of liberating eastern Tennessee from Confederate control. In mid-August, again under the threat of being relieved of command, Rosecrans moved. By now Burnside also was on the march. Neither force met significant immediate resistance. On September 3 Burnside occupied Knoxville, while most of the small Confederate garrison there, commanded by Major General Simon B. Buckner, joined Bragg's army at Chattanooga.

Encircled by mountains and their outlying ridges, Chattanooga appeared to be eminently defensible. Bragg took the opposite view. Glum from the loss of central Tennessee, edgy over the disharmony within his command, and physically tired, he looked upon the mountains as blinds for the advancing Federal columns. He said a mountain with its gaps was like a wall full of rat holes. "The rat lies hidden at his hole, ready to pop out when no one is watching. Who can tell what lies hidden behind that hole?"

What lay behind the holes was Rosecrans's approaching army. He now was moving rapidly and skillfully, sending detachments north of

Chattanooga to create the impression he intended crossing the Tennessee River there in order to combine his efforts with Burnside's. Actually, Rosecrans was directing the bulk of his army south of the city to turn Bragg's position by seizing or threatening the railroad to Atlanta. In early September Bragg became aware of the danger only when he learned that heavy Union forces were below the Tennessee River at Bridgeport, Alabama, twenty miles west and slightly south of Chattanooga. On September 8 Bragg abandoned the city and moved south in order to avoid being trapped. He established his headquarters at Lee and Gordon's Mill twelve miles below Chattanooga.

Rosecrans now made a mistake that ultimately undid him and almost spelled catastrophe to his army. Deciding that Bragg was in a precipitous retreat and that still another relatively bloodless Union victory could be gained by rapid maneuver, Rosecrans took one of his three corps, that of Major General Thomas L. Crittenden, to occupy Chattanooga while the two corps of Thomas and Major General Alexander M. McCook marched across Lookout Mountain southwest of the city and struck at the railroad. Spread more than forty miles apart in rugged terrain with few connecting roads, the various units were beyond effective supporting distance of one another.

These circumstances presented Bragg with an opportunity to mount a counterstroke of major dimensions. The overall strategic situation enabled Confederate authorities to strengthen Bragg's counterstroke measurably. After the fall of Vicksburg, Grant suggested a move by his army against Mobile, but Halleck withheld approval and instead ordered Grant to send reinforcements to General Banks for a move against the Confederates west of the Mississippi. After Gettysburg, Meade failed to press Lee vigorously in Virginia, causing Lincoln to suggest that a portion of the Army of the Potomac simply stand on the defensive, thereby freeing the remainder to be employed elsewhere. In a most unusual letter to Halleck he wrote: "General Meade has three men to General Lee's two.... If the enemy's 60,000 are sufficient to keep our 90,000 away from Richmond, why...may not 40,000 of ours keep their 60,000 away from Washington, leaving us 50,000 to be put to some other use?" Again, however, Lincoln repeated his conviction that the defeat of Lee's army was Meade's true object.

Before Lincoln's advice could be acted upon, Davis and his generals moved to take advantage of the respite given them by the idleness of the Union forces in Virginia and Mississippi. Two divisions from Johnston's army in Mississippi returned to Bragg, and Lee now approved the previously rejected plan for dispatching reinforcements from his army to the West. Longstreet with approximately 12,000 men was to move by rail to join Bragg in Georgia just south of Chattanooga. Because Knoxville was in Union hands, thus denying the Confederates the use of the most direct rail route between their armies, the troops and all their arms and equipment must travel roundabout through the Carolinas and the city of Atlanta, a distance of almost 1,000 miles.

While awaiting Longstreet's arrival, Bragg attempted unsuccessfully to carry out a plan for crippling his opponent by defeating separate segments of the Union army by turns. He had occasions to do so. Learning that a single division of Thomas's corps was isolated in a mountain cove south of Chattanooga, Bragg ordered an attack on it by the division commanded by Major General Thomas C. Hindman, reinforced by troops from Lieutenant General D. H. Hill's corps. When Hill proved unable to move, Buckner's corps was designated instead. But Hindman procrastinated and never delivered the attack. Bragg then tried to mass against a division of Crittenden's corps as it moved south out of Chattanooga, but again the Confederate commander was unable to activate his subordinates. Corps commander Leonidas Polk simply ignored his orders. Rosecrans took advantage of these failures to reconcentrate his force. By nightfall of September 18, with only one of Longstreet's divisions present, the two armies, Bragg with about 62,000 men, Rosecrans with about 58,000, faced each other across a small stream bearing the Indian name Chickamauga, "Sluggish Water" or "Dead Water," soon to be translated "River of Death."

The following morning the Confederates attacked, and the battle raged throughout the day. Bragg directed his main effort against the Union left or northern flank, seeking to envelop it and cut off Rosecrans's line of communications or retreat to Chattanooga. But Bragg's orders were vague, the assault was uncoordinated, and the tactical results during the day were meager. Longstreet and an additional division arrived during the night, and the reinforcements were placed in the left sector of the Confederate line. Putting Longstreet in charge of this wing of the army, Bragg repeated on the following day the same general plan he had devised for the first day.

Again the friction of war intervened. Through misinformation and a confusion of orders the morning of September 20, Rosecrans shifted a division of his troops in such a way as inadvertently to leave a gap near the center of his line, directly in the path of Longstreet's main effort. Almost without opposition the Confederates burst through the gap, achieving a classic "penetration of opportunity" that completely severed the Union line. The Union right dissolved as two entire divisions began a headlong retreat into Chattanooga, surging over the army headquarters and carrying the hapless Rosecrans with them. From the city he wired Washington, "We have met with a serious disaster."

It turned out to be less serious than Rosecrans believed, though not through any act of generalship on his part. Throughout the day it was serious enough. Longstreet, with what Napoleon would have called a gift of *coup d'oeil*, evaluated the situation at a glance and ordered his column to wheel right instead of left as Bragg had planned, thus improvising an envelopment of the remainder of the Union line. Rosecrans's departure from the field left Thomas in command and gave him an opportunity to win eternal fame. Deliberate and methodical, known throughout the army by the nickname "Slow Trot," the Virginia Unionist was a sound tactician and an indomitable fighter. Concentrating the Union left wing around the strong defensive terrain of Snodgrass Hill where he was reinforced by the reserve under Granger, who without orders marched "to the sound of the guns," Thomas repelled repeated Confederate attacks and after dark withdrew in good order into a new defensive position outside of Chattanooga. He had forever become "the Rock of Chickamauga."

Ironically, the culmination of the battle during the afternoon occurred with neither army commander on the field. Bragg in midafternoon retired to his headquarters and made no effort either to reinforce Longstreet in his assaults against Thomas or to pursue after Thomas withdrew. Bragg's subordinates were furious over these command failures, and the entire Confederate army was left in a mood of frustration and demoralization. "What does he fight battles for?" asked the ever-aggressive Forrest, who vowed never to serve under Bragg again, and who shortly would be sent to the Department of Mississippi and Alabama.

Chickamauga was an electrifying tactical victory for the Confederacy, the last one of its kind. But the engagement cost more than 18,000 Confederate casualties that could not be replaced as compared with more than 16,000 Union casualties that could be replaced, and it left the important city of Chattanooga still in Union hands, however unsurely at the moment. Strategically, Chickamauga was a hollow triumph for the South.

Deciding now to lay siege to the defeated Union army in Chattanooga, Bragg moved up and disposed his force about the city in an effort to cut off Union supplies. His main body occupied Missionary Ridge, a rugged escarpment lying east and south of the city and in a position that commanded the railroads to Atlanta and Knoxville. An outpost line was established on Orchard Knob, a hill three-quarters of a mile in front of Missionary Ridge. Bragg also placed a force at Brown's Ferry across the bend of the Tennessee opposite the city, and another force on the slope between the peak of Lookout Mountain and the river, thus blocking both the river and the Memphis and Charleston Railroad, which was the Union line of communication with its railhead at Bridgeport, Alabama, and indirectly with its primary base at Nashville.

Bragg's force was insufficient to invest the city completely. The besieged Union army there was able to bring in a trickle of supplies from its railhead by a roundabout sixty-mile trail through the mountains which was vulnerable to Confederate cavalry raids. On October 3 Major General Joseph Wheeler's horsemen caught and destroyed a

Union supply convoy of 500 or more loaded wagons. The daily fare of a northern soldier in Chattanooga shrank to less than half the usual ration.

The Union situation was not desperate, but for more than a month it was extremely serious, and Lincoln moved decisively to remedy it. A contingent of some 17,000 troops which was already under way from Virginia under Hooker soon arrived at Bridgeport. More important, Lincoln brought Grant from Mississippi to take command at Chattanooga, because, said Lincoln, Rosecrans since Chickamauga had lost his nerve and was acting "confused and stunned like a duck hit on the head." Grant, before his arrival, sent an order replacing Rosecrans with Thomas and telling the new commander to hold out at all hazards, to which the doughty warrior replied, "We will hold the town until we starve."

Using the circuitous route from Bridgeport, Grant reached Chattanooga on October 23. He immediately approved a plan that opened an adequate supply route to the railhead. He did this by boating a force down river at night to Brown's Ferry and sending a column there by land across the neck formed by the river's loop. Together these troops drove away the Confederates guarding the ferry site, then constructed pontoon bridges across the river at the places where it formed the ankle of Moccasin Point. The soldiers named the new supply route the "cracker line." Already Grant had ordered Sherman from Mississippi with an additional 20,000 troops. He obviously was preparing an assault to break the siege.

Meanwhile, events in the Army of Tennessee and at the supreme Confederate command were preparing this army for certain defeat. Once the Union supply line was opened, the Confederate siege became a pretense; Longstreet described it acidly, "We were trying to starve the enemy out by investing him on the only side from which he could not have gathered supplies." The corps commanders had already sent a petition to Davis calling for Bragg's removal. Longstreet forgot his disagreement with Lee at Gettysburg and wrote the secretary of war, saying: "I am convinced that nothing but the hand of God can save us or help as long as we have our present commander....Can't you send us General Lee? The army in Virginia can operate defensively, while our operations here should be offensive—until we recover Tennessee at all events. We need some great mind as General Lee's (nothing more) to accomplish this."

Davis responded to these overtures by paying Bragg and his subordinates a visit in early October. He dealt with the criticisms by leaving Bragg in command and removing his severest critics. Polk was ordered to Mississippi; D. H. Hill was relieved and left without a command. With Davis's approval, Bragg dispatched Longstreet with 15,000 troops to retake Knoxville. The Union army at Chattanooga, soon increased to approximately 70,000, would outnumber its opponent by almost one-third. Thus Union forces were being concentrated at the point of decision under their three most capable generals, while Confederate forces were being dispersed there and kept under the weakest of the field commanders.

In late November Grant launched his coordinated attack. Sherman was to lead the main effort in crossing the river north of the city to strike the northern end of the Confederate line on Missionary Ridge. At the same time Hooker was to drive off the Confederate force of about 2,700, principally the troops of Major General Carter L. Stevenson and Brigadier General Edward C. Walthall, holding the position between Lookout Mountain and the river, then move against the southern flank of the Confederate position on Missionary Ridge. Thomas was to seize Orchard Knob, then demonstrate against the center of the Confederate line in order to prevent Bragg from reinforcing his vulnerable flanks. On November 23 Thomas's troops took Orchard Knob; the following day Hooker accomplished the first part of his mission with relative ease. That night a detachment of his troops scaled the mountain, drove off the handful of Confederates there, and planted the stars and stripes amid the mists of Point Lookout. The entire operation soon became known by the romanticized name, the "Battle above the Clouds."

Sherman's repeated assaults on the 25th against the Confederate right (Hardee's corps) were fierce, but the line held. The troops of Confederate division commander Major General Patrick Cleburne, known by his associates as the "Stonewall Jackson of the West," fought with particular stubbornness. Hooker was slow in approaching the Confederate left, and was only lightly engaged in the final attack. The decisive action of the day, and one of the most remarkable actions of the entire war, occurred by Thomas's troops in the center against Breckinridge's corps. After advancing and seizing the Confederate line of rifle pits along the base of Missionary Ridge, the troops charged without orders but with invincible spirit up the steep slope of the ridge, while, ironically, Grant and Thomas watched in alarm, and Grant said somebody would "pay for" the blunder if the assault failed.

It did not fail. The Confederates at the center of the line were improperly located along the comb of the ridge instead of the brow or "tactical crest," the line on the forward slope allowing the longest unobstructed field of observation and fire. Perhaps most damaging of all to the Confederates was a general demoralization and lack of faith in their leader. In a moment of panic at the climax of the Union charge, the center of the Confederate line broke and fled. The siege of Chattanooga ended with the Union "miracle of Missionary Ridge."

With Cleburne's division fighting a grim and effective rearguard action at the Ringgold Gap fourteen miles below Chattanooga, Bragg was able to withdraw his disorganized army back to the vicinity of Dalton,

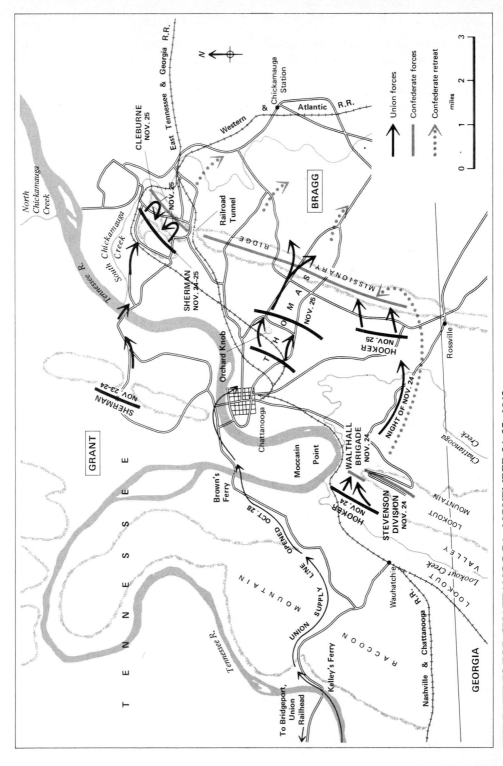

THE BATTLES FOR CHATTANOOGA, NOVEMBER 24–25, 1863

157

Georgia, located on the railroad twenty-five miles south of the city. Disheartened and disgraced, he now asked to be relieved of command, and confided to Davis, "... the disaster [at Missionary Ridge] admits of no palliation, and is justly disparaging to me as a commander.... I fear we both erred in the conclusion for me to retain command here after the clamor raised against me." On Lee's advice, Davis recalled Joseph E. Johnston from inactivity and placed him at the head of the downcast Army of Tennessee.

The ultimate outcome of the Chattanooga campaign brought to a favorable conclusion for the Union the final three out of four of the great strategic operations of 1863. With Lee's army repulsed and crippled in the eastern theater, Vicksburg and Port Hudson taken and the Confederacy split along the line of the Mississippi River, and Chattanooga, the gateway to the lower southeast, firmly in Union hands, the Confederacy was severely, if not mortally, wounded. But the tiger is said to be most dangerous when wounded; some of the bloodiest fighting of the entire war had still to be endured.

Lincoln was keenly aware that much remained to be done to bring the contest to a successful consummation for the Union. He sought constantly for ways to exalt the Union war aims, unite the North behind his administration in pursuit of these aims, and steel the population for the mighty effort yet needed for victory. In the fall of 1863 he took advantage of an opportunity to do so when he was invited to speak at the dedication of the recently established battle cemetery at Gettysburg. There on November 19, surrounded by thousands of fresh graves, in an address of remarkable brevity, eloquence, and meaning, he identified the Union cause as that of liberty, equality, and democratic government for all humankind, thus transmuting the northern war goals into universal ideals.

IX

The Contest for European Favor

———— ❖ ————

The major nations of Europe recognized the importance of the American struggle in respect to the future balance of world power. Both Union and Confederate leaders were aware that the attitude and behavior of the European states would play a significant role in determining the outcome of the conflict. Southern authorities, mindful of the French alliance that had assured American victory in the war for independence against England, hoped for comparable European support in the Confederacy's war for independence against the Union. The Confederacy strove through diplomacy to gain financial aid, mediation, formal recognition, and possibly armed intervention by Great Britain and France. The Union strove to maintain friendly relations with the European powers, and made their neutrality, at the very least, the condition of this friendship.

British sentiment toward the war was mixed, with leading figures in the government itself divided in their sympathies. Queen Victoria, influenced by her husband, Prince Consort Albert, favored the Union, as did Lord John Russell, the minister of foreign affairs, and Lord Richard Lyons, the minister to the United States. Viscount Henry Palmerston, the prime minister, and William E. Gladstone, the chancellor of the exchequer, leaned toward the Confederacy. A sizable portion of the upper classes favored the Confederacy; many of the landed aristocrats felt a certain kinship with the plantation society of the South. British textile manufacturers, representing one of the nation's major industries, relied heavily on the South for their supply of cotton, and other industrialists welcomed the prospect of an extensive southern free-trade market for their wares.

Many observers saw an advantage to Great Britain in the breakup of a united American nation. The Russian minister in Washington, Edouard de Stoeckl, predicted that Great Britain would receive great benefit from such an outcome. He wrote his government: "The Cabinet of London is watching attentively the internal dissensions of the Union and awaits the result with an impatience which it has difficulty disguising." The American minister to Russia, Cassius M. Clay, advised President Lincoln, "I saw at a glance where the feeling of England was. They hoped for our ruin! They are jealous of our power. They care neither for the South nor the North. They hate both." A British editor reflected something of this point of view when he explained: "We do not see why three or four independent republics...will not answer better than one absorbing and overwhelming dominion," which, in his opinion, had produced "a conviction of boundless power and unmatched grandeur which now inflates the bosom, disturbs the brain and damages the principles of nearly every American citizen."

The laboring classes were divided in their attitudes toward the result of the Civil War. Some workers favored the Union and applauded the speeches of such liberal British reformers as John Bright, Richard Cobden, and W. E. Forster, who identified the northern cause with that of democracy for laborers and common citizens everywhere. Bright called the Confederate effort "odious and...blasphemous," and expressed the hope that a reunited American nation would become "the hope of freedom, and a refuge for the oppressed of every race and of every clime." But the prospect of the closing of the cotton mills for want of southern fiber, followed by the actual closing of large numbers of them, created the fear of unemployment and starvation among the workers, and many if not most of them yearned for a speedy cessation of hostilities and sympathized with the Confederacy. Most Britons of all classes opposed slavery, but the policies of the Lincoln administration early in the war convinced them that the institution would not be affected by a Union victory.

The Confederacy solicited the approval of the British public through the columns of such sympathetic newspapers as the London *Times* and the *Manchester Guardian,* which published accounts of the military campaigns that exaggerated southern victories and minimized northern successes. The Confederacy in 1862 hired a British agent, James Spence, to write a book titled *The American Union,* which affirmed the constitutionality of secession and presented an image of southern culture that was superior to that of the North.

The most astute of Confederate propaganda agents was Henry Hotze, a Swiss immigrant to the United States who before the war had worked on the staff of the *Mobile Register.* Commissioned in the fall of 1862 by the Confederate secretary of state, Hotze settled in London and began contributing articles on the war to the leading English journals. Establishing his own newspaper, the *Index,* he shrewdly converted many English writers into Confederate propagandists by inviting them to submit articles for publication in his newspaper. He wrote brilliant editorials expounding the southern position and urging European men, especially the Irish, not to migrate to America and join the Union army. He also sent back to the Confederate government keen observations on the state of British public opinion. Later in the war he moved to France, where he carried on his activities with equal skill.

The French government held an equivocal attitude toward the American Civil War. At the outset, the French foreign minister, Edouard Thouvenel, issued a pronouncement of regret over the division of the American union and declared that the reestablishment of harmony in this country would be to his nation's advantage. But these smooth words masked the true sentiments of his government. The Union minister to France, William L. Dayton, convinced of French duplicity toward the North, later wrote in exasperation, "Truthfulness is not, as you know, an element in French diplomacy.... No man but a Frenchman would ever have thought of Talleyrand's famous bon mot that the object of language is to conceal thought." The war provided the French emperor Napoleon III with an opportunity to carry out an ambition to make Mexico into a French protectorate, which in 1863 he attempted to do by supporting Archduke Maximilian of Austria as the emperor of Mexico.

Napoleon favored the Confederacy because a united American nation, opposed to European penetration in the Western Hemisphere, stood in his way. Also, the French textile industry, like that of England, depended heavily on southern cotton. From the beginning the French emperor was ready to intervene on the Confederate side except that French involvement in European power politics made the venture too risky without the cooperation of Great Britain and its fleet. Thus the behavior of both major European economic and military powers depended upon the decision of Great Britain.

Next to President Lincoln, the chief figure in the conduct of the Union's foreign affairs, Secretary of State Seward, seemed at first something of a liability, especially in dealing with the British, whom he regarded with undisguised hostility. He was quoted as boasting that he would twist the tail of the British lion. The American minister to Great Britain, Charles Francis Adams, said Seward was looked upon there as "an ogre fully resolved to eat all Englishmen raw." Seward's notorious proposal for issuing an ultimatum to the leading powers of Europe was known and deplored there. Lord Lyons wrote from Washington that Seward would be "a dangerous foreign minister."

But in the end, Seward's attitude was an asset to Union diplomacy. He and Lincoln were agreed on the fundamental point that the United States was to break relations with any nation that granted recognition to the Confederacy. Seward implacably rejected every offer of mediation by European powers and every suggestion that the rebellion would succeed.

When after the failure of McClellan's campaign on the Virginia Peninsula, the French minister in Washington, Count Henri Mercier, suggested the impossibility of a Union victory, Seward said: "Do not believe for a moment that either the Federal Congress, myself or any person connected with this government will in any case entertain any proposition or suggestion of arrangement or accommodation or adjustment from within or without upon the basis of a surrender of the Federal Union." Told by European diplomats that the United States was too large for a single nation, Seward replied that it was too small for two. He wrote to Adams, "Those who favor and give aid to the insurrection, upon whatever pretext, assail the nation in an hour of danger, and therefore they cannot be held or regarded as its friends." European statesmen were inclined to tread lightly in the presence of such a threatening figure.

Fortunately for the Union, Adams was an ideal choice for the post of minister to Great Britain. Son of one American president and grandson of another, himself a distinguished journalist and astute politician, Adams proved to be a superb diplomat. Frequently smoothing Seward's abrasive language, Adams presented the Union's case with consummate skill and ultimate success. Dayton also conducted his affairs in France with competence and discretion. But Great Britain was the critical nation in American Civil War diplomacy, and Adams was the supreme overseas agent of that diplomacy. Historians James G. Randall and David Herbert Donald have concluded that Adams's character and ability were as valuable to the Union cause as were its military victories. The combination of Seward's truculence and Adams's tact turned out to be exactly what Union diplomacy needed.

But it was with considerable optimism that Davis and Confederate Secretary of State Toombs in March 1861 dispatched three emissaries, William L. Yancey of Alabama, Judge Pierre Rost of Louisiana, and A. Dudley Mann of Georgia, on a preliminary visit to the major European capitals. Unfortunately for the Confederacy, though these men were versed in domestic politics and law, they lacked the polish and breadth of vision for effective diplomatic work.

Toombs instructed the emissaries to present in England the case for secession as a constitutional right justified by northern aggression and to emphasize the protective tariff as an instrument for exacting tribute from the region and an impediment to English trade with the United States. Their crowning argument was to be made on the role of the South's great staple, cotton, in the world economy, with a "delicate allusion" to the dependence of English prosperity on the cotton trade and the disastrous consequences that would result from a long war between the North and South.

The reference to cotton was no idle threat. It grew out of one of the Old South's supreme articles of faith, the belief that cotton was the dominating economic force of the western world. Senator James Henry Hammond of South Carolina spoke for his entire region when in 1858 he uttered the boast, "You dare not make war on cotton. Cotton is King." Traveling throughout the South in 1861, correspondent William Howard Russell of the *Times* reported that southerners looked upon England as being a mere appanage of the Cotton Kingdom; he quoted one of them as having said to him, "Why, sir, we have only to shut off your supply of cotton for a few weeks and we can create a revolution in Great Britain. There are four millions of your people depending on us for their bread, not to speak of the many millions of dollars. No, sir, we know that England must recognize us."

So strong was this belief that it led southerners into a diplomacy of coercion instead of persuasion. During the summer and fall of 1861 great numbers of spokesmen urged an embargo on cotton. Although the Confederate authorities decided that an official embargo would be impolitic, they encouraged a voluntary one. The southern people responded by withholding from the market most of that year's heavy crop, so that virtually none of it reached Europe.

That such a diplomacy would have succeeded under any conditions is extremely problematical. The conditions under which it was attempted were particularly unfavorable. Bountiful cotton crops during the late 1850s had created a heavy surplus of fiber in the British warehouses; for the moment, the factories could keep busy in spite of a break with their source of supply, and the statesmen could remain patient. In early May, Lord Russell gave audience to the Confederate emissaries. He did it warily, with an eye on the Union secretary of state. "If it can possibly be helped," Russell had written to Lyons, "Mr. Seward must not be allowed to get us into a quarrel. I shall see the southerners when they come, but unofficially and keep them at a proper distance." So he did, without any commitment on British recognition.

Angry that the Confederate emissaries were received even unofficially, Seward drafted a letter threatening to sever diplomatic relations if it happened again. Lincoln toned down the letter and Adams relayed its message in his own words, saying that any further meetings with the Confederate "pseudo-commissioners" would be looked upon by the United States as a manifestation of hostility. Russell did not meet with the Confederates again, and soon he announced a hands-off policy, saying, "We have not been involved in any way in [the American] contest...and for God's sake, let us if possible, keep out of it."

The Confederates' failure to gain immediate British recognition of independence was partly offset by gaining certain lesser diplomatic advantages. When President Lincoln declared the blockade against the Confederacy, Queen Victoria's government ignored United States representations and responded with a declaration of neutrality that recognized the Confederacy as a belligerent power, thus freeing British merchants to sell arms and supplies to the South as well as the North. The French government promptly took a similar step.

In the fall of 1861 Davis replaced the preliminary emissaries with what he intended as regular Confederate ministers to Great Britain and France. He chose two eminent southern political figures, both former United States senators, James M. Mason of Virginia to represent the Confederacy in England and John Slidell in France. Mason was a planter-aristocrat; he was also the grandson of George Mason, author of the Virginia Declaration of Rights. But in the British mind these connections were overshadowed by the knowledge that he was the drafter of the ill-famed fugitive slave act of 1850. Slidell was a native of New York who at an early age migrated to Louisiana, where he married into the Creole gentry, learned to speak French acceptably, and became a dominant figure in Democratic party politics in both state and national circles.

Ironically, Mason and Slidell perhaps came nearest accomplishing their mission before they reached Europe. Making their way to Havana, they took passage there for England on the British mail packet *Trent*. On November 8, the second day at sea, it was overhauled by a United States warship under the command of Captain Charles Wilkes, who arrested the two Confederates and carried them to Boston, where they were placed behind bars. A commotion followed, with popular applause in the North for Captain Wilkes and an angry outburst by the bellicose British prime minister, who began ostentatious preparations for war. Minister Adams expressed profound sadness over the event, and his son Henry called those who exulted over it a "bloody set of fools." The New York diarist George Templeton Strong recorded his fear that British ironclads would soon be steaming up the Narrows of New York harbor and throwing shells into Union Square.

Lincoln kept his head and cautioned Seward, "One war at a time." Both Seward and Minister Adams assured the British government that Wilkes had acted without authorization. In a cabinet meeting on Christmas Day, at which Senator Charles Sumner read friendly letters received from Bright and Cobden, the administration wisely decided to set the Confederates free in order to avoid any possibility of war with England. Seward wrote Lord Lyons, saying they would be "cheerfully liberated"; at the same time Seward expressed a sentiment in the letter, which he made public, that soothed American sensibilities by emphasizing that the Confederates would be held if the safety of the Union depended on such a course. They were promptly released, and the danger of a confrontation between the United States and Great Britain was averted.

The freed Confederate emissaries arrived in Europe in January 1862 and were cordially received. Mason enjoyed the hospitality of a number of British merchants, shipowners, and members of Parliament who favored the southern cause; Slidell got an even more promising welcome in France where he was admitted to interviews with the emperor himself. Both emissaries talked with the foreign ministers of the countries to which they were dispatched.

But the Confederate goals of diplomatic recognition and European intervention remained elusive. Following the instructions of Confederate Secretary of State R. M. T. Hunter, the Confederate emissaries described the Union restrictions as being a mere "paper" blockade and hence a violation of international law. Yet when asked why more cotton was not therefore reaching Europe, they equivocated because they could not afford to confess the existence of a southern embargo.

In March southern sympathizers in Parliament urged the government to take action against the blockade on grounds that it was ineffectual and illegal. But the British officials were reluctant to admit a principle that might well backfire against them in future wars of their own. Lord Russell had already declared the Union blockade adequate to prevent access to Confederate ports or create an evident danger to ships entering or leaving the ports; he now affirmed that the blockade was real and therefore legal. The move for intervention collapsed.

The appointment in the early spring of 1862 of Judah P. Benjamin as secretary of state brought Confederate diplomatic affairs under a particularly keen intelligence, but the European need for southern cotton remained the foundation of Confederate diplomacy. The alleged illegality of the Union blockade remained the primary Confederate diplomatic argument.

The pinch of a cotton shortage in the French textile industry combined with Napoleon III's interest in Mexico to cause him to make a move toward mediation. Minister Mercier actually approached Seward with such a proposal, only to meet with a sharp rebuke over the French recognition of Confederate belligerency, which, said Seward, had the effect of prolonging the war. The quickest way to get cotton to the French mills, he advised, was to end this source of southern hope.

When an attempt by Confederate sympathizers in Parliament failed to bring about a joint British-French mediation offer, Benjamin temporarily concentrated his efforts on obtaining intervention by France alone, in the hope that Britain would then follow suit. Slidell was authorized to offer the emperor a treaty of free trade with the Confederacy, plus a bonus of 100,000 bales of cotton. The French navy was to break the blockade, escort merchant vessels laden with arms and other supplies to the South, then accompany the same vessels, bearing cotton, back to France. Ultimately, suggested Benjamin, the cotton traffic between the two nations could reach a million bales.

A few days later the Confederate congress authorized Davis to make commercial treaties, including trade concessions, with Great Britain, France, and Spain. Clearly, the Confederate policy of diplomatic coercion by embargo had given way to a policy of enticement by supply. Slidell put Benjamin's offer directly to Napoleon, who expressed interest but was still too wary to move without the collaboration of Great Britain.

The most precarious moment in the wartime foreign relations of the Union, and the most favorable moment in those of the Confederacy, came during the Confederate triple counteroffensive of the fall of 1862. The French minister Mercier, who had visited Richmond and talked with Benjamin and other southern leaders, and was convinced of the Confederacy's invincibility, urged his government to intervene. Napoleon was persuaded to make a formal proposal of joint British-French-Russian intervention.

Palmerston and his colleagues actually were planning the very sort of move Napoleon had in mind. Confederate military successes during the summer of 1862 caused the *Times* to urge intervention. Minister Adams wrote, "There is no doubt that the idea here is as strong as ever that we must ultimately fail, and unless a very few weeks show some great military result we shall have our hands full in this quarter." He believed that only a decisive Union victory in the field could forestall European action.

As Lee marched into Maryland, the British cabinet decided that if he should win another significant victory or capture a major northern city, an overture would be made to both belligerents asking them to cease hostilities and arrive at terms of separation, with England and France, and possibly Russia, serving as mediators. If the North should reject the proposal and the South accept it, the European parties would recognize the independence of the Confederacy. If in the coming encounter the Union forces should prevail, said Palmerston, "We may wait awhile and see what may follow...."

On October 7 Gladstone, who later would become one of England's great prime ministers, uttered a premature public statement saying Davis and other leaders of the South had made an army, were making a navy, and "what is more than either, they have made a nation.... We may anticipate with certainty the success of the Southern States so far as regards their separation from the North." Russell now formally proposed an armistice.

But Palmerston, impulsive and truculent in speech, was more cautious in action. Minister Adams was quietly threatening, leaking word of packing his luggage for departure, and making clear that the Lincoln administration would not accept mediation in the war. Lee's failure in the Maryland campaign, followed by the announcement of the preliminary emancipation proclamation, gave Palmerston pause. Immediately after receiving word of the outcome at Antietam, he said the time was not ripe for British action: "Ten days or a fortnight more may throw a light upon future prospects." On October 22 he wrote to Russell, "We must continue [for the present] to be lookers-on till the war shall have taken a more decided turn."

The British decision came in a cabinet meeting of November 11. In addition to Palmerston's doubts concerning the Confederate military outlook, the British statesmen were influenced by the attitude of Russia. Here the Union found an unlikely ally. The Russian government traditionally looked upon the United States as a counterweight to British power, which in turn was viewed as a major threat to Russian security. Czar Nicholas I was reported to have said on an earlier occasion, "Not only are our [Russian and American] interests alike, our enemies are the same."

From the beginning of the Civil War the Russian statesmen had expressed strong sympathy for the Union. Norman Graebner identifies this pragmatic accord between the world's greatest despotism and its leading democracy as being an example of "Realpolitik at its diplomatic best" because it served the interest of both nations. The Russian government had already rejected the French proposal for intervention. The British government now did the same. The Union's severest diplomatic crisis was over.

Quite likely England and France would have granted recognition to the Confederacy if Lee's campaign had been successful. What the consequences of this action would have been is problematical. The historian E. D. Adams wrote that mediation and recognition by England would have resulted in war with the Union, and that the independence of the Confederacy would have been assured. But Palmerston made clear that diplomatic recognition would not affect England's neutrality in the war itself. Without armed intervention, the outcome of the struggle probably would have remained unchanged. Only if the Union government had insisted on going to war with the European powers, an eventuality that Lincoln carefully avoided, would recognition have guaranteed Confederate independence.

Second only to the threat of intervention as a source of friction between the Union and Great Britain was the practice of private British shipbuilders in supplying the Confederates with naval vessels, and the tardiness of the British government in stopping the practice. Constructed to the specifications of a Confederate naval agent, Captain James Bulloch, these vessels sailed under temporary names and without armaments to rendezvous points off the Azores or in the British West Indies, where they were armed, turned over to Confederate officers, and given Confederate names. They were then employed as raiders against American shipping. The most famous of them was the *Enrica*; renamed the *Alabama* and commanded by Captain (later Rear Admiral) Raphael Semmes, it became the scourge of the seas. The raider *Florida* was almost as destructive.

RAPHAEL SEMMES   (The
Kunhardt Collection)

Bulloch's plans included vessels potentially more dangerous than
the commerce raiders. He contracted with shipbuilders in both England
and France for the construction of a fleet of ironclad rams capable of
crippling or destroying the wooden ships of the Union blockade. By the
autumn of 1863 two of these formidable craft were almost finished by
the Laird firm of Birkenhead, England. Through informers and double
agents, the resourceful United States consul at Liverpool, Thomas H.
Dudley, learned of the existence of the English rams and passed the information on to Minister Adams, who repeatedly sent Lord Russell
veiled warnings of war if they should fall into Confederate hands.

These warnings were consistent with the policy of Secretary of State Seward, who believed the British were motivated by the dread of such a war, and who instructed Adams to inform Russell that his government's attitude toward this affair so complicated the relations between the two countries as to make difficult the preservation of their friendship.

Bulloch adopted the subterfuge of selling the ships to a French firm for resale to the pasha of Egypt, and the British government at first refused to take action against them. But Adams's persistent protests eventually bore fruit, as did the earlier passage by the United States Congress of a bill authorizing the commissioning of privateers to augment the Union blockade. Finally, on September 5 Adams sent a note to Russell that ended, "It would be superfluous in me to point out to your Lordship that this is war." Already the British government had decided to seize the vessels, though it had not yet done so. They were seized the day after the receipt of Adams's ominous note and were turned over later to the British navy. No European-built rams got to the Confederacy. Again, the British statesmen were motivated in part by the determination to avoid creating any precedents which might in the future be used against England.

Many lesser sources of diplomatic tension remained, some of them capable of producing major problems. The blockade continued to strain Union relations with Europe, especially with Great Britain. Union naval vessels in 1863 took the measure, unprecedented in current diplomatic affairs, of seizing merchant ships of neutral nations if the ships were bound for Cuba, the British West Indies, or Matamoros, Mexico, with cargoes intended to be transferred to Confederate blockade runners or sold to Confederate agents operating below the Rio Grande. Union prize courts ruled the seizures legal on grounds that the supplies were destined for enemy use. Although the Confederate government protested strenuously and British merchants and the pro-Confederate British press called for reprisals, the British government refused to move. Doubtless Palmerston and Russell foresaw the time when such an extended form of blockade would be useful to their nation.

Confederate diplomacy involved efforts to secure foreign financial aid as well as diplomatic recognition and intervention. Many millions of dollars were raised through the sale of Confederate bonds to private individuals overseas, especially to British friends of the Confederacy. But the major Confederate venture in overseas finance, the Erlanger Loan, occurred in France. The prominent French banking firm of Emile Erlanger & Company agreed in the spring of 1863 to market in Europe $25 million in bonds bearing 8 percent interest, the bonds to be exchangeable for Confederate-owned cotton at a fixed, low price. Secretary Benjamin bridled at both the high commission—23 percent—and the interest rate, but yielding to Slidell's belief that the loan would favorably influence the emperor, Benjamin accepted the arrangement. Little came of it. The price of the bonds declined steadily; Confederate military reverses during the summer caused it to plummet. Out of the transaction the Confederacy received less than $3 million in cash. Eventually, the purchasers of the bonds lost their entire investment.

Still the fortunes of battle continued to affect the vicissitudes of diplomacy. Lee's stunning victory at Chancellorsville in May 1863 revived the hopes of southern diplomats and friends abroad. Sympathetic Britons stirred up mass meetings of unemployed textile workers and planned moves in Parliament to coincide with an overture by Napoleon to reopen the question of British-French intervention. Again Slidell met with Napoleon and urged a French move, without British cooperation, if necessary. Two days later the two chief Confederate sympathizers in Parliament, William S. Lindsay and John A. Roebuck, had audience with Napoleon, who avowed his continued willingness to join England in intervening in behalf of the Confederacy, but who denounced the British government for its alleged equivocation and perfidy in the matter.

On June 30 Roebuck introduced in Parliament a formal motion for the recognition of Confederate independence. An intemperate man, a vehement pro-Confederate who once said the Union army was composed of "the scum and refuse of Europe," he now warned that a united America was a menace to world security. He disclosed the substance of his confidential interview with Napoleon, including the emperor's reflection on the integrity of the British authorities. Roebuck's indiscretion deterred even most Confederate sympathizers among his colleagues.

Palmerston was unshaken in his decision to remain aloof from the American struggle. On July 3 Minister Adams, who had stood by anxiously throughout these episodes, wrote that the affair in Parliament had ended "by no means to our disadvantage." He said Roebuck had exposed himself to ridicule and contempt, and added perceptively, "The rebel cause cannot be restored this season by any action had in its favor on this side of the water. It may yet be helped by events on the other, should their last desperate enterprise be crowned with any success." At the moment Adams penned these words, what he referred to as the Confederates' "last desperate enterprise" was being repulsed at Gettysburg, to be followed in a day by the capture of Vicksburg. Palmerston's judgment had been sustained by the weight of iron.

Fully aware at last of the improbability of gaining British recognition, Benjamin in August instructed Mason to leave England, and the commissioner soon joined Slidell in Paris. A month later Benjamin severed the last tenuous ties between the Confederacy and Great Britain by expelling all British consuls from the South.

Afterward, Benjamin concentrated all his efforts on using the Mexican pawn to induce Napoleon to extend unilateral French recognition to the Confederacy. When Slidell was unable to move Napoleon by warning him that a Union victory would doom the French enterprise in Mexico, Benjamin appointed an envoy, William Preston of Kentucky, to approach Emperor Maximilian in the hope of persuading him to use his influence in gaining French recognition of the Confederacy. This scheme too was futile. Instead of journeying to Mexico, Preston sought out Maximilian's agents in Europe, who, upon Napoleon's orders, rejected all Confederate overtures.

Confederate diplomatic hopes disappeared altogether with the Confederate military reverses of the final months of the war. Tension between the Union and Great Britain relaxed; Minister Adams received compliments in Parliament for his able services in keeping peace between the two nations. The most serious Union difficulty in foreign affairs late in the war occurred over the activities of Confederate agents in Canada, especially a raid by some of them in October 1864 across the border to pillage the town of St. Albans, Vermont. Furious over the release of the raiders by a Canadian magistrate, Seward wrote Adams to give notice of the American intention to abandon the venerable Rush-Bagot agreement of 1817, which drastically limited armaments along the border of the United States and Canada. The threat was sufficient; under pressure from the British government as well as that of local sentiment, the Canadian authorities tightened their surveillance and the Confederate raids ceased.

The Union success in averting foreign recognition of and military assistance to the Confederacy was crucial to the outcome of the war. Norman Graebner has written persuasively that even a limited armed intervention by the Europeans might have enabled the South to win its independence. During the war, he concluded, the nation's future rested as much on the efficiency of its diplomatic corps as on that of its military corps. Confederate leaders and their people had exaggerated the power of King Cotton to bring the world to terms. It was a fatal miscalculation.

X

Military Success and Political Victory

❖

The tumultuous events of 1863 brought the opposing presidents of the Union and Confederacy to a critical point of decision. Both now had to decide whether to continue the war efforts as they had been carried on to that moment, efforts in which the presidents themselves had to a great extent acted as their own generals in chief, notwithstanding Lincoln's attempts to do otherwise, or to appoint authentic generals in chief and turn over to them the conduct of the military operations. Both presidents in fact did make appointments to what appeared to be the position of general in chief, but the qualifications of the appointees and the conditions of appointment were significantly different. The differences were telling if not crucial.

In early March 1864 Lincoln promoted Grant to the newly resurrected rank of lieutenant general in the Regular Army, last held by George Washington, and appointed him general in chief of Union armies. Halleck now became the Union chief of staff, with strictly administrative duties. The president had with increasing admiration watched Grant's progress in command. His leadership had made the difference in both the Vicksburg and Chattanooga campaigns; Meade, the other logical choice for the position of general in chief, had, in Lincoln's judgment, faltered badly after Gettysburg. Lincoln expressed his supreme confidence in Grant when later he wrote to him, saying: "The particulars of your plan I neither know nor seek to know.... I wish not to obtrude any constraints or restraints upon you...."

Davis firmly opposed creating the position of general in chief. This attitude was in part the result of a strict interpretation of the Confederate constitution, which, like the Federal model, declared the president to be the commander in chief of armed forces. Davis's view also arose from personal preference and pride in his own career as a distinguished soldier and secretary of war. He once said, "I have neither the authority nor the will to delegate the supreme command."

Davis was aware of the necessity for a greater coordination of Confederate military efforts. He now found himself also needing to provide employment for his old friend Braxton Bragg, a full general and an officer of unquestioned ability in the training, discipline, and organization of armies and in strategic planning. Thinking to remedy both problems, Davis in February 1864 issued an order placing Bragg in charge of the conduct of Confederate military operations, with the exalted title commander in chief. Thus he chose a general who had only recently resigned his command because of failure in the field, while Lincoln chose for the highest position the general he considered to be the most capable of the Union army commanders.

Impressive as Bragg's new title was, he was not general in chief of Confederate armies. Moreover, Davis's order said explicitly that Bragg would act "under the authority of the President," an expression that actually meant Davis would remain the real general in chief. The war entered its final year with a conspicuous contrast in the Union and Confederate command structures.

Grant's initial recommendations were not auspicious, at least not from Lincoln's point of view. Grant wished to launch invasions of the Southeast from both Mobile and Chattanooga and to remain personally in the West and exercise from there his authority as general in chief. As for the East, his plan called for landing a force of 60,000 on the Atlantic coast below Richmond to move inland and seize the Weldon Railroad, Lee's supply line with the port of Wilmington, North Carolina, and with the entire South Atlantic area.

Halleck's reply represented Lincoln's long-expressed conviction that Lee's army was the true target of the Union army in Virginia and that Grant's proposal would require the splitting of the Army of the Potomac, place Lee on interior lines between the two segments, and dangerously expose Washington to invasion. Also, Grant was informed that he was expected to command from the East instead of the West. Hence, notwithstanding Lincoln's declaration of a hands-off policy in dealing with his new general in chief, the president in fact made vital contributions to the military strategy that Grant ultimately would put into effect. Later Grant would acknowledge that the campaign directly against Lee's army was essential to Union victory in the war.

Grant left Meade in command of the Army of the Potomac but made his own headquarters there. In this way he avoided the immediate interference of the Washington bureaucracy, and incidentally of the president; Grant at the same time located himself where he could look over Meade's shoulder and supervise the operations against Lee. Eventually, he became in fact, though not in title, the commander of the Army of the Potomac, with Meade primarily carrying out his orders. Grant also brought a tough and proven officer, General Philip Sheridan, from the West to take command of the cavalry in Virginia.

Grant planned a concerted attack on all fronts, to be reinforced by the choking blockade of the Union navy. Direct assaults would be made upon the major Confederate armies. Meade (and Grant) would assail Lee's army in Virginia, while William Tecumseh Sherman with the combined weight of the Army of the Ohio, Army of the Tennessee, and Army of the Cumberland was to move from Chattanooga against the other major Confederate field force, Joseph E. Johnston's Army of Tennessee in northern Georgia, and "break it up."

At the same time, all available Union forces were to strike at Confederate communications and sources of supply in order to weaken the entire southern war effort. Sherman, in particular, was instructed to "get into the interior of the enemy's country as far as you can, inflicting all the damage you can against their war resources." His drive was to merge at Atlanta with a Union movement from Mobile. This was Winfield Scott's Anaconda strategy resurrected and enlarged on a scale far beyond what anyone at the beginning of the war would have dreamed.

One part of Grant's strategy, the launching of the movement from Mobile, was aborted before the overall plan was put into effect. Halleck, influenced by Lincoln's hope of restoring Louisiana to the Union before the war ended, had already approved a move to eliminate the Confederate Trans-Mississippi Department. General Banks was to lead a joint army-navy expedition from New Orleans up the Red River into eastern Texas. At the same time Major General Frederick Steele was to advance from Arkansas to seize Shreveport, headquarters of the Trans-Mississippi Department, located on the Red River in the northwestern corner of Louisiana. Grant intended that Banks and his 28,000 troops, along with Rear Admiral Porter and his fleet of gunboats and transports, be back in New Orleans in time to move against Mobile in coordination with the other Union campaigns.

Banks dawdled in New Orleans until March 12, then mismanaged the entire affair. Once the movement began, he seemed to be as interested in seizing Confederate cotton as in conducting tactical operations. In early April Confederate General Richard Taylor with about 12,000 troops caught the Union column on the march at Sabine Crossroads near Mansfield in northwestern Louisiana and administered a sharp defeat. Retreating ten miles to Pleasant Hill, Banks held off a second attack by Taylor, then staged a hasty retreat to the fleet in the Red River near Natchitoches. The withdrawing expedition found an alarming situation awaiting it at Alexandria in the center of the state. The river there was too low for the ironclads to pass through the rapids.

Taylor pursued Banks and repeatedly urged his superior, General Kirby Smith, to provide sufficient reinforcements to attack the appar-

ently trapped Union column. Instead, Kirby Smith sent his available reserves to Sterling Price to deal with the threat from the north against
Shreveport; on April 18 Price accomplished this mission effectively by
attacking and routing Steele's troops in the battle of Poison Spring in
southern Arkansas. Banks's expedition escaped intact in mid-May after
a resourceful army engineer, Lieutenant Colonel Joseph Bailey, improvised a dam and jetties that created a chute deep enough to free the
gunboats. By the time Banks got back to New Orleans, the other campaigns in Grant's grand strategy were well under way.

The Confederate Trans-Mississippi Department would remain un-
conquered throughout the war, and would outlive the Confederacy itself. The department would also remain virtually autonomous, known
whimsically as "Kirby-Smithdom" because within it the general controlled impressment, conscription, tax collection, cotton exports, transportation, diplomatic missions to Mexico, and the exchange of prisoners of war. The region produced bountiful crops and carried on a brisk
trade with European merchants in Mexico. Kirby Smith supplied his
troops by purchasing or impressing cotton and exchanging it for arms
and supplies south of the border. But the Federal control of the Mississippi denied all but a trickle of these resources to the main body of the
Confederacy.

In Virginia, Grant was aware that to destroy or decisively defeat Lee
and the Army of Northern Virginia would require fighting of extraordinary severity and persistence. He found among the officers of the Army
of the Potomac an inhibiting spirit of apprehension and admiration for
their famed opponent. "Well, Grant has never met Bobby Lee yet,"
they said to Grant's staff officers. Determined to banish this feeling
from their minds, he said to Meade, "Lee's army will be your objective
point. Wherever Lee goes, there you will go also."

By early May the Union and Confederate armies in Virginia were at
full numerical strength. Burnside's corps had been ordered by Grant
from Tennessee, bringing the Army of the Potomac, now massed in the
familiar area north of the Rappahannock and Rapidan above Fredericksburg, up to approximately 120,000. Longstreet's corps, minus Pickett's
division, had returned to Lee from the West, and many regiments had
been brought up from the lower Atlantic coast. The Army of Northern
Virginia was some 65,000 strong. It was located south of the Rappahannock and Rapidan, and, in order to protect its lines of communication and its supply area, it was spread across a fifty-mile front from
Fredericksburg southwest to the vicinity of Gordonsville.

On May 4, the date set for the opening of Grant's grand offensive,
the Army of the Potomac once again crossed the Rapidan into the very
Wilderness area of the Chancellorsville campaign. Grant's aim was to
pass the Confederates' right flank and threaten Richmond or draw
them into a battle in the open against overwhelming numbers. Two simultaneous diversionary campaigns were designed to weaken Lee's

army: Major General Franz Sigel was to advance with a column from West Virginia into the Shenandoah Valley, Lee's major source of rations; and Major General Benjamin F. Butler was to move with a force named the Army of the James up the south side of the James River to threaten Richmond from below and ultimately join forces with the Army of the Potomac as it pushed south. Lincoln described these secondary moves in a country metaphor: "Those not skinning can hold a leg."

Lee determined to strike the Army of the Potomac in the tangled woods of the Wilderness, where mobility and organization would be difficult and the effects of the superiority of Union numbers and artillery at a minimum. He sent the corps of Ewell and A. P. Hill marching east, Ewell along the Orange Turnpike and Hill along the roughly parallel Orange Plank Road, to approach Grant's column from his right. Longstreet with the reserve corps followed. Fighting began the morning of May 5 and raged throughout the day, Ewell engaged with Major General Gouverneur K. Warren's corps, and Hill with Hancock's corps, in separate encounters scarcely a mile apart. At nightfall the battle was a standoff; both Lee and Grant planned attacks for the following morning.

At 5:00 A.M. Meade attacked with the three corps of Warren, Sedgwick, and Hancock. Ewell held, but Hill soon faced defeat. Lee then became involved personally in rallying his disorganized and exhausted troops. At this moment the head of Longstreet's column appeared, and Lee ordered an attack through Hill's position against Hancock's corps. Caught up in the fury of the combat, and seeking to inspire his troops to superhuman effort, Lee rode forward with them as if to lead the assault. "Go back, General Lee, go back," they cried, but he retired only after Longstreet arrived and told him bluntly to do so.

Initially the Confederate counterattack was successful. Swinging his attack so as to take Hancock's line in the flank, Longstreet rolled it back to the important Brock Road junction, where the retreat was halted with the aid of reserves sent from Burnside's corps. The entire action recalled Jackson's assault at almost the same spot the year before. The similarity was to become even more striking. In the early afternoon, as Longstreet moved about the front working to regain the momentum, he, like Jackson, was hit and severely wounded by fire from his own ranks. By late afternoon the strength of the attack was spent; further efforts by Longstreet's successor, General Richard Anderson, to take the road junction were repulsed.

Unable to overwhelm the Federal left, Lee directed his attention to the opposite end of the line. There, to his frustration, he found that brigade commander Brigadier General John B. Gordon during the morning had reported the Federal right to be in the air and had requested permission to attack it, only to be overruled by Early and Ewell. Once again, Lee felt the absence of Jackson. Lee now ordered the attack even though the day was almost spent. Gordon promptly struck Sedgwick's corps and drove in its exposed flank, but nightfall and stiffening Union resistance brought the movement to a halt. The Confederates now consolidated their lines and entrenched.

The battle of the Wilderness was over. Neither commander could see any prospect of a decisive conclusion there. The fighting in the dense woods and scrub had been fierce, confused, and terrifying, beset with the ghosts, and sometimes the skeletons, of soldiers killed in the battle of Chancellorsville. Increasing the horror, fires from exploding shells swept over parts of the battlefield, sometimes consuming the bodies of the fallen and causing the wounded to prepare to shoot themselves to avoid being burned alive. Union casualties were severe, approximately 18,000. Confederate casualties, approximately 10,800, were proportionately even heavier. After such encounters in the past, Union generals in Virginia had, with perhaps less cause, withdrawn from the battlefield. Would Grant and Meade do the same?

The answer was not long in coming. Instead of pulling back to reorganize, Grant now purposed to shift left in an effort to turn the Confederate right flank by moving the Army of the Potomac south along Brock Road. On the night of May 7 the two corps of Warren and Sedgwick pulled out of the line, formed column, and began the march with Grant and Meade riding in the lead; the troops sent up a cheer over the knowledge that they were headed toward Richmond and not being withdrawn as usual.

Sensing Grant's purpose, Lee already had instructed his engineers to prepare a shortcut through the woods and had ordered Anderson to move his corps into bivouac for a few hours of rest during the night and to march before dawn to occupy Brock Road at the village of Spotsylvania Courthouse. Fitzhugh Lee's cavalry was dispatched to harass and delay the Union march.

Lee's intuition and preparation combined with the caprices of war—Clausewitz's chance and uncertainty at work again—to pay the Confederates great dividends. Anderson, discovering his intended bivouac area on fire, marched without pause to his assigned battle station; at the same time, the Union infantry movement was delayed on the road in the darkness for two hours by an altercation and fistfight between two of Sheridan's cavalry regiments. The following morning heavy musket fire greeted the approach of Warren's advance guard at Spotsylvania and served notice that the Confederates had won the race, if by the slimmest of margins.

Fighting was continuous throughout the afternoon of May 8 as the remaining corps of both armies arrived on the scene and the Union commanders extended their line in an effort to envelop the Confederate right. By the following day both lines, heavily entrenched, described the

THE WILDERNESS AND SPOTSYLVANIA, MAY 5–12, 1864

form of rough V's that lay across Brock Road and enclosed Spotsylvania within their angles. The Confederates held the inverted and interior V; the Federals held the corresponding outer V. The soldiers called the angle in Lee's formation a "mule shoe." The following day was filled with skirmishing, and with sharpshooting that produced a major Union casualty. Sedgwick, attempting to steady his men who were dodging from the humming Minié balls, declared boldly that the Confederates "couldn't hit an elephant at this distance." An instant later he fell mortally wounded from a shot through the head.

Unsuccessful in turning Lee's position, Grant and Meade now assaulted it repeatedly. On the 10th, using a tactical formation of massed and shortened ranks, moving at double quick with muskets uncapped and thus unable to fire, young Colonel Emory Upton led his brigade in an attack that broke through the west face of the mule shoe near its apex. But the attack was not properly supported, and Upton was forced to retire after a bloody fight in the trenches.

Two days later Grant and Meade launched a massive coordinated assault using tactics similar to Upton's. Hancock's corps penetrated the mule shoe at the apex, held by Ewell's corps, while the Union corps of Major General Horatio G. Wright, Sedgwick's successor, struck furiously at the "bloody angle" on the west side of the V, and Burnside's corps exerted pressure on the east side. The Confederate line was broken; the entire army faced disaster. But a desperate countercharge, led by Gordon with Lee present until he was persuaded by the entreaties of the soldiers to move back, sealed off the penetration long enough for the Confederates to prepare and occupy a new line across the base of the salient. For another week the two armies fought doggedly in this location as the Federals searched for a weakness in the Confederate position.

On May 11 Grant had written Halleck that he proposed "to fight it out on this line, if it takes all summer." Now he changed his mind, and the night of the 20th the Army of the Potomac began another march designed to turn the Confederate position on its right. Swinging to the east of the Mattapony River, the Union column headed south for Hanover Junction, the important rail intersection only twenty miles above Richmond. Anticipating Grant's object, Lee withdrew along the chord of the Union arc, the military "interior line," and by the 22d the Army of Northern Virginia was deployed in another inverted V on strong terrain south of the North Anna River, awaiting the appearance of the Federals. A few days of probing convinced Grant the position was too formidable for a direct assault, so during the night of May 26 he began still another move to pass the Confederate right.

As the Army of the Potomac marched east on a route north of the North Anna and Pamunkey rivers, Lee repeated his operation of moving along the chord of the Union arc. When the Federals crossed the

Pamunkey at Hanover Town, they found Lee's army entrenched south of Totopotomoy Creek. Again Grant sought to turn the Confederate position by edging around its right. But when on the 31st he reached the village of Cold Harbor near the old Gaines' Mill battleground, he once more found the Confederates ahead of him. Protected by earthworks, their line stretched from the Totopotomoy Creek on the left to the Chickahominy River on the right. A scant nine miles behind them lay Richmond. Half of Grant's army of 100,000 was now concentrated against the center of an attenuated Confederate line. The situation was tempting. A point-blank assault against this line just might break it, scatter the Army of Northern Virginia, seize the rebel capital, and end the war.

Grant had hoped to weaken Lee's army with the operations of Sigel in the Valley and Butler on the James. Also, during the Spotsylvania operations Grant had dispatched Sheridan with 10,000 cavalry to strike deep at Lee's communications and threaten Richmond from the north while Butler menaced it from the south. All these efforts failed to accomplish their primary aim, though Sheridan's sweep did force Lee to send Stuart after him with approximately 4,500 troopers. In a fierce encounter on May 11 at Yellow Tavern five miles north of the Confederate capital, Stuart deflected the invading Union cavalry. But he did so at the cost of his own life. Upon word of his death, Lee wrote, "A more zealous, ardent, brave and devoted soldier than Stuart the Confederacy cannot have." The plumed cavalier had atoned for whatever sins he may have committed during the Gettysburg campaign.

Meanwhile, Sigel's force of approximately 10,000 pressed into the Shenandoah Valley from West Virginia. Neglecting to keep his columns within supporting distance of one another, Sigel with about 7,000 was attacked and defeated on May 15 at New Market by Confederate Major General John C. Breckinridge with a force of 5,000, including the corps of cadets from the Virginia Military Institute at Lexington. Breckinridge then hastened with 2,500 troops to join Lee in the Cold Harbor line.

Butler was no more successful below Richmond than Sigel was in the Valley. Moving his force of 36,000 tentatively up the south side of the James, Butler allowed his opponent, General Beauregard, who had been ordered up from the defense of Charleston, sufficient time to bring reinforcements from North Carolina to the Confederate position at Drewry's Bluff. On May 16 Beauregard with 18,000 men attacked the Federals and drove them back into an area known as the Bermuda Hundred, which lay within the angle formed by the confluence of the Appomattox River with the James. Promptly establishing an entrenched line across the neck of the position, Beauregard so effectively penned Butler's force into it that Grant would say he was "corked up like a cork in a bottle." With Richmond temporarily safe, Davis now sent additional reinforcements from Beauregard to Lee.

Thus by early June, Lee at Cold Harbor was stronger by some 10,000 or more troops than Grant had anticipated. Otherwise, the Confederate line there might have been vulnerable. Fully aware of the failure of his diversions, Grant nevertheless yielded to the temptation for a direct assault. His soldiers obeyed with remarkable gallantry, though like some of the Confederates at Gettysburg, they sensed the ghastly futility of it; some of them pathetically pinned cards of identification to the backs of their tunics. The attack began at dawn on June 3, but it quickly broke under a devastating fire of musketry and artillery that left approximately 7,000 Union casualties on the field. The Confederates lost only about 1,500 men in this action. Grant later conceded his error of judgment.

Cold Harbor ended a month of the most sustained combat of the entire struggle. In a sense the fighting represented a new mode of warfare on both sides. No longer able to wage offensives, Lee had resorted to the kind of strategy of conservation of forces that Clausewitz said was suitable for the weaker contestant. By fighting only on the defensive and from behind earthworks, Lee sought to exact such a toll that he would wear down the northern determination to continue the war. Grant had responded with repeated attacks, declaring he would win by "sheer attrition," if necessary, and had displayed "dogged pertinacity," which Lincoln would later say was the key to his generalship. The entire campaign had been converted into a continual series of battles.

Lee had responded to Grant's moves with unexcelled anticipation and skill, and had inflicted fearsome casualties, approximately 55,000, on the Army of the Potomac. But the losses of the Army of Northern Virginia, approximately 32,000, were proportionately heavier. In military resources alone, the strategy of attrition was working against Lee. He found himself engaged in a mode of warfare he could not win so long as the soldiers and civilian population of the North had the will to keep it up.

Yet Grant could not afford many Cold Harbors. In some quarters he was already being called "the butcher." To avoid another direct assault, he now planned and executed a brilliant turning movement that temporarily stole a march on Lee. Sending Sheridan to raid along the Virginia Central Railroad and occupy Lee's cavalry, Grant during the period June 13–17 pulled the Army of the Potomac out of its lines and marched it in an extensive arc east and south, across the Chickahominy River, then across the broad and deep lower James on a bridge improvised by the Union engineers and described ruefully by one Confederate as the greatest span since Xerxes's invasion of ancient Greece. Grant's objective was the town of Petersburg, a rail center of crucial importance on Lee's line of communication, located twenty-three miles south of Richmond. Grant intended the assault to be made by the corps of Major General William F. "Baldy" Smith from Butler's Army of the James, reinforced by elements of the Army of the Potomac.

But the Union attack itself was as ineffectual as the preceding march had been skillful. Again Butler recoiled from moving against the thin

Confederate force on his front at Bermuda Hundred. Grant delegated to Meade the conduct of his attack against Petersburg, and Meade was unable to achieve a coordinated assault. On the 15th when the attack began, General Smith moved hesitantly against the lightly manned Confederate earthworks; attacks on the 16th and 17th as the bulk of the Army of the Potomac joined the battle forced the Confederates back to their last line of trenches, but failed to break through to Petersburg. Not until the night of the 17th did Grant arrive and plan a fully coordinated assault for the following day.

Even then the attack was piecemeal. That afternoon Meade lost his poise completely and sent the following order to his corps commanders: "I find it useless to appoint an hour to effect co-operation.... What additional orders to attack you require I cannot imagine.... Finding it impossible to effect co-operation by appointing an hour for attack, I have sent an order to each corps commander to attack at all hazards, and without reference to each other." In the words of historian Bruce Catton, the entire affair after the passage of the James was "hopelessly bungled"; he suggests that the Army of the Potomac, "as an army," was hardly commanded at all. The situation was perhaps comparable to that in the Army of Northern Virginia the last two days at Gettysburg.

During the entire period, Beauregard waged a defense of extraordinary boldness and tenacity. Leaving a mere 1,000 men facing Butler at Bermuda Hundred, he concentrated his remaining 14,000 in front of Petersburg and repulsed all early Union efforts to take the city. Meanwhile, he repeatedly wired Lee of the danger on the Petersburg front and urged him to send reinforcements.

Lee was in a severe quandary. Again he had anticipated Grant's purpose. "We must destroy this army of Grant's before he gets to James River," he said prophetically. "If he gets there, it will become a siege, and then it will be a mere question of time." In an effort to weaken the Union force on his front, Lee attempted another diversion similar to Jackson's famous Valley campaign during the summer of 1862. On June 13, the very day the Army of the Potomac began its march to the James, Lee ordered General Jubal Early with 13,000 troops to move into the Shenandoah Valley, clear it of the enemy, and threaten Washington from that quarter.

Yet because Lee feared that the Union pressure on Petersburg was only a diversion in favor of a direct assault north of the James against Richmond, he responded tardily to Beauregard's messages and calls for troops, though Lee did begin to send some reinforcements. Beauregard's dispatches were at first vague as to the identity of the forces in front of him. But a telegram the evening of June 17 named Hancock's corps among them, and by the time the Union attack began the following morning, Anderson's corps from Lee's army was there to help repel it. By the time a second Union assault was made that afternoon, Hill's corps was there and Lee with it. Every Union effort failed; Grant's great turning movement across the James had ended in a stalemate.

Lee's failure to detect that the Army of the Potomac was crossing the river below Richmond may have cost him the golden opportunity he had been hoping for since the battle of the Wilderness, an opportunity to strike his opponent on the march and undeployed for combat. Although Early carried out his mission energetically by crossing the Potomac and marching to the very outskirts of Washington before he was checked, the move did not divert a significant number of troops from Grant's army. Instead, Grant now held the Army of Northern Virginia locked in siege; the outcome was indeed a "mere question of time."

The great siege of Richmond and Petersburg would last until virtually the end of the war. Both sides constructed elaborate earthworks that ultimately ran continuously for some thirty miles. Lee's vital lines of supply were the Weldon Railroad and the Southside Railroad. The Weldon Railroad connected with the one remaining Confederate port, Wilmington, North Carolina, and gave access to the Atlantic seaboard of the Confederacy. The Southside Railroad connected, fifty miles west of Petersburg, with the Richmond and Danville Railroad and the Virginia and Tennessee Railroad. The Richmond and Danville Railroad led through central Virginia and made a connection that went through central North Carolina and into South Carolina. The Virginia and Tennessee Railroad led through western Virginia and linked the Virginia theater with what was left of the Confederacy west of the Alleghenies.

Grant's vital line of supply was by water, the Potomac River and Chesapeake Bay, to his base at City Point on the lower James. From there his line was by the City Point Railroad. He also had access to the Chesapeake via the Norfolk Railroad. Shortly after establishing his siege position he had his engineers construct a local rail line, the Military Railroad, that ran a short distance behind and parallel to his entrenchments, thus vastly simplifying his logistical problems. This entire supply and communications network was beyond the reach of Confederate operations.

With Lee's battle line spread invitingly thin, Grant from time to time attempted to break it with some kind of direct assault. The most spectacular of these occurred on July 30 on the Petersburg front in the explosion of a mine consisting of four tons of gunpowder that had been planted under the Confederate position by way of a tunnel of several hundred feet. But the Union attack through the resulting crater was incompetently led and poorly coordinated. A Confederate countermove ordered by Lee and executed by Brigadier General William Mahone's division sealed off the penetration and inflicted heavy casualties on the Union troops, many of them blacks, caught in and around the crater. The ill-fated Union General Burnside, whose corps was involved, paid

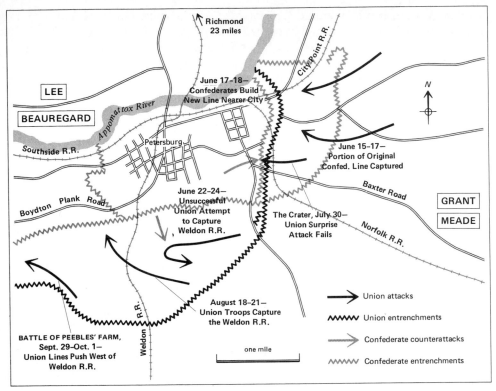

PETERSBURG, 1864

for the failure in being relieved of command. A few months later he resigned.

In late September Grant concentrated two corps north of the James River for a direct blow at Richmond. He captured Fort Harrison, a key stronghold in the Confederate line, but though determined counterattacks were repelled, the Union drive was unable to proceed beyond that point.

Grant's most effective tactical operations on the siege front consisted of extending his line to the south and west in order to menace or cut Lee's lines of supply, and of executing turning movements around Lee's flank. In shifting troops to meet Grant's direct attacks, Lee was obliged to weaken his flanks, enabling Grant to send columns around them. On August 18 Warren's corps seized the Weldon line at Globe Tavern and held it against repeated Confederate counterattacks. But the Union efforts to seize the Southside Railroad were defeated almost to the very end, and Lee was able to reestablish contact with the Weldon by way of an improvised, roundabout wagon route.

Meanwhile, Grant took another important step to weaken Lee's army. He determined to seize control of the Shenandoah Valley and destroy its usefulness to the Confederacy. Throughout the entire war it had been a major source of supplies for the southern forces in Virginia, and a channel for invading Maryland and Pennsylvania and threatening Washington. By the summer of 1864 it was the chief theater of operations for the most successful of the Confederate guerrilla activities, those of Colonel John S. Mosby and his partisan rangers. In August Grant sent Sheridan to take command in the Valley, combine the scattered Union forces there, and defeat the Confederate defenders. The redoubtable cavalryman was instructed to pursue the Confederates relentlessly, and to cross the Blue Ridge and destroy the Orange and Alexandria Railroad at Charlottesville. He also was instructed to leave the entire Valley "a barren waste," to the point that "crows flying over it...will have to carry their provender with them."

Sheridan was the man for the job. Collecting a force of more than 41,000, he moved against Early's army of fewer than half this strength. For over a month the two forces maneuvered back and forth, but on September 19 Sheridan overtook Early at Winchester and administered a sharp defeat, then followed it with another defeat four days later at Fisher's Hill.

While Sheridan proceeded to create the barren waste by burning thousands of barns, destroying immense quantities of crops in the field, and killing or driving off most of the cattle, his opponent, Early, received a brigade of reinforcements from Lee. On October 19 Early struck the Union army by surprise at Cedar Creek just above Strasburg. Initially routed, the Federals were rallied spectacularly by Sheridan, who was absent on a trip to Washington when the attack occurred, but who providentially arrived on the scene just in time to turn the retreating column around and halt the Confederate pursuit. A Federal counterattack quickly converted defeat into victory. For Sheridan, Cedar Creek was the narrowest of escapes; for "Old Jube" Early it was the last bolt. Lee was now obliged to strip Early's command to strengthen the lines at Petersburg; by the following spring, Sheridan's "mopping up" operations had ended all organized Confederate resistance in the famous Valley.

Late summer brought other significant Union successes. One of the most dramatic of these occurred in early August when Farragut steamed his Gulf fleet into Mobile Bay and engaged the Confederate defenses, primarily Fort Morgan at the mouth of the bay and a formidable though extremely sluggish ironclad ram, the *Tennessee*, in the largest naval battle of the war. With characteristic audacity the admiral ran past the fort and, allegedly shouting, "Damn the torpedoes. Full speed ahead," ordered his ships forward. Silencing the defending vessels, he took control of the bay though the city itself would remain in Confederate hands until the following spring.

As the armies in Virginia struggled in their iron embrace and the Union navy tightened the blockade and seized Mobile Bay, the forces in

Georgia executed an accompanying minuet of fire and movement. On May 5 Sherman's force, comprising the Amy of the Cumberland under Thomas, the Army of the Tennessee under McPherson, and the Army of the Ohio under soon-to-be Major General John M. Schofield, some 108,000 in all, marched south out of Chattanooga in coordination with Grant's move across the Rapidan.

Sherman's advance came as no surprise to the Confederate authorities. Months earlier, immediately after the loss of Chattanooga, Lee warned Davis of the menace to Georgia and its factories and provisions, saying the fate of the Confederacy was at stake. He urged that reinforcements be sent there from the many scattered garrisons along the Atlantic and Gulf coasts, and said presciently, "Upon the defence of the country threatened by [the coming enemy movement from Chattanooga] depends the safety of the points now held by us on the Atlantic."

The Confederate force defending Georgia, the Army of Tennessee, commanded by General Johnston, was now reinforced to a strength of 60,000. Two of its three corps were led by veteran corps commanders Hardee and Polk, the third by Lieutenant General Hood, who had distinguished himself in the fighting in Virginia and at Chickamauga. The army was entrenched along a commanding ridge about the town of Dalton, Georgia, situated on the Western and Atlantic Railroad twenty-five miles southeast of Chattanooga and seventy-five miles north of Atlanta. Johnston hoped to lure Sherman into making a costly direct assault on the position.

Sherman wisely rejected such a move, and instead forced Johnston out of position with a turning movement around his left flank that threatened the railroad behind him. These operations were repeated at Resaca fifteen miles below Dalton, with the Confederate army retreating on May 15 to Cassville twenty-five miles south of Resaca. Here Johnston set a trap for attacking Schofield's army, which temporarily was separated from the main Union force, but Hood, whose corps was supposed to spring the trap, failed to do so because of misinformation that he was being menaced from the rear by an enemy column. Johnston then withdrew his army to a stronger position at the Allatoona Pass, where the Etowah River and the railroad run through a rugged mountain ridge. Sherman responded with another turning movement by crossing the river west of the Confederate position and marching south toward the town of Dallas.

Still hoping to induce the Federals to make a disastrous assault, Johnston withdrew from the Allatoona Pass and occupied a position in the vicinity of Dallas and New Hope Church, directly in Sherman's line of advance. On May 25, unaware that the main body of the Confederate army was present, Hooker's corps of the Army of the Cumberland attacked and was repulsed. Yet Sherman avoided a general engagement. After three days of widespread skirmishing, he undertook to maneuver

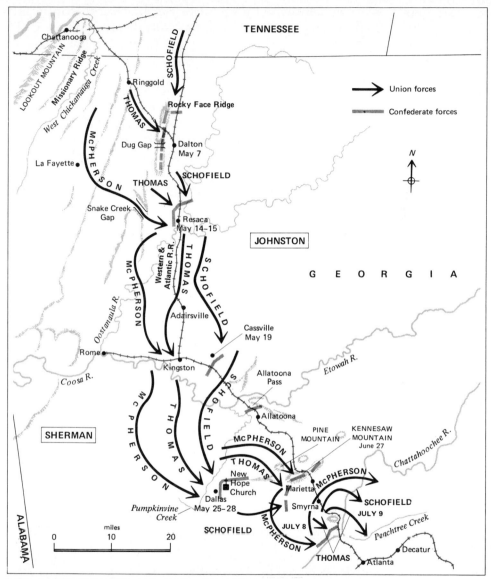

THE CAMPAIGN FOR ATLANTA, MAY–JULY 1864

his army in an envelopment of Johnston's right flank that would cut him off from the railroad, which was exposed by the Confederate move to the Dallas and New Hope Church area.

Alert to the threat to his lifeline, Johnston matched Sherman's moves, and by June 6 the two armies were again astride the railroad. With the Confederate right flank anchored on Kennesaw Mountain commanding the railroad just north of Marietta, and less than twenty miles north of Atlanta, and the remainder of the line curved back to defend the railroad against a Union thrust from the west, Johnston held a position of vital tactical and strategic importance as well as formidable defensive strength.

For two weeks Sherman probed and searched for a weakness in the Confederate line, then on June 27, believing the section at Kennesaw Mountain to be overextended and vulnerable, he made the kind of direct assault that Johnston had long invited. The result was predictable; the attack was repulsed with 3,000 Union casualties and only 800 Confederate losses. Sherman would not repeat this mistake.

Instead, he resumed his turning tactics by sending McPherson's force around Johnston's left flank to threaten the railroad in his rear. Johnston resumed his withdrawal and on July 4 established an entrenched line north of the Chattahoochee River at the point where the railroad crossed the stream. Sherman was now a scant ten miles from Atlanta, the most important rail center of the lower Confederacy; the river was the last serious natural obstacle between him and his immediate prize.

The Chattahoochee did not long deter the Union advance. Sherman now swung a column around Johnston's right flank, with Thomas on the 8th crossing the stream a few miles above the Confederate position and McPherson crossing farther up at Roswell. Johnston responded the following day by abandoning the line of the Chattahoochee and occupying a position behind Peachtree Creek and immediately north of the city. Sherman promptly began another turning movement around the Confederate right by sending McPherson to seize Decatur on the railroad running east to the Atlantic coast.

To this point the campaign had been conducted with great skill and prudence by both commanders. It was largely a campaign of marching, digging entrenchments, and constructing abatis—obstacles bristling with logs and tree limbs. Despite constant skirmishing and occasional engagements such as that at Kennesaw Mountain, casualties in both armies were remarkably light in comparison with the toll in Virginia. But Johnston had not been able to halt Sherman's steady advance, and the Confederates had run out of space for withdrawing if Atlanta was to be saved. Without a reckless frontal assault by Sherman, which he was not likely to make, or a successful counterattack by Johnston, the city was doomed.

There had been friction between Jefferson Davis and Johnston since the very beginning of the war. Never confident of Johnston's willingness to fight, Davis became increasingly impatient with a Fabian policy of yielding ground without a showdown battle. As Sherman neared Atlanta, Davis repeatedly inquired Johnston's intentions; the general, possibly fearing to divulge his plans lest they fall into enemy hands, replied

equivocally. On July 17 Davis took the fateful step of removing Johnston from command and replacing him with Hood.

Hood was a renowned fighter. He possessed extraordinary personal
courage, as attested by an arm disabled at Gettysburg and the stump of
a leg shot off at Chickamauga. He knew how to arouse his troops to
superhuman effort; his Texas brigade in Lee's army had often been the
spearhead of the assault. But from his cadet days at West Point, Hood
had held a reputation for rashness. Everyone, including Sherman, was
aware that Hood's elevation to command was the signal for an attack.

Significantly, Lee was averse to the replacement of Johnston with
Hood. In reply to Davis's inquiry, Lee offered a remarkably candid and
accurate evaluation of Hood. He said the Texan was a bold fighter, but
that his other qualities were in doubt, and added an ominous prophecy,
"We may lose Atlanta and the army too." Bruce Catton believed that
the removal of Johnston and the appointment of Hood in his place was
perhaps the gravest mistake made by either administration during the
entire war. This is a sweeping judgment. Other mistakes come to mind:
Lincoln's appointment of Hooker to command the Army of the Potomac, or Davis's decision to leave Bragg in command at Chattanooga.
But the elevation of Hood to lead the Army of Tennessee ranks high on
the list of errors.

Lee also told Davis that he yet hoped Johnston would be able to
strike a blow that would save Atlanta. If the city could not be saved,
said Lee, he supposed Johnston would fall back upon Augusta on the
border of Georgia and South Carolina, and, Lee advised, all available
Confederate cavalry ought to be set upon the Union line of communication. This was wise strategy. It would have kept a powerful striking
force on Sherman's flank, and would have put the Confederate cavalry
in the West to its most effectual strategic use. Sherman, because of his
deep respect for the Confederate horsemen, feared such a strategy. He
said the southern cavalry was superior to the Union cavalry both in
quantity and quality; he explained, "[The Confederate cavalry] will
travel a hundred miles where ours will ten."

But Lee's suggestion went unheeded. Hood was now in command
in Georgia. On July 20, following a plan which Johnston said he was
already considering, and taking advantage of a gap of three miles between the forces of Thomas and Schofield, Hood attacked Thomas on
his left flank in the battle of Peachtree Creek but was beaten off. Falling
back into the city's entrenchments, Hood sent Hardee's corps through
Atlanta to attack the left flank of McPherson's army three miles east of
the city. Hardee struck at noon on the 22d, while Major General Benjamin F. Cheatham's corps, formerly Hood's, made an assault directly
out of the entrenchments and up the line of the railroad to Decatur. In
these fierce actions, together known as the battle of Atlanta, the Confederates were repulsed with a loss of some 8,000 casualties. Union

losses, only half as numerous, included the death of the outstanding young commander—the top cadet in his West Point class—General James B. McPherson.

Sherman now reversed the direction of his thrust by sending the Army of the Tennessee, commanded by Howard in place of McPherson, in a wide three-quarter circle north and west and south, completely around the city of Atlanta. This move threatened Hood's one remaining important line of communication, the Macon and Western Railroad, which ran south from Atlanta and branched west to Montgomery and east to Savannah. In an effort to abort the move, Hood on July 28 attacked a portion of Howard's entrenched force in the battle of Ezra Church west of Atlanta but again was defeated with severe losses.

Still the coveted rail line was intact in Confederate hands. Sherman made repeated attempts to cut it with cavalry, only to be foiled by the brilliant action of Joseph Wheeler's horsemen. Eventually, after a month of siege and bombardment, Howard's infantry moved to seize the line at Jonesboro twenty miles south of Atlanta. On the last day of the month, in a final effort to protect it, Hardee with half of Hood's remaining troops attacked Howard's right flank division in the battle of Jonesboro and was beaten back. Meanwhile, Thomas and Schofield closed upon the railroad between Jonesboro and Atlanta.

Hood, with his army severely depleted by casualties and his communications virtually severed, marched that night along the Macon road southeast out of an Atlanta that was lit by the fires of blazing warehouses and shaken by the explosions of burning ammunition trains. The following day Sherman's lead units moved into the city. On September 2 he wired Halleck, "Atlanta is ours, and fairly won."

The capture of Atlanta was a tremendous Union victory in every sense of the word. It represented a clear tactical victory over one of the two major Confederate armies; it was a strategic victory as a successful part of Grant's comprehensive plan for simultaneous, coordinated offensives against the South. It placed in Union hands and deprived the Confederacy of one of the key communications centers and an important manufacturing center of the lower South. The capture also provided a powerful boost to Union morale at a moment when Grant's costly offensive in Virginia seemed indefinitely stopped; conversely, the loss of Atlanta by the Confederates struck a numbing blow to the southern spirit. Finally, the taking of Atlanta helped assure, if it was not decisive in, the reelection of Lincoln in the 1864 presidential race in the North.

His reelection was by no means a certainty. Only a master of the political arts could have weathered the storms of controversy and intrigue that swept the North throughout the Civil War. Fortunately for the Union cause, Lincoln met that qualification. By holding undeviatingly to his primary goal—preservation of the Union—while resorting to delay, equivocation, subterfuge, and compromise on other goals, he was able to contain if not control, the forces of opposition both in the Democratic party and within the ranks of his own party.

Much of the time the Republican opposition was the more formidable because large numbers of northern Democrats, the "War Democrats," supported the Lincoln administration and, in effect, merged with the Republicans under the name "Union party." Early in the war, however, the combination of reverses on the battlefield and unpopular measures such as military arrests and emancipation severely jeopardized Republican control of Congress. In the congressional elections of 1862 the Republicans were able to retain a slender majority only through victories in the border slave states, where voters were intimidated by threats and the monitoring of the polls by Union troops. The improving military situation and the changed popular attitude on emancipation and the enlistment of blacks as soldiers helped assure Republican success later in the war.

But many Republicans chafed at what they looked upon as Lincoln's ineptitude. Even his supporters shared this view to some extent. In November 1862 the *New York Times*, generally a friend of the administration, published editorials referring to its "inactivity and inefficiency," and to Lincoln's indecisiveness and willingness to accept alibis for failures. Led by the congressional Radicals in collusion with Secretary of the Treasury Chase, the Republicans after the disaster at Fredericksburg began to urge Lincoln to drop Seward, his chief confidant, who came to admire Lincoln as the strongest figure in the government, but who had been suspect in the eyes of the Radicals since his compromise efforts during the Fort Sumter affair. Their goal was a reorganized cabinet with Chase in command. Lincoln recognized the entire game as an attack on his own leadership. "They wish to get rid of me," he said, "and I am sometimes half disposed to gratify them."

He did not, however, gratify them. Instead, on December 20 he countered with a game of his own. He assembled a cabinet meeting with a committee of the disaffected congressmen, but with Seward, who had submitted a letter of resignation, absent. Lincoln assured the group of harmony within the cabinet, and that Seward was an essential member of the team. When Lincoln then called upon the cabinet to confirm this judgment, Chase found himself outmaneuvered and trapped into doing so. The next day, in his chagrin, he made the mistake of handing Lincoln his own letter of resignation. Lincoln rejected the resignation but kept the letter. He was exultant over the outcome of the confrontation; any further pressure to oust Seward would be equalized by the fear that Chase too would be ousted. Lincoln filed both letters and kept both men in the cabinet. He explained his advantage in rustic terms: "Now I can ride; I have a pumpkin in each end of my bag."

An uneasy harmony prevailed for months between Lincoln and the Chase-Radical faction. Eventually the harmony dissolved. Many administration measures during 1863 aroused criticism and doubt concerning

Lincoln's competence. Among these were the growth of federal intervention in state affairs, the mounting taxes and swelling national debt,
the continuation of military arrests, and the adoption of conscription.
Although the shocking Union defeats at Chancellorsville in May and
Chickamauga in September were more than redressed by the back-to-
back victories at Gettysburg and Vicksburg in July and finally at Chattanooga in November, the end of the war was nowhere in sight, nor
was the outcome yet clear.

The deepest rift between Lincoln and the Radicals occurred over the
question of reconstruction: how and under what conditions a seceded
state was to be reunited with the Union. Lincoln acted again according
to his interpretation of broad presidential authority and his conviction
that the seceded states were not actually out of the Union, but merely
out of their proper relation to it.

In December 1863 he announced his plan of reconstruction. It was a
remarkably lenient program, both because he still looked upon the
preservation of the Union as the primary war aim, and because he
hoped to weaken the southern will to resist by offering southerners an
easy and relatively nonpunitive way to regain their proper places in the
nation. The central features of the plan were its provision for the application in each state of a simple oath of allegiance to the Constitution of
the United States and the Union; and the promise that when the oath
was taken by a number of persons equal to one-tenth of that state's voters in the presidential election of 1860, permission would be granted to
establish a state government without slavery, which the president
would recognize as legitimate.

The Radicals firmly disagreed with Lincoln on all aspects of reconstruction. They looked upon the seceded states as having committed
"state suicide" or being "conquered provinces," and demanded a
strong congressional voice in the process of bringing the states back
into the Union. The announcement of Lincoln's plan kindled a movement in the Republican party to dump him in favor of Chase as the 1864
presidential candidate. With Chase's tacit if not explicit encouragement,
Senator S. C. Pomeroy of Kansas distributed a circular declaring Lincoln
could not be reelected and that Chase was the right man for the job.

The Lincoln supporters responded in a diatribe against Chase delivered February 27, 1864, in Congress by Brigadier General Francis P.
Blair, Jr. (nephew of the postmaster general), who, through Lincoln's
sleight of hand had left his command in Sherman's army to return temporarily to his seat in the House of Representatives. Again Chase offered his resignation from the cabinet; again Lincoln managed to talk
him into staying. Soon the "Chase for President" movement subsided.
But Chase's feelings toward the administration were too strong to be
contained. In late June the secretary again tendered his resignation.
This time, to his discomfiture, Lincoln accommodated him.

Nor did the unhappiness with the Lincoln leadership subside. The mounting cost of the war during the spring of 1864 added to the disaffection; in late May a group of Radical Republicans and some Democrats met in Cleveland, named themselves the Radical Democratic party, and nominated General Frémont on a platform calling for absolute equality of all men before the law and the confiscation and redistribution of rebel-owned property. As an overture to the Democrats, the platform also condemned military arrests and suspension of habeas corpus. However, Frémont was perceived as being forceful but unstable, the Radical parts of the platform were offensive to many northern voters, and no prominent Republican joined the movement. Consequently, it gained little momentum.

Assisted by a liberal use of patronage in the army command and in federal civilian jobs, Lincoln and his supporters were able to keep a firm hand on the party reins. Henry J. Raymond of the *New York Times*, chairman of the Republican National Executive Committee, Lincoln's "Lieutenant General in Politics," exercised a deft control when the Union (Republican) party convention met in Baltimore in early June. Lincoln was renominated for president, and his choice, the War Democrat Andrew Johnson of Tennessee, for vice president. The party platform expressed confidence in administration war measures, called for unconditional surrender of the Confederacy, and endorsed a constitutional amendment abolishing slavery. But it avoided any mention of racial equality and ignored the explosive issue of reconstruction.

The Radicals in Congress did not ignore the issue of reconstruction. Lincoln had proceeded with his 10 percent plan, and three states—Louisiana, Arkansas, and Tennessee—were moving to comply with it, along with Virginia where a loyal administration had been in existence within Union lines since early in the war. The preceding spring both Louisiana and Arkansas had adopted constitutions that met Lincoln's demands. To the extreme displeasure of the Radicals, these states had not enfranchised the former slaves, though Lincoln had written to the newly elected "loyal" governor of Louisiana: "I barely suggest for your consideration whether some of the colored people may not be let in— as, for instance, the very intelligent, and especially those who have fought gallantly in our ranks."

The Radicals countered in early July by passing the Wade-Davis bill (named after Senator Benjamin Wade and Representative Henry Winter Davis), which embodied their plan of reconstruction. It called for a majority of a state's voters to take an oath of loyalty to the Union, denied the vote to all persons who had voluntarily borne arms for the Confederacy, and prohibited slavery in any restored state. Though black suffrage was on the Radical agenda, they veered away from a demand for it in their reconstruction bill because it would have been unpopular with many northern voters, especially in states where it was not allowed.

With the war still raging and large areas in the southern states under Confederate control, the Wade-Davis requirements were immediately unattainable. To demand them was to delay reconstruction until
the war was over, which is actually what the Radicals desired. Lincoln
refused to sign the Wade-Davis bill and allowed it to die by pocket veto.
He explained in a proclamation that the program in the bill was suitable
for any state choosing to adopt it, but he refused to repudiate the reconstruction governments authorized in his own plan, and he denied
the authority of Congress to prohibit slavery in a state.

Furious, the Radicals responded by publishing a statement known
as the Wade-Davis Manifesto, which charged Lincoln with usurping authority and denounced his proclamation as the most "studied outrage
on the legislative authority of the people" that had ever been committed. Refusing to read the manifesto, Lincoln said, "To be wounded in
the house of one's friends is perhaps the most grievous affliction that
can befall a man."

Friction within the Republican party combined with the ghastly casualties of the summer, the apparent stalemate of the fighting, and the
mounting war weariness of the northern population to inflame the debate on measures for ending the struggle. Peace advocates, including
such prominent figures as Horace Greeley and Charles Francis Adams,
now called for renewed efforts along this line. Lincoln supported these
moves, even to the point of approving meetings with Confederate
agents and the visit of emissaries to Jefferson Davis, though he doubted
that anything would come of the meetings. Nothing did come of them,
but the aftermath of one of them had serious political consequences for
him.

Lincoln responded to Greeley's importunities by authorizing him to
meet with Confederate agents in Niagara Falls, Canada, to discuss
terms for ending the war. The meeting accomplished nothing; the Confederate agents were without authority, and Lincoln's terms were unacceptable to the Confederacy anyway. When word of the conference
leaked to the public, Lincoln felt obliged to reveal his instructions to
Greeley, which demanded the "integrity of the whole Union and the
abandonment of slavery." These terms were not new, but the explicit-
ness with which they were now presented, the length and severity of
the war, and the precariousness of the political situation combined to
make them decidedly untimely for Lincoln. In the words of V. Jacque
Voegeli, "It was one thing to argue in good times that emancipation
would shorten the war and help restore the Union, but quite another to
declare in a period of gloom that the fighting would not cease under
any circumstances until slavery was abolished."

A final movement now arose within the Republican party to jettison
Lincoln as the party nominee. Momentarily representing both Peace Republicans and Radicals, it sprang in large part from the conviction that

Lincoln could not be reelected. Thurlow Weed, the astute New York Republican editor and politician, wrote, "Lincoln's re-election is an impossibility." Henry J. Raymond wrote Lincoln saying, "The tide is setting strongly against us." Raymond perceptively analyzed the causes of the popular disaffection as being the apparent military stalemate and the administration's stand on emancipation. A number of Republicans, including Greeley, approved efforts to assemble a convention in Cincinnati for the purpose of nominating someone else, possibly Grant, Sherman, even General Benjamin F. Butler. But the convention never occurred, and the Republicans approached the election with increasing apprehension.

The Democrats hoped to capture the administration by seizing upon war weariness, the emancipation issue, and Republican discord along with Lincoln's alleged intransigence, incompetence, and authoritarianism. To succeed, the Democrats must win back their own numbers who supported the war—the War Democrats—without alienating the peace wing. They attempted to do so in a convention held August 29–31 in Chicago. Nominating the unemployed General McClellan to appeal to the War Democrats, the convention turned the writing of the platform over to the Peace Democrats led by the returned exile Clement L. Vallandigham. The peace plank was a clever equivocation that called for an armistice: "to the end that at the earliest possible moment peace may be restored on the basis of the Federal Union of the States." Conspicuously missing was any reference to emancipation.

At first the Democrats appeared to have struck just the right note. Greeley and other distinguished journalists continued to urge northern political leaders to replace Lincoln with a more promising candidate. Lincoln himself had already despaired of being reelected. Shortly before the Democratic convention he penned a letter for future use and, remarkably, prevailed on his cabinet to sign the back of it without reading it. The letter said: "This morning, as for some days past, it seems exceedingly probable that this Administration will not be re-elected. Then it will be my duty to so co-operate with the President elect, as to save the Union between the election and the inauguration; as he will have secured his election on such ground that he cannot possibly save it afterwards."

Lincoln was sorely tempted to retreat on emancipation. On August 17 he drafted a letter in which he reinterpreted his Niagara statement and indicated he would welcome an overture from the Confederate authorities proposing peace with reunion and saying nothing about slavery. Apparently, he never sent the letter. A week later, at Raymond's suggestion, he wrote authorizing a commission to go to Richmond and offer peace to the South on the sole condition of submission to the Union. All other issues—in other words, slavery—were to remain open for settlement "by peaceful means."

Convinced that Davis would reject this offer, Raymond hoped to disarm political critics who said the war was being carried on, not primarily to save the Union, but for the actual purpose of assuring emancipation. Again, Lincoln never sent the letter. After thinking it over carefully, he decided against it and explained to Raymond that the overture would be interpreted in the North as an abandonment of emancipation, which, he said, would be worse than defeat in the election: "it would be ignominiously surrendering it in advance."

Misgivings about Lincoln's reelection turned out to be groundless. He won the electoral votes of all the states except New Jersey, Delaware, and Kentucky, and received a popular majority of 55 percent. Also, the Republicans won sweeping victories in the contests for state legislatures and Congress. Possibly Lincoln and the other Republicans would have been reelected under any likely circumstances; the course of events during the last weeks of the campaign assured this outcome. Although McClellan minimized the Democratic peace plank and emphasized the preservation of the Union, the Republicans made political capital out of references to their opponents' "Copperhead platform." The soldiers' votes, whether taken in the field or back home on furlough—with furloughs freely granted—went largely to the Republicans. So did the votes of government employees, who were given the alternative of losing their jobs.

Perhaps the greatest reason for the Republican triumph was the determination of a majority of northern voters, particularly the soldiers, to fight the war to a complete victory, and a surge of confidence that the Lincoln administration was making genuine progress in doing so. Timely Union military successes, victory at Mobile Bay and in the Shenandoah Valley, and especially the capture of Atlanta, helped create this surge. George Templeton Strong believed the taking of Atlanta, coming when it did, was the greatest event of the war. Lincoln said the victories at Mobile Bay and Atlanta were achieved "under divine favor" and set aside a day of national thanksgiving.

XI

The Resurgent North

❖

Only rarely and peripherally did the civilian population of the North actually witness the war or feel the direct fury of it. To the minds of many citizens of the Union, the area of actual combat was a faraway and exotic land. Measured by the facilities of transportation and communications of the 1860s, the battlefields of the South were as remote to New Englanders as were those of Europe in World War II. In news time and immediacy, the Civil War battlefields were infinitely more remote and indistinct to northerners than were those of Vietnam to Americans a century later.

Despite the remoteness of the military campaigns, northerners felt the war keenly in a multitude of ways. The most poignant way came from the cost in casualties, especially the heavy death toll from both wounds and disease, which brought anguish and sorrow to hundreds of thousands of firesides. The absence of the additional hundreds of thousands of sons or husbands away in service created loneliness and anxiety at home and serious dislocations in the work force of farm or factory.

Added to these woes were the burdens of increased taxes, fluctuations in the value of the currency, price inflation, the reduced purchasing power of the laboring classes, and vicissitudes in business and domestic affairs. All combined with disagreements over war aims, opposition to many of the administration's war measures, and, late in the conflict, a numbing war weariness to stamp the imprint of the conflict deeply on the psyche of the North.

The North had responded to secession with shock and anger, along with a determination to stamp it out and preserve the integrity of the Union. The diarist George Templeton Strong doubtless expressed the majority attitude of the region in saying, "That termagant little South Carolina has declared herself out of the Union....O, for an hour of Andrew Jackson, whom I held (when I was a boy and he was 'taking the responsibility') to be the embodiment of everything bad, arrogant, and low." News of Fort Sumter provoked the wish that Charleston itself had been fired upon: "...that damnable little hornet's nest of treason deserves to be shelled. It's a political Sodom...." Strong accurately and hopefully predicted that the southern attack would fan the flames of abolitionism, and wrote: "John Brown would be worth his weight in gold just now. What a pity he precipitated matters and got himself prematurely hanged!"

The outbreak of hostilities, followed by Lincoln's proclamation and call for troops, had galvanized most of the northern population into a flurry of patriotic activity. Mass meetings, both planned and spontaneous, occurred in communities throughout the land. A Detroit editorial captured the mood to say: "The Star-Spangled Banner rages most furiously. The old inspiring national anthem is played by the bands, whistled by the juveniles, sung in the theatres... sentimentally lisped at every piano by patriotic young ladies, ground out on church organs... hammered on tin pans by small boys, and we had almost said barked by dogs. The banner itself... floats proudly and beautifully in every direction... from the roofs of houses... from all public places.... Omnibus men decorate their vehicles and horses."

Individuals who were or had been sympathetic or equivocal toward the South or secession now felt the sting of popular disapproval, and were sometimes ridden out of town on rails, pelted with eggs, or ostracized by their associates. Men and boys who exhibited too little patriotism were shunned and shamed by the women and girls, who, according to Professor Bell I. Wiley, were the most spirited of patriots. Dissenters were brought into line or silenced.

Outspoken opponents of Lincoln and his policies now found it the better part of valor to close ranks against the rebellious South. Among the most notable examples of this change was Democratic Mayor Fernando Wood of New York City, who earlier in the secession crisis had gone so far as to suggest that New York ought to take advantage of the situation to become a free city. Now he recommended to the city council an appropriation of $1 million to equip Union regiments. Prosouthern or wavering newspapers, including one owned by Wood's brother, were visited by patriotic crowds and obliged to fly the stars and stripes.

The most fervent patriotic demonstrations were those involving the raising of regiments for the army, the enlistment of volunteers into these units, and their departure for rendezvous, training, and deployment. Enlistments usually occurred at mass meetings, picnics, or other public gatherings, with military music by brass bands, impassioned oratory, and appeals from the women to induce the men to sign up. The entraining or embarkation of the completed units at the railway depots or steamboat landings was accompanied by similar ceremonies, often featuring an address by the state governor or some other prominent official, and the presentation of the regimental colors by women of the community.

Early in the war the uncertainties and dislocations of secession caused business stagnation and spread a general economic depression throughout the North. But within a few months the region's industries were astir from the immense government war purchases combined with elevated tariffs against foreign competition. At the same time, northern farmers, processors, and shippers received and filled unprecedented orders of produce for the army and for Europe, where crop failures in Great Britain and shortages on the continent created an unusual demand. In 1862, as one example, the city of Chicago shipped out almost twice as much grain and flour as it had shipped in 1860, along with comparable quantities of beef and pork. Other cities of the Northwest reported similar sales.

Fortunately for the Union, its farms throughout the war produced bumper crops that amply supplied both domestic and foreign needs. In the absence from the farms of hundreds of thousands of male laborers, the recently invented American agricultural machinery such as the McCormick reaper made a significant contribution to the production of this bounty. But the women and boys left at home also contributed vitally by taking the places usually occupied by men on the reapers and mowers and at the plows and hoes. According to the *Detroit Free Press* in 1864, a great part of the corn produced in Michigan that year was cultivated by women.

All elements of American industry burgeoned from the purchases of arms and the panoply of equipment for waging war on the grand scale. Virtually every industrial product was in demand, from guns of all calibers, ammunition, swords, and bayonets to locomotives, iron rails, shoes, and canned desiccated vegetables. The Pennsylvania iron industry doubled its output of rails, and with Pittsburgh at the forefront the state became the premier iron producer of the nation. The construction of buildings both for business and residences went up constantly, creating an insatiable demand for lumber and all other kinds of materials. What the *Chicago Tribune* wrote of its area could have been said of any other northern city: "On every street and avenue one sees new buildings going up, immense stone, brick, and iron business blocks, marble palaces and new residences everywhere.... The unmistakable signs of active, thriving trade are everywhere manifest...where the enterprise of man can gain a foothold."

Bold and resourceful captains of industry and business came to the top. Corporations multiplied, the stock market soared, New York emerged as the nation's undisputed financial capital. Many heralded American fortunes and companies had their beginnings in sales to the army at this time. Philip D. Armour, then in his early thirties, reaped a $2 million profit by purchasing pork low and selling to the army at a previously established high contract price. Clement Studebaker built and sold wagons to begin the accumulation of the capital that eventually would produce and market one of the world's most famous automobiles. Collis P. Huntington negotiated government subsidies for the development of the Central Pacific Railroad. Although the young John D. Rockefeller, Andrew Carnegie, and J. P. Morgan did not become financial titans during the war, they did have experiences and learn lessons then that pointed them in the direction they were soon to go.

The truly spectacular profits went to a relatively few entrepreneurs, but the flourishing businesses, high dividends, and full employment spread an extraordinary prosperity throughout much of the northern population. The *New York Times* commented in 1864 that in the midst of a gigantic war the people of the North were never better fed, sheltered, or clothed.

Speculation in commodities became both a business and a pastime, and shrewd or lucky operators grew rich overnight. Fluctuations in the value of government securities in relation to gold invited gambling that made and squandered fortunes in the gold market. The progressive rise in the tax on newly manufactured whiskey, but not on stocks already in existence—levies lobbied and logrolled through Congress—yielded the owners of the extant stocks a profit of $100 million.

Lincoln and the top civilian and military officials were, with the exception of Secretary of War Cameron early in the war, men of scrupulous honesty. But hardly a government agency escaped the taint of corruption at the lower levels. Countless scandals arose out of an illicit cotton trade with Confederate brokers. Colonel Andrew Jackson Butler, brother of General Benjamin F. Butler, with his headquarters in New Orleans, was believed to be one of the most flagrant culprits in the cotton traffic; the Treasury Department agents that swarmed after General Banks's expedition up the Red River in the spring of 1864 were accused of similar activities.

General Grant at one time became so exasperated by the conduct of traders in his department, many of whom were Jews, that he issued an ill-advised order banning all Jewish traders. Lincoln was obliged to revoke it. But the president was painfully aware of the dark side of American democracy at war, and he once explained in striking metaphors the necessity of extraordinary measures of search and seizure to restrain contraband trade with the Confederates. "Every foul bird comes abroad," he wrote, "and every dirty reptile rises up."

Pleasure and diversion irresistibly lured a people with unaccustomed amounts of money in their pockets and excited by the intoxication of war or seeking escape from the grim news of the battlefields and casualty lists. "This war," wrote a correspondent of the London *Times,* "has brought the levity of the American character out in bald relief. There is something saddening, indeed revolting, in the high glee, real or affected, with which the people here look upon what ought to be, at any rate, a grievous national calamity. The indulgence in every variety of pleasure, luxury, and extravagance is simply shocking." Late in 1863, at a time of Union military success, Assistant Secretary of State Frederick W. Seward wrote, "Gayety has become as epidemic in Washington this winter as gloom was last winter....people are inclined to eat, drink and be merry."

Every place of amusement was thronged with customers. Grand opera, theaters of both high and low drama, blackface minstrels, dance halls, race courses, P. T. Barnum's museum of curiosities in New York City, and such renowned watering places as Saratoga and Lake George, New York, all were in full swing. The popular English actress Laura Keene played to sold-out houses; a favorite role was in the comedy *Our American Cousin*. Picnics featuring baskets piled high with food crowded the parks and groves. One of the more spectacular social occasions of the war was the marriage in Grace Church, New York, of the mock "General" Tom Thumb (Charles S. Stratton, a celebrity midget in Barnum's museum) to his diminutive bride, Lavinia Warren. Many prominent figures, including General Burnside, were in attendance. Another famous event was a grand ball given in New York City in honor of the officers and men of the Russian naval fleet that anchored there late in the war, a visit looked upon as a friendly gesture by the czar's government.

The styles blossomed. A correspondent wrote from Saratoga, "Of fashions here there is no end." He spoke of women's gowns "just from Europe" that had cost the wearers as much as $4,000, and he reported caustically, "Girls, none too young to be in the nursery, make their toilettes three or four times a day, having hats and gloves for each dress, and assume affectations that would disgrace an actress at the Bowery." He was describing conditions at one of the nation's top pleasure resorts; not many other places, if any, would have matched Saratoga in the plumage and preening of its clients. But countless others emulated it.

The Civil War, like all wars, brought a relaxation of private as well as public morals, if not in fact, at least in appearance and in the awareness of social critics. Gambling, drinking, and philandering were favorite targets of their comments. "In flirtation," said the Saratoga observer, "the married women are decidedly the most au fait; in fact, from the manner of a certain set of New York fashionables, one would suppose that he had dropped into one of the Spas of Europe....What the women spend in dress, the men spend in 'liquoring up,'...in horses and in gambling."

Prostitution waxed in the cities and especially those places near the army bases and camps. Professor Wiley has written that the mobilization of men for military service was paralleled by a mobilization of women for pandering to their grosser appetites. Every city had its "tenderloin" district, and frequently the prostitutes plied their skills at large. A Cincinnati newspaper complained they were so rampant in that city that they were "elbowing all decent women from the public promenade." New York, Chicago, and Boston were said to be swarming with women of loose virtue. Washington perhaps exceeded all other communities in their prevalence. "Entire blocks on the south side of Pennsylvania Avenue were devoted to the business [of prostitution]," wrote the historian Margaret Leech, and she quoted an eponymic pun that was destined to become famous: "One whole section [of the area] was christened Hooker's Division."

Many northern leaders and observers agreed with the newspaper critics in expressing shock and dismay at the extravagance, garishness, and unseemly gaiety that prevailed in numerous quarters. One commentator remarked: "It makes one's heart sick to see the folly which reigns triumphant....One would hardly think...that the country's heart was being torn asunder." The respected poet and journalist William Cullen Bryant, writing in the *New York Evening Post,* sternly reprimanded his fellow northerners' wanton indulgence in luxury. "What business have Americans at any time with such vain show, with such useless magnificence? But especially how can they justify it to themselves in this time of war?...Is there nothing worthier than personal adornment in which to invest their means? Are there no enterprises open to these men of fortune which would benefit the country and their fellows as well as themselves?"

The 340,000 free blacks in the Union, especially the 222,000 in the nonslave states, enjoyed at least a small measure of the prevailing prosperity. Many job opportunities that were traditionally closed to them were opened by the increased demands for labor. But the blacks had interests in the Union war effort that transcended material gain. Their leading spokesman, the eloquent orator and journalist Frederick Douglass, himself a former slave, had long seen in the power of the federal government a source of hope for curbing if not eliminating slavery. From the beginning of the conflict Douglass had urged that emancipation be made a foremost war aim. He represented the black community generally in feeling a natural sympathy for their enslaved kinsmen, and also in believing that emancipation would tend to erase the stigma of bondage which most white Americans associated with the black race.

Douglass especially believed that service in the Union military forces would generate respect for the blacks and earn them the full rights of citizenship. His was one of the strongest voices importuning Lincoln to employ black fighting men. After the president did so, Douglass took a leading role in urging young blacks to enlist. "In your hands [the] musket means liberty," he told them. He went on to imply that if their constitutional rights should be denied them after the war ended, they might use their arms to guarantee those rights. More then 34,000 free blacks went into the Union forces where by their conduct they earned the respect, and at times gained the admiration, of their white fellow soldiers.

Yet, as already seen, blacks in the armed forces suffered from a great variety of discriminatory practices throughout the war. So did

FREDERICK DOUGLASS
(Library of Congress)

northern blacks who remained at home. Racial antipathies ran too deep
to be eliminated in such a brief period and in the midst of such conditions. Inflamed by the war and, among many whites, by the government policies of emancipation and the employment of blacks as soldiers
and sailors, these antipathies broke into open hostility and violence in a
number of cities, reaching a peak in the New York riots of July 1863.
Black gains in employment too often proved to be temporary when
whites returned from the army.

   But emancipation and military service by the blacks did begin to improve their lot in the northern society. At the beginning of the war only
five northern states, all in New England and containing but 6 percent of
the free-state black population, permitted blacks to vote. They also bore
many other legal and extralegal disabilities. During the war the leading
abolitionists urged the northern states to grant full civil rights to blacks,
and pointed out the inconsistency of demanding rights for them in the
South while denying them at home. A number of states removed many
of the legal restrictions. A number of states also provided for referenda

on the question of extending the vote to blacks; two states, Iowa and Minnesota, approved black suffrage shortly after the war. Still, the vast majority of the northern blacks remained disfranchised until the adoption in 1870 of the Fifteenth Amendment to the Constitution.

Despite the remaining restrictions, the wartime experience of the northern blacks strengthened their sense of ethnic community and left them with an enduring pride in their accomplishments in support of the war effort and in pursuit of its goals. Ultimately, their aspirations for full citizenship under the law would be fulfilled. But this awaited another time and another set of circumstances.

The war affected northern women in many special ways. It gave them a multitude of new employment opportunities besides the additional demands it made for their work on the farms. The immense government orders for equipment opened to women more than 100,000 jobs in factories, sewing rooms, and arsenals; many of these jobs were of the kind traditionally monopolized by men. The absence of men who were now in uniform allowed women to enter the teaching profession in far greater numbers than ever before. Scattered throughout the country were women teamsters, steamboat captains, pawnbrokers, bankers, brokers, morticians, saloon keepers, and boardinghouse proprietors.

The war also helped to admit women into government employment, particularly through the policies of the Treasurer of the United States, Francis Spinner, who by 1865 was using 447 women in Washington alone. Gradually other government departments took women into their ranks. Although the women in the Washington offices of the government received compensation equal to that of the men, most of the women employed in "men's jobs" in private industry and business faced discrimination in pay and working conditions. They especially encountered the jibes, rude practical jokes, and bullying of their male co-workers. At the end of the war, the women were the first to be dismissed, especially as the armies were disbanded and veterans returned to the work force.

Understandably, the women who became the most famous through their wartime work were the nurses. In the beginning of the war all army nurses were males, and there was a strong prejudice against the use of women in these jobs. But the extraordinary wartime needs of the armed forces combined with the zeal of the women to break down the barriers. Throughout the war the renowned New England reformer Dorothea Dix served the Union army as superintendent of women nurses, a job of great responsibility, especially after Surgeon General William A. Hammond ordered that at least one-third of all nursing positions be filled by women.

Among the most famous nurses of the war was Clara Barton, who worked as superintendent of nurses for the Army of the James and years after the war led in organizing the American Red Cross, which

she served as president for almost a quarter-century. Another acclaimed nurse, one of the many who worked with the United States
Sanitary Commission, was Mary Ann Bickerdyke, a middle-aged
widow from Ohio. She became so well known for her no-nonsense efficiency and authoritativeness that on one occasion when an army surgeon incurred her displeasure and appealed for General Grant's intervention, the general is quoted as saying: "My God, man, Mother
Bickerdyke outranks everybody, even Lincoln. If you have run amuck
of her I advise you to get out quickly before she has you under arrest."

Despite the many wartime gains made by women in employment
and the many contributions made by them to the war effort, those who
hoped for immediate gains in legal and political status were doomed to
disappointment. In 1863 the leaders of the prewar women's rights
movement, including Susan B. Anthony, Elizabeth Cady Stanton, and
Lucy Stone, organized the Women's Loyal League dedicated to persuading Congress to enact the Thirteenth Amendment abolishing slavery everywhere in the United States. They hoped to link women's
rights to emancipation and ultimately to black suffrage. But their hopes
for women's suffrage were soon blasted; another half-century would
elapse before these aspirations were fulfilled.

Notwithstanding such setbacks, the wartime experience of northern
women broke them forever out of the sphere of activity that was traditionally reserved for women only. Long after the war, Clara Barton declared that it had accelerated the cause of women by at least fifty years;
Julia Ward Howe said that after being engaged in the countless activities that accompanied the war, the American woman refused to return
to her "chimney corner life of the fifties." An eminent authority on the
wartime role of both northern and southern women, Mary Elizabeth
Massey, has concluded that the war did serve as an important "springboard" for the advancement of women in American life.

One portion of the northern society, the wage laborers in the factories, shops, and arsenals, on railroads, wharves, and other public facilities, and in the construction industry, did not enjoy the general afflu-
ence of the period. Wages rose more slowly than the soaring prices of
necessities, at times dropping more than 30 percent below the level of
inflation. Many workers, especially women whose husbands were in
service, and unskilled European immigrants, endured genuine hardship. There was serious labor unrest, particularly among the immigrants, many of whom were cool or hostile toward emancipation and
other war measures.

Labor attempted to cope with the emergency by reviving the movement for collective action, which was moribund at the outbreak of the
war. Skilled workers such as locomotive engineers, tailors, and brick
masons—69 occupations in all—formed themselves into unions which
by the end of the struggle counted some 300 local groups. An ineffec-

tual effort was made to consolidate these into a national organization calling itself the International Industrial Assembly of North America.

These activities met with sharp antiunion legislation by the state governments, and the unrest led to a number of strikes. When strikes occurred in industries directly affecting the war effort, the Lincoln administration moved with alacrity and severity to suppress them. Troops were dispatched to break a strike in the Parrott cannon factory at Cold Spring, New York, and the labor leaders there were arrested and held in a military prison. In a number of instances, commanding generals prohibited strikes within their theaters of operation and enforced the orders by military arrests. Troops broke a strike of coal miners in Pennsylvania; the government seized and ran the Reading Railroad in that state. Arrested army deserters under military guard unloaded transports at New York City when the longshoremen struck. Troops were sent from Gettysburg to suppress the rioting that occurred in New York City, a state of affairs brought on partly by opposition to conscription but also in protest against the use of blacks as strikebreakers.

European radical theorists viewed the Union war effort as a crusade in behalf of the proletariat. Late in the war Karl Marx, the famed expositor of classic communism, wrote to Lincoln, hailing him as a son of the working class who was engaged in a "matchless struggle for the rescue of an enchained race and the reconstruction of a social world." According to Marx, the workingmen of Europe were sure that "as the American War of Independence initiated a new era of ascendancy for the middle class, so the American anti-slavery war will do for the working classes." Marx failed to anticipate that the Union victory actually would represent a triumph for American capitalism as well as for American nationalism. Emerson D. Fite concluded in his thorough study of social and economic conditions during the conflict: "The war closed with labor still regarding itself as aggrieved and persecuted, still arrayed against capital, still on the defensive and probably, from the standpoint of labor alone...worse off than in 1860."

If a rapacious or irresponsible minority took advantage of the war to make exorbitant profits, resort to wine, women, and song, and flaunt their finery, the great majority of the northern citizens turned their energies to the dedicated support of the war effort. Volunteer groups undertook a great variety of activities for raising money for the Union cause; women formed Ladies' Aid Societies that busied themselves with making bandages, shirts, underwear, bedclothes, towels, and other needed items for the soldiers. Charities both for the soldiers and their families sprang up. State and local governments created homes for soldiers incapacitated by wounds or disease and orphanages for the children of soldiers who died in the war. Great sums of money and quantities of food were collected and dispensed to the families threatened with destitution by the enlistment or conscription of their breadwinners.

The most noteworthy charity organizations were national and private in character and ministered directly to the soldiers themselves. The United States Sanitary Commission, under the presidency of the influential New York preacher Dr. H. W. Bellows, raised immense quantities of money through donations and the staging of "sanitary fairs" and lotteries. With its numerous warehouses and widespread network of agents and laborers, the commission provided soldiers with fruit and vegetables to enrich their diet and with countless other commodities not issued by the government, dispatched physicians to the army hospitals to inspect and report on their conditions, and provided surgeons and nurses to supplement the army medical personnel. The commission has been called the forerunner of the modern Red Cross.

The United States Christian Commission, also supported by donations, built and staffed chapels in the army camps and distributed Bibles and religious tracts; its personnel were active in visiting, comforting, and caring for the wounded, sick, and dying in the hospitals. Other groups, anticipating the services of such World War II institutions as the United Service Organizations (USO), fed, assisted, and entertained thousands of transient soldiers who were on furlough or sick leave or were being transferred from one unit to another. Women were particularly active in this work. The most famous of these volunteer way stations, the Cooper's Shop in Philadelphia, gave hospitality to more than 87,000 men in uniform during a single year.

The nation's main cultural centers lay in the North, and because most of the individuals prominent in the region's literary and educational circles were abolitionist as well as nationalist in sentiment, they zealously supported the Union war effort with their emotions, tongues, and pens. Ralph Waldo Emerson switched quickly from a belief in local autonomy to an advocacy of "the absolute powers of a [national] Dictator"; he preached total war against the rebels and declared unconstitutional any negotiation with them, even including agreements about the exchange of prisoners and the sanctuary of hospitals, or truces for burying the dead on the battlefield.

The poet Walt Whitman, serving as a nurse in Union army hospitals, witnessed firsthand the effects of the fighting, an experience that Professor Daniel Aaron says strengthened the "mystic Unionism" of his postwar works. Historian Francis Parkman grieved because he was physically disqualified from military service. He welcomed the war, which, he said, "like a keen fresh breeze...has stirred our clogged and humid atmosphere."

Among the major writers, only Nathaniel Hawthorne and Herman Melville refused to join ranks with their fellows in unrestrained zeal for the Union cause. Both were opposed to secession and hoped for Union victory, but both were philosophical pessimists whose vision was focused on the dark side of man's nature, whether northern or southern. Hawthorne was something of a literary "doughface"; earlier he in fact had written a sympathetic biography of President Franklin Pierce, who wore the stigma of that epithet.

Hawthorne doubted that freedom would improve the lot of the blacks; he pronounced it "sentimental nonsense" to risk American lives to emancipate them. His view of the war caused Professor Aaron to dub him "Lonely Dissenter." Melville agonized over the war's terrible waste in lives, questioned the necessity of the devastations practiced late in the conflict, and recoiled from the mechanization of society implicit in a northern victory. In Aaron's words, Melville employed the conflict to write "a parable of human blindness."

No great and lasting war novels or poetry appeared during the war, though an abundance of perfervid patriotic verse was written. The war poems composed later by major writers, except for such works of Whitman as "Drug-Taps" and sections of his most famous paean to democracy, "Leaves of Grass," were remote in perception as well as place and time. Of James Russell Lowell's "Harvard Commemoration Ode," Aaron says, "The War looms like a splendid abstraction. The fallen soldiers appear dimly through the fog of sentiment. The poet's anguish is diluted in rhetoric."

John Greenleaf Whittier's Quaker religion perhaps inhibited him from composing a corpus of true war poems. He did, however, in a small book entitled *In War Time and Other Poems* celebrate national success, and especially emancipation.

> Not as we hoped; but what are we?
> Above our broken dreams and plans
> God lays, with wiser hand than man's
> The corner-stones of liberty.

One of his poems was touched with fire. "Barbara Frietchie" was the ballad of an incident in which an elderly woman was alleged to have risked her life displaying the national flag during the southern invasion of Maryland. According to the poem, a famous Confederate intervened to save her.

> Up the street came the rebel tread,
> Stonewall Jackson riding ahead.
>
> .   .   .   .
>
> "Shoot, if you must, this old gray head,
> But spare your country's flag," she said.
>
> .   .   .   .
>
> "Who touches a hair on yon gray head
> Dies like a dog! March on!" he said.

One war novel—John W. De Forest's *Miss Ravenel's Conversion from Secession to Loyalty*—drew upon the author's combat experiences to re-create battle and hospital scenes with harrowing realism. Even so, according to Aaron, no novelist in more than a century since the war has been able to capture the common soldier of the struggle so vividly as has the historian Bell Wiley in his books *The Life of Johnny Reb* and *The Life of Billy Yank*.

The most impressive writing done by a northerner during the war was that of the diarist George Templeton Strong. A lawyer by profession, he served as treasurer of the United States Sanitary Commission, a position that brought him in touch with Lincoln, Seward, Stanton, and Grant, and gave an unusual depth to his perspective on the conflict.

Strong produced the most readable and most perceptive account of northern attitudes and emotions behind the lines. In Aaron's words, it "unfolds like a historical novel." Upon news of the Union defeat at Second Bull Run: "It has been a day of depressing malignant dyspepsia.... we the people have been in a state of nausea and irritation all day long....Stonewall Jackson (our national bugaboo) about to invade Maryland, 40,000 strong." Upon the news of Lee's surrender: "...the rebel army of the Peninsula, Antietam, Fredericksburg, Chancellorsville, the Wilderness...and other battles, has ceased to exist....God be praised." Upon the surrender of the last Confederate forces: "PEACE. Peace herself at last....So here I hope and believe ends, by God's great and undeserved mercy, the chapter of this journal I opened with the heading of War on the night of April 13, 1861."

Wartime music in the North added an immense patriotic dimension to the sentimental themes that were already strong in the music of the times. The most popular pieces blended the two elements. Most of the songs were composed by professional songwriters. Among the favorites was "Tenting on the Old Camp Ground," by Walter Kittredge.

> We're tenting tonight on the old Camp ground
> Give us a song to cheer
> Our weary hearts, a song of home
> And friends we love so dear.
>
> .   .   .   .
>
> Tenting tonight,
> Tenting tonight,
> Tenting on the old Camp ground.
>
> .   .   .   .
>
> Dying tonight
> Dying tonight
> Dying on the old Camp ground.

The most prolific, and possibly most popular, songwriter was George F. Root. Among the favorites produced by him were "Just Be-

fore the Battle, Mother," "Tramp! Tramp! Tramp!" and "The Battle Cry
of Freedom," which was perhaps the most stirring of all the Union
marching songs.

> Yes we'll rally round the flag, boys, we'll rally
>   once again,
> Shouting the battle cry of Freedom,
> We will rally from the hillside, we'll gather from
>   the plain,
> Shouting the battle cry of Freedom.
>
>   .   .   .
>
> The Union forever, Hurrah, boys, Hurrah!
> Down with the traitor, up with the star;
> While we rally round the flag boys, rally once again,
> Shouting the battle cry of Freedom.

The marching song most suggestive of the war mission of emancipation, "John Brown's Body," was anonymously and spontaneously
composed and set to a traditional air. Julia Ward Howe adapted its melody to lyrics that came to her in a midnight flash of inspiration after
witnessing a review of troops in Washington. Her "Battle Hymn of the
Republic," fusing martial ardor with moral passion, became the immortal song of the Union.

> Mine eyes have seen the glory of the coming of
>   the Lord;
> He is trampling out the vintage where the grapes of
>   wrath are stored;
> He hath loosed the fateful lightning of His terrible
>   swift sword:
> His truth is marching on.
>
>   .   .   .
>
> Glory! Glory Hallelujah! Glory! Glory Hallelujah!
> Glory! Glory Hallelujah! His truth is marching on.

The northern press was, with some exceptions already noted, free
to express its views on the war and on the administration's measures
for waging it. The vast majority of the newspapers staunchly approved
the goal of crushing secession, and the Republican press, including
such influential newspapers as the *New York Times*, the *Philadelphia Inquirer*, the *Washington Chronicle*, and the *Chicago Tribune*, was generally
favorable to the Lincoln administration and its measures, though even
the *Times*, which may be considered an unofficial voice of the administration, was critical of what it considered shortcomings. The *Chronicle*
was perhaps the nearest thing to an administration mouthpiece.

The *New York Daily Tribune*, edited by the gadfly of reform, Horace Greeley, and the *New York Evening Post*, edited by the austere and dignified William Cullen Bryant, were strongly abolitionist in their viewpoints and were at first critical of Lincoln because of his reluctance to resort to emancipation. As previously indicated, Greeley in 1864, believing Lincoln could not be reelected, joined the movement to replace him as the Republican presidential candidate.

Most of the Democratic press, including such newspapers as the *New York Express*, the *Cincinnati Enquirer*, the *Chicago Times*, and the *Detroit Free Press*, supported the goal of preserving the integrity of the nation, but opposed Lincoln and many of his measures for doing so, including emancipation, the employment of blacks as soldiers, conscription, and military arrests and the suspension of habeas corpus. The *Times* denounced the Emancipation Proclamation as "a wicked, atrocious, and revolting deed," which had converted a war for the Union into a struggle "for the liberation of three million negro barbarians and their enfranchisement as citizens."

James Gordon Bennett's *New York Herald*, a Democratic paper and the archetype of sensationalist "yellow journalism," at first equivocated in its loyalties. "[The *Herald*] is non-committal this morning," Strong recorded in his diary at the time of Fort Sumter. Then vitriolically, "It may well be upholding the Administration and denouncing the Democratic party within a week. It takes naturally to eating dirt and its own words (the same thing)." The *Herald* soon adopted a loyal tone, but not until it was threatened with a mobbing. The *New York Daily News* shared many of the views of the *Herald*; during the 1864 presidential campaign, the *Daily News* described Lincoln as the "compound of cunning, heartlessness, and folly that [the voters] now execrate in the person of their Chief Magistrate."

Every major newspaper sent reporters into the field to write narratives of the campaigns and battles. Inevitably, the editors generated strong opinions on strategy; Greeley and others were in part responsible for the repudiation of General Scott's "anaconda plan," and for the precipitous march on Richmond that ended in disaster at First Bull Run. The editors and reporters also developed favorites among the officers and wrote commentaries that were eulogistic or critical according to their views. General McClellan flattered the reporters, and they in turn named him the "young Napoleon." Henry J. Raymond made an all-night, and futile, trip from New York to Washington to warn Lincoln of Hooker's inadequacies.

Although the commanding generals attempted to exert censorship in matters of military security, they were unable to do so effectively. Lee partly relied on the northern newspapers for information on Union troop strength and movements and on proposed operations. Initial battle accounts, necessarily written in haste, usually contained a multitude of errors, and sometimes led to premature and unwise decisions by the higher authorities. Some of the accounts of the battle of Shiloh were especially overdrawn and sensational; according to J. Cutler Andrews, many of them were written by persons who came no closer to the battlefield than Cairo, Illinois, thus giving rise to the expression "Cairo war correspondent" for reporters who wrote from afar.

Photography, like the nation itself, came of age during the Civil War. Invented in France a quarter-century earlier, the camera, along with the press, became the great recorder of the war as many of America's then more than three thousand photographers worked to portray it. Hundreds of thousands of pictures, possibly in excess of one million, recorded the appearance of the war's leading figures and most haunting events, creating for posterity impressions that add an incalculable emotional dimension to this, the most emotional chapter of American history. The most famous name associated with Civil War photography is that of Mathew B. Brady, a New York photographic entrepreneur who, ironically, because of his nearsightedness, may not have taken a single war exposure, but whose cameramen, including James and Alexander Gardner, Timothy O'Sullivan, George N. Barnard, David B. Woodbury, T. C. Roche, and James Gibson, took thousands. Brady and his employees, plus innumerable other photographers, left an indelible legacy of war images.

Northern churches found themselves caught in the raging tides of wartime emotion. Their very spiritual values were steeped in American nationalism, and they viewed secession with abhorrence. Also, they were in the forefront of antislavery sentiment. Yet in the opening months of the war the martial atmosphere seemed to stifle religious impulses. Worship services and revival meetings palled before the pageantry of enlistment, mustering, and the cadenced marching of troops to stirring military airs. Additions to membership and attendance at assembly dropped; ministers and church publications complained of a dwindling interest in affairs of the soul. One observer commented that besides these distractions, "the suspense of the public mind, the exciting intelligence from time to time received, indeed the very idea of war, all tend to obliterate seriousness, and to close the ear and the heart to the appeals of the Gospel of Christ." Said another, "The humiliating confession must be made that the church and the world seem, to a great extent, to have fallen into a common slumber."

As the conflict lengthened and the novelty and initial excitement yielded to the deeper sentiments of national purpose, including that of emancipation, the religious impulse reasserted itself. Beginning in early 1863 and continuing throughout the struggle, revivals occurred with increasing frequency, and the churches became bulwarks of support for the many wartime charities as well as for the Union war effort itself.

Many of the most prominent religious leaders called for emancipation as a Union war aim and gave it their ardent support once it became so. The struggle brought to consummation the crusade of such famed abolitionist evangelists as Theodore Dwight Weld, who wrote, "I profoundly believe in the righteousness of such a war.... [We] exult in this mighty Northern uprising, notwithstanding its mixtures of motives, and base alloys and half truths, and whole lies, thrown to the surface by the force beneath...." Henry Ward Beecher said, "I utterly abhor peace on any such grounds [as acquiescence in secession]. Give me war redder than blood and fiercer than fire...." Upon word of early Confederate victories, he scored Lincoln for alleged incompetence: "At present, the North is beaten.... Let it be known that the Nation wasted away by an incurable consumption of Central Imbecility."

Abolitionist exhorters railed at Lincoln also for delaying in adopting emancipation. Beecher cried, "Never was a time when men's prayers so fervently asked God for a Leader! He has refused our petition!" Eventually these preachers changed their minds about Lincoln. After he issued the preliminary Emancipation Proclamation, Weld traversed much of the North, giving fiery addresses supporting the Union war effort and campaigning for Republican congressional candidates in the 1862 elections. At the war's end, Secretary Stanton honored a request by Beecher in sending a shipload of northern churchmen to Fort Sumter, where on the fourth anniversary of Major Anderson's surrender, Beecher stood in the masonry ruins under a billowing American flag and delivered a eulogy to the president he had previously denounced.

Northern schools and colleges suffered from the emotions of war in the minds of the students and younger faculty, many of whom quickly joined the army. The outbreak of hostilities created a variety of campus responses: at Bowdoin College the ringing of the chapel bell, display of national colors, waving of a skull-and-crossbones banner, and the beginning of military drills; at Oxford, Ohio, the organization of a college rifle company with 160 enlistments within minutes; at the University of Michigan the formation of five companies during the first few weeks of war. In the four years of the struggle the Yale enrollment dropped from 521 to 438; the Harvard enrollment from 443 to 385. The College of New Jersey (Princeton) instantly lost one-third of its 312 students when the southerners among them left to join the Confederacy.

But the demands on northern manpower were not sufficient to depopulate the educational institutions of the region. The majority of the students remained at their books; northern education, like the northern economy, actually flourished during the conflict. The campus rivalries in football, baseball, and boating—the most popular sport in the eastern colleges—went on without serious interruption. The schools received unprecedented financial support from both private philanthropists and state legislatures. Emerson Fite concluded that war was a stimulus to northern intellectual life.

All forms of northern resources, social, emotional, and cultural as well as physical and financial, came to the support of the war effort. Initially, the population answered the call to arms with fiery zeal; as the struggle progressed, it drew deeply upon the region's great reserves of strength in manpower, economy, and morale. Yet the length and severity of the conflict, and the harshness of the measures demanded for victory, tested the popular will almost, if not absolutely, to the limit. So marked was the northern war weariness in the late stages of the struggle that even the most unshakable patriots were close to despair of ultimate Union success. When at last it came, George Templeton Strong spoke for his entire generation when he wrote, "We have lived a century of common life since [the beginning of hostilities]."

XII

The Beleaguered South

❖

The South endured war to the full. All but two of the greatest battles of the Civil War and virtually all of the countless skirmishes were fought there. War took the lives of one-fourth of the young white men of the South, and of an indeterminable number of white women and of blacks, both men and women. War blasted and scorched many of the fields and woods and cities; it violated homes, churches, and schools, sometimes with destruction, often with vandalism and desecration. At first the pomp and glory of war united with the zeal of creating a new nation to kindle an intense enthusiasm among the southern people; later, the enormous waste of life and property, and finally the experience of defeat, saddened and humbled them and left them broken. The war burned deep scars on the face of the land; it burned even deeper scars on the emotions of the population. The twentieth-century southern poet Allen Tate has said the South retains a knowledge of history "carried to the heart." Certainly the memories of the war were carried to the heart. War permeated every fiber of southern life.

Southerners frequently answered the call to arms with wafting spirits and slight apprehension of the seriousness of their commitment. The novel and film *Gone with the Wind* faithfully capture the mood of the plantation hotbloods whooping in delight over the news of Fort Sumter. Wiser heads who warned of northern strength and southern weakness were scorned as timid old women; the Yankees were a race of peddlers too base to withstand the crucible of war. Many young southerners welcomed the occasion to demonstrate regional superiority on the battlefield; they feared the war would be over before they had an opportunity to smell gunpowder.

The South, like the North, went to war with both gaiety and determination. As the region bustled with the mustering of militia units and the formation of volunteer regiments, the civilian population turned to its own spontaneous and voluntary activities in a great folk movement to support the Confederate war effort. Parades and barbecues featured patriotic harangues by distinguished public figures urging the young men to enlist; wealthy planters, merchants, and professionals pledged money for the purchase of arms and uniforms. Every form of social event—balls, banquets, musicals, tableaux, charades, candy pullings—provided an occasion for raising funds for the cause. Women formed sewing societies and made uniforms; young girls rolled bandages.

Auctions, raffles, and drawings were favorite means of raising money for the Confederacy. An excellent example of this occurred when the women of the "Campaign Sewing Society" of Baton Rouge, Louisiana, reinforced their needlework by staging what they called a "tombola"—a lottery in which the prizes were donated and tickets sold for chances. "The hall soon was overflowing with minor articles from houses and shops," recalled a member of the society. "Nothing either was too costly or too insignificant to be refused. A glass showcase glittered with jewelry of all styles and patterns, and bits of rare old silver. Pictures and engravings, old and faded, new and valuable, hung side by side on the walls. Odd pieces of furniture, work-boxes, lamps and candelabra, were arranged here and there, to stand out in bold relief amid an immense array of pencils, tweezers, scissors, penknives, toothpicks, darning-needles, and such trifles. The stalls of the stable were tenanted by mules, cows, hogs, with whole litters of pigs, and varieties of poultry. The warehouse groaned under the weight of barrels of sugar, molasses, and rice, and bushels of meal, potatoes, turnips, and corn. As is ever the case, the blind goddess was capricious: with the exception of an old negro woman, who won a set of pearls, I can not remember any one who secured a prize worth the price of the ticket. I invested in twenty tickets, for which I received nineteen leadpencils and a frolicsome old goat, with beard hanging to his knees...." The tombola made a profit of $6,000—in Confederate treasury notes of quickly disappearing value.

Ceremony and pageantry accompanied the mustering and departure of volunteer units with such fiercely colorful names as the Georgia Hussars, the Tiger Rifles, the Gros Tête Fencibles, or the Southern Avengers. Martial music, florid patriotic orations and sermons, and flag presentations by hoopskirted belles marked these occasions. Said one young woman at such a time: "Receive then, from your mothers and sisters, from those whose affections greet you, these colors woven by our feeble but reliant hands.... And when this bright flag shall float before you on the battlefield... let it inspire you... with the brave and patriotic ambition of a soldier [who is] aspiring to his own and his country's honor and glory...." To which the color sergeant replied: "Ladies, with high-beating hearts and pulses throbbing with emotion, we receive from your hands this beautiful flag, the proud emblem of our young republic...." War was remote, the image of it romantic, when these stirring words were spoken.

War was not long remote from the South, nor did its romantic image long remain untarnished. By early 1862 the southern ports were under blockade, southern farms short of workers, and southern produce without adequate markets. Inflation became rampant as the supply of manufactured wares and other necessities shrank and the Confederate government launched repeated issues of paper currency. Prices soared. The cost of farm equipment, shoes, clothing, drugs, and the entire supply of goods usually imported by the agricultural South went out of reach to the majority of the population. In mid-1864, butter in Richmond cost $15 per pound, potatoes $25 per bushel, shoes $125 a pair, and trousers $100. This was at a time when Confederate private soldiers received $11 per month and armory workers $3 per day.

Kindled by these circumstances, corruption flourished, especially late in the war, as many southerners took advantage of the times to engage in speculation, hoarding of supplies, and "gouging" or profiteering. Trading with the enemy, particularly in cotton, became commonplace. As early as 1862 a Georgian wrote with exaggeration, but with a considerable grain of truth, that lying, swindling, and speculation were the only happenings in his part of the Confederacy; he ended with what he must have considered the most damning of all comments, "There is a heap of Yankees here as well as in [the] North." Toil, want, and demoralization were the measure of an increasing number of southerners as the war ground on.

In the absence of the customary family breadwinners, the wives and children along with the older men of the great non-slave-owning majority of the southern population ran the plantations and farms, improvised countless substitutes for the usual commodities of life, and played an indispensable part in sustaining both the armies and the crippled civilian economy. Food remained plentiful in rural areas beyond the immediate reach of the armies, though salt, the common meat preservative, became extremely rare and precious.

Wants were met by ingenuity, abstinence, and "making do." Quantities of salt were obtained from southern mines, salt springs, seawater through evaporation, and, sometimes, the boiling of salt-saturated soil dug from the floor of smokehouses. The word *Confederate* took on a new definition in the vocabulary of patriotic austerity: as an adjective it came to mean substitute, crude, obsolete, out-of-fashion. Bolted cornmeal became "Confederate" flour; a rope halter, a "Confederate" bridle; a farm wagon drawn by mules, a "Confederate" carriage; tin cups and spoons, "Confederate" silver; outmoded dresses, "Confederate" gowns. One plantation girl even tried eating hailstones in her desire for ice.

Perhaps the most acute shortage in the Confederacy was that of medicine. As early as 1862 the price of quinine was $20 per ounce; two years later it was $100 per ounce. To most citizens it was utterly unobtainable, a cruel privation in an area historically plagued by malaria. The Confederate government and some of the state governments set up medical laboratories. Various substitutes were devised out of extracts from common roots or herbs. A multitude of outmoded home remedies reappeared, some of them as barbaric as they were useless. As a treatment for diphtheria, one soldier wrote his wife recommending that the patient be smeared in lard and administered heavy doses of calomel twice a day. At least one planter stretched his supply of small-pox vaccine by using the scabs from his own family to vaccinate the slaves.

Life was even more austere for most southern city dwellers than for the farm families. The increase in city population because of the war industries, the inadequacies of southern transportation, and the stringencies of inflation combined to create extreme hardship among the urban masses. Whole families in Richmond and other cities lived in single rooms, using fireplaces for both warmth and cooking, and subsisting on corn fritters, boiled potatoes, and beans. Social occasions tended to become "starvation parties," with water as the only refreshment served. With dark humor, the citizens of Richmond said they once carried their money to market in their wallets and their groceries home in baskets; now they carried their money in baskets and their groceries in wallets.

The war blighted southern social life but did not kill it. Such folk amusements as picnics, barbecues, cornhuskings, hoedowns, and quilting parties continued in the rural areas, along with hunting, fishing, and attending religious revival meetings. During much of the war, it actually enlivened the social scene in the larger cities. Richmond was the social capital of the Confederacy as well as the political capital. Its population more than tripled, and its streets and buildings teemed with politicians, military officers, government clerks, factory workers, soldiers on furlough, and the families of soldiers in nearby camps or hospitals. The city also attracted great numbers of gamblers, confidence men, and prostitutes; casinos and brothels flourished in the rank atmosphere of war.

State and local governments appropriated funds for the support of families left destitute by the absence of husbands and fathers. Added to these official actions were those of many of the more fortunate private citizens, who donated money or produce, formed voluntary benevolence associations, and set up charity markets. But as the regional economy staggered under the burden of war and collapsed in the face of enemy invasion, these relief measures fell woefully short of the needs. Perhaps nothing could have met these needs. The Confederate government, preoccupied with the ominous military situation and hampered by the doctrine of state rights, made little or no attempt to do so. On one occasion, April 1863, Davis was obliged to call out troops to stop the looting of Richmond stores by a band of desperate women. Almost from the beginning of the war, hunger and want helped to blight civilian morale.

Areas in the presence of the armies endured the most severe tribulations of the war, and eventually the armies went almost everywhere in the region. Union soldiers and liberated slaves foraged and pillaged wantonly; ultimately Grant, Sherman, and other generals incorporated these activities into their strategy for victory. But southerners also learned a truth later expressed by the philosopher Santayana, that being host to a friendly army is almost as burdensome as being host to a hostile one. In January 1863 a Louisiana planter whose place had recently been the campsite of a Confederate brigade wrote: "Our troops have stripped me, by robbery, of nearly every resource for living from day to day, & what is in reserve for me from the common enemy, is yet to be ascertained.—From a condition of ease, comfort and abundance, I am suddenly reduced to one of hardship, want & privation." During the summer and fall of 1864 many of the citizens of Georgia reached the conclusion that Wheeler's Confederate cavalry was almost as much to be feared as Sherman's bummers.

The approach of a Union force caused great numbers of southerners with their slaves to abandon their homes and become refugees in areas not yet threatened by invasion. Thousands of residents of the upper South "refugeed" farther south; other thousands fled to Texas. This exodus bore many similarities to civilian flights in the wars of the twentieth century: roads jammed with wagons and carts piled high with belongings, and the exiles, white and black, trudging along the sides. Frequently organized into caravans, they camped in the open fields at night. Uprooted from homes left prey to vandalism and neglect, moving into makeshift quarters in strange places, and suffering exposure, privation, and anxiety, the refugees—especially the women and children among them—presented one of the saddest civilian spectacles of the war.

Anxiety and loneliness increased the hardship and mental anguish of families left behind as the armies maneuvered and fought for advantage. In areas where slaves made up a majority or a large part of the population, there was the nagging dread of servile insurrection. Mail had always been slow in the rural South; now it became glacially slow. Late in the war, letters from soldiers frequently required weeks to reach their destination, and sometimes then only by passing from hand to hand among friends and acquaintances.

Plantations and farms, always isolated, now became places of tormenting solitude. A woman wrote, "Lacking new books to read and mail to bring us letters, newspapers or magazines, there yet came into our lives an intenser interest in what was before us so constantly." It was, of course, the war that was before them so constantly. Another woman recalled living for months without any word of the outside world, only to discover that friends and relatives had died and been buried without her knowledge. A lonely planter recorded pensively in his diary, "Solitude is not good for man." But solitude was the lot of most of the residents of the great rural expanses of the Confederacy.

Law and order frequently broke down in isolated areas stripped of most of the male population and uncontrolled by either army. Deserters and guerrillas sometimes became marauders raiding and plundering the plantations and farms. Late in the struggle a woman in rural western Louisiana wrote: "For more than a year past, lawless men have been permitted to band themselves together, and roam at will... insulting, chastising, robbing, burning houses, murdering the families of our soldiers; and in some instances despoiling in the most brutal manner, wives, daughters and sisters of that which is dearer than life itself—their honor." Hers was a vivid description of the ugly backwash of war.

Finally, there was grief. The war filled the land with widows and orphans and heartbroken parents. A teenage girl who had moved to Texas as a refugee with her family recorded in her diary, "Never a letter but brings news of death." An anguished mother wrote, "Every breeze chants the requiem of dying heroes." A young wife whose husband fell on the ramparts at Port Hudson cried, "Why does anybody live when Paul is dead?—dead, dead, forever?" Richmond repeatedly witnessed funeral processions of Confederates killed in battle or dead of disease, occasions marked by riderless horses with boots reversed in the stirrups, and bands rendering the sweet, sad strains of the "Dead March" from Handel's oratorio *Saul*. An observant southerner of the time said grief killed as many southern women as bullets killed southern men. The South learned the tragic cost of war.

Although the Confederate authorities attempted no systematic employment of cultural and intellectual resources, southerners in religious, literary, artistic, and educational pursuits willingly lent their talents to the cause. Emory Thomas has written that the churches are the likeliest places to look for the origins of southern nationalism. Theologians traditionally provided religious arguments justifying the institution of slavery and the righteousness of southern independence. Believing the Lord would bless the South in its struggle against the alleged atheism and fanaticism of the North, they urged their followers to support the Confederacy with might and main; they importuned the soldiers of the South to demonstrate steadfastness and valor and, if necessary, to sacrifice themselves on the battlefield. Preachers "sounded the trumpets" that called the South to war.

Upon the secession of the South, the Episcopal, Presbyterian, and other Protestant churches followed the earlier course of the Methodists and Baptists in establishing southern denominations. Although the international character of the Catholic church prohibited a formal division along regional lines, southern Catholics supported the Confederacy as if they were in fact a separate body.

Religion played a powerful role in the lives of many Confederate civil and military leaders. Reared in a Baptist family, Jefferson Davis was not a formal church member at the outbreak of the war; in Richmond he was converted to the Episcopal faith, thus taking the final symbolic step in joining the southern aristocracy even as he enlisted religion in the cause of southern independence. He attended services regularly at St. Paul's Episcopal church, and he issued a number of proclamations setting aside special days for fasting and prayer on behalf of Confederate victory. Lee was a devout Episcopalian, Jackson an austere Presbyterian. Though both strove mightily for victory, both fervently believed the outcome of the war was in God's hands.

A number of Confederate generals were able to blend religion with war in one fashion or another. The Reverend Robert Louis Dabney, a renowned Presbyterian theologian, was a member of Jackson's staff. Brigadier General William Nelson Pendleton, a graduate of the United States Military Academy and Lee's nominal chief of artillery, was an Episcopal minister who early in the war carried out the ultimate religious-military theme by naming the guns of his battery Matthew, Mark, Luke, and John. He prayed for the souls of the enemy even as he ordered fire upon their bodies. Leonidas Polk, promoted in October 1862 to the rank of lieutenant general, also a graduate of the United States Military Academy where he was one of Albert Sidney Johnston's roommates, was the Episcopal bishop of Louisiana at the beginning of the war. Occasionally during the war he reverted to his ecclesiastical role. When Generals Joseph E. Johnston and John Bell Hood turned to religion in their efforts to stop Sherman in Georgia, the "Fighting Bishop" laid aside his uniform and donned his robes long enough to perform the rites of baptism.

Countless congregational prayer meetings begged favor on the southern effort, and great revivals swept the camps as civilian missionaries joined with the service chaplains in the work of saving souls and urging the Lord to uphold Confederate arms. Although religion failed to bring victory to the South, it unquestionably gave the region an immense measure of strength. Governor Pickens of South Carolina said the preachers converted the southern struggle for independence into a holy war. In reflecting on their role in sustaining the cause, a Confederate congressman said, "Not even the bayonets have done more." So intimate was the bond between religion and the Confederacy that the churches would long remain major custodians of the spirit of the defunct southern nation; the lost cause of the Confederacy, says Professor Charles Reagan Wilson, became the civil religion of the postwar South.

Though at first the southern press was divided in its views on the wisdom of secession, the overwhelming majority of the region's newspapers gave their unwavering support to the Confederacy once it was established. But Confederate journalism continued to exhibit the fiery individualism that led Professor Robert S. Cotterill almost a century later to say that virtually every editorial published in the Old South contained the ingredients of an invitation to a duel or a homicide. The editors disagreed vehemently in their views toward the Davis administration. Nathaniel Tyler's *Richmond Enquirer*, Richard M. Smith's *Richmond Sentinel*, and Richard Yeadon's *Charleston Courier* supported the president with such firmness that they were considered administration spokesmen.

Edward Pollard and John M. Daniel of the *Richmond Examiner* were just as relentless in their criticism of Davis and his measures. They accused him of incompetence and of arbitrariness amounting to military tyranny. The great old fire-eater, Robert Barnwell Rhett, writing in his son's *Charleston Mercury*, was implacable in his jeremiads against Davis. Ironically, the allegedly despotic Confederate government made no move to silence these hostile editors, though unquestionably they weakened the southern war effort by sowing seeds of doubt and dissension among the population.

Southern creative writers responded to the war with works of deep emotion. Poetry was especially popular. Though most of it was hastily written and tritely sentimental, that of the two South Carolinians, Paul Hamilton Hayne and Henry Timrod, gave true esthetic expression to the exaltation and sense of tragedy aroused by the events of the epoch. Haynes's "The Battle of Charleston Harbor" celebrated the heroic defense of that site. Timrod, the so-called poet laureate of the Confederacy, set forth his version of the distinctive southern virtues in the poems "The Cotton Boll" and "Ethnogenesis." In "A Cry to Arms" he issued a poetic call to action.

> The despot roves your fairest lands;
>   And till he flies or fears,
> Your fields must grow but armèd bands,
>   Your sheaves be sheaves of spears!
> Give up to mildew and to rust
>   The useless tools of gain;
> And feed your country's sacred dust
>   With floods of crimson rain!

His "Ode" to the Confederate dead buried in the Magnolia Cemetery at Charleston, written after the war, is said by the literary critic Ludwig Lewisohn to possess "the carved and cool completeness of Latin verse."

> Sleep sweetly in your humble graves,
> Sleep, martyrs to a fallen cause,
> Though yet no marble column craves
> The Pilgrim here to pause.

In seeds of laurel in the earth
The blossom of your fame is blown
And somewhere, waiting for its birth
The shaft is in the stone!

Southern wartime fiction lacked the spirit and literary quality of the best wartime poetry. Possibly there was not enough time for a significant novel to mature. The region's most famed prewar novelist, William Gilmore Simms of Charleston, was the author of moving works of fiction drawn from the history of South Carolina. He lived through the war and wrote some poetry and many editorials supporting the Confederacy. But his genuine talents seemed blighted by the conflict; he died in 1870 having attempted no major work on it. The best-known southern novel written during the war was Augusta Jane Evans's *Macaria; or, Altars of Sacrifice,* a complicated story of romance and family antagonisms in which the Confederate hero dies in the conflict as did the Greek heroine for whom the work was named.

Understandably, the grimness of life in the Confederacy inhibited the creation of a humorous literature that equaled in verve and color the tales of the renowned humorists of the Old South. But humor did not disappear. The most noteworthy professional humorist was "Bill Arp" (Charles H. Smith of Georgia), who aimed newspaper barbs at "Mr. Abe Linkhorn," asking him on one occasion to send some stinking codfish to drive away the skunks; or, suggested Arp, Secretary of State Seward might be sent in lieu of the fish. Arp also twitted southern leaders for their foibles, once quoting the secretary of the treasury as saying he was not sure whether the Confederate banknotes in circulation amounted to six hundred million dollars or six thousand million dollars.

The spontaneous humor of the nonprofessionals is more appealing today. For example, a bold headline in a Jackson, Mississippi, newspaper, which read: "RAILROAD ACCIDENT: The 10:00 o'clock train from Meridian arrived on time today." Or the naughtily clever poem written in reply to a request by one John Harrolson of the Niter and Mining Bureau for the women of Selma, Alabama, to save the contents of their chamber pots for use in making explosives. One verse said:

John Harrolson! John Harrolson!
   Do pray invent a neater
And somewhat more modest mode
   Of making your saltpetre;
For tis an awful idea, John,
   gunpowdery and cranky
That when a lady lifts her shift
   she's killing off a Yankee.

A gem of southern feminine humor rendered an account of a sermon in which the preacher used as his text the Old Testament story of Joseph the Hebrew slave's refusal to commit adultery with his Egyptian master's wife. When the preacher concluded that Joseph had resisted the greatest temptation known to man, a whimsical young woman in the audience said in a stage whisper, "Fiddlesticks!...Old Mrs. Pharaoh was forty."

The most abiding of Confederate literature was not produced as formal literature. It included the diaries and correspondence of talented southerners describing the epochal events of their times and the emotions kindled by them. A majority of the diaries were written by women, thus revealing many of the innermost thoughts and sentiments of a portion of the feminine element of the southern society. The most famous of these records is that of Mary Boykin Chesnut of South Carolina, whose husband was a former United States senator and who served most of the war as an aide to Jefferson Davis. Published later, it is one of the most readable and most perceptive of all works written by Confederates. Comparable diaries, also published later, were kept by Judith White McGuire of Virginia, Sarah Morgan Dawson and Sarah Katherine Stone, both of Louisiana, and Catherine Ann Devereux Edmondston of North Carolina.

Mrs. Chesnut described with refreshing candor the social affairs of the Confederate capital. She also discerned with remarkable insight and noted with admirable honesty one of the major weaknesses of the Confederacy, that of internal dissension. "We crippled ourselves—," she wrote, "blew ourselves up—by intestine strife." Unfortunately for posterity, in rewriting her work for publication some years later she destroyed a large portion of the original. Enough of it remains, however, to suggest that the revised copy is essentially accurate. C. Vann Woodward, in a carefully edited version, says Mrs. Chesnut demonstrated a "reassuring faithfulness" to her perceptions of her wartime experiences, and that in doing so, "She brings to life the historic crisis of her age...."

Possibly even more gripping than the Chesnut diary is a collection of the wartime letters and brief portions of journals left by the Charles Colcock Jones family of Georgia. Jones was a prominent Presbyterian minister and the author of a widely used catechism for the religious instruction of slaves. The Joneses were ardent secessionists. Applauding the withdrawal of South Carolina, the matriarch Mary Jones wrote her son: "When your brother and you were very little fellows, we took you into old Independence Hall; and at the foot of Washington's statue I pledged you both to support and defend the Union. That Union has passed away, and you are free from your mother's vow." Grateful to God for early Confederate victories, she faced the later trials and disappointments of the war with heartache but fortitude. After receiving the news of Gettysburg she wrote, "How long will this awful conflict last? And to what depths of misery are we to be reduced ere the Sovereign Judge of all the earth will give us deliverance.... I can look extinction for me and mine in the face, but submission never!"

Yet submission came, and no one described it more feelingly than one of Mary Jones's daughters in a letter to her mother. "It is with sad and heavy hearts we mark the dark, crowding events of this most disastrous year. We have seen hope after hope fall blighted and withering about us, until our country is no more—merely a heap of ruins and ashes.... The degradation of a whole country and a proud people is indeed a mighty, an all-enveloping sorrow." The Jones papers, published more than a century after the war, prompted the modern novelist Madison Jones to say that though the story of the Old South and its destruction has been told and retold, these writings tell it "in the fullness of its poignance and tragedy [and] with a vividness and force that are surely unparalleled."

Without a strong southern tradition in the fine arts, the Confederacy did not live long enough to develop one of its own. Architecture in the great Georgian, West Indian, and neoclassical plantation houses, town residences, and public buildings constituted the Old South's major form of esthetic expression. Construction ceased during the war, and much of what was already in existence suffered destruction or damage. Yet the fine arts did serve the Confederate cause. Theaters continued to operate in Richmond and other cities, with occasional productions of Shakespearean and other great dramas. These were overshadowed by hastily composed works that appealed to the majority by combining southern patriotism and comedy, such as John Hill Hewitt's *King Linkum the First*, Joseph Hodgson's *The Confederate Vivandiere*, and J. J. Delchamp's *Great Expectations: or, Getting Promoted*. Blackface minstrels were also popular. Doubtless these farces partially diverted southern minds from the grim realities surrounding them.

Southern painters and sculptors employed their talents in support of the Confederacy by producing war scenes or representations of Confederate heroes. The most notable example of such work was William Washington's *The Burial of Latané*, a painting that depicted the pride and pathos accompanying the funeral of a young officer killed during Stuart's ride around McClellan early in the war.

Although Confederate photography produced no figure so prominent as the northern photographic entrepreneur Mathew B. Brady, Confederate cameramen were busy recording their views of the conflict. The very earliest war pictures, scenes of Fort Sumter shortly after the bombardment, were taken by a photographer representing the Charleston firm Osborn and Durbec. The names of such southerners as

George Cook, J. D. Edwards, F. K. Houston, and J. W. Petty deserve to be remembered along with those of the northern photographers for their success in creating a vivid pictorial record of the war.

Music was the most popular of the fine arts in the South, and it was easily adapted to the martial spirit of the times. The music for which the South would ultimately be most renowned, its folk music, was not then in formal composition. Ironically, the most stirring airs of the Confederacy were the work of outsiders or immigrants, offering a convincing illustration of the dependence of the Old South upon imports from abroad. A jaunty prewar minstrel song, "Dixie's Land," better known by the shortened title, "Dixie," written by Daniel Emmett of Ohio, became the Confederacy's unofficial "national anthem" after it was played at Jefferson Davis's inauguration as provisional president at Montgomery. The opening verse went

> I wish I was in the land of cotton, old times there
>   are not forgotten,
> Look away, look away, look away, Dixie Land.
> In Dixie Land where I was born in, early on a frosty
>   mornin',
> Look away, look away, look away, Dixie Land.
>
> (Chorus)
> Then I wish I was in Dixie, hooray! hooray!
> In Dixie Land I'll take my stand to live and die in
>   Dixie,
> Away, away, away down South in Dixie,
> Away, away, away down South in Dixie.

Perhaps the most dashing of Confederate songs was "The Bonnie Blue Flag," written by an Irish immigrant named Harry McCarthy, a prewar southern comedian. Celebrating a flag that was displayed above the Mississippi state capitol upon the occasion of secession, the lilting melody suggests the Celtic origin of the composer:

> Hurrah! Hurrah! For Southern rights hurrah!
> Hurrah for the Bonnie Blue Flag
> That bears a single star!

The most famous of the Confederate marching songs was a catchy piece named "The Yellow Rose of Texas," which was also a minstrel number. Unfortunately, the identity of the composer is unknown. The final lines of the chorus went:

> You may talk about your dearest May,
> And sing of Rosalee,

But the Yellow Rose of Texas
Beats the Belles of Tennessee!

Many other songs kindled southern spirits or expressed southern
emotions. Among these were James Ryder Randall's "Maryland, My
Maryland," the sometimes-called "Marseillaise" of the Confederacy;
the stately "General Lee's Grand March," by Hermann L. Schreiner; the
sentimental love ballad, "Lorena," by H. D. L. Webster; and the heart-
breaking story of a young soldier's death, "Somebody's Darling," by
Marie Ravenel. Music exerted a sustaining force in the lives of
southerners at war.

Southern schools, like all other southern institutions, quickly went
to war. Many of the native southerners among the teachers enlisted or
were drafted into the Confederate army or provided some other form of
essential service to the cause. Professor John W. Mallet of the University of Alabama drew upon his scientific knowledge to invent an improved artillery shell and supervise the preparation of chemicals for use
in making explosives. The LeConte brothers, John and Joseph, distinguished South Carolina scientists, employed their expertise in important work for the Confederate Niter and Mining Bureau.

Many of the college professors of the South were from elsewhere
and did not share the region's views on secession. A number of the
most distinguished of them resigned their positions and went north at
the beginning of the war. These included the famed scientist Louis
Agassiz, who was on the faculty of the Medical College of Charleston,
and the equally famed political scientist Francis Lieber, who taught at
the University of South Carolina. Both Agassiz and Lieber were Europeans who had been attracted to the United States years before the war.
Others who left southern institutions of higher learning included
Frederick A. P. Barnard, president of the University of Mississippi, who
later enjoyed a highly distinguished career as the president of Columbia
College; and William Tecumseh Sherman, president of the Louisiana
State Seminary and Military Academy, who soon donned a blue uniform to become the nemesis of the Confederacy.

Southern teachers who remained in the classroom supported the
Confederacy with pedagogy. They reinforced southern political and social beliefs and Confederate ideals in the minds of their students. Some
of the teachers wrote textbooks to supplant the volumes customarily
imported from northern publishers. A Confederate substitute for Noah
Webster's famed blue-back speller was soon in print, along with a
southern edition of *Caesar's Gallic War*. Professor William Bingham of the
Bingham School in North Carolina produced an acceptable Latin grammar.

The southern authors eliminated every vestige of northern sentiment and replaced it with appropriate southern sentiment. They justi-

fied slavery and extolled Confederate valor. Even the writers of arithmetic books and geographies found ways to inculcate southern principles. *Johnson's Elementary Arithmetic* contained such problems as: "If one Confederate soldier can whip 7 Yankees, how many soldiers can whip 49 Yankees?" This was an adaptation of a well-known volume published before the war by Professor Daniel Harvey Hill of Washington College and then of Davidson College, who later became a Confederate general. His *Elements of Algebra* contained an illustration drawn from an episode in the Mexican War when a formation of Indiana volunteers fled before an enemy charge while a Mississippi regiment stood fast. He used another illustration in which shrewd Yankee peddlers were selling wooden nutmegs to innocent southern housewives.

Most of the region's colleges closed their doors before the war ended. The pleas of university officials that students be exempted from military service were turned down. Even if they had been granted, most of the students probably would have enlisted, and the surging emotions of the times would have made serious study impossible for those who remained in the classroom. Some of the school buildings were destroyed and many severely vandalized; virtually all that escaped this kind of treatment were subject to idleness and neglect.

Although most of the students in the primary and secondary schools were too young for military service, these institutions suffered all the other ill effects of the war. Many of the three thousand private academies, the mainstay of precollege training, closed for want of money or teachers, as did many of the emerging public schools. Frequently untrained women or old men replaced teachers now in uniform; school terms were sharply abbreviated; enrollments thinned as the children's labor became increasingly needed in home, field, and shop.

Only in North Carolina, where Superintendent Calvin Wiley's influence with Governor Vance kept the public schools in the state budget, were they able to continue more or less as usual. Throughout the South generally, formal education was a major casualty of the conflict.

Blacks in the Confederacy, particularly the three and a half million slaves among them, ultimately gained the most—their freedom—from the outcome of the Civil War. But in the early stages of the struggle the lives of the slaves were only remotely touched by it. The "friction and abrasion" of war, to borrow Lincoln's expression, did not of itself destroy slavery, though it severely weakened it and prepared the way for its extinction.

Even before the Union armies made strong headway into the South, slavery began to erode somewhat under the impact of war. How much the behavior and labor of the slaves were affected by the mere knowledge that a war related to their status was in progress is impossible to measure. But accounts by the owners reveal unmistakably that the slaves were aware of the war in its very early stages when it was still far from their own areas; that they seemed to possess a sort of mental telepathy which kept them at least partially informed. It is also clear from such telling expressions as "the demoralization of the negroes" or "the unrest among my people" that to some extent they were responding to this awareness.

More tangible effects on slave conduct came as the result of the heavy demands for military service made by the war upon the white population. Although the Confederate draft laws exempted one white man for each large or middle-sized plantation, many planters and their sons enlisted in the army, leaving the slaves to be managed by the plantation mistress with or without an overseer. Many of these functionaries also went into uniform; wartime plantation journals and correspondence are peppered with complaints about the unavailability of overseers or the incompetence and negligence of those who were available.

The "refugeeing" of white families from the threat of invasion upset the relationship between the owners and their chattels. Everything about the move and the new and strange environment worked against the usual routine. The slaves frequently were further "demoralized" in these moves by being forced to separate from wives and children who belonged to some other owner. The situation also afforded extraordinary opportunities for escape to those slaves who were disposed to attempt it.

The exigencies of war brought improved working and living conditions to at least some of the slaves. Because of the shortage of white labor, many slaves were hired from their owners to work in factories producing armaments, equipment, or supplies for the Confederacy. Here they were able to take advantage of an incentive system that had long existed on many plantations and in a number of southern industries by inducing employers to give cash bonuses for production above the assigned tasks.

Some slaves also benefited during the war from a heightened effort on the part of conscientious white southerners, especially religious leaders, to eliminate the abuses in the system and make it conform to southern theories of the existence of a true Christian brotherhood embracing both masters and slaves, and to the southern claims of the uplifting effect of slavery on the blacks. All of these improvements in the conditions of the slaves tended, of course, to redound to the advantage of the owners and employers by maintaining or increasing their output. Thus, through a great variety of measures, the owners and managers and the slaves made adaptations to the demands and opportunities of war.

Despite the wartime difficulties that appeared in the slave system, slave productivity remained high in the interior of the Confederacy as long as the actual combat was at a distance. During the fall and winter of 1861–62, slaves harvested and processed the largest sugar crop ever grown in Louisiana. As late as the summer of 1863, Union soldiers in the deep South expressed amazement over the immensity of corn crops being grown there by slave labor. With good reason, the soldiers scoffed at the appearance of "ponderous articles" in northern newspapers saying the Confederacy could be starved into submission.

In addition to producing food on the plantations and serving for hire in many southern factories, great numbers of slaves were impressed by the Confederate government to dig earthworks and construct fortifications, build and maintain railroads, and perform a wide range of other heavy labor. The living and working conditions of many of these slaves were harsher than the conditions on the plantations from which they were taken. Slaves also served as teamsters, cooks, and in numerous menial capacities for the Confederate army. Those northerners were right who justified emancipation on the argument that the slaves were being used to support the Confederate war effort; one of the abiding paradoxes of the conflict lies in the important role they played in making that effort formidable.

The arrival of the Union army quickly disproved the traditional southern claim that the slaves were content with slavery, at least among the masses of the bondsmen. The moment a blue-clad force approached a particular area the slaves began to slip away singly and in twos and threes, usually during the night, and make their way to the Union camps. Some of the runaways soon became disillusioned with their reception and returned to the plantations with such remarks as, "We've seen the elephant and we are glad to be home."

Most did not return. Early in the war General Benjamin F. Butler at Fortress Monroe on the Virginia Peninsula set the precedent of using black refugees from the plantations as laborers for the Union army; he avoided the difficult legal and political question of emancipation by calling them "contraband of war," a name that would stick throughout the struggle. After the capture in late 1861 of Port Royal, South Carolina, the Treasury Department official in charge of the abandoned plantations there, Edward L. Pierce of Boston, established schools for the blacks and brought down northern entrepreneurs to run the plantations by using the former slaves as wage laborers. Also, many of them were given plots of land to cultivate for themselves. This experiment became, in the words of historian Willie Lee Rose, a "rehearsal for reconstruction."

The penetration of the northern forces into the heart of the Confederacy gave additional hundreds of thousands of slaves an opportunity to escape. Though many remained loyal to their owners, multitudes of others fled from the plantations and thronged around the military encampments in a vast "jubilee" of freedom; according to one account, the march of a Union column through the southern countryside stirred up swarms of blacks "like thrusting a walking-cane into an ant-hill."

The presence of such masses of unemployed blacks in the vicinity of the army created a situation that obliged the commanders, from military necessity if not always from compassion, to assign special officers to supervise the handling of the runaways. In December 1862 Grant appointed an Ohio chaplain, Captain John Eaton, to serve as superintendent of contrabands in the entire department of western Tennessee and Mississippi. This action set a precedent that would be followed in all the other Union military departments in the South and would culminate in March 1865 in the creation within the War Department of the Bureau of Refugees, Freedmen, and Abandoned Lands, better known as the Freedmen's Bureau.

Through the efforts of such officers as Eaton and their staffs, the Union army provided the blacks with rations, medical care, and the rudiments of schooling. The blacks welcomed with keen enthusiasm the instruction in reading, writing, and ciphering; great numbers of children and a few adults got their first taste of formal education under these extraordinary circumstances. At the same time the army established many of the blacks in colonies to work the abandoned or confiscated plantations either for themselves or, more often, as hired laborers for northern entrepreneurs who rented or leased the lands.

Thus while the war raged about them, southern freedmen took the first halting steps on the long and tortuous journey to full American citizenship. A few became landowners; others became participants in collective farming experiments; others became contract laborers on the proprietors' land and received their pay in cash or kind; others worked individual plots for a division of the produce, an early form of sharecropping.

Blacks also began to exercise one of their most prized liberties, that of worship free of white domination or tutelage. Even as they settled within the Union lines they frequently held great religious meetings by campfire, accompanied by powerful sermons from the mouths of black exhorters, by impassioned, plaintive, and rhythmic singing of their spirituals, and by fervent prayers of thanksgiving to Jesus and God Almighty and "Mr. Linkum" for their delivery from bondage. In many instances, long before the war was over they established fixed places for their services. In these activities lay the chief origin of the independent southern black churches that were to play a vital role in the affairs of the race after the war.

The Union army protected the blacks and fostered their well-being as best it could. But the army was unable to prevent their suffering great hardships. This was especially true on those occasions when the Confederates recaptured territory or when guerrilla bands evaded the Union patrols and outposts. When in December 1862 the raids of Van

Dorn and Forrest obliged Grant to abandon certain places in western Tennessee, the blacks were in terror of being left behind. They swarmed over the passenger and freight cars of the troop trains, clinging to every available space and even crouching on the roofs. The trains were moved very slowly and with the utmost caution, but even so, wrote Captain Eaton, "the exposure of these people—men, women, and children [to the winter cold]—was indescribable." Their fears were justified, for the Confederates were known to follow a practice of executing blacks who were reported to have been guilty of violence or pillaging, or of leadership in abandoning their owners.

Torn from their moorings and destitute of the means of livelihood, great numbers of blacks succumbed to exposure, malnutrition, and disease. In addition, they often were exploited by the Union soldiers, many of whom turned to the women for sexual gratification. A Louisiana planter wrote in indignation and pity that the occupants of a runaway camp across the Mississippi River from New Orleans were living in "the most abject misery Degredation & Filth...in the most Loathsome manner and committing the most Dreadfull excesses of Depravity & Lechery in connexion with the soldiers...." He said the blacks were dying by the hundreds. Northern soldiers left comparable, if less vivid or censorious, accounts. Such scenes caused some of the soldiers to predict an early end for the entire race in the South. James M. McPherson estimates a death rate of 25 percent among the residents of the contraband communities. Perhaps this was an inescapable price of freedom.

The most remarkable thing about the behavior of the liberated blacks was their refusal to resort to insurrection or widespread violence. Thomas Jefferson, a severe critic of slavery, had predicted that emancipation would bring bloodshed in its wake if the freed slaves were not deported from the country, and southerners now lived in fear of the fulfillment of his prediction. Moved by this dread, the southern authorities early in the war tightened the restrictions in their slave codes, activated their customarily lackadaisical night patrols, and established homeguard military organizations to put down anticipated uprisings.

Many northern observers, especially the abolitionists, believed the entire slave population had always seethed with rage and the urge to rebel. The abolitionists fully expected an insurrection at this time; doubtless many of them hoped for one. Joshua Giddings of Ohio, a prominent antislavery politician, was convinced that the appearance of even a small army of liberation in the South would set off a gigantic upheaval among the blacks. Others held similar views; in the spring of 1861 Ulysses S. Grant wrote that the greatest danger following the anticipated quick collapse of the Confederacy would be a slave revolt, which, he said, might have to be suppressed by a northern army. David M. Potter has called this expectation of rebellion the "Spartacus Delusion," an expression taken from the name of the leader of a famous slave insurrection in ancient Rome.

Southern blacks were not passive recipients of freedom. In addition to rebelling "with their legs" by abandoning the plantations and other places of work, they participated in many ways in their own liberation. Besides the 134,000 of them who served in the Union army, perhaps as many as 200,000 assisted the invading forces as laborers, cooks, teamsters, and the like. Many individual blacks committed acts of sabotage against the Confederate forces or against their masters. The most celebrated case of this sort was that of Robert Smalls of Charleston, the assistant pilot on a southern steamer, who delivered the ship into the hands of Union blockaders. After the war Smalls would serve as a congressman from his state.

At times blacks behind the Confederate lines became openly hostile to their masters and on some occasions committed acts of violence. Mary Boykin Chesnut recorded an instance of murder by the slaves on a South Carolina plantation; a few episodes of rape took place. The blacks often pillaged houses in the vicinity of the protecting Union troops, especially places that had been abandoned by their owners; drawing upon the Old Testament account of the liberation of the Children of Israel, the looters spoke gleefully of "spilin the Gyptians [spoiling the Egyptians]." There were scattered and ineffectual efforts to stage a rebellion.

But there was no slave uprising. Usually the slaves left the plantations quietly and peacefully. Exactly why an insurrection did not take place is difficult to determine; black slaves in Saint-Domingue (modern Haiti) and elsewhere had demonstrated convincingly that they were capable of staging successful uprisings. The southern slaves generally seemed unwilling to take the risk; or, perhaps more accurately, they considered the risk unnecessary. A slave was quoted as saying fatalistically, "I see no use of us going and getting ourselves into trouble. If so be it we are to get free, we get it anyhow.... We think it betterer to stay home on the plantation, and get our food and our clothes. If we are to get freedom, dar we are! But, if we run away...where is we?"

The presence of the northern civil and military authorities discouraged violence among the slaves; once a Union force was firmly established in an area, it imposed order on them as well as the local whites. Lincoln's Emancipation Proclamation instructed the slaves to remain peaceful until liberated, except to defend themselves.

Doubtless the conduct of many slaves was prompted by genuine affection for kind masters. Bonds of friendship and love often extended through the barriers of race and thralldom. The "faithfulness" of the slaves became legendary in the postwar South. Mary Boykin Chesnut recorded remarkable personal instances in which slaves protected valuable property belonging to the master. One slave returned to Mrs. Chesnut a box of silver which she had placed in his keeping during the Union invasion; another slave returned her mistress's diamonds; "handed them back to me with as little apparent interest in the matter as if they were garden peas." The famed diarist wrote that the "fidelity" of the blacks was a principal topic of conversation among the white population of South Carolina after the war.

Both Henry W. Grady, a major spokesman among postwar white southerners, and Booker T. Washington, the major spokesman among postwar black southerners, spoke movingly of the peaceful conduct of the slaves during the war. Contrasting this behavior to what the slaves might have done by rebelling, Grady exclaimed, "A thousand torches behind the lines would have disbanded the Confederate armies."

Unqualified statements of wartime slave loyalty were as glaring in their exaggeration as were the sweeping prewar abolitionist predictions of slave rebellion. Still, the slaves did not take advantage of their opportunity to rebel and exact vengeance. Perhaps Bell Wiley offers the most complete summary of why they did not do so: "That the slaves in the interior did not 'rise up' against their masters is not surprising when one takes into consideration their lack of facilities for rapid communication and concerted action, the affection which the most intelligent ones had for their masters' families, the fear inspired by the summary execution of those whose plots to rebel were detected, and the tremendous advantages which the whites had over them in every respect, save that of numbers." Whatever the reasons, the South was spared the horrors and ineradicable hatreds of a war between the races as the slaves became free.

Southern women played a special role in the drama of the Confederacy. Most of them supported secession with unsurpassed zeal, upheld the righteousness of the Confederate cause, urged the men to enlist, and shamed those who were reluctant to do so. The women formed "sulk and pout" clubs to manifest their displeasure with unpatriotic men, and sometimes sent them female undergarments as tokens of contempt. The women spoke of joining the Confederate military ranks, if necessary, and a few of the more zealous of them actually did so disguised as men. European travelers and northern soldiers in the South agreed that women were the most militant of all Confederates. General Nathaniel P. Banks, commanding the occupied portion of Louisiana, said southern women had caused the war and were the major force in keeping it going. The poet Timrod paid tribute to their fervor with these lines:

> Does any falter? let him turn
> to some brave maiden's eyes,
> And catch the holy fires that burn
> In those sublunar skies.

Oh! could you like your women feel,
and in their spirit march.
A day might see your lines of steel
Beneath the victor's arch.

The most telling contribution made by women to the Confederate effort was in taking the places of the hundreds of thousands of men who were called away from the farms, shops, and stores. For most southern women, this was a matter of managing plantations or working farms, but thousands of others made uniforms for the Quartermaster Department or cartridges for the Ordnance Department, or they served as clerks in the government bureaus. Still others taught school, made clothing, baked bread, and filled every kind of job usually done by men. Perhaps the farm wives had the hardest lot of all as they ran the household, managed the children, plowed and hoed the fields, cooked the meals, tanned leather, spun thread, wove cloth, sewed clothing, treated the sick, and became home teachers for children who had been left without schools.

A number of women served the Confederacy glamorously as spies. The most celebrated of these, a Virginia girl named Bell Boyd, repeatedly brought important military information through the Union lines. Mrs. Rose O'Neal Greenhow, a Washington socialite, was credited with providing the Confederate commanders with intelligence that helped them win the battle of First Bull Run. Imprisoned temporarily as a spy, she was later deported to Richmond. Eventually she was drowned off the North Carolina coast while attempting to run the blockade on a mission for the Confederacy.

Doubtless the most memorable Confederate heroines were the women who served as nurses and attendants to the wounded soldiers. In the beginning, before the establishment of military hospitals, great numbers of women worked as volunteers to care for the multitudes of casualties, often incurring grave risks in treating soldiers on the battlefield. The most celebrated example of this sort of feminine valor was that of Mrs. Arthur F. Hopkins of Virginia and Alabama, twice wounded in the course of her work, and named by General Joseph E. Johnston the "Angel of the South."

Women improvised the first behind-the-lines hospitals by taking the disabled into their homes for further care. In recognition of the work of Sally L. Tompkins, who rented a house in Richmond and set up in it a twenty-two bed infirmary for soldiers, Jefferson Davis made her a captain, the only female commissioned officer of the war. Women served as the matrons of many of the hospitals created later by the Confederate government.

Ella King Newsom of Arkansas became known as the "Florence Nightingale of the Southern Army" as the result of her work in setting up hospitals and aid stations throughout the Confederacy. Among the more famous hospital matrons were Kate Cumming of Mobile, Phoebe Pember, a dynamic and charming Jewish woman who served the great Chimborazo Hospital in Richmond, and Louisa Susanna McCord of South Carolina. An Englishwoman in the Confederacy wrote perceptively, "Heaven only knows what the soldiers of the South would have done without the exertions of the women in their behalf."

Not all southern women were heroines. The conduct of a number of them reflected the general deterioration of moral standards caused by the war. Some of them engaged in illicit sexual affairs out of a sense of excitement and adventure. In many instances, however, they did so out of a genuine need for money or food. Prostitution became widespread, especially in the vicinity of the army camps; late in the war the mayor of Richmond wrote that prostitutes thronged daily in the vicinity of the capitol, "promenading up & down the shady walks jostling respectable ladies into the gutter." Some southern women went so far as to barter their favors to Union soldiers; from near Atlanta in 1864 a Confederate soldier's wife wrote her husband that some of her married neighbors were "horin" with the Federals in return for food. Similar occurrences were also taking place throughout the South.

Notwithstanding the fervor with which southern women supported the Confederate war effort, it is probably impossible to know how the masses of southern women truly felt about the institution of slavery. Anne Firor Scott has found, paradoxically, that most of those who left a record of their views on the subject were opposed to slavery and were happy when it ended. One plantation mistress said that "at heart" all southern women were abolitionists. In the patriarchal society of the Old South, even though women were idealized and "placed on a pedestal" in the scale of social values, they shared, to some extent, a subordinate status with the slaves. Mary Boykin Chesnut said expressly that southern women were slaves. There also seems to have existed a closer emotional bond between the plantation mistresses and their female house servants than between the planters and their slaves. Possibly these relations fostered among southern women a stronger sympathy for the slaves than was held by southern men.

The war and its hardships stimulated an introspection among the women that caused some of them to reveal their dislike for slavery. Their motives varied from individual to individual. Some condemned the institution out of compassion for the slaves and a moral revulsion against the inherent wrong of the system. A Louisiana woman wrote that her earliest memory was that of pity for her family's chattels, and said she had always felt the guilt of slavery and how impossible it was for a slave owner to go to heaven. Other women were happy to see slavery ended because they considered it a curse upon the South and an onerous burden to the slave owners themselves.

Many southern women opposed slavery because it often resulted in sexual relations between their husbands and the female slaves. Mrs.

Chesnut, though she held most blacks in very low esteem, hated slavery which she called a "monstrous system," and said, "Like the patriarchs of old, our men live all in one house with their wives & their concubines....My disgust sometimes is boiling over."

Ultimately the fierce Confederate patriotism of southern women broke before the stern realities of war. Shaken by the sight of innumerable women late in the struggle appealing to have their husbands or sons exempted from military service, a War Department official observed, "The iron is gone deep into the heart of society." Letters from distraught wives deluged the armies and became a major cause for desertion. Only a heart of granite could have remained steadfast under such entreaties as the following: "Before God, Edward, Unless you come home we must die. Last night I was aroused by little Eddie's crying....He said 'Oh, mamma, I'm so hungry!' And Lucy, Edward, your darling Lucy, she never complains, but she is growing thinner and thinner every day." The demoralization of the women was a major cause of the final collapse of the Confederacy.

The permanent effect of the southern women's wartime activities is beyond precise measurement. Although they had never been the fragile and ineffectual creatures they were sometimes pictured as being, the war cast them in roles that were far removed from those usually assigned to them. Possibly this experience combined with the defeat of southern men on the battlefield and the physical or psychological inability of many of the men to adjust to postwar conditions to weaken somewhat the region's traditional patriarchal family system and to turn southern women in the direction of public endeavor.

Significantly, one of the most assertive organizations of the New South, the United Daughters of the Confederacy, was formed by women for the purpose of commemorating the courage and virtue of the short-lived southern republic. Mary Elizabeth Massey had in mind southern women as well as northern women when she expressed the conviction that the Civil War helped to launch American women permanently into spheres previously reserved to men.

Southern emotions rose or fell with the tides of victory or defeat in the field. Early successes, purchased with heavy sacrifice in the blood of husbands and sons, brought a wave of mingled joy and grief that in its intensity resembled a religious experience. The toll of prolonged war and the prospect of collapse plunged southerners into depression. A Louisiana planter expressed the general feeling when he wrote: "The days (emphatically days of darkness & gloom) succeed each other bringing nothing but despondency with regard to the future....The Lord help us.—Such is war, civil war." The supreme act of despair was that of Edmund Ruffin, arch-secessionist and firer of one of the war's first shots. He wrapped himself in a Confederate flag and shot himself through the head.

XIII

The Union Triumphant

---·❖·---

*I*n defeating Hood's army and capturing Atlanta, Sherman was not able to carry out the primary mission Grant had given him, to destroy the Confederate army in Georgia. Hood, having avoided destruction by abandoning Atlanta, now doubled back to the north and attacked Sherman's supply line, the railroad from Chattanooga. When Sherman came up from Atlanta to protect the line, Hood proposed to march back into Tennessee in the hope of luring the Federals out of the lower South altogether, and perhaps of recapturing the important city of Nashville, which long had served as a key Union base.

Hood's plan was approved by General Beauregard, now commander of the recently created and shadowy Military Division of the West, and by Jefferson Davis, who met with Hood in the town of Palmetto, Georgia, to discuss the details of the operation. Leaving only Wheeler's cavalry to protect the entire lower southeast, Hood on November 19 crossed the Tennessee River at Tuscumbia, Alabama, with about 38,000 troops, including Forrest's cavalry from Mississippi, for a bold counter turning movement into Tennessee.

While Grant believed that Sherman ought to pursue and destroy Hood's army, Sherman now proposed a drastically different plan of operations, a plan that would add a new and vital dimension to the entire Union strategy. He suggested that the Union forces in Tennessee be made adequate for the defense of that state, with Thomas in command and two corps of the Army of the Cumberland as the nucleus, but that the main body of his own army abandon the chase after Hood and march from Atlanta to Savannah on the sea, foraging for supplies as it went. On October 11, after an exchange of correspondence in which Sherman explained and urged his plan, Grant assented.

Sherman's goal was far more than the mere capture of a city or an area. He envisioned the disruption of Confederate communications, the destruction of factories and all other military resources, and, perhaps most important of all, the crushing of civilian as well as soldier morale—the extinction of the southern will to continue the war. The idea had been maturing in his mind for some time; early in the conflict he had written, "We must reconquer the country...as we did from the Indians." His meaning in this statement is not entirely clear, but, significantly, the most effective tactics that had been employed against the Indians had been the ravaging of their villages and food supplies, measures that Sherman after the war would repeat with singular effectiveness against the western tribes.

In truth, the conflict was now far beyond the observance of the so-called rules of war, or of that measure of civility which had prevailed earlier in the struggle. Sherman the previous year had rehearsed his terroristic methods against the civilian population in the interior of Mississippi, and Union forces in Louisiana had carried out similar practices. General Early's Confederate cavalry showed their appreciation of such methods by burning Chambersburg, Pennsylvania, in the raid on Washington and collecting ransom from other towns along the route to prevent a similar fate. Grant was already applying Sherman's kind of warfare in Virginia.

Sherman amplified his meaning in his official correspondence. "We are not only fighting hostile armies," he wrote, "but a hostile people. We cannot change the hearts of those people of the South, but we can make war so terrible...that generations would pass away before they would again appeal to it." In a sentence that revealed a truly Clausewitzian understanding of the broader nature of war—war as an extension of politics as well as the ultimate exercise in violence—Sherman said, "If we can march a well-appointed army right through [the lower South], it is a demonstration to the world, foreign and domestic, that we have a power which Davis cannot resist. This may not be war, but rather statesmanship." He strongly believed the operation was feasible, and explained, "...the utter destruction of [Georgia's] roads, houses, and people, will cripple their military resources....I can make this march, and make Georgia howl!"

Davis perceived in Sherman's move an opportunity for the Confederacy, not only to recapture Tennessee and perhaps take Kentucky, but to trap Sherman's army as well. Before returning to Richmond after his conference with Hood, Davis visited a number of southern cities, including Macon and Augusta, Georgia, Montgomery, Alabama, and Columbia, South Carolina, and delivered addresses to large crowds there. Previously he had shown little awareness of the importance of speaking directly to the people, or perhaps he had felt his other duties were more pressing.

He now made vigorous statements of confidence as well as moving appeals for a renewal of hope and effort by the population: "Our cause is not lost. Sherman cannot keep up his long line of communication; and retreat sooner or later he must. And when that day comes, the fate that befell the army of the French Empire in its retreat from Moscow will be reenacted"; "Is this a time to ask what the law demands of you...? Rather is it not the time for every man capable of bearing arms to say: 'My country needs my services, and my country shall have them!'"

Sherman said he could make the march through Georgia, and make it he did. On November 15 his 60,000 veterans marched out of the ashes of Atlanta singing "John Brown's body lies amouldering in the grave....His soul is marching on." Moving in four parallel columns across a front of sixty miles, without serious military opposition, and living off the land, they brought fright and havoc to the population. Sherman's orders authorized only the gathering of rations and forbade the destruction of private property, and his corps commanders and their subordinates made gestures of enforcing them.

But the general attitude of retribution that suffused the army at all ranks and grades rendered such proprieties of little effect. After the war Sherman explained: "The Rebels wanted us to detach a division here, a brigade there, to protect their families and property while they were fighting....This is a one-sided game of war, and many of us... kindhearted, just and manly...ceased to quarrel with our own men about such minor things and went in to subdue the enemy, leaving minor depredations to be charged up to the account of rebels who had forced us into war, and who deserved all they got and worse." His specific instructions to a subordinate for dealing with snipers, issued early in the Georgia campaign, were more to the point: "Cannot you send [an expedition] over about Fairmouth and Adairsville, burn ten or twelve houses of known Secessionists, kill a few at random, and let them know it will be repeated every time a train is fired on...."

Multitudes of blacks exulting in freedom trudged in the wake of the army, and a host of stragglers and deserters swarmed across the countryside. Both groups added to the pillage and destruction wrought by the army. So did the Confederate cavalry in its efforts to carry out a "scorched earth" policy ordered by the authorities in Richmond. Georgia writhed under the lash of war.

As Sherman marched south, Hood marched north. He hoped to overwhelm the scattered opposing forces in Tennessee before Thomas could get them concentrated around Nashville. At Spring Hill the night of November 29 Hood appeared to have trapped two Federal corps (approximately 34,000) under General Schofield, but unaccountably Hood allowed them to march away without an attack. The following day he caught up with them at Franklin well entrenched on favorable defensive terrain. In anger and frustration, he launched a hastily planned, suicidal frontal assault that lasted from late afternoon until well after dark. His casualties were staggering: over 6,000 against scarcely more than a third as many Federals. Six Confederate generals, including the redoubtable Cleburne, died of wounds that day; the bodies of four of them lay in a row on the front porch of Carnton House within the Confederate position.

Hood followed Schofield as he withdrew to Nashville, where his arrival, in addition to reinforcements from Missouri, brought Thomas's strength to approximately 50,000. In an attempt to lure Thomas into making a costly assault, Hood placed his force in position across the two railroads running south from Nashville, thus severing the communications between Thomas and Sherman. But Hood unwisely weakened himself by dispatching Forrest with most of his cavalry and two brigades of infantry to attack a Federal detachment that was still holding Murfreesboro thirty miles to the southeast. With fewer than half his opponent's numbers, Hood was obliged to stretch his line dangerously thin in an effort to avoid having it enveloped or turned.

Meanwhile, Grant, chafing over Thomas's deliberateness, twice wired him direct orders to attack. When Thomas still delayed because of a winter storm, Grant ordered Major General John Logan to Nashville to relieve Thomas of command. Finally, on December 15 Grant started from Petersburg for Nashville to take the command there in person, but news reached him in Washington that stopped him. Thomas had attacked Hood and had won a great victory.

On the day Grant left Petersburg, Thomas, fixing the Confederates with a holding attack against their right, launched a massed assault upon their overextended left, shattering the line and driving it completely out of position. The following day he repeated these tactics to drive the Confederates from their new position. A stubborn rearguard resistance by Forrest's cavalry, now returned from the futile Murfreesboro mission, enabled Hood to get his army back across the Tennessee River into northern Alabama and eventually to Tupelo, Mississippi. But it was a mere remnant (15,000 men) of the once-proud Army of Tennessee; tactically, the battle of Nashville was the most decisive of the war. The bold venture into Tennessee had ended in a Confederate disaster, to which the ragged, marching soldiers paid grim-humored recognition in their parody of "The Yellow Rose of Texas":

> You may talk about your Beauregard,
> And sing of General Lee,
> But the Gallant Hood of Texas
> Played hell in Tennessee!

Hood paid a different form of recognition to total defeat. From Tupelo, on January 13, 1865, he wired Richmond, saying, "I respectfully request to be relieved from the command of this army." His request was granted.

What effect a Confederate victory in Tennessee would have had on Sherman is problematical. Possibly, as John G. Barrett believes, it would have obliged Sherman to abandon his grand march. What can be said with certainty is that Hood's failure in Tennessee assured Sherman's success beyond peradventure. On December 13, two days before Thomas opened the battle of Nashville, Sherman's army took Fort McAlister on the Ogeechee River below Savannah and established contact with a Union fleet and its welcome supply vessels. When on the 21st the army closed upon the city itself, a defending Confederate force of 15,000, commanded by Hardee, marched out to the north in order to avoid capture. That day Sherman wired Lincoln: "I beg to present you as a Christmas gift the City of Savannah...."

Sherman turned north from Savannah toward a reckoning with the mother state of secession, South Carolina. Describing the mood of his soldiers, he wrote, "The whole army is burning with an insatiable desire to wreak vengeance upon South Carolina. I almost tremble at her fate, but feel that she deserves all that seems in store for her." With skillful feints in the direction of Charleston to the east and Augusta, Georgia, to the west, Sherman confused and scattered the defending southern troops, most of them state militia, and struck inland for Columbia, the state capital, which fell on February 17.

South Carolina had much in store from what Sherman would call "minor depredations." A Pennsylvania soldier wrote that after his unit crossed into the state, the division commander rode along the line of troops saying, "Boys, are you well supplied with matches as we are now in South Carolina?" At the end of the march through the state a soldier wrote, "We burnt every house, barn, mill that we passed...."

The night Columbia was taken most of the city went up in flames, whether by the action of Confederate General Wade Hampton in firing bales of cotton to keep them from the enemy, or by the action of drunken Union soldiers rioting in the streets, or possibly a combination of the two. Parts of various other South Carolina towns suffered equally, and many of the state's most venerable plantation mansions were destroyed. Of the burning of Columbia, an Ohio soldier wrote home to say, "Our men had such a spite against the place they swore they would burn the city, if they should enter it, and they did." A Wisconsin soldier wrote, "Fire and soldiery had full swing, or sweep if you like that better, and vied with each other in mischief. Never in modern times did soldiers have such fun." These accounts may have been exaggerated for the benefit of the folk back home. But deservedly or not, Sherman's march created an enduring legend of wanton vandalism.

The Union grand strategy now culminated in a massing of forces against the diminishing area and resources of a weakened and mortally wounded Confederacy. The vulnerability of the Confederacy was immeasurably increased by the work of the Union navy, especially the silent and unspectacular but remorseless grip of the blockade. In the beginning the navy had only forty-two vessels in service and the blockade was hardly more than a gesture. In May 1861 the entire North Carolina coastline was being guarded by only two ships. Never was the blockade tight enough to stop the blockade runners altogether. With a total of some 8,500 of these craft of all descriptions, the Confederacy was able to export more than a million bales of cotton and bring in impressive amounts of arms, munitions, and other supplies. One calculation indicates that 84 percent of all attempts by blockade runners operating from the North Carolina coast were successful. Confederate diplomats cited such accomplishments to support their argument that the blockade existed merely on paper, and was therefore illegal.

Confederate Secretary of the Navy Stephen Mallory faced the impossible task of combating the Union navy without a navy of his own and with the meagerest of facilities for building one. In 1860 the states that were to become the Confederacy produced less than one-tenth of the ships and boats constructed in the United States. Mallory attacked the problem with considerable vigor and imagination, though he seems never to have recognized fully the need for an effectual river fleet. Keenly aware that he could not equal his adversary in conventional vessels, he resorted to novel and at times radical measures, including, as previously explained, the building of commerce raiders and ironclad rams in England, and the commissioning of privateers. He also authorized the production of torpedoes (marine mines) and even of submarines.

Ultimately Mallory's plan failed to stop the Union navy or to destroy the blockade. But it did make some striking accomplishments, including the construction of a number of rams and submarines in makeshift Confederate shipyards, though the homemade rams were so deficient in engine power that they had to be used principally as floating batteries in defense of southern rivers and harbors. The Confederate navy would have been formidable if it had acquired the services of the rams built in England under the directions of Captain Bulloch. Most of the submarines were experimental, though one of them, the *C.S.S. Hunley,* in February 1864, sank a Union warship, the *Housatonic,* off Charleston harbor, a significant token of what was to come in naval warfare. The most successful part of Mallory's strategy was the work of the commerce raiders, which so seriously damaged the Union merchant marine that most shipowners transferred to the British flag.

Despite all Confederate efforts, the blockade grew steadily in effectiveness throughout the conflict. In December 1864 the Union navy had 671 ships on station, and the Confederacy held but a single remaining port, that of Wilmington, North Carolina, which was soon to fall to an amphibious assault. One out of every two attempts to run the blockade now ended in capture.

Even more damaging to the Confederacy than the loss of blockade runners was the effect of the blockade on major shipping to southern ports, which virtually stopped during the war. One student of the conflict has written: "The measure of the blockade's effectiveness...lay not in the number of ships seized but rather in the number of cargoes rotting on Liverpool docks and the number of British vessels that never got under way for [trade with the Confederacy]. Shipowners who ordinarily would have deposited freight at Carolina wharves were deterred by nightmares of capture...." Thus, notwithstanding the Confederate accusations that the blockade was ineffectual, it actually exerted a stranglehold on the entire southern economy.

In mid-January a Union joint navy and army assault took Fort Fisher guarding the port of Wilmington, North Carolina. Five days after Sherman's capture of Columbia, South Carolina, General Schofield and his corps, transported all the way from Nashville by rail and ship, overwhelmed an improvised force commanded by General Bragg and took Wilmington itself, closing the Confederacy's lone remaining outlet to the world.

From the ashes of Columbia, Sherman was on the move north into central North Carolina, his progress marked by a towering pillar of smoke from the state's burning pine forests. He reached Fayetteville on March 11 and headed for Goldsboro on the Weldon Railroad—still an important Confederate supply line into the interior of North Carolina. In Sherman's words, his movement was "as much an attack on Lee's army as though I were operating within the sound of his artillery." This appraisal was accurate enough; the march induced tens of thousands of additional Confederates to leave the ranks in the determination to assist their destitute families. Some estimates of Confederate desertion by the spring of 1865 go as high as 40 percent of the number on the rolls.

Grant had long envisaged using Mobile as a springboard for another damaging raid into the interior of the lower Confederacy, and in January he ordered General Edward Canby, now commanding the Department of the Gulf, to proceed against the city from New Orleans. Canby moved slowly, but in early April he landed an army of 45,000 in Mobile Bay, drove out the city's 10,000 defenders led by General Richard Taylor, and captured Mobile.

But as events turned out, the expedition that Grant desired against the Confederate communications, factories, and supplies of Alabama came from Tennessee instead of Mobile. Under General Thomas's orders, Brevet Major General James H. Wilson on March 18 crossed the Tennessee River into northern Alabama with a force of 14,000 cavalry and struck south for Selma, an important center for the manufacture of Confederate weapons and munitions.

Wilson's opponent was the foremost Confederate cavalry leader, Nathan B. Forrest, but even his skills and implacable spirit were now inadequate. Heavily outnumbered by Union troopers, most of whom were armed with repeating carbines, his men and mounts famished and exhausted, and his soldiers demoralized by the certain knowledge that they were fighting for a lost cause, Forrest for the first time was clearly defeated. On April 2 Wilson took Selma, then swept east to Montgomery and into Georgia. He rivaled his more famous senior colleagues, Sherman and Sheridan, in the thoroughness of his destruction of Confederate resources.

Wartime politics reflected the events of the battlefield. Lincoln's reelection demonstrated sharply the contrast between the rising spirit of unity and determination in the North and the growing dissension and demoralization in the South. If in the fall of 1864 a presidential election had been held in the Confederacy, Davis doubtless would have been crushingly defeated.

Lincoln, with his cabinet solidified by Chase's resignation, balanced by that of the conservative Montgomery Blair, and with a popular mandate of approval for the measures of his administration, was now firmly in the saddle. He did not gloat; the war and life itself had taken too heavy a toll to allow gloating. The endless casualty lists were a source of deepening agony, besides his continuing grief over the death in 1862 of his son Willie. Lincoln's countenance, always haggard, and his public appearances, always solemn, became perceptibly more grave.

Lincoln's handling of the peace proposals reflected the marked shift in the wind represented by his reelection and by the recent and continuing Union military successes. On February 3, 1865, following arrangements approved by him and carried out by Francis P. Blair, Sr., Lincoln and Seward met on a Union steamer at Hampton Roads, Virginia, with Confederate Vice President Stephens—the leading southern peace advocate—and two other delegates appointed by Davis. Lincoln expressed the hope of a "spirit of sincere liberality" in dealing with the seceded states, even indicating, according to Stephens, a willingness to compensate slave owners for their freed slaves; but on emancipation as well as submission to the Union, Lincoln was unshakable. These terms were anathema to Davis, and perhaps to a majority of the southern population, and the war continued.

Davis, on the evening of February 6, before a mass meeting at the African church in Richmond, responded to the failure of the peace conference with a final appeal to the southern people to brace themselves for further effort and sacrifice. He regretted he was not speaking to a victory celebration, but said he was thankful that there were still citizens willing to lay all they possessed on the altar of their country. He said Lincoln had invited a peace proposal but had rejected all honorable overtures, and now the struggle must go on. Let the absent soldiers of the Confederacy return to their regiments, Davis declared, and the South would be free within a year. "Let us then unite our hands and hearts, lock our shields together and we may well believe that before another summer solstice falls upon us, it will be the enemy who will be asking us for conferences and occasions in which to make known our demands."

This was the most impassioned address of Davis's career. His words came from the heart; they were direct and sincere, and they excited the admiration even of some of his most intractable critics. Pollard of the *Richmond Examiner* wrote that never had he been so moved by the power of as many words. Alexander Stephens said the speech was "bold and undaunted in tone...[that it] had a loftiness of sentiment ...as well as magnetic influence in delivery...." He compared it with the appeals of such historic orators and patriots as Rienzi and Demosthenes.

A short time later, Lincoln also presented another of his masterful addresses. On March 4 he stood before the Capitol, its great dome now finished largely at his insistence, to deliver his second inaugural. Its expression of generosity and contriteness—the war pictured as a divine punishment visited upon both North and South for the sin of slavery; its powerful religious overtones—"woe unto the world because of offenses"; its words of compassion—"with malice toward none, with charity for all"; and its vow of determination to continue the war, if God willed, "until every drop of blood drawn with the lash shall be paid by another drawn with the sword," and until the nation was purged and regenerated: all combined to rank this oration beside that of the Gettysburg cemetery dedication in its inspirational power and declaration of high national purpose.

Lincoln could speak for himself, and doubtless for a majority of the northern people, but not for his entire party. He gave his unqualified support to the passage by Congress of the Thirteenth Amendment to the Constitution abolishing slavery everywhere in the nation, and he expressed gratification over the hope that it would be ratified by the states. Still his tug with the Radicals over the nature of reconstruction did not abate. They succeeded in blocking the seating of delegates elected to Congress under his reconstruction plan, though he urged acceptance, saying of the new Louisiana state constitution that even with its flaws "it is better for the poor black man than we have in Illinois." The Civil War ended without a resolution of the issue.

Two measures of desperation adopted by the Confederacy in the twilight weeks of the war were deeply marked by hostility between Davis and the Congress. These were the proposal to enroll slaves in the Confederate army and the creation of the position of general in chief. The move to arm the slaves was the most revolutionary of all Confederate acts for waging the war. Conceived early in the struggle by General Cleburne, the idea had been rejected by Davis for fear of demoralizing the white troops and arousing dissent among the southern population. Impending defeat brought a reconsideration of the issue.

Governor William Smith of Virginia took the initiative by asking the legislature to arm the slaves of his state, and in January 1865, in response to a letter from a Virginia legislator, Lee wrote urging the employment of blacks as soldiers, with emancipation to them at once, accompanied by a plan of gradual and general emancipation.

The immense irony of the Confederate move toward emancipation is obvious, but it offers an excellent illustration of Clausewitz's point that war generates a dynamic and momentum of its own. To say the South desired independence solely for the preservation of slavery goes too far; yet in the beginning no man would have dreamed that one day the Confederacy would consider abolishing slavery as the price of independence. The irony is deepened by the reflection that by the summer of 1864, prior to the decisive Union military victories, a majority of the population of both North and South probably would have accepted reunion without emancipation as a condition of peace.

Davis gave his support to a bill for arming the slaves and emancipating them, and in late February wrote, "It is now becoming daily more evident to all reflecting persons that we are reduced to choosing whether the negroes shall fight for or against us, and that all arguments as to the positive advantages or disadvantages of employing them are beside the question." Cogent as this statement was, it did not stop the arguments. Foote and Wigfall led a bitter fight in Congress against the bill, and the *Charleston Mercury* denounced it unsparingly, even to the point of rebuking Lee for suggesting "this scheme of nigger soldiers and emancipation."

Congress in early March approved the enlistment of 300,000 slaves in the Confederate army, but emancipation was left to the decision of the individual states. A few companies of blacks were enrolled and paraded through Richmond in uniform; none got into combat. An emissary, Duncan Kenner of Louisiana, had been sent to Europe in the forlorn hope that the promise of Confederate emancipation might bring foreign recognition, but the hope was soon extinguished in interviews between Mason and Palmerston and Slidell and Napoleon III.

The threat of immediate disaster brought the Confederacy to the final and logical, if futile, stage in its military command structure. Defeat in the field and demoralization on the home front now kindled a demand that Davis be deposed and Lee made dictator in the manner of ancient Rome. Instead, the congress passed a compromise measure creating the position of general in chief, confident that Lee would be appointed to it. Rightly interpreting the act as a rebuke of his own leadership, Davis was sorely tempted to veto it; Mrs. Davis was quoted as saying, "If I were he I would die or be hung before I would submit to the humiliation." In the end Davis signed the act, and on February 6, as Grant tightened his grip on the lines below Petersburg, as Sheridan pursued his mission of waste in the Shenandoah Valley, and as Sherman's columns converged on ill-fated Columbia, Davis named Lee general in chief of Confederate forces.

Lee was a reluctant generalissimo. Because he was aware of Davis's objections, he had resisted Davis's earlier overtures that he take a position in charge of all military operations. Lee now softened the blow to Davis's pride by saying, "I am indebted alone to the kindness of his Excellency, the President, for my nomination to this high and arduous office."

Just as Grant had elected to go into the field with the Army of the Potomac, Lee elected to remain commander of the Army of Northern Virginia. Perhaps the reason he did so was best expressed by General Joseph E. Johnston, who had been idle since his removal from command in front of Atlanta. Johnston wrote to a friend, "Do not expect much of Lee in this capacity. He cannot give up the command of the Army of Northern Virginia without becoming merely a minor official...." Johnston's comment unquestionably grew in part out of his animosity for Davis; it doubtless exaggerated the extent to which Davis would have interfered with Lee if Lee had chosen to make his headquarters in Richmond. But Johnston's statement did accurately identify Davis's compulsion to play an active role in military command.

Lee could do little at this stage to alter the situation. Yet he began to contemplate the radical strategic move of abandoning the cities of the Confederacy and combining the remnants of all the southern armies into a single striking force. The first step toward this object was to urge Davis to bring Johnston out of retirement and place him in command of the forces opposing Sherman in the Carolinas. Davis made the appointment, doing so, he explained, in the hope that the defects he had seen in Johnston as an independent commander would be remedied under Lee's control. In the effort to stop or impede Sherman, Lee authorized Johnston to collect all available Confederate troops east of the Mississippi River, except those of the Army of Northern Virginia itself.

Johnston's performance, considering the state of Confederate transportation and supply, was truly impressive. Within a month he collected a force of some 45,000 troops, including Hardee's command from Charleston and what remained of the old Army of Tennessee, which had made the exhausting journey by rail and foot all the way from northern Mississippi. Seeking to prevent a junction of the armies of Sherman and Schofield at Goldsboro, Johnston set a small delaying force in front of Schofield and concentrated some 27,000 for a blow against Sherman's left wing, commanded by Major General Henry W. Slocum, near the town of Bentonville. The Confederate attack on March 19 was initially successful, but as Sherman rapidly brought up the bulk of his army, Johnston was forced to retreat. Four days later Sherman and Schofield joined forces in Goldsboro, where Sherman rested his army for three weeks in preparation for the final move to join Grant and close the ring on Lee.

As events turned out, Sherman's march to close the ring was never made. It was not required, and Grant wished the honor of defeating the Army of Northern Virginia to go to the Army of the Potomac alone, that the soldiers of the western army be given no occasion to claim credit for it. The extent of Confederate weakness became evident when Lee began operations for escape from the Petersburg siege. On March 25 he launched a concentrated attack on Fort Stedman at the center of the Petersburg line. Commanded by John B. Gordon, now a major general, because Hill was sick and Longstreet unrecovered from his wound, the immediate objective was to achieve a quick penetration that would force Grant to shift troops there and weaken his grip at the western extremity of his line, thus making it possible for Lee to extricate the bulk of his army.

Fort Stedman was taken by surprise and captured, but the endeavor was useless. Grant was able to counterattack and recover it almost immediately and at the same time to increase his pressure on the Confederate position southwest of Petersburg. Lee's desperate gamble had failed. Even more ominous, Sheridan now arrived at Grant's headquarters with his entire cavalry force and a corps of infantry on the way. This gave Grant the strength to deliver the *coup de grâce* to his stricken opponent, and Grant said to Sheridan, "I now feel like ending the matter." Anticipating Lee's attempt to escape, Grant ordered Sheridan's cavalry and the entire Army of the James, now commanded by Butler's successor, Major General Edward Ord, to sweep south of the Appomattox River and strike at the line of Confederate withdrawal and supply, the Southside Railroad.

Despite the failure at Fort Stedman, Lee on March 28 began his move. To protect his vulnerable right flank, he thinned his emaciated siege line to form a mobile force under General Fitzhugh Lee, which he sent to drive back the Union threat, and he instructed General George Pickett, the division commander on the right, to hold Five Forks, the key blocking position, "at all hazards," in order to prevent the Union forces from reaching the Southside Railroad.

Perhaps by now the holding of Five Forks was beyond Confederate capabilities, but the manner in which the position was lost shed no glory on the commanders who were responsible for defending it. Late in the afternoon of April 1, while Fitzhugh Lee and Pickett attended a shad bake at the headquarters of Major General Thomas L. Rosser, one of Fitzhugh Lee's cavalry commanders, Sheridan's corps overwhelmed the unprepared Confederates and took Five Forks. The following morning Grant broke the Confederate line in front of Petersburg with a frontal assault. Lee's entire position was now untenable, his army face to face with destruction. That night the Army of Northern Virginia, now only some 35,000 courageous but bedraggled troops, pulled out of their lines and marched west.

As the final scenes were being enacted in the Richmond entrenchments, the final scenes were also being enacted in the Richmond halls of legislation and administration. The exhausting debate over the arming of the slaves was the last activity of any significance attempted by the Confederate congress. On March 18 it adjourned to meet no more. For a few days Davis and his cabinet continued to assemble, engaged in what had now become a charade of deliberations. The morning of Sunday, April 2, Davis was as usual in his pew at St. Paul's Episcopal church when he received Lee's terse message that the capital must be abandoned at once. Davis rose and strode out of the church, his face as "impassive as an iron mask." That night he and his cabinet left the doomed city on a train headed south. The Confederate government had ceased to govern.

Lee's intention in withdrawing from the capital was to gain the Richmond and Danville Railroad and move south to a junction with Johnston. Sensing this purpose, Grant pressed forward relentlessly in two infantry columns and with Sheridan's cavalry harassing the retreating Confederates at every step. Lee reached the railroad at Amelia Courthouse, but there he lost a precious day because his orders for provisions had gone amiss, and he felt it imperative to forage rations for his starving men. This delay enabled Ord's column to seize the railroad at Burkeville, forcing Lee to continue his march west in the grim hope of joining Johnston by a roundabout route through Lynchburg.

The retreat now became a spectacle of hunger, exhaustion, and despair. Only reverence for its commander held the destitute Confederate army together. "Lee was somewhere to the front, so his army followed." Many soldiers did not follow, but, overcome with hardship and the futility of it all, dropped out of ranks by the hundreds. After a week of marching and skirmishing, and a pitched battle on April 6 with Sheridan's force at Sayler's Creek, only about three-fourths of the original Confederate formation remained. Meanwhile, Grant drove himself and his army unsparingly to outmarch Lee's faltering column. On the 8th Sheridan reached Appomattox Station ahead of the Confederates; by the following morning Ord's infantry also had arrived and was moving into position.

Two days earlier Grant had sent Lee an invitation to surrender because, as Grant expressed it, of the "hopelessness of further resistance," and in order to avoid the responsibility of additional bloodshed. Lee refused it. Believing that only Sheridan's cavalry was in front of him, Lee attacked on the morning of the 9th in the hope of breaking clear. As the Union horsemen gave way, the masses of blue-clad infantry deployed behind them came into view. Lee now made his most difficult decision as the commander of the Army of Northern Virginia, the decision to surrender.

Beyond a doubt, many of his troops at a word from him would have sacrificed themselves in a final, suicidal assault against the Union line. General E. Porter Alexander, Longstreet's outstanding chief of artillery, offered an alternative to surrender or a suicidal assault. Simply disband the army, suggested Alexander, and let the men report under arms to their state governors. In other words, let the South continue the struggle by guerrilla warfare.

Lee rejected the suggestion. As Christian men, he said, the commanders must consider the effect of such a decision upon the country as a whole, which was already demoralized from four years of war. Without rations and under no control, the men would be obliged to become marauders. Federal cavalry would pursue them and overrun many sections which otherwise might remain uninvaded. Such an action would bring on a state of affairs that would take the country years for recovery. The younger officers might "go to bushwhacking," said Lee, but for him, the only dignified course was to meet General Grant, surrender himself, and take the consequences of his acts.

The climax of the war occurred that afternoon in the parlor of the McLean house in the village of Appomattox Courthouse. In perhaps the most memorable scene of American history, Lee the patrician surrendered himself and his army to the magnanimous commoner who had overcome them. Grant permitted all officers and men to be paroled and to return to their homes; Confederate officers might retain their sidearms and horses. Upon Lee's quiet hint, Grant also permitted every Confederate soldier who claimed a horse or mule to keep the animal for working his farm. Lee remarked, "This will have the best possible effect upon the men. It will be very gratifying and will do much toward conciliating our people."

Federal troops occupied Richmond immediately after the Confederate withdrawal. Much of the city had gone up in flames that spread from burning arsenals, bridges, and warehouses. Lincoln visited Richmond on April 4 and sat in Davis's chair to the cheers of Union veterans. Two weeks later Lee rode home through the charred streets, saluted by the lifted caps of Confederate and Union troops alike.

The night of April 11, after returning from Richmond and receiving the electrifying news of Lee's surrender, Lincoln stood at a White House window and addressed the large crowd gathered on the lawn below. He chiefly talked about the problems of reconstruction. "It is fraught with great difficulty," he said. "Nor is it a small additional embarrassment that we, the loyal people, differ among ourselves as to the mode, manner, and means...." He dismissed as "a merely pernicious abstraction" the Radicals' theories concerning the legal status of the se-

RUINS OF RICHMOND   (Library of Congress)

ceded states; he repeated arguments he had made earlier defending his own plan of reconstruction; while admitting that the new Louisiana constitution was not perfect, he said of it, "We shall sooner have the fowl by hatching the egg than by smashing it."

Yet Lincoln also made statements indicating he was moving somewhat toward the views of his political opponents; that he was willing to modify his plan if it turned out to be "adverse to the public interest." He closed by saying that in the present situation, "it may be my duty to make some new announcement to the people of the South. I am considering, and shall not fail to act, when satisfied that the action will be proper."

Lincoln held his last cabinet meeting the morning of April 14, with General Grant in attendance. In discussing reconstruction, Lincoln admitted he had perhaps tried to move too fast. He approved a recommendation by Stanton for keeping an army of occupation in the South temporarily, but he disapproved of Stanton's suggestion that state boundaries be eliminated as a part of the process. The question of black suffrage was not discussed. As for the treatment of the Confederates themselves, Lincoln spoke kindly of Lee and other officers, and of the men in the ranks who had fought so gallantly for their cause. He said he desired no reprisals, no "bloody work," not even for the guiltiest secessionists, though he said he would like to see them frightened out of the country, and his hands made a sweeping gesture like that of shooing chickens.

Lincoln had no further opportunity to reveal his thoughts on the momentous events and issues of the times. That night at Ford's Theater, while enjoying Laura Keene's performance in *Our American*

Cousin, he was shot by John Wilkes Booth. That same night Seward was seriously wounded in an unsuccessful attempt on his life. Lincoln died the following day.

A moment after Lincoln's death, Stanton declared at his bedside, "Now he belongs to the ages," words that have been echoed ever since in the hearts of countless Americans. Overwhelmed by the news, George Templeton Strong wrote in his diary: "LINCOLN AND SEWARD ASSASSINATED LAST NIGHT!!! The South has nearly filled up the measure of her iniquities at last....I am stunned, as by a fearful personal calamity....We shall appreciate [Lincoln] at last."

Doubtless many northern Democrats shed few tears at the time; certainly those northerners who supported the Confederacy and those who had felt the heavy hand of arbitrary arrest and incarceration were unmoved. But the event was greeted with anguish and rage by millions of Lincoln's fellow citizens in the North, including many of his former critics and mockers; the ceremony of his lying in state in the Capitol and his funeral procession by shrouded train from Washington throughout the Northeast as far as Albany, then west to Chicago, and finally to his home town, Springfield, Illinois, for burial were attended by multitudes of grieving citizens.

The southern response to Lincoln's death was mixed. Many Confederates were happy to see an intractable foe cut down. One of them, expressing a mood doubtless shared by thousands, wrote, "Lincoln's death seemed...like a gleam of sunshine on a winter's day." A plantation girl said Booth had earned the applause of generations of southerners and that she hoped he would find refuge in the South. On the other hand, mass meetings occurred in most southern cities and adopted resolutions of regret and censure over the assassination. Unquestionably, this was done, at least in part, out of expediency. A young woman of New Orleans observed that the city was full of the tokens of mourning, and commented sardonically, "The more violently 'secesh' the inmates, the more thankful they are for Lincoln's death, the more profusely the houses are decked with emblems of woe....Men who have hated Lincoln with all their souls, under terror of confiscation and imprisonment...tie black crepe from every practicable knob and point to save their homes."

But many southerners had begun to discern a generosity of spirit and lack of vindictiveness in Lincoln's program for reconstruction. Possibly they had been moved also by the compassionate sections of his second inaugural. To these southerners he had emerged as a protector of the South against the malice of the Radicals; they considered his death a blow to the region as well as to the nation. Many of the high civil and military leaders of the Confederacy expressed what may reasonably be accepted as sincere regrets over the event; General Joseph E.

Johnston said it was "the greatest possible calamity to the South." Mary Boykin Chesnut said the ascension to the presidency of Andrew Johnson, "that vulgar renegade," would bring misery upon the South.

One of the most poignant expressions of dismay by a southerner over Lincoln's assassination occurred in the diary of a planter who had opposed secession but had loyally supported the Confederacy. He wrote: "[Lincoln's] death, is...in my judgment one of the greatest misfortunes that could have befallen the country....[It is] in my opinion, a great loss to the whole country & especially to the South—as from him, we had a right to expect better terms of peace than from any one else at all likely to come into power.—Oh! my poor country—What have you yet to Suffer."

Lincoln's death removed the very linchpin of the Union war effort, though the event occurred too late to affect the course of the war itself. What effect it had on the aftermath of the war has been the subject of endless controversy: whether Lincoln would have succeeded in maintaining a conciliatory reconstruction program for the seceded states; or in pursuit of such a program, would, like his successor, have been overridden and subjected to impeachment; or would ultimately have joined the Radicals in pursuit of their program.

The Radicals believed his death removed a serious obstacle to their plans. The day he died a group of them met in caucus; one of them, Congressman George W. Julian of Indiana, wrote of the meeting, "While everybody was shocked at his murder, the feeling was nearly universal that the accession of [Andrew] Johnson to the Presidency would prove a godsend to the country. Aside from Mr. Lincoln's known policy of tenderness to the Rebels...his...views of the subject of reconstruction were as distasteful as possible to radical Republicans."

In the shadow of tumultuous events in the field and in Washington, Jefferson Davis refused to give up. From Danville, Virginia, on April 5 he issued a proclamation in which he admitted the grave injury sustained by the Confederacy through the loss of its capital, but he called for a "new phase" of the struggle, outlining a fluid form of warfare, and saying, "Relieved of the necessity of guarding particular points, our army will be free to move from point to point, to strike the enemy far from his base."

Meeting a week later with General Joseph E. Johnston in Greensboro, North Carolina, Davis urged that the war be continued. But it now became clear that the surrender of Lee's army, and the prevailing war weariness and demoralization of the southern population, made further resistance out of the question. Johnston rejected Davis's overtures. On the 18th Johnston surrendered his force to General Sherman on terms far more favorable to the South than those offered to Lee, even agreeing to the recognition of the existing state governments if their officials would take the oath of allegiance to the Union, and assuring individual citizens of their personal, property, and political rights. Rebuffed by the Washington government, Sherman on the 26th applied terms similar to Grant's. On May 4 at the town of Citronelle, Alabama, a short distance north of Mobile, General Richard Taylor surrendered to General Canby the remaining Confederate army east of the Mississippi.

Still Davis pressed on. He and his wife and a small retinue of companions moved by rail through the Carolinas, then headed cross-country for the Trans-Mississippi Department, where he hoped for a revived Confederacy supported by General Kirby Smith and the one remaining organized Confederate force. This vision was soon dashed. On May 10, near the village of Irwinsville, Georgia, Davis and his party were discovered and captured by a detachment of Wilson's Union cavalry. On May 26 at Baton Rouge, General Kirby Smith surrendered his command to General Canby. The war was over.

XIV

Reflections on Men and Measures

———— ❖ ————

A period of a century and a quarter has passed since the end of the Civil War, and countless scholars, soldiers, and laymen alike have attempted to explain the causes for Union victory and Confederate defeat. Grady McWhiney and Perry D. Jamieson have observed that there are almost as many explanations for the outcome as there are historians writing about the conflict; and someone has calculated that books about the war have been written at a rate of more than one per day since the end of the war. Most of these works contain explanations, either explicit or implicit, for the result.

Robert E. Lee said in his final address to his troops at Appomattox that after four years of unsurpassed courage and fortitude they had been compelled to yield to overwhelming numbers and resources. Jefferson Davis, in his history of the rise and fall of the Confederate government, described the war as a contest of "unequal combats" by the Confederate armies and an "unequal struggle" by the Confederate population. Inadequacy of numbers and resources became the traditional explanation of the southern people for the region's failure to win.

Northerners of the war generation looked upon the Union victory as being the reward for superior virtue. The fervent abolitionist and nationalist Henry Wilson believed God Almighty had intervened to destroy both the sinful institution of slavery and the equally sinful effort of the South to withdraw from the Union. The popular historian James Ford Rhodes believed the moral ascendancy of Abraham Lincoln over Jefferson Davis was a critical factor in the Union triumph.

Twentieth-century scholars, both northern and southern, being further removed from the war and presumably freer of the passions and prejudices aroused by it, have usually tended to minimize northern superiority in numbers and resources as the key to Union victory. In 1919 Nathaniel W. Stephenson wrote that Confederate inner dissension and the strangling effects of the Union blockade accounted for the defeat of the South. A few years later Frank L. Owsley produced his explanation of Confederate defeat as being the result of the political doctrine of state rights.

Others have emphasized southern social and economic weaknesses as causes for Confederate defeat. Bell Wiley noted the disadvantage of the South as an agrarian and provincial society, "bound by its old ways and concepts... not sufficiently flexible to wage a modern war against the modern nation that its adversary had become." Peter J. Parish offers a corollary to this explanation, saying, "In military as in political leadership, the North eventually showed a resilience, a flexibility and a breadth of comprehension which the South could not match." It is fair to say that in some ways the Confederates were less revolutionary in their methods of waging revolution than the Federals in suppressing revolution.

Some students of the Civil War identify weaknesses in the fabric of the Confederacy even more fundamental than state rights, defective political administration, or social conservatism. McWhiney and Jamieson believe the Confederacy was a victim of its ethnic makeup, allegedly predominantly Celtic, which impelled its soldiers to launch suicidal charges mindlessly and repeatedly against newly adopted weapons, the rifled musket and Minié ball, that had made offensive tactics in close formation obsolete.

Professor Wiley suggested that southern unity was weakened by an exaggerated individualism; David Herbert Donald has followed a parallel argument to the conclusion that the Confederacy destroyed itself through an excess of democracy among its statesmen and soldiers. Wiley also believed that the southern will was palsied by feelings of guilt over the institution of slavery and the political heresy of secession. Beringer, Hattaway, Jones, and Still apotheosize this last idea in their statement that the epitaph of the Confederacy ought to read: "Died of Guilt and Failure of Will." Professor Drew Gilpin Faust has concluded that the very ideology of the Confederacy "was defeated in large measure by the internal contradictions that wartime circumstances brought so prominently to the fore."

These many theories have not been spun out of thin air. They are the conclusions reached by knowledgeable and serious students of the war. Unquestionably, there is evidence to be found for all of them. Perhaps the best place to begin still another discourse on the reasons for the outcome of the war is with the recognition that all such explanations represent conjecture, more or less informed opinion; that none of the various discrete explanations is final, and none is necessarily exclusive of the others.

The one factor acknowledged by all students of the war is that the Union possessed a heavy advantage in numbers and an awesome advantage in wealth and material resources. These disparities exceeded those said by Clausewitz to be adequate to guarantee victory under any circumstances. It cannot be demonstrated that a Confederate triumph was possible because, clearly, Confederate success required advantages in skill, unity, and will that were great enough to overcome the Union advantages in numbers, wealth, arms, and supplies. Equally clearly, the Confederacy failed to generate the necessary skill, unity, and will. Union victory was the result of a superiority in the sum of its war-making capacity, including numerical, material, and nonmaterial resources.

There is compelling evidence to believe that in addition to its numerical and material advantages, the Union ultimately succeeded in developing a more effective national strategy than the Confederacy, a strategy that skillfully combined domestic and diplomatic policies and resources behind the war effort. The Union also succeeded ultimately in developing a more comprehensive, and thus more effective, military strategy. These superior strategies were in part outgrowths of superior northern wealth, industry, transportation, and commerce, plus the experience derived from them. The strategies were also the products of more modern political and social systems. They demonstrated the accuracy of Clausewitz's generalization that societies tend to make war in a manner consistent with their own fundamental characteristics.

The Union strategies were also the fruit of superior leadership, in which Abraham Lincoln was the towering figure. Despite his lack of administrative or military experience, or, as some would say, because of his freedom from the blinders of such experience, he was able to see the war as a whole and to create a national strategy appropriate to Union needs. More clearly, perhaps, than any other single individual he perceived the preservation of the Union to be the primary and overarching war aim; and he held to that aim with remarkable tenacity and singleness of purpose, subordinating all other considerations to the achievement of it.

Just as important, Lincoln possessed an extraordinary ability to communicate his goals and plans to the masses of the northern population and persuade them to follow. Whether in the exalted phrases of his major addresses or the earthy sayings conveying his satisfaction or displeasure over issues or with generals, politicians, or editors, he touched the minds and hearts of a majority of the people. A master of the English prose, like Roosevelt and Churchill in a later struggle, Lincoln mobilized the language and sent it forth to war.

Lincoln was equally skillful in leading, inducing, cajoling, or coercing recalcitrant congressmen, cabinet members, generals, and other citizens to cooperate in carrying out his programs. He could be idealistic or pragmatic, intractable or flexible, arbitrary or negotiative, depending upon the issue and the situation. He sometimes captured and assumed the direction of movements—emancipation, for example—that were initiated by others. If on occasion he followed the precepts of Moses or Jesus Christ, at other times he moved in the spirit of Machiavelli or Bismarck.

Because Davis proved unable to achieve the goal of southern independence, because of the abrasive nature of his personality, and perhaps because after the war he was viewed as the archetypal unreconstructed rebel, many scholars have been tempted to caricature him as a bumbling and ineffectual war leader.

The historian David M. Potter once passed a withering judgment on Davis, say-ing: "There is no real evidence that [he] ever at any one time gave extended consideration to the basic question of what the South would have to do in order to win the war....It hardly seems unrealistic to suppose that if the Union and the Confederacy had exchanged Presidents with one another, the Confederacy might have won its independence."

This indictment is subject to challenge. Other respected scholars have ren-dered far more favorable opinions on Davis's leadership. Rembert Patrick made a cogent argument that in light of the Confederacy's many weaknesses and dis-abilities, Davis administered its government with genuine effectiveness. Hatta-way and Jones admit that Davis was politically less skillful than Lincoln, but they conclude that "the vigor and success of [Davis's] leadership in the military sphere suggest no shortcomings," and they go so far as to make the debatable judgment that the Confederate war effort was better mobilized and more effec-tually directed than the Union war effort.

Davis was obliged to work with the southern society as he found it, a soci-ety of many inherent weaknesses, especially for withstanding the massive stress of a conflict such as the Civil War. These weaknesses included the state rights political philosophy, agrarian hostility to taxation and distrust of govern-ment credit, resentment among the poor over real or alleged privileges to the rich, an individualistic and localistic folk culture that worked against coopera-tion among its leaders and citizens and fostered resentment toward regimenta-tion and discipline, and a parochial world view that exaggerated the degree of southern influence over the international economy.

The Confederacy was weakened also by the persistence of an open union-ism among many southerners and a latent unionism among an indeterminable number of others. All of these factors contributed to the shortcoming which a number of scholars today emphasize as the primary cause of Confederate de-feat: the failure to develop an invincible spirit of southern nationalism.

Unquestionably, Davis was a key figure in generating a redoubtable meas-ure of strength in the Confederacy. He was as firmly dedicated to southern sep-aration as Lincoln was to national preservation, and Davis imparted to the Con-federate cause much of the force of his personal character and determination. He appealed to the southern population in powerful addresses that drew for inspiration upon the revered themes of national independence and individual liberty.

Davis showed admirable resourcefulness in directing the process by which the Confederacy armed itself and sustained a prolonged and mighty war effort, an effort that is particularly impressive when the cost and duration of the Civil War are gauged by European conflicts of the same era—the Austro-Prussian War, which ended in Prussian victory in seven weeks, and the Franco-Prussian War, which ended in Prussian victory in six months. One may question whether in proportion to numbers and resources any other people to that time had developed greater conventional military prowess than did the Confed-eracy.

Although Davis was aware of the necessity of kindling and fostering an indomitable spirit of Confederate nationalism among southerners, and although he devoted much of his energy to this endeavor, his efforts were not equal to the task. Thus his failure as a political leader contributed to his failure as a war leader. His imperious attitude and implacable emphasis on prerogative, aggravated perhaps by physical illness, made him aloof, brittle, and inflexible. He could be broken, it was said, but never bent. That anyone could have maintained harmonious relations with the many spitfires among the politicians and generals of the Confederacy is highly doubtful; Davis's demeanor toward them made friction inevitable and ruinous.

Despite the sincerity and vigor of Davis's appeals and declarations, they fell short of Lincoln's greatest efforts in communication. Davis's most recent biographer, Clement Eaton, wrote that Davis was technically Lincoln's superior in this art, but that the loftiness of the Union cause elevated Lincoln's addresses above Davis's. Whatever the explanation, Davis did not match Lincoln in the rhetoric of statesmanship. Davis's communications with the common people were markedly less effective still, at least until it was too late to matter. Professor Wiley said Davis seemed oblivious of the necessity of taking them into his confidence. Alluding to an acclaimed practice of President Roosevelt's during World War II, Wiley said that a "fireside chat" by Davis would have been unthinkable.

The most striking contrast between Lincoln and Davis as commanders in chief was in Lincoln's insistence on appointing a general in chief and Davis's refusal to accept one until it was too late to exert any significant effect on the course of the war. Eventually, Lincoln found in Grant the ideal man to serve as the Union general in chief; Grant provided the concert of effort and the exercise of will required for victory.

The Confederacy's preeminent general, Lee, probably should have been appointed general in chief early in the war. As an army commander he was without superior, possibly without peer. Hattaway and Jones, who are at times quite critical of him, conclude nevertheless that in operational skill he stands out above all other generals of the war. Whether Lee could have devised and executed a more comprehensive and effectual overall strategy is a matter of controversy among students of the conflict. But his appointment would have given the Confederacy a genuine unity of command, and there seems little doubt that he would have achieved a far greater degree of coordination and cooperation, both among his subordinate generals and with Davis.

Because the actual Confederate strategy was unable to achieve victory it has been the target of much criticism, especially in recent years. The criticisms usually reflect a marked degree of historical presentism; they tend to measure Confederate strategy by the concepts prevailing at the critic's own time. The doctrines of total war that emerged from the American experience in World War II and were reinforced by the American interpretation of the writings of Clausewitz, especially his emphasis on the destruction of the enemy's armed forces as the ultimate means of gaining victory, inspired military historians to reexamine the Civil War in these lights.

Accordingly, Lincoln, Grant, and Sherman came to be viewed as modern war makers; Davis, Lee, and Jackson as old-fashioned soldiers. The foremost Union generals were thought to have been Clausewitzian without knowing it; the Confederates, Jominian by training, mentality, and habit. Many scholars favored the strategy of western concentration that the Confederate authorities were accused of rejecting, though the most recent analyst of this question, Richard M. McMurry, argues that the Davis administration did not in fact neglect the West. Advocates of a more complete western concentration see in such a move an application of "global" strategy, in the symbolic sense, to the geography and other circumstances of the Civil War.

Conjecturally, the adoption by the Confederacy of some form of military strategy different from that actually employed might have been a wise move. Yet, that any strategy could have achieved a Confederate victory through battles of decision in the field is questionable. Besides the Confederate disadvantages in numbers, arms, and supplies, the southern political, economic, and social structure probably was too fragile to sustain indefinitely a struggle of this kind with the North, a struggle in which the southern people suffered an immensely disproportionate burden in casualties, destruction, and disruption.

Recent military experiences throughout the world, especially those of the United States in Vietnam and of the Soviet Union in Afghanistan, have lent weight to still another form of criticism of Confederate strategy. As the weaker contestant, goes this line of thought, the Confederacy might have adopted the classic strategy of the weak: that of avoiding battles of decision, freely yielding territory for a time, employing hit-and-run tactics, and resorting to wholesale guerrilla warfare. In this way, it is believed, the will of the Union ultimately may have been extinguished by attrition.

The argument in favor of guerrilla warfare by the Confederacy is by no means a new one. General Alexander suggested guerrilla warfare to Lee at Appomattox, and Davis had some such mode of warfare in mind for continuing Confederate resistance. Union authorities feared it would occur. The argument is plausible; an intractably determined people waging guerrilla warfare can be exterminated but not conquered. Southerners during the American Revolution had demonstrated both a staunch determination and marked skills in guerrilla operations. Guerrilla activities actually carried out by the Confederacy on a limited scale indicated that southerners still possessed comparable skills. Lee no doubt could have inspired a formidable guerrilla movement, though both his reason and his sense of honor prohibited him from resorting to it. Unquestionably, the Forrests, Morgans, Wheelers, Mosbys, and other Confederates of similar talent were ideally suited to such a program.

There is, however, serious question whether a dependence on general guerrilla warfare was at all feasible for the Confederate leaders. It would have been out of the question at the beginning of the war when most southerners earnestly believed they were capable of winning by conventional means. Any Confederate administration proposing to give up the land to the enemy without decisive battles probably would have been ousted, as, most likely, would a present-day national administration proposing such a strategy against an invader of superior resources. Equally questionable is the view that after four years of voluminous bloodshed and property destruction, and decisive defeat in the field, the majority of the southern people would have been willing to undertake an endless guerrilla war.

Though theoretically by guerrilla warfare the Confederacy may have been capable of winning its independence, in fact the effort would have been hamstrung by many of the same weaknesses that reduced the effectiveness of Confederate action in conventional warfare. Moreover, the risks of guerrilla warfare were far greater than those of conventional warfare. It has been suggested that the Confederacy may have been obliged to carry out such operations for decades in order to achieve its goal. This would have provoked an indefinitely extended federal military occupation accompanied by martial law. It doubtless would have resulted in wholesale executions and imprisonments, civil strife between southern classes and factions, widespread confiscation and redistribution of property, and arming of the freedmen to bolster the counterforce and constabulary: in brief, the massive and permanent disruption, the obliteration, of the southern way of life. If unsuccessful in achieving independence, guerrilla warfare would have been devastating beyond measure.

It can, of course, be argued problematically that such federal policies would have aroused among southern whites the very irrepressible spirit of solidarity and resistance required for winning independence. But even if ultimately successful in this object, guerrilla warfare would have wrought havoc in the region; Clausewitz said this kind of operation might be considered as "a state of legalized anarchy that is as much a threat to the social order at home as it is to the enemy."

Quite likely, this form of resistance would have been more destructive to southerners than purchasing peace with a surrender that they conceived as permitting them to retain their dignity and sense of honor, their place in the political structure of the nation, their homes and other property except slaves, which were owned by only a minority of the white families, and most of the ingredients of their traditional way of life. Lee did not explicitly say all this in rejecting the appeal for guerrilla warfare, but the idea may be read between his lines. It can be detected also in the behavior of the southern population in embracing his decision.

The Civil War was fought at immense cost in blood and treasure. On both sides it inspired prodigies of valor and sacrifice, and aroused a profound spirit of ruthlessness and brutality. Out of the relatively small population of that day, more Americans, Union and Confederate, died of wounds and disease in the Civil War than in all other American wars together prior to Vietnam. The estimated toll in the lives of Union servicemen was 360,000; in the lives of Confederate servicemen, 258,000. Losses by the United States population in 1990 in proportion to Union losses would be almost 4 million; in proportion to losses by the southern white population, above 11 million.

The war settled two issues, those of slavery and the permanence of the Union, that had to be resolved in order for the United States to become the nation it has become: a nation committed, however halting and incomplete the fulfillment, to the ideals expressed by Lincoln at Gettysburg. Whether in time the issues that caused the war could have been settled peacefully has been the subject of a continuing debate that yields no absolute answer. Most Americans, North and South, perceive the conflict as a tragic but inevitable and heroic episode in the life of the country. The story of the war is the American Iliad.

Sources

———— ❖ ————

According to the latest count, approximately 90,000 books and articles have been written on the multifarious aspects of the Civil War, and the number still grows at a remarkable rate. Obviously, the presentation here of an exhaustive bibliography is impossible. Offered instead is a selective body of works covering the present study.

The most complete bibliographical guide to the literature on the Civil War is Allan Nevins, Bell I. Wiley, and James I. Robertson, *Civil War Books: A Critical Bibliography* (2 vols.; 1967–1969). The greatest of all sources on the war is *The War of the Rebellion: A Compilation of the Official Records of the Union and Confederate Armies* (128 vols. and index; 1880–1901). The companion source on the war at sea is *Official Records of the Union and Confederate Navies in the War of the Rebellion* (30 vols.; 1894–1922). Although the *Official Records* deal primarily with military policies and campaigns, they also contain a wealth of information on nonmilitary affairs that were related to the war. Other public documents of great value include the *Congressional Globe* and the published miscellaneous documents of both the United States Senate and the House of Representatives.

The background of the Civil War and the course of the war itself are set forth in great detail in James Ford Rhodes, *History of the United States from the Compromise of 1850* (9 vols.; 1893–1900). A recent work of comparable scope is Allan Nevins, *The Ordeal of the Union* (8 vols.; 1947–1971). An excellent study of the breakdown of national harmony is Roy F. Nicholls, *The Disruption of American Democracy* (1948). Opposing points of view on the inevitability of the war are offered in Arthur C. Cole, *The Irrepressible Conflict, 1850–1865* (1934), and Avery O. Craven, *The Coming of the Civil War* (1942), *The Repressible Conflict, 1830–1861* (1939), and *The Growth of Southern Nationalism* (1953). The most complete discussion of the Dred Scott decision is Don E. Fehrenbacher, *The Dred Scott Case: Its Significance in American Law and Politics* (1978). A full and insightful analysis of the intensification of sectional controversy during the thirteen years immediately preceding the war is David M. Potter, *The Impending Crisis, 1848–1861* (1976).

A number of recent studies broaden the perspective on the background to the war by analyzing the political motivations of both northerners and southerners beyond the concern over slavery. Among the more useful of these works are William E. Gienapp, *The Origins of the Republican Party, 1852–1856* (1987), and "Who Voted for Lincoln?" in John L. Thomas, *Abraham Lincoln and the American Political Tradition* (1986); Eric Foner, *Free Soil, Free Labor, Free Men: The Ideology of the Republican Party before the Civil War* (1970); William J. Cooper, *The South and the Politics of Slavery* (1978), and *Liberty and Slavery:*

Southern Politics to 1860 (New York, 1983); Michael F. Holt, *The Political Crisis of the 1850s* (1978); and J. Mills Thornton, *Politics and Power in a Slave Society: Alabama, 1800–1860* (1977). Robert F. Durden, *The Self-Inflicted Wound: Southern Politics in the Nineteenth Century* (1985), emphasizes the role of racism in southern politics of the period.

Works concentrating on secession or the response to it include Dwight L. Dumond, *The Secession Movement, 1860–1861* (1931); Ralph Wooster, *The Secession Conventions of the South* (1962); Steven A. Channing, *Crisis of Fear: Secession in South Carolina* (1970); Joseph Carlyle Sitterson, *The Secession Movement in North Carolina* (1939); William L. Barney, *The Secessionist Impulse: Alabama and Mississippi in 1860* (1974); Michael P. Johnson, *Toward a Patriarchal Republic: The Secession of Georgia* (1977); and Donald E. Reynolds, *Editors Make War: Southern Newspapers in the Secession Crisis, 1860–1861* (1970). The best account of the North's immediate reaction to secession is Kenneth M. Stampp, *And the War Came: The North and the Secession Crisis, 1860–1861* (1950).

There is a wealth of general works on the Civil War. The best of the older treatments is Rhodes, *History of the United States from the Compromise of 1850*. Jefferson Davis, *The Rise and Fall of the Confederate Government* (2 vols.; 1881), though strongly reflecting Davis's own views, presents valuable information and insights on the conflict. The most detailed modern work on the war is Allan Nevins, *The War for the Union* (4 vols.; 1959–1971), which constitutes the last four volumes of *The Ordeal of the Union.* Among the most readable multiple-volume accounts are Bruce Catton, *The Centennial History of the Civil War* (3 vols.; 1961–1965); and Shelby Foote, *The Civil War: A Narrative* (3 vols.; 1958–1974).

A landmark work among single-volume, comprehensive histories of the conflict is James G. Randall and David Herbert Donald, *The Civil War and Reconstruction* (2d ed.; 1961). Other excellent single-volume works include James M. McPherson, *Ordeal by Fire: The Civil War and Reconstruction* (1982) and *Battle Cry of Freedom: The Civil War Era* (1988); and Peter J. Parish, *The American Civil War* (1975). Richard H. Sewell, *A House Divided: Sectionalism and Civil War, 1848–1865* (1988), provides a concise discussion of the war and its causes.

A brief and highly useful account of the military campaigns, though now dated in some of its interpretations, is R. Ernest Dupuy and Trevor N. Dupuy, *The Compact History of the Civil War* (1960). An extremely helpful campaign-by-campaign narrative is Thomas E. Griess (ed.), *The American Civil War* (1988), a volume in the West Point Military History Series.

Pictorial histories of the war abound. There are countless thousands of images of the myriad aspects of the struggle, and great numbers of them have been reproduced in books that combine photographs with textual narratives. The most eminent early work of this sort is Francis T. Miller, *The Photographic History of the Civil War* (10 vols.; 1912), reissued in 1957 with an introduction by Henry Steele Commager. Other publications include Richard M. Ketchum (ed.), *The American Heritage Picture History of the Civil War,* text by Bruce Catton (1960); Hirst D. Milhollen and Milton Kaplan (eds.), *Divided We Fought: A Pictorial History of the War, 1861–1865,* text by David Herbert Donald (1956); and Bell I. Wiley, *The Common Soldier of the Civil War* (1975), and *The Embattled Confederates: An Illustrated History of Southerners at War,* illustrations compiled by Hirst D. Milhollen (1964). A recent work that includes many heretofore unpublished photographs and is accompanied by excellent essays on the major aspects of the war is William C. Davis (ed.), *The Image of War, 1861–1865* (6 vols.; 1981–1984).

The Confederate experience has been recorded in a number of general accounts. Among the better older books are Nathaniel W. Stephenson, *The Day of the Confederacy* (1920); and Robert S. Henry, *The Story of the Confederacy* (1931). More recent works include Clement Eaton, *A History of the Southern Confederacy* (1954); Charles P. Roland, *The Confederacy* (1960); Frank E. Vandiver, *Their Tattered Flags: The Epic of the Confederacy* (1970); and Emory M. Thomas, *The Confederate Nation, 1861–1865* (1979). The fullest treatment of internal affairs in the Confederacy is E. Merton Coulter, *The Confederate States of America, 1861–1865* (1950). Other useful works are Clifford Dowdey, *Experiment in Rebellion* (1946), and *The Land They Fought For: The Story of the South as the Confederacy, 1832–1865* (1955).

Biographies of the civil leaders North and South provide a wealth of information on all aspects of the war. Studies of Lincoln and Davis are particularly enlightening. The most complete works on Lincoln, dated but still useful, are John G. Nicolay and John Hay, *Abraham Lincoln: A History* (10 vols.; 1917); and Roy P. Basler and others (eds.), *The Collected Works of Abraham Lincoln* (9 vols.; 1953–1955). James G. Randall, *Lincoln the President* (4 vols., last vol. completed by Richard N. Current; 1945–1955), is the most detailed and most critically scholarly of the studies of Lincoln in the White House. An excellent single-volume biography is Benjamin P. Thomas, *Abraham Lincoln: A Biography* (1952). Highly readable but more controversial is Stephen B. Oates, *With Malice Toward None: The Life of Abraham Lincoln* (1977). Extremely colorful but uncritical is Carl Sandburg, *Abraham Lincoln: The Prairie Years* (2 vols.; 1926), and *Abraham Lincoln: The War Years* (4 vols.; 1939).

Interesting and valuable works on various phases of Lincoln's career include David M. Potter, *Lincoln and His Cabinet in the Secession Crisis* (1942); David Herbert Donald, *Lincoln Reconsidered: Essays on the Civil War* (1956); Richard N. Current, *The Lincoln Nobody Knows* (1958), and *Lincoln and the First Shot* (1963); and T. Harry Williams, *Lincoln and the Radicals* (1941), and *Lincoln and His Generals* (1952).

No definitive biography of Davis has been written. Early studies include William E. Dodd, *Jefferson Davis* (1907); Hamilton J. Eckenrode, *Jefferson Davis: President of the South* (1923); and Robert McElroy, *Jefferson Davis, the Unreal and the Real* (2 vols.; 1937). Colorful but uncritical is Hudson Strode, *Jefferson Davis* (3 vols.; 1955–1964). Sympathetic but balanced is Clement Eaton, *Jefferson Davis* (1977). Davis's papers have been published by Dunbar Rowland (ed.), *Jefferson Davis, Constitutionalist: His Letters, Papers, and Speeches* (10 vols.; 1923). A later and more critical issue of Davis's papers, now under way and complete to the mid-1850s by Haskell M. Monroe, Jr., James T. McIntosh, Lynda L. Crist, Mary S. Dix, and Richard E. Beringer (eds.) is *The Papers of Jefferson Davis* (6 vols. to date; 1971–1989).

Useful studies of major figures in Lincoln's cabinet include Glyndon G. Van Deusen, *William Henry Seward* (1967); Albert B. Hart, *Salmon Portland Chase* (1899); Thomas G. Belden and Marva R. Belden, *So Fell the Angels* (1966); Frederick J. Blue, *Salmon P. Chase: A Life in Politics* (1987); Benjamin P. Thomas and Harold M. Hyman, *Stanton: The Life and Times of Lincoln's Secretary of War*

(1962); and John Niven, *Gideon Welles: Lincoln's Secretary of the Navy* (1973). The views of participants in the Union administration occur in Gideon Welles, *Diary of Gideon Welles: Secretary of the Navy under Lincoln and Johnson* (3 vols.; 1911); and David Herbert Donald (ed.), *Inside Lincoln's Cabinet: The Civil War Diaries of Salmon P. Chase* (1954). Helpful works on important figures in Davis's cabinet include Robert D. Meade, *Judah P. Benjamin: Confederate Statesman* (1943); Eli Evans, *Judah P. Benjamin: The Jewish Confederate* (1987); Joseph T. Durkin, *Stephen R. Mallory: Confederate Navy Chief* (1954); and George G. Shackelford, *George Wythe Randolph and the Confederate Elite* (1988).

Among the most helpful specific campaign and battle accounts are Edwin B. Coddington, *The Gettysburg Campaign: A Study in Command* (1968); Harry W. Pfanz, *Gettysburg: The Second Day* (1987); Stephen W. Sears, *Landscape Turned Red: The Battle of Antietam* (1983); James Lee McDonough, *Shiloh: In Hell before Night* (1977), *Stones River: Bloody Winter in Tennessee* (1980), *Chattanooga: A Death Grip on the Confederacy* (1984), and, with Thomas L. Connelly, *Five Tragic Hours: The Battle of Franklin* (1983); Stanley Horn, *The Decisive Battle of Nashville* (1956); Earl Schenck Miers, *Web of Victory: Grant at Vicksburg* (1955); Peter F. Walker, *Vicksburg: A People at War* (1960); Samuel Carter, *The Final Fortress* (1980); Lawrence L. Hewitt, *Port Hudson: Confederate Bastion on the Mississippi* (1987); Fairfax Downey, *Storming the Gateway: Chattanooga, 1863* (1960); Joseph T. Glatthaar, *The March to the Sea and Beyond: Sherman's Troops in the Savannah & Carolina Campaigns* (1987); and John G. Barrett, *Sherman's March through the Carolinas* (1956).

The story of the Army of the Potomac is movingly told by Bruce Catton, *Mr. Lincoln's Army* (1951), *Glory Road: The Bloody Route from Fredericksburg to Gettysburg* (1952), and *A Stillness at Appomattox* (1953). The story of the Army of Tennessee is related by Stanley Horn, *The Army of Tennessee: A Military History* (1941); and, more critically and in greater detail, by Thomas L. Connelly, *Army of the Heartland: The Army of Tennessee, 1861–1862* (1967), and *Autumn of Glory: The Army of Tennessee, 1862–1865* (1971). Richard M. McMurry, *Two Great Rebel Armies: An Essay in Confederate Military History* (1989), offers a brief but insightful comparison of the two major Confederate field forces.

Biographies and published memoirs of the military leaders contain detailed accounts of the campaigns and battles of the war. The most famous of the published memoirs are *Personal Memoirs of U. S. Grant* (2 vols.; 1885–1886); and *Memoirs of W. T. Sherman, Written by Himself* (2 vols.; 1875). Confederate memoirs include John Bell Hood, *Advance and Retreat: Personal Experiences in the United States and Confederate States Armies* (1880); and Joseph E. Johnston, *Narrative of Military Operations...during the Late War between the States* (1874). General Beauregard's memoirs were published by proxy Alfred Roman, *The Military Operations of General Beauregard in the War between the States, 1861–1865* (2 vols.; 1884). Richard Taylor, *Destruction and Reconstruction: Personal Experiences of the Late War* (1879), is a masterpiece of Confederate reminiscence. Edward Porter Alexander, *Military Memoirs of a Confederate: A Critical Narrative* (1918), and *Fighting for the Confederacy: The Personal Recollections of General Edward Porter Alexander*, ed. by Gary W. Gallagher (1989), offer both excellent narrative and thoughtful criticism on Confederate operations. Informative and insightful articles on the campaigns, produced by officers on both sides, are found in *The Annals of the War Written by Leading Participants North and South* (1879); also by participants, but more polemical and less reliable, are articles in *Battles and Leaders of the Civil War*, ed. by R. U. Johnson and C. C. Buel (4 vols.; 1887–1888).

Preeminent among the biographies, though vulnerable to criticism for being too uncritical toward its subject, is Douglas S. Freeman, *R. E. Lee: A Biography* (4 vols.; 1934–1935), and its supplement, *Lee's Lieutenants* (3 vols.; 1942–1944). Other studies of top-ranking generals on both sides include Warren W. Hassler, Jr:, *General George B. McClellan: Shield of the Union* (1957); Stephen W. Sears, *George B. McClellan: The Young Napoleon* (1988); Stephen E. Ambrose, *Halleck: Lincoln's Chief of Staff* (1962); J. F. C. Fuller, *The Generalship of Ulysses S. Grant* (2d ed.; 1958), and *Grant and Lee: A Study in Personality and Generalship* (1933); William S. McFeely, *Grant: A Biography* (1981); Basil H. Liddell Hart, *Sherman: Soldier, Realist, American* (1929); Lloyd Lewis, *Sherman, Fighting Prophet* (1932); James M. Merrill, *William Tecumseh Sherman* (1971); T. Harry Williams, *P. G. T. Beauregard: Napoleon in Gray* (1955); Joseph H. Parks, *General Edmund Kirby Smith, C.S.A.* (1954); Gilbert E. Govan and James W. Livingood, *A Different Valor: The Story of General Joseph E. Johnston, C.S.A.* (1956); Charles P. Roland, *Albert Sidney Johnston: Soldier of Three Republics* (1964); Grady McWhiney, *Braxton Bragg and Confederate Defeat* (1969); and Richard M. McMurry, *John Bell Hood and the War for Southern Independence* (1982).

Books are available on virtually all of the most important lower-ranking generals on both sides. Among these works are Richard O'Connor, *Sheridan the Inevitable* (1953); Freeman Cleaves, *Rock of Chickamauga: The Life of General George H. Thomas* (1948), and *Meade of Gettysburg* (1960); Glenn Tucker, *Hancock the Superb* (1960); Richard Elliott Winslow, *General John Sedgwick: The Story of a Union Corps Commander* (1982); Russell F. Weigley, *Quartermaster-General of the Union Army: A Biography of Montgomery C. Meigs* (1959); G. F. R. Henderson, *Stonewall Jackson and the American Civil War* (2 vols.; 1919); Frank E. Vandiver, *Mighty Stonewall* (1957); H. J. Eckenrode and Bryan Conrad, *James Longstreet: Lee's War Horse* (1936); Donald B. Sanger and Thomas R. Hay, *James Longstreet* (1952); William Garrett Piston, *Lee's Tarnished Lieutenant: James Longstreet and His Place in Southern History* (1987); Nathaniel Cheairs Hughes, Jr., *General William J. Hardee: Old Reliable* (1965); Robert S. Henry, *"First with the Most" Forrest* (1944); Emory M. Thomas, *Bold Dragoon: The Life of J. E. B. Stuart* (1986); James I. Robertson, *General A. P. Hill: The Story of a Confederate Warrior* (1987); and Gary W. Gallagher, *Stephen Dodson Ramseur: Lee's Gallant General* (1985).

Brief biographies of all the general officers in both armies are in Ezra J. Warner, *Generals in Gray: Lives of the Confederate Commanders* (1959), and *Generals in Blue: Lives of the Union Commanders* (1964).

The classic treatments of the lives of the soldiers on both sides are Bell I. Wiley, *The Life of Johnny Reb: The Common Soldier of the Confederacy* (1943), and *The Life of Billy Yank: The Common Soldier of the Union* (1952). A splendid work updating and enhancing Wiley's studies is James I. Robertson, Jr., *Soldiers Blue and Gray* (1988). Gerald F. Linderman, *Embattled Courage: The Experience of Combat in the American Civil War* (1987); and Reid Mitchell, *Civil War Soldiers: Their Expectations and Experiences* (1988), analyze motivation through intensive examinations of letters and diaries of both Union and Confederate soldiers.

Among the studies of the naval war is the trilogy, *The Navy in the Civil War* (1883), which includes Daniel Ammen, *The Atlantic Coast*; A. T. Mahan, *The Gulf and Inland Waters*; and James R. Soley, *The Blockade and the Cruisers.* Another older work is Charles B. Boynton, *The History of the Navy during the Rebellion* (2 vols.; 1867–1868). A comprehensive modern study is Virgil Carrington Jones, *The Civil War at Sea* (3 vols.; 1960–1962). An excellent essay on the Union blockade is James M. Merrill, "Strangling the South," in William C. Davis (ed.), *The Embattled Confederacy*, vol. 3 of *The Image of War.* The standard work on the river operations is H. Allen Gosnell, *Guns on the Western Waters: The Story of River Gunboats in the Civil War* (1949). Rowena Reed, *Combined Operations in the Civil War* (1978), deals with army-navy operations.

Studies of Confederate efforts at sea include J. T. Scharf, *History of the Confederate States Navy* (1887); Tom H. Wells, *The Confederate Navy: A Study in Organization* (1971); William N. Still, *Confederate Shipbuilding* (1969), and *Iron Afloat: The Story of the Confederate Armorclads* (1971); and Stephen R. Wise, *Lifeline of the Confederacy: Blockade Running during the War* (1988).

Works on the vital role of the railroads in the war include Thomas Weber, *The Northern Railroads in the Civil War, 1861–1865* (1952); George E. Turner, *Victory Rode the Rails: The Strategic Place of the Railroads in the Civil War* (1953); and Robert C. Black III, *The Railroads of the Confederacy* (1952).

Specialized works that throw light on, or raise thoughtful questions about, Civil War administration, strategy, tactics, logistics, and operations include J. G. Randall, *Constitutional Problems under Lincoln* (rev. ed.; 1951); Rembert W. Patrick, *Jefferson Davis and His Cabinet* (1944); Emory M. Thomas, *The Confederacy as a Revolutionary Experience* (1970); Raimondo Luraghi, *The Rise and Fall of the Plantation South* (1978); Archer Jones, *Confederate Strategy from Shiloh to Vicksburg* (1961); Bruce Catton, *Reflections on the Civil War* (1981); and Grady McWhiney (ed.), *Grant, Lee, Lincoln and the Radicals* (1964). William A. Tidwell, with James O. Hall and David Winfred Gaddy, *Come Retribution: The Confederate Secret Service and the Assassination of Lincoln* (1988), employs circumstantial evidence to link the Confederate government with a plot to kidnap the president.

Among the studies that especially address the reasons for Union victory and Confederate defeat are Bell I. Wiley, *The Road to Appomattox* (1956); David M. Potter, "Jefferson Davis and the Political Factors in Confederate Defeat," in *The South and the Sectional Conflict* (1968); David Herbert Donald (ed.), *Why the North Won the Civil War* (1960); Paul D. Escott, *After Secession: Jefferson Davis and the Failure of Confederate Nationalism* (1978); Herman Hattaway and Archer Jones, *How the North Won: A Military History of the Civil War* (1983); Grady McWhiney and Perry D. Jamieson, *Attack and Die: Civil War Military Tactics and the Southern Heritage* (1982); Richard E. Beringer, Herman Hattaway, Archer Jones, and William N. Still, Jr., *Why the South Lost the Civil War* (1986); and Drew Gilpin Faust, *The Creation of Confederate Nationalism: Ideology and Identity in the Civil War South* (1988).

Studies that give information and insights into the nature of life on the home front during the war include Emerson D. Fite, *Social and Industrial Conditions in the North during the Civil War* (1910); Margaret Leech, *Reveille in Washington, 1860–1865* (1941); Wood Gray, *The Hidden Civil War: The Story of the Copperheads* (1942); Frank L. Klement, *The Copperheads in the Middle West* (1960), and *The Limits of Dissent: Clement L. Vallandigham and the Civil War* (1970); George M. Frederickson, *The Inner Civil War: Northern Intellectuals and the Crisis of the Union*

(1965); Daniel Aaron, *The Unwritten War: American Writers and the Civil War* (1973); J. Cutler Andrews, *The North Reports the Civil War* (1955), and *The South Reports the Civil War* (1970); Bell I. Wiley, *The Plain People of the Confederacy* (1944), and *Confederate Women* (1975); Charles W. Ramsdell, *Behind the Lines in the Southern Confederacy* (1944); and Charles P. Roland, "The South at War," in *The Embattled Confederacy*.

Mary Elizabeth Massey, *Refugee Life in the Confederacy* (1964), gives an account of the experiences of the South's uprooted population. The same author's *Bonnet Brigades* (1966) presents the wartime story of women in both the Union and the Confederacy. Anne Firor Scott, *The Southern Lady: From Pedestal to Politics, 1830–1930* (1970), contains important information on women in the Confederacy, and especially their attitude toward slavery. Randall C. Jimerson, *The Private Civil War: Popular Thought during the Sectional Conflict* (1988), probes the ideology that motivated both sides in the war.

Among the works dealing with the peculiar experience of blacks during the war are Bell I. Wiley, *Southern Negroes, 1861–1865* (1938); Benjamin Quarles, *The Negro in the Civil War* (1953); Dudley T. Cornish, *The Sable Arm: Negro Troops in the Union Army, 1861–1865* (1956), and "Slaves No More," in *The Embattled Confederacy*; Joseph T. Glatthaar, *Forged in Battle: The Civil War Alliance of Black Soldiers and White Officers* (1989); Willie Lee Rose, *Rehearsal for Reconstruction: The Port Royal Experiment* (1964); James H. Brewer, *The Confederate Negro: Virginia's Craftsmen and Military Laborers, 1861–1865* (1969); and Clarence L. Mohr, *On the Threshold of Freedom: Masters and Slaves in Civil War Georgia* (1986). V. Jacque Voegeli, *Free but Not Equal: The Midwest and the Negro during the Civil War* (1967), analyzes brilliantly the shifting attitudes of the citizens of the Midwest toward slavery and blacks, and the response of the Lincoln administration to the political implications of these attitudes.

James M. McPherson, *The Struggle for Equality: Abolitionists and the Negro in the Civil War and Reconstruction* (1964), discusses the efforts of northern blacks and abolitionists to secure black rights during the war. Lawanda C. Cox, *Lincoln and Black Freedom: A Study in Presidential Leadership* (1981), states the case for Lincoln as a supporter of rights for blacks. John Cimprich and R. L. Mansfort, "Fort Pillow Revisited," in *Civil War History*, 28 (December 1982), pp. 293–306, throws additional light on a tragic and controversial episode of the war.

Incomparable sources of information on the home front are the diaries, memoirs, and letters written during the war, many of which have been published. The outstanding northern diary is Allan Nevins and Milton Halsey Thomas (eds.), *The Diary of George Templeton Strong: The Civil War 1860–1865* (1952). The best published version of the diary of Mary Boykin Chesnut, the most famous Confederate diary, is C. Vann Woodward (ed.), *Mary Chesnut's Civil War* (1981). The published letters of the Charles Colcock Jones family, the outstanding collection of Confederate letters, are Robert Manson Myers (ed.), *The Children of Pride: A True Story of Georgia and the Civil War* (1972), and an abridged edition of the same work with a number of previously unpublished letters (1984).

Selected older works dealing with the diplomatic affairs of the war include Ephraim D. Adams, *Great Britain and the American Civil War* (2 vols.; 1925); and Frank L. Owsley, *King Cotton Diplomacy: Foreign Relations of the Confederate States of America* (1931). Karl Marx and Friedrich Engels, *The Civil War in the United*

States, ed. by Richard Enmale (1937), reveals the attitude of these historic European radicals toward the American conflict. Among the more recent studies are David P. Crook, *The North, the South, and the Powers* (1974); Norman A. Graebner, "Northern Diplomacy and European Neutrality," in David Herbert Donald (ed.), *Why the North Won the Civil War*; Lynn M. Case and Warren F. Spencer, *The United States and France: Civil War Diplomacy* (1970); Frank J. Merli, *Great Britain and the Confederate Navy, 1861–1865* (1970); Martin Duberman, *Charles Francis Adams, 1807–1886* (1961); Mary Ellison, *Support for Secession: Lancashire and the American Civil War* (1972); and Brian A. Jenkins, *Britain and the War for the Union* (2 vols.; 1974–1980).

An excellent scholarly study of both persistent and changing attitudes toward the Civil War is Thomas J. Pressly, *Americans Interpret Their Civil War* (1954). The most moving evocation of the feelings of the American people on the meaning of the struggle is Stephen Vincent Benét's epic poem, *John Brown's Body* (1928).

Index

❖

Aaron, Daniel, 207–209
Abolition: and Lincoln, 194; northern attitudes, 197; and the northern press, 211; and the Republican party platform of 1864, 193; and the Thirteenth Amendment, 246
Abolitionists, 232, 234
Adams, Charles Francis: biographical sketch of, 162; and the Confederate ironclads, 168, 169; as minister to Great Britain, 161–164, 166, 168–171; and the *Trent* incident, 164
Adams, Charles Francis, Jr.: and black soldiers, 101; and the peace movement, 194; at Petersburg, battle for, 101
Adams, E. D., 167
Adams, John Quincy, 2, 97
Afghanistan, 261
Agassiz, Louis, 227
Agriculture, 40–41, 199
Alabama, secession of, 23
Alabama, C.S.S., 167
Albert, Prince Consort, 159
Alexander, E. Porter: at First Bull Run, 52; and guerrilla warfare, 261; proposal to disband the Army of Northern Virginia, 251
American Red Cross, 204–205, 207
American Revolution, and guerrilla warfare, 261
American Union, The, 160
Anderson, Joseph R., and Tredegar Iron Works, 106
Anderson, Richard H.: and battle of Gettysburg, 143; at battle of the Wil-

Anderson, Richard H. (*Continued*): derness, 176; at Chancellorsville, 124, 126; at Petersburg, 182; at Spotsylvania Courthouse, 177
Anderson, Robert: at Fort Sumter, 30, 32, 213; and Kentucky-Tennessee campaign, 57
Andersonville Prison, 108–109
Andrew, John, 94
Andrews, J. Cutler, 212
Anthony, Susan B., 205
Antietam, battle of, 80–83, 86; and emancipation proclamation, 99; impact on diplomacy, 166; photograph of Confederate dead at Dunker Church, 82
Appomattox Courthouse, Lee's surrender at, 251
Arkansas: and presidential reconstruction, 193; and secession, 36
Armour, Philip D., 199
Army of Northern Virginia, 134, 175, 249; Lee appointed commander of, 69; surrender of, 250–251; as target of Union strategy, 173; and the western strategy, 133. *See also entries on individual generals, campaigns, and battles*
Army of Tennessee, 155, 174, 186; after Chattanooga, 158; decline of, 121; retreats into Alabama, 241; surrender of, 254. *See also entries on individual generals, campaigns, and battles*
Army of the Cumberland, 174, 186, 238
Army of the James, at Petersburg, 249
Army of the Ohio, 78, 151, 174, 186

Army of the Potomac, 175; and the defeat of Lee, 249; Grant's relationship with, 173–174; organized and trained by McClellan, 54–56. *See also entries on individual generals, campaigns, and battles*

Army of the Tennessee, 174, 186; under Grant, 78; under Henry Halleck, 78

Atlanta, campaign for, 186–190, 238; fall of, 190, 196; importance of, 190

Austro-Prussian War, 259

Bailey, Joseph, 175

Baker, Edward, 56

Ball's Bluff, battle of, 55, 90

Banks, Nathaniel P., 68, 75, 174, 234; and Mobile campaign, 174; and Red River campaign, 200; at Pleasant Hill, 174; at Sabine Crossroads, 174; and siege of Port Hudson, 133

Baptist Church, 3, 220–221

Barksdale, Ethelbert, 117

Barnard, Frederick A.P., 227

Barnard, George N., 212

Barnum, P. T., 201

Barnwell, Robert, 117

Barrett, John G., 241–242

Bates, Edward, 19, 32

"Battle Above the Clouds," *see* Chattanooga campaign

"Battle of Charleston Harbor, The," 222

"Battle Cry of Freedom, The," 210

"Battle Hymn of the Republic," 210

Beauregard, P. G. T., 135, 180, 182, 238; and First Bull Run, 51–52, 112; at Fort Sumter, 33; and Jefferson Davis, 112; and Kentucky-Tennessee campaign, 59; at Petersburg, 182; at battle of Shiloh, 60–63; on strategy, 42, 129

Bee, Barnard E., 52

Beecher, Henry Ward, 12, 213

"Beecher's Bibles," 12

Bell, John, election of 1860, 20–21

Bellows, H. W., 207

Benjamin, Judah P.: biographical sketch of, 111; as Confederate attorney general, 30, 111; as Confederate secretary of state, 111, 165–166, 169–171; as Confederate secretary of war, 111; and the Erlanger loan, 169–170; and financing the war effort, 169–170

Bennett, James Gordon, 211

Bentonville, battle of, 248

Beringer, Richard E., on state rights, with Hattaway, Jones, and Still, 113, 257

Bermuda Hundred, battle of, 180–182

Bickerdyke, Mary Ann, 205

Big Bethel Church, battle of, 51

Big Black River, battle of, 147

Bingham, William, 227

Bismarck, Otto von, 258

Black sailors, 100–101, 203

Black soldiers, 39, 100–102, 233; discrimination against, 202; and efforts at full rights of citizenship, 202; Fifty-fourth Massachusetts Volunteer Infantry Regiment, 101; and Fort Pillow massacre, 101; impact on northern ideas, 202; and Lincoln's reelection, 191; and the northern press, 211; at Petersburg, 183; proposed use by Confederacy, 246–247; as prisoners of war, 109; and suffrage, 193

Black, Robert C., 108

Blacks, 233; abuse by the Confederate Army, 232; arrest of by Confederates in Pennsylvania, 136; benefits from northern prosperity, 202; civil rights of, 203; conduct of, 232; as contrabands, 230–231; discrimination against, 203; and emancipation, 202; free blacks and northern prosperity, 202; hardships faced, 231, 232; and religious freedom, 231; southern, 228–234; suffrage of, 193; and the Union war effort, 202. *See also* Abolition; Black Soldiers; Emancipation; Slavery

Blair, Francis P., Jr.: and the Union offensive in Missouri, 51; as U.S. representative, 192

Blair, Francis P., Sr., 245

Blair, Montgomery, 32, 245

"Bleeding Kansas," *see* Kansas

Blockade of the South, 43, 66, 163, 165, 168–169, 174, 185, 242–244; as reason for Union victory, 257

Blockade runners, 243

Bocock, Thomas S., 117

"Bonnie Blue Flag, The," 226

Booth, John Wilkes, 253

Border states: and secession, 37–38; suppression of Copperheads, 92

Bowdoin College, 213

Boyd, Belle, 205

Brady, Mathew B., 212, 225

Bragg, Braxton, 34, 78, 84, 244; and battle of Chickamauga, 152–154; and campaign for Chattanooga, 112, 156–158, 189; as commander in chief of Confederate forces, 112, 173; criticisms of, 112, 151, 154–155, 158; invites the Northwest to join the Confederacy, 84; and Jefferson Davis, 112, 173; at Perryville, 85–86; relieved of command, 158. *See also entries on individual campaigns and battles*

Bragg, Thomas, as Confederate attorney general, 111

Brandy Station, battle of, 136

Breckinridge, John C.: and battle of Missionary Ridge, 156; and battle of New Market, 180; and battle of Stone's River, 121; as Confederate secretary of war, 111; election of 1860, 20–21

Bright, John, 160, 164

Brooks, Preston, 13

Brown, John: agitation created by, 198; at Harpers Ferry, 18–19; "John Brown's Body," 210; and murders at Pottawatomie Creek, 13

Brown, Joseph E., 104; and conscription, 114; and martial law, 115; and state rights, 114

Brown's Ferry, 155

Bryant, William Cullen, 211

Buchanan, James: and Dred Scott decision, 14–15; election of 1856, 13–14; and Fort Sumter, 30; and Kansas controversy, 15; and possession of federal properties in the South, 30; and secession, 25–26

Buckner, Simon Bolivar: at Chickamauga, 153; at Fort Donelson, 59; and the occupation of Knoxville, 151

Buell, Don Carlos, 58, 84, 87; and the Army of the Cumberland, 59; and the Army of the Ohio, 78; at battle of Perryville, 85–86; at battle of Shiloh, 59, 63; and the Chattanooga campaign, 83–84

Buford, John, and battle of Gettysburg, 138

Bull Run, first battle of, 51–54, 235

Bull Run, second battle of, 75–77

Bulloch, James, 167–169, 243

Burial of Lantané, The, 225

Burns, Anthony, 9, 17

Burnside, Ambrose E., 118, 176, 201; at Antietam, 82; and Army of the Ohio, 151; and Army of the Potomac, 87, 118, 122, 175; arrest of Clement L. Vallandigham, 92; at Bermuda Hundred, 180–182; biographical sketch of, 118; and battle of Fredericksburg, 87, 118–120; as commander of the Department of Ohio, 92; occupies Knoxville, 151; resignation of, 184. See also entries on individual campaigns and battles

Butler, Andrew Jackson, 13, 200

Butler, Benjamin F., 176, 180, 249; advance on Richmond, 176; at Fortress Monroe, 230; on the James River, 180; occupation of New Orleans, 65; as possible Republican nominee in 1864, 195; and slaves as contraband of war, 230

Caesar's Gallic War, southern edition, 227

Calhoun, John C., 4–6, 8, 10; and theory of concurrent majority, 26

California, admission as a free state, 4

Cameron, Simon, as secretary of war, 32, 90, 200

Campaign Sewing Society of Baton Rouge, 216

Canada: and Confederate agents, 171; and Confederate raid on St. Albans, Vermont, 171

Canby, Edward R. S., 255; accepts final Confederate surrender, 255; at Glorieta Pass, 64; captures Mobile, 244

Carnegie, Andrew, 200

Carrick's Ford, battle of, 51

Catholics, 10, 12, 19, 220

Catton, Bruce, 182, 189

Cavalry, 124–126, 136–137, 144–145, 180–181, 189, 244–245; Confederate, 72, 83–84, 101, 120–122, 189–190, 231–232, 261; Union, 83, 154, 174, 177, 185, 247–250. See also entries for individual generals, campaigns, and battles

Cedar Creek, battle of, 185

Cemetery Hill, 139–140

Cemetery Ridge, 142

Chancellorsville, battle of, 124–128, 135, 177, 192; impact on diplomacy, 170

Chandler, Zachariah, 89

Channing, Edward, 109

Charleston Courier, 222

Charleston Mercury, 115–116, 222, 247

Charleston, Medical College of, 227

Chase, Salmon P., 19; condemns Kansas-Nebraska Act, 11; efforts to remove Seward from cabinet, 191; and McClellan, 76; as possible presidential candidate in 1864, 192; resignation of, 191, 192; as secretary of the treasury, 32, 89–90, 95–97

Chattanooga campaign, 149–158, 172, 192

Cheatham, Benjamin F., 189

Cherokee Indians, 38

Chesnut, Mary Boykin, 107, 224, 233–234, 236–237; on Andrew Johnson as president, 254

Chicago Times, 211

Chicago Tribune, 199, 210

Chickamauga, battle of, 150–151, 153–154, 192

Chickasaw Indians, 38

Chimborazo Hospital (Richmond), 236

Choctaw Indians, 38

Cincinnati Enquirer, 211

City Point Railroad, 183

Clara Barton, 204–205

Clausewitz, Karl von, 68, 79, 177, 181, 257–258, 261; and Confederate strategy, 260; and guerrilla warfare, 262; theories on war and generalship, 40, 44, 45

Clay, Cassius M., 160

Clay, Henry, and Compromise of 1850, 1, 4–5

Cleburne, Patrick: and battle of Missionary Ridge, 156; death of, 240; proposes use of slaves in Confederate Army, 246

Cobb, Howell, 6, 110; and formation of the Confederacy, 27; and secession, 23; as U.S. secretary of the treasury, 25

Cobden, Richard, 160, 164

Coddington, Edwin B., 139, 147

Cold Harbor, battle of, 180–181

Columbia College, 227

Committee on the Conduct of the War, 56, 90

Compromise of 1850, 1, 4–10, 17

Confederacy: administration of, see Confederacy, government of; agents in Canada, 171; agriculture of, 217; blacks, 231–232; blockade runners, 243; colleges and universities in, 227, 228; considers emancipating slaves, 246–247; constitution of, 27, 29, 45, 172–173; cultural activities in, 220–228; diplomacy of, 78, 83, 159–171, 175, 243; disintegration of, 220, 250–255; economy of, 2, 40, 217–218, 257; explanations for defeat, 256–262; finances of, 104–105, 169–170; formation of, 26–27, 30; and freedom of the press, 116; government of, 27–30, 103–117; and guerrilla warfare, 261–262; industrialization of, 106, 147; and inflation, 105, 216–218, 223; literature of, 222–225; medical shortages, 217–218; military command structure of, 247; morale of, 190, 215–216, 245, 247; and the press, 221–222; propaganda of, 160–161; provisional government of, 27–30; and railroads, 108; refugees during the war, 219, 229; and religion, 220–221; social life of, 218; and state rights, 94, 113–114, 218; strategy of, 78, 129, 133–134, 260–261; surrender of, 251–255; Union blockade of, 216–217, 242–244; and voluntary benevolence associations, 218; war aims, 41; and wartime corruption, 217; weaknesses of, 259–262; women in the, 224, 234–237. See also South

Confederate Army: abuse of black soldiers, 101, 232; administration of, 110–111; camp life, 46, 103, 107; cavalry of, 189, 219; command structure of, 131, 173; and conscription, 103–104; considers use of black soldiers in, 246–247; desertion from, 244; disease, 107; enlistment in, 103–104, 215–216, 247; formation of 30, 42–43, 46; The Life of

Confederate Army (Continued): Johnny Reb, 209; medical care of, 235–236; and prisoners of war, 108–109; shortages, 106–108, 114; supply of, 106–107, 114, 138, 175, 185; training, 47. See also entries on individual campaigns and battles

Confederate Navy, 243; blockade runners, 169, 243; British and French shipbuilders, 167–168; commerce raiders, 167–168, 243; shipbuilding programs, 167–168, 243; and the Union blockade, 168, 243. See also Blockade of the South

Confederate Vivandiere, The, 225

Congress, Confederate: adjourns permanently on March 18, 1865, 250; and arming the slaves, 247, 250; and conflict with Davis, 117, 246; and conscription, 103–104, 115; creates position of general in chief, 247; and emancipation, 247; and financing the war, 104–105; and foreign affairs, 165; and partisan politics, 117; and railroads, 108; secrecy of, 115; and suspension of the writ of habeas corpus, 115–116

Congress, U.S., 91; and confiscation acts, 90; and emancipation, 98; and Enrollment Act, 93; and financing the war, 96–97; and Lincoln-Chase conflict, 192; and privateers and the Union blockade, 169; Republican control of, 191; and stock speculation, 200; and the Thirteenth Amendment, 246; war aims of, 89; and the war effort, 93

Conscription: Confederate, 103–104; Union, 93–94, 192, 211

Constitution, Confederate, 27, 29, 45, 172–173

Constitution, U.S., 1, 8, 21, 29, 102; and abolition, 97; and Dred Scott decision, 14; Fifteenth Amendment, 203; proposed amendment for gradual emancipation, 99; and reconstruction, 192; Thirteenth Amendment, 98, 205, 246

Constitutional Union party, 20–21

Cook, George, 226

Cooke, Jay, 96

Cooper's Shop, 207

Copperheads, 91–92

Corinth, battle of, 86–87

Cotterill, Robert S., 221–222

Cotton: and Confederate diplomacy, 160–163, 165–166, 171; embargo of, 163; illegal speculation and trading in, 217; and the Old South, 2, 162, 163; and the Trans-Mississippi Department, 175

"Cotton Boll, The," 222

Couch, Darius N., 123, 125
Coulter, E. Merton, 44, 113
Crampton's Gap, 80
Crater, battle of, 183
Creek Indians, 38
Crittenden Compromise, 26
Crittenden, George, 58
Crittenden, John J., 26
Crittenden, Thomas L.: and the Chattanooga campaign, 152–153; at Chickamauga, 153
"Cry to Arms, A," 222
Cuba, 11
Cumberland Gap, 86
Cummings, Kate, 236
Curtin, Andrew Gregg, 94
Curtis, Samuel R., 61

Dabney, Robert Louis, 221
Daniel, John M., 222
Davidson College, 228
Davis, George, 111
Davis, Henry Winter, 193
Davis, Jefferson, 11, 112, 114, 189; as administrator, 106–108, 110–113; biographical sketch of, 27–28; and Braxton Bragg, 86, 107, 112, 155, 158, 173, 189; cabinet of, 29–30, 110–111; capture of, 255; characteristics of, 110–111; and Compromise of 1850, 4, 8; and Confederate defeat, 256; and Congress, 110, 116–117, 246; and conscription, 103; criticisms of, 111–112, 115–116, 222; and the Crittenden Compromise, 26; death of son, 110; diplomacy of, 162, 164–166; elected president of the Confederacy, 45; and the elections of 1863, 117; evaluation of, 259–260; and Fort Sumter, 33–35; and Hood's Tennessee campaign, 238–239; inaugural address of, 35, 226; and Joseph E. Johnston, 112, 158, 188–189, 248; and Lee's surrender, 254; and martial law, 115; military experience of, 46; and peace proposals, 79, 194, 196, 245–246; as provisional president of Confederacy, 27, 226; relations with Robert E. Lee, 69, 72, 79, 112, 135–136, 248; in role of general in chief, 172–173, 246–248, 260; and southern nationalism, 45–46, 260; and state rights, 113, 114; strategy of, 44, 129, 152; supports use of blacks in the Confederate Army, 246–247; and suspension of writ of habeas corpus, 115–116; and Robert Toombs, 112; and the Trans-Mississippi Department, 149, 255; wartime leadership of, 103, 110, 112, 116, 166, 172–173, 189, 239–240, 248, 254–255, 258–261; wife, Varina Howell, 110

Davis, Varina Howell, 110
Dawson, Sarah Morgan, 224
Dayton, William L., 161, 162
De Bow, J. D. B., 17
De Forest, John W., 208
Delaware, 37
Delchamp, J.J., 225
Democratic party, 10, 12, 102; and conscription, 94; and "Copperhead platform," 196; and Democratic press, 211; and election of 1852, 8; and election of 1854, 12; splits in election of 1860, 19–21; and election of 1962, 99; and election of 1864, 191, 195–196; and Emancipation Proclamation, 99–100; and financing the war, 97
Desertion, 48, 244
Detroit Free Press, 199, 211
Diplomacy: of the Confederacy, see Confederacy, diplomacy of; of the Union, see Union, diplomacy of
Disease, 47, 49, 109, 197, 217–218
Dix, Dorothea, 204
"Dixie," 226
Donald, David Herbert, 162, 257
Doubleday, Abner, 138
Douglas, Stephen A., 4; Compromise of 1850, 5–6; debate with Lincoln, 15–17; election of 1858, 16; election of 1860, 20–22; Freeport Doctrine, 16; Kansas-Nebraska Act, 11; popular sovereignty, 12; supports Lincoln, 35
Douglass, Frederick, 202
Draft, see Conscription
Dred Scott decision, 14–16, 31
"Drum-Traps," 208
Dudley, Thomas H., 168
DuPont, Samuel F., 66

Early, Jubal A.: and battle of Cedar Creek, 185; and battle of Chancellorsville, 126; and battle of Fisher's Hill, 185; and battle of Gettysburg, 139; and battle of the Wilderness, 176; at Chambersburg, Pennsylvania, 239; at Marye's Heights, 124, 126; in Shenandoah Valley campaign of 1864, 182–185
East Tennessee, 151
Eaton, Clement, 260
Eaton, John, 231–232
Edmondston, Catherine Ann Devereux, 224
Edwards, J. D., 226
Election of 1852, 8
Election of 1854, 11–12
Election of 1856, 13
Election of 1860, 14, 19–22
Election of 1862, 99, 213
Election of 1863, Confederate, 117

Election of 1864, 190, 194–196
Elements of Algebra, 228
Eleventh Corps, Army of the Potomac, at
    Gettysburg, 138
Elkhorn Tavern, battle of, *see* Pea Ridge,
    battle of
Ellis, John M., 36
Elmira Barracks, 109
Emancipation Proclamation, 98–100, 233, 211,
    213
Emancipation, 55, 57, 89, 97–102, 194,
    230–234; Confederate moves toward,
    246–247; and the Confederate war
    effort, 230, 247; and contraband of
    war, 230; and the election of 1864, 195;
    and Frederick Douglass, 202; and free
    blacks, 202; hostilities over, 203; and
    northern churches, 212, 213; and the
    northern press, 211; political fallout
    from, 191; and Thomas Jefferson, 232;
    and Union war aims, 196; views of
    Nathaniel Hawthorne, 208; and the
    Women's Loyal League, 205
Emerson, Ralph Waldo, 17–18; and the
    Union war effort, 207
Emmett, Daniel, 226
Enfield rifle, 47
England, *see* Great Britain
English bill, 15
Enrollment Act, 93. *See also* Conscription
Episcopal Church, 220–221
Ericsson, John, 67
Erlanger loan, 169–170
Erlanger, Emile, 105
"Ethnogenesis," 222
Europe, 159–171
Evans, Augusta Jane, 223
Evans, Nathan G., 52
Everett, Edward, 20
Ewell, Richard, 136, 139; and battle of
    Gettysburg, 138–140, 143–144; at
    Spotsylvania Courthouse, 179; and the
    Wilderness campaign, 176
Ex parte Milligan, 92–93

Fair Oaks, *see* Seven Pines, battle of
Farragut, David Glasgow: attack on Forts
    Jackson and St. Philip, 65; victory at
    Mobile Bay, 185
Faust, Drew Gilpin, 257
Fifteenth Amendment to the Constitution, 203
Fifth Corps, Army of the Potomac, in
    Richmond campaign, 72
Fillmore, Millard, 8; election of 1856, 13
Fisher's Hill, battle of, 185
Fite, Emerson D., 206, 213
Fitzhugh, George, 18
Florida, secession of, 23
Florida, C.S.S., 167
Floyd, John, 25, 59

Foote, Andrew, 247; at Fort Donelson, 59;
    at Fort Henry, 58–59; at Island No. 10,
    64
Foote, Henry Stuart, 117
Ford's Theater, 252
Forrest, Nathan Bedford: and battle of
    Nashville, 241; at battle of Shiloh, 63;
    on Braxton Bragg, 154; at Fort
    Donelson, 59; and Fort Pillow
    massacre, 101; and guerrilla warfare,
    261; and Hood's Tennessee campaign,
    238; operations in Tennessee and
    Kentucky, 83; operations in western
    Tennessee, 231–232; raids against
    Rosecrans, 120; raids on Union
    communications, 122; and the Selma
    campaign, 244–245
Forster, W. E., 160
Fort Donelson, 44, 56, 58–59
Fort Fisher, 244
Fort Harrison, 184
Fort Henry, 44, 56, 58–59
Fort Jackson, 65
Fort McAlister, 242
Fort Morgan, 185
Fort Pickens, 30–32, 34
Fort Pillow, 64, 101
Fort St. Philip, 65
Fort Stedman, 249
Fort Sumter, 197; bombardment of, 33; crisis
    surrounding, 30–35; fourth anniversary
    of surrender, 213; impact on Southern
    attitudes, 215
Fortress Monroe, 68
Fox's Gap, 80
France, 159; diplomacy with, 159, 161–162,
    165–167, 170–171; and southern cotton,
    161–163, 165
Franco-Prussian War, 259
Franklin, battle of, 240–241
Franklin, William B., 83, 119
Fredericksburg, battle of, 118–120, 128
Free Soil party, 8
Freedom of the press, *see* Press, freedom of
Freeman, Douglas Southall, 72, 80, 125, 145
Frémont, John C.: and the Department of the
    West, 57; and the election of 1856, 13;
    and the election of 1864, 193;
    emancipation orders of, 90; and the
    Kentucky-Tennessee campaign, 56;
    and Republican party, 21; and the
    Shenandoah Valley campaign of 1862,
    69
Fugitive slave law, 5, 9, 17

Gardner, Alexander, 212
Gardner, James, 212
Garfield, James A., 64
Garrison, William Lloyd, 3
"General Lee's Grand March," 227

Georgia, 23, 26
Georgia Hussars, 216
Gettysburg, battle of, 137–147, 155, 172, 192;
    impact on foreign policy, 170
Gettysburg Address, 158, 263
Gettysburg campaign, 135–137, 149, 158
Gibbon, John, 144
Giddings, Joshua, 232
Gladstone, William E., 159, 166
Glendale, battle of, 74
Glorieta Pass, battle of, 64
Gone with the Wind, 215
Gordon, John B.: at Fort Stedman, 249; at
    Spotsylvania Courthouse, 179; and the
    Wilderness campaign, 176–177
Gorgas, Josiah, 106
Grady, Henry W., 234
Graebner, Norman, 167, 171
Granger, Gordon S.: at battle of
    Chickamauga, 154; and the
    Chattanooga campaign, 149
Grant, Ulysses S., 147, 180, 205, 241, 249; at
    Appomattox Courthouse, 250–251; and
    the Army of the Tennessee, 59; and
    the Army of the Potomac, 174–175,
    248–249; and attack on Cold Harbor,
    180–181; and battle of Shiloh 59–64,
    114; and battle for Vicksburg, 149;
    biographical sketch of, 57; and black
    soldiers, 101; captures Fort Donelson,
    59; and the Chattanooga campaign,
    155–156; and contrabands, 231;
    criticisms of, 181; at Fort Henry, 58;
    generalship of, 149, 172, 261; and
    Jewish traders, 200; Lincoln's view of,
    66; securing the Mississippi River,
    121–122; at Petersburg, 181–184, 241,
    247, 249; possible Republican nominee
    in 1864, 195; and prisoners of war, 109;
    promoted to lieutenant general, 172;
    and the Shenandoah Valley, 184–185;
    and slavery, 232; at Spotsylvania
    Courthouse, 177, 179–180; strategy of,
    152, 173–175, 181, 190, 219, 244;
    surrender of the Army of Northern
    Virginia, 249–251; tactics of, 57, 130;
    "Unconditional surrender," 59; as
    Union general in chief, 172–175, 190,
    244, 248, 260; and Vicksburg
    campaign, 129–132, 134, 147, 148, 152;
    in Virginia, 239; in the West, 83; and
    the Wilderness campaign, 176–177. See
    also entries for individual campaigns and
    battles
Great Britain, 83, 159, 160; and the blockade,
    165; diplomacy with, 159–167, 169–171;
    and Rush-Bagot treaty, 171; and
    slavery, 160; and southern cotton,
    159–163, 165; and the Trent incident,
    96, 164

Great Expectations: or, Getting Promoted, 225
Greeley, Horace, 98; advocates replacing
    Lincoln in 1864, 195, 211; and battle of
    First Bull Run, 211; as editor of the
    New York Daily Tribune, 211; and the
    peace movement, 194; and the
    repudiation of the "anaconda plan,"
    211
Greenbacks, 97
Greenhow, Rose O'Neal, 52, 235
Gregg, David M., 145
Grierson, Benjamin H., 131
Gros Tête Fencibles, 216
Guerrilla warfare, 231, 261–262; evaluation of,
    261–262; as proposed by E. Porter
    Alexander, 251; and southern values,
    262

Halleck, Henry, 122, 128, 149, 190;
    commander of Western theater, 59; as
    general in chief, 74–75, 78, 122; at
    Shiloh, 78; as Union Army chief of
    staff, 172–173; and the war in the
    West, 78, 83; western strategy after
    Vicksburg, 152
Hamlin, Hannibal, 19
Hammond, James Henry, 163
Hammond, William A., 204
Hampton, Wade, 242
Hampton Roads, battle of, 67–68
Hampton Roads peace conference, 245
Hancock, Winfield Scott: and battle of
    Gettysburg, 139–140, 144, 146; at
    Petersburg, 182; at Spotsylvania
    Courthouse, 179; and Wilderness
    campaign, 176
Handel, George Frederick, 220
Hardee, William J., 47; abandons Savannah,
    242; at battle of Atlanta, 186, 189; in
    the battles for Chattanooga, 156; at
    battle of Jonesboro, 190; and battle of
    Stone's River, 120; criticisms of Bragg,
    151; in Johnston's campaign in the
    Carolinas, 248; and the Kentucky-
    Tennessee campaign, 56; at Perryville,
    85
Harpers Ferry, 51, 137; John Brown's attack,
    18, 19; captured by Jackson, 79–80
Harris, Isham G., 36
Harrisburg, Pennsylvania, 79
Harrolson, John, 223
"Harvard Commemoration Ode," 208
Harvard University, 213
Hattaway, Herman, and Archer Jones: on
    Davis, 46, 72, 259; on Lee, 72, 134,
    260; on Montgomery C. Meigs, 95; and
    state rights, with Jones, Beringer, and
    Still, 113, 257
Hatteras Inlet, 66
Hawes, Richard, 85

Hawthorne, Nathaniel, 207–208
Hayne, Paul Hamilton, 222
Heth, Henry, 138
Hewitt, John Hill, 225
Hicks, Thomas H., 37
Hill, A. P.: at Antietam, 82; at
    Chancellorsville, 126; in the
    Gettysburg campaign, 136, 138–140,
    143–145; at Harpers Ferry, 82; at
    Petersburg, 182, 249; and Pickett's
    charge, 145; in Seven Days' battles,
    72; and the Wilderness campaign,
    176
Hill, Benjamin H.: and Jefferson Davis, 117;
    opposes secession of Georgia, 23
Hill, Daniel Harvey, 228; at Chickamauga,
    153; and Elements of Algebra, 228;
    relieved of command, 155; in Seven
    Days' battles, 72
Hindman, Thomas C., 153
Hodgson, Joseph, 225
Hofstadter, Richard, 5
Holden, William W., 116
Hollins, George N., 65
Homestead Act of 1862, 91
Hood, John Bell, 198; and battle of Ezra
    Church, 190; and battle of Franklin,
    240–241; and battle of Gettysburg, 140,
    142, 189; at battle of Nashville, 241;
    and the campaign for Atlanta, 186,
    189–190, 221, 238; at Chickamauga,
    189; resigns as commander of the
    Army of Tennessee, 241; and the
    Tennessee campaign, 238–241; Texas
    Brigade of, 189
Hooker, Joseph: abilities of, 128; at Antietam,
    82; and the Army of the Potomac,
    122–123; biographical sketch of, 123;
    and Burnside, 123; at Chancellorsville,
    123–129; and the Chattanooga
    campaign, 155–156; at Fredericksburg,
    119; and the Gettysburg campaign,
    137; resignation of, 137; at Sharpsburg,
    80
Hopkins, Mrs. Arthur F., 235
Hotze, Henry, 160–161
Housatonic, U.S.S., 243
Houston, F. K., 226
Houston, Sam, and secession, 24
Howard, Oliver O.: and battle of Ezra
    Church, 190; and battle of Gettysburg,
    138–139; at battle of Jonesboro, 190;
    and the campaign for Atlanta, 190; at
    Chancellorsville, 123, 125
Howe, Julia Ward, 205, 210
Howell, Varina (Mrs. Jefferson Davis), 27
Hunley, C.S.S., 243
Hunter, David, 90
Hunter, R.M.T., 111, 165
Huntington, Collis P., 199

Illinois, black exclusion laws, 99
Immigrants, 10, 19, 161; and Confederate
    music, 226; as laborers, 205
In War Time and Other Poems, 208
Index [London], 160
Indians, as party of the Confederacy, 38
Industry, 40–41
International Industrial Assembly of North
    America, 205–206
Ironclads, battle of Hampton Roads, 67–68
Iuka, battle of, 86

Jackson, Claiborne F., 37, 51
Jackson, Thomas J. "Stonewall," 111, 139,
    176–177; at Antietam, 82; in "Barbara
    Frietchie," 208; at Cedar Mountain, 75;
    at Chancellorsville, 124–126, 128; death
    of, 126, 128; at First Bull Run 52, 54; at
    Fredericksburg, 118–120; generalship
    of, 261; at Harpers Ferry, 79–80;
    Presbyterian background of, 221; and
    the Richmond campaign, 68–69, 72; at
    Second Bull Run, 75–76; in Seven
    Days' battles, 72; at Sharpsburg, 80; in
    the Shenandoah Valley campaign,
    68–70, 182; strict morals of, 49
Jamieson, Perry D., with Grady McWhiney,
    44, 256–257
Jefferson, Thomas, 1–2; on emancipation, 232
"John Brown's Body," 210
Johnson, Andrew: becomes president, 254; as
    Union party nominee for vice
    president, 193
Johnson, George W., 85
Johnson, Herschel V., 20, 23
Johnson's Elementary Arithmetic, 228
Johnston, Albert Sidney, 221; in battle of
    Shiloh 60–61, 63, 114; death of, 63, 69;
    and Fort Donelson, 59, 112; and Fort
    Henry, 112; and the Kentucky-
    Tennessee campaign, 56–59
Johnston, Joseph E., 67, 117, 120; and the
    Army of Tennessee, 158, 174, 254; at
    battle of Bentonville, 248; and battle of
    Seven Pines, 69; and the campaign for
    Atlanta, 186–189, 221; Confederate
    commander in the West, 129; and
    Jefferson Davis, 112, 248; at First Bull
    Run, 51–52, 54; on Lee's appointment
    as general in chief, 248; and Lincoln's
    death, 253–254; surrender of, 254; and
    the Vicksburg campaign, 131, 132,
    147–149
Jomini, Antoine Henri, 45, 68, 261; on tactics, 60
Jones, Archer, see Hattaway, Herman
Jones, Charles Colcock, 224–225
Jones, Madison, 225
Jonesboro, battle of, 190
Julian, George W., 89
"Just Before the Battle, Mother," 209

Kansas controversy, 12–15
Kansas-Nebraska Act, 11–13, 17
Keene, Laura, 201, 252
Kenner, Duncan, 247
Kennesaw Mountain, battle of, 187–188
Kentucky campaign, of fall 1862, 83–87
Kentucky: inauguration of Richard Hawes as
     Confederate Governor, 85; and
     secession, 37; support for the
     Confederacy, 85
Kentucky-Tennessee campaign of February
     1862, 56–59
Killer Angels, The, 146
"King Cotton," see Cotton
King Linkum the First, 225
Kittredge, Walter, 209
Knights of the Golden Circle, 91
Know-Nothings (Native American party), 10,
     12–13, 19–21
Knoxville, Union occupation of, 151–152, 155

Labor unions, 205–206
Ladies' Aid Societies, 206
Lane, Joseph, 20
"Leaves of Grass," 208
Lecompton constitution, 15. See also Kansas
     controversy
LeConte, John and Joseph, 227
Lee, Fitzhugh: at Five Forks, 249; at
     Petersburg, 249; at Spotsylvania
     Courthouse, 177
Lee, Robert E., 103, 128, 173, 189, 216, 256;
     and the Army of Northern Virginia,
     69, 72, 174–175, 248; and the Atlantic
     coastal defenses, 66; at battle of
     Sayler's Creek, 250; biographical
     sketch of, 69, 71–72; and the campaign
     for Atlanta, 186, 189; as Confederate
     general in chief, 247–248, 260; at Cold
     Harbor, 180–181; criticisms of, 134; and
     Davis, 112, 248; evaluates Hood, 189;
     evaluation of, 260; at Fort Stedman,
     249; at Fredericksburg, 118–120;
     generalship of, 75, 176, 261; and
     Gettysburg campaign, 133–134,
     136–138, 144–146; and Grant's strategy
     of attrition, 181; rejects guerrilla
     warfare, 251, 261–262; on J. E. B.
     Stuart, 180; on Jackson's death, 128;
     and Joseph E. Johnston, 158; and
     Maryland campaign, 78–80, 83, 166; on
     McClellan, 79; at Petersburg, 182–185,
     249; proposal to enroll blacks in the
     Confederate Army, 247; and Richmond
     campaign, 68–69, 72; at Second Bull
     Run, 75–76; sentiments on war, 119; in
     Seven Days' battles, 72–74; at
     Sharpsburg, 80, 83; at Spotsylvania
     Courthouse, 177, 179; strategy as
     general in chief, 248; strategy for

Lee, Robert E. (Continued):
     Gettysburg campaign, 135; strategy for
     the Atlanta campaign, 189; strategic
     ideas of, 72, 129, 136; and Stuart, 137;
     surrender of the Army of Northern
     Virginia, 250–251; and the western
     strategy, 129, 133, 134, 152; and
     western Virginia, 51; and the
     Wilderness campaign, 176, 177
Leech, Margaret, 202
Letcher, John, 36
Lewisohn, Ludwig, 222
Lieber, Francis, 227
Life of Billy Yank, The, 209
Life of Johnny Reb, The, 209
Lincoln, Abraham, 87, 89, 163; and abolition,
     97; and the Army of the Potomac, 152,
     189; biographical sketch of, 15; and
     black soldiers, 100, 193; and black
     suffrage, 193; and the border states,
     37; cabinet of, 32, 245, 252; and
     Salmon P. Chase, 191–192, 245; and
     the Chattanooga campaign, 149, 151,
     155; and colonization of slaves, 98–99;
     compared with Davis, 259–260; and
     the Constitution, 98, 192; and the
     Copperheads, 91–92; criticisms of, 94,
     191, 213; and Crittenden Compromise,
     26; death of, 252–254; death of son,
     Willie, 110, 245; diplomacy of, 163,
     166–167; and Dred Scott decision, 14;
     and the election of 1858, 16; and the
     election of 1860, 19–21; and the
     election of 1864, 195–196, 211; and
     emancipation, 83, 90–91, 97–98, 100,
     195–196, 213, 233, 245, 258; evaluation
     of as war leader, 258; and foreign
     policy, 160–161; and Fort Sumter,
     32–35, 88–89; and the Gettysburg
     Address, 158, 246, 263; and Grant, 66,
     149, 172, 260; on Grant's strategy, 176,
     181; and his generals in chief, 172, 260;
     inaugurations of, 30–31, 246; and
     Jewish traders, 200; and labor unrest,
     206; on Lee, 252; and Lee's surrender,
     251; and the liberation of East
     Tennessee, 151; and the Louisiana
     constitution, 192, 246, 252; and Karl
     Marx, 206; master of English prose,
     258, 260; military leadership of, 261;
     Niagara statement of, 195; and
     northern religious leaders, 213; and
     peace efforts, 194–195, 245; as a
     politician, 190–191, 193, 195, 258; and
     the preservation of the Union, 259;
     and presidential powers, 89, 92, 102,
     192; and the press, 210–211;
     proclamation and call for troops, 198;
     public opinion of, 88, 92; racial
     attitudes of, 16; and Radical

Lincoln, Abraham (*Continued*):
Republicans, 76, 100, 191–193, 246; and reconstruction, 116, 192–193, 246, 251–254; reelection in 1864, 190–191, 193, 196, 245; relations with McClellan, 54–56, 67–68, 74–76, 78, 87; and the Republican party, 193; and secession, 26, 30–32, 37, 252; and Seward, 191; and slavery, 98, 246; and Harriet Beecher Stowe, 9–10; strategic ideas of, 43, 74, 152, 173, 258; and suspension of writ of habeas corpus, 37, 89, 91–92, 193; and the Thirteenth Amendment, 246; and George H. Thomas, 84; and the *Trent* incident, 164; and the Union, 102; and the Union victory, 256; visits Richmond, 251; and Clement L. Vallandigham, 92–93; and the Wade-Davis Bill, 194; war aims of, 89, 97, 100, 152, 158, 190, 192, 258; and wartime corruption, 200; wartime leadership of, 88–89, 91–92, 94, 102, 172–173, 190–193, 195, 198, 258. *See also entries for individual generals, campaigns, and battles*
Lincoln, Mary Todd, 15
Lincoln-Douglas debates, 15–16
Lindsay, William S., 170
Logan, John, 241
Logan's Crossroads, battle of, 58
London *Times*, 160, 163, 166, 200
Longstreet, James: at Antietam, 82; at Chancellorsville, 124; at Chattanooga, 155; at Chickamauga, 153–154; and criticism of Braxton Bragg, 155; at Fredericksburg, 118–119; and the Gettysburg campaign, 136–137, 139, 140, 142–145; at Knoxville, 155; and Robert E. Lee, 155; and the move to join Bragg's army, 153; at Petersburg, 249; and Pickett's charge, 144–145; rejoins the Army of Northern Virginia, 175; reputation of, 139; at Second Bull Run, 75; in Seven Days' battles, 72; at Suffolk, 124; and the western strategy, 129, 133, 139, 152; and the Wilderness campaign, 176; wounded, 176
"Lorena," 227
Louisiana: reconstruction of, 193, 246, 252; secession, 23, 24, 26
Louisiana State Seminary and Military Academy, 227
Louisiana, C.S.S., 65
Lovell, Mansfield, 65
Lowell, James Russell, 208
Luraghi, Raimondo, 106
Lyon, Nathaniel: death of, 54; and the Union offensive in Missouri, 49, 51; at Wilson's Creek, 54
Lyons, Lord Richard, 159, 161, 163–164; and the *Trent* incident, 164

Macaria; or Altars of Sacrifice, 223
Machiavelli, Niccolò, 258
Magoffin, Beriah, 37
Magruder, James B., 68
Mahone, William, 183
Malaria, 217
Mallet, John W., 227
Mallory, Stephen R., 30; as Confederate secretary of the navy, 111, 243; on Jefferson Davis, 110
Manassas, C.S.S., 65
Manchester Guardian, 160
Mann, A. Dudley, 162
Mansfield, Joseph K. F., 80
March to the sea, 238–240, 242
Marx, Karl, 206
Maryland: invited to join the Confederacy, 78; and secession, 37
Maryland campaign, 78–79, 83, 166; impact on diplomacy, 166–167
"Maryland, My Maryland," 37, 227
Mason, George, 164
Mason, James M., 5, 164; as emissary to Great Britain, 164–165, 169, 247; and the *Trent* incident, 164
Massey, Mary Elizabeth, 205, 237
Maximilian: as Archduke of Austria, 161; as Emperor of Mexico, 171
McCarthy, Henry, 226
McClellan, George B.: on abstinence from alcohol, 49; at Antietam, 82; appointed general in chief, 55; and Ball's Bluff, 55; and battle for Yorktown, 68; biographical sketch of, 55; at Carrick's Ford, 51; as commander of the Army of the Potomac, 54–56, 76; and the election of 1864, 195–196; and Lee's Maryland campaign orders, 79; and the Maryland campaign, 79–80; and the northern press, 211; and politics, 55, 74, 76, 90; removed from command, 87; and the Richmond campaign, 67–69, 72–74; and Second Bull Run, 76; at Seven Pines, 69; at Sharpsburg, 80, 83; target of Committee on the Conduct of the War, 90
McClernand, John A., 129; relieved of command, 148; and the Vicksburg campaign, 129–131, 147–148
McCook, Alexander M., 152
McCord, Louisa Susanna, 236
McCormick, Cyrus H., 199
McCulloch, Ben, 54; death of, 61
McDowell, Irvin: at First Bull Run, 51–52; and the Richmond campaign, 68, 73
McGuire, Judith White, 224
McLaws, Lafayette, 126
McMurry, Richard M., 261
McPherson, James B.: and the Atlanta campaign, 186–188, 190; death of, 190;

McPherson, James B. (*Continued*):
seizes Decatur, 188; and the Vicksburg campaign, 131, 148
McPherson, James M., 97
McWhiney, Grady, with Perry D. Jamieson, 44, 256–257; and the Celtic thesis on Confederate defeat, 257
Meade, George Gordon: and the Army of the Potomac, 137, 173–175; at Chancellorsville, 123, 125; criticisms of, 146–147; at Fredericksburg, 119; in the Gettysburg campaign, 137–140, 142–144, 146–147, 172; at Petersburg, 182; at Spotsylvania Courthouse, 179; and the Wilderness campaign, 176–177
Medical care, 109; in the Confederacy, 217–218, 235–236; at Shiloh, 64; in the training camps, 47; United States Sanitary Commission, 207
Meigs, Montgomery C., 95
Melville, Herman, 207–208
Memminger, Christopher G., and Confederate finance, 30, 104–105
Mercier, Count Henri, 162, 165–166
Merrimack, U.S.S., 67
Merryman, John, 92
Methodist church, 3, 220
Mexico: and Archduke Maximilian, 161, 165; and diplomacy of the Trans-Mississippi Department, 175; and Napoleon III, 169, 171; territorial cession of 1848, 4, 8
Miami University at Oxford, 213
Michigan, University of, 213
Military Railroad, 183
Mill Springs, battle of, 58
Milliken's Bend, battle of, 101
Minié balls, 47, 179
Miss Ravenel's Conversion from Secession to Loyalty, 208
Mississippi, secession of, 22
Mississippi campaign, *see* Corinth, battle of
Mississippi, University of, 227
Missouri: and battle of Pea Ridge, 61; and battle of Wilson's Creek, 54; early Union victories, 51; and secession, 37
Missouri Compromise, 1–2, 4, 7; and Dred Scott decision, 14. *See map, p. 7*
Mobile Bay, battle of, 185; effect of Union victory, 196
Mobile campaign, 174
Mobile Register, 160
Monitor, U.S.S., 67–68
Montgomery convention, 45
Morgan, J. P., 200
Morgan, John Hunt: at battle of Shiloh, 63; and guerrilla warfare, 261; and the Kentucky campaign, 84; raids against Rosecrans, 120; raids in Tennessee and Kentucky, 83; and Kirby Smith, 84

Morrill Act, 91
Morton, Oliver, 94
Mosby, John S., guerrilla activities, 185, 261
Munitions: improvements in, 227; rifled muskets, 43. *See also* Weapons
Murfreesboro, battle of, *see* Stone's River, battle of
Music, 209–210, 220, 226–227
Myers, Abraham C., 106–107

Napoleon III, Emperor of France, 161, 165–166, 247; and British-French intervention, 170; and British-French-Russian intervention, 166; and Mexico, 196, 171
Nashville, battle of, 241
Nashville Convention, 4, 8
Nebraska Territory, 11
New England Emigrant Aid Company, 12
New Market, battle of, 180
New Orleans, occupation of, 65
New Orleans Bee, 21–22, 24
New York City: riots of July 1863, 93, 203–206; social life during the war, 201; Fernando Wood, as Mayor of, 198
New York Daily News, 211
New York Daily Tribune, 38, 98, 211
New York Evening Post, 202; abolitionist views of, 211
New York Express, 211
New York Herald, 211
New York Journal of Commerce, 92
New York Times, 210; and Fort Sumter, 34; and Lincoln, 191, 193, 210; and standard of living in the North, 200
New York World, 92
Newsom, Ella King, 235
Niagara Falls peace negotiations, 194
Nicholas I, Czar of Russia, 167
Norfolk Railroad, 183
North: agricultural production, 40, 199; attitude toward Lincoln, 88; attitudes about the war, 38, 66, 191; colleges and universities of, 213; Confederate sympathizers in, 91–93, 198; and conscription, 94; cultural and intellectual activities of, 207–209; and dissenters, 198; diversion and entertainment, 200–202, 206; economy of, 2–3, 97, 198–200; and emancipation, 99, 100; and fashions for women, 201; financing the war, 96–97, 197; and free blacks, 202–204; and freedom of the press, 198; impact of early defeats, 54; impact of the war on, 74, 197–214; increased taxes, 197; industry of, 199; and inflation, 197; and labor, 205–206; material resources of, 40–41; morale after Chancellorsville, 135; patriotism in, 198; peace movement in, 194; and

North (*Continued*):
the press, 198, 210–212; public reaction to Fort Sumter, 34; racial attitudes, 3; reaction to Lincoln's death, 253; relaxing of morals in, 201; and religion, 212–213; and slavery, 9, 97, 99; standard of living, 200, 205; and state rights, 94; suppression of Copperheads, 91–93; volunteer groups in, 206–207; war aims, 41, 89–91, 100, 158, 196, 212; war effort of, 95, 102, 202; and wartime corruption, 200; and wartime prostitution, 201–202; war weariness, 195, 214; will to continue the war, 136; women in society, 203, 205. *See also* Union

North Carolina, and secession, 36
Northrop, Lucius B., 107, 112

O'Sullivan, Timothy, 212
"Ode" to Confederate dead, 222
Old South, 223; architecture of, 225; literature of, 225; music of, 226; role of women, 236
Ord, Edward, 86, 249; troops at Appomattox Courthouse, 250
Order of American Knights, 91
Osborn and Durbec, photographs by, 225
Our American Cousin, 201, 252
Owsley, Frank L., 112–113, 257

Palmerston, Viscount Henry, 159, 166–167, 169–170, 247
Parish, Peter J., 257
Parkman, Francis, 207
Parrott cannon factory, 206
Patrick, Rembert, 259
Patterson, Robert, 51, 52
Pea Ridge, battle of, 61
Peace efforts, 26, 194
Peace Democrats, 195; in the South, 116
Peachtree Creek, battle of, 189
Pember, Phoebe, 236
Pemberton, John C.: at battle of Big Black River, 147; and Vicksburg campaign, 131–132, 147–149
Pendleton, William Nelson, 221
Penninsula campaign, *see* Richmond campaign; Seven Days' battles
People's party, 12
Perryville, battle of, 85–86
Petersburg, battle of, 101, 181–184, 249
Pettigrew, James Johnston, 138–139
Petty, J. W., 226
Pfanz, Harry W., 142
Philadelphia Evening Journal, 92
Philadelphia Inquirer, 210
Phillips, Wendell, 18
Photography, 212, 225–226
Pickens, Francis, 35, 221

Pickett, George E., 175; and battle of Gettysburg, 144–145; at Five Forks, 249; at Petersburg, 249
Pickett's charge, 144–145
Pierce, Edward L., 230
Pierce, Franklin: biography by Nathaniel Hawthorne, 208; and Jefferson Davis, 28
Pinkerton, Allan, 68
Pittsburg Landing, battle of, 59–64. *See also* Shiloh
Pleasant Hill, battle of, 174
Pleasonton, Alfred: at battle of Brandy Station, 136; at Antietam, 83
Poison Spring, battle of, 175
Polk, Leonidas: and Atlanta campaign, 186; and battle of Stone's River, 120; biographical sketch of, 221; at Chickamauga, 153; criticisms of Bragg, 151, 155; and the Kentucky-Tennessee campaign, 56–57; at Perryville, 85; transferred to Mississippi, 155
Pollard, Edward A., 112, 222; and criticisms of Davis, 116; as editor of the *Richmond Examiner*, 246
Pomeroy, S. C., 192
Pope, John: as commander of Army of the Potomac, 74–75; at Island No. 10, 64; at Second Bull Run, 75–76
Popular sovereignty, 4, 12, 16
Port Hudson, 130–131; siege of, 101, 133; surrender of, 149
Port Royal Sound, seizure of, 66
Port Royal, South Carolina, 230
Porter, David D.: and Mobile campaign, 174; and Red River campaign, 174–175; and Vicksburg campaign, 130–131, 148
Porter, Fitz John: court-martial of, 76; at Second Bull Run, 76; in Seven Days' battles, 72; at Sharpsburg, 83
Potter, David M., 232, 259
Powhatan, U.S.S., 33
Presbyterian church, 3, 220
Press: Army censorship of, 211; battle accounts of, 211–212; freedom ot, 92, 116, 198, 210–211, 222; in the North, 92, 198, 210–212; in the South, 116, 221–222
Preston, John S., 115
Preston, William, 171
Price, Sterling: at battle of Poison Spring, 175; at Iuka, 86; and the Missouri campaign, 51; and the Trans-Mississippi campaign, 175; at Wilson's Creek, 54
Princeton (College of New Jersey), 213
Prisoners of war, 101, 108–109; at Andersonville prison, 108–109

Quakers (The Society of Friends), 208

Racial attitudes, 2, 202–203; in the North, 91
Radical Democrats, 193
Radical Republicans, 55; and Andrew
    Johnson, 254; and black suffrage, 193;
    and the Committee on the Conduct of
    the War, 56, 90; conflict with Lincoln,
    90, 191–192, 194; efforts to oust
    Seward after Fredericksburg, 191; and
    emancipation, 89, 100; and Lincoln's
    death, 254; and McClellan, 74, 76; and
    reconstruction, 192–193, 246, 251–254;
    and slavery, 90; and the Union war
    effort, 90; and the Wade-Davis Bill,
    193–194
Railroads, 41, 52; and the campaign for
    Atlanta, 186–188, 190; at Chattanooga,
    121, 151, 154; and the Confederate war
    effort, 107–108; and Longstreet's move
    to the West, 152–153; and Petersburg,
    181, 183–184; strategic use of by Bragg,
    84
Raleigh Standard, 116
Randall, James G., 162
Randall, James Ryder, 37, 227
Randolph, George W., 111
Ravenel, Marie, 227
Raymond, Henry J., 193, 195–196, 211
Reagan, John H., 30, 111
Reconstruction: and black suffrage, 193; and
    the Louisiana constitution, 246, 252;
    presidential, 192–193, 251–254; Radical,
    192–194; rehearsal for at Port Royal,
    South Carolina, 230; and the
    Republican party platform of 1864, 193;
    and the 10 percent plan, 193; and the
    Wade-Davis Bill, 193–194
Rector, Henry M., 36
Red River campaign, 174–175
Religion: anti-Catholicism, 12, 19; in the
    armies, 49; effort to end slave abuses
    during the war, 229; of former slaves,
    231; impact on southern leaders, 221;
    Irish Catholic immigrants, 10; and the
    northern churches, 212–213; Quakers
    (Society of Friends), 16; and reform
    movements, 3; and slavery, 3; and
    southern churches, 220; and southern
    nationalism, 220; and the United States
    Christian Commission, 207
Republican party, 12–13, 102; control of
    Congress, 191; convention in Baltimore
    in 1864, 193; and Dred Scott decision,
    14; and election of 1854, 11–12; and
    election of 1856, 13; and election of
    1860, 14, 19, 21; and election of 1862,
    99, 191; and election of 1864, 191–193,
    196; and financing the war, 97; friction
    between Lincoln and Radicals, 194;
    northern governors during the war,

Republican party (Continued):
    94; opposition to Lincoln, 191, 194–195;
    and the press, 210; and secession, 26
Reynolds, John, 138
Rhett, Robert Barnwell, 8; and criticisms of
    Davis, 116; as editor of Charleston
    Mercury, 222; and formation of
    Confederacy, 27; and Fort Sumter, 35;
    at Nashville Convention, 22; and
    secession, 22; on strategy, 44
Rhodes, James Ford, 256
Richmond, Kentucky, 84
Richmond, Virginia: battle for, 183–184;
    looting in April 1863, 218; and
    prostitution, 236; social life of, 218,
    224; Union occupation of, 251; wartime
    living conditions, 218
Richmond and Danville Railroad, 183
Richmond campaign, 68–69, 73–74
Richmond Enquirer, 222
Richmond Examiner, 112, 116, 222, 246
Richmond Sentinel, 222
Rich Mountain, battle of, 51
Roanoke Island, 44, 66
Robertson, James I., 48–49
Roche, T. C., 212
Rockefeller, John D., 200
Rodes, Robert E., 139
Roebuck, John A., 170
Root, George F., 209–210
Rose, Willie Lee, 230
Rosecrans, William S., 129, 134; and battle of
    Chickamauga, 151–153; and battle of
    Stone's River, 120–121, 149; and
    Chattanooga campaign, 149–155; at
    Corinth, 86–87; at Iuka, 86; replaces
    Buell in command, 87
Rosser, Thomas L., at Five Forks, 249
Rost, Pierre, 162
Ruffin, Edmund, 19; and Fort Sumter, 33;
    suicide of, 237
Rush-Bagot treaty, 171
Russell, Lord John, 159, 163, 165–167; and
    Confederate ironclads, 168–169
Russell, William Howard, 163
Russia, 159–160; diplomacy with, 166–167;
    visit of fleet to New York City, 201

Sabine Crossroads, battle of, 174
Sanitation, 46–47
Santayana, George, 219
Saul, 220
Sayler's Creek, battle of, 250
Schofield, John M.: and battle of Franklin,
    240; and battle of Nashville, 241; and
    campaign for Atlanta, 186–190; at
    Goldsboro, 248; at Wilmington, North
    Carolina, 244
Schreiner, Hermann L., 227

Scott, Winfield, 8, 32, 69; and the "anaconda plan," 43, 174, 211; author of *Infantry Tactics*, 47; on Lee in Mexican war, 69

Secession: Buchanan's response, 25–26; efforts at compromise, 26; and Nashville Convention, 4, 8; and northern churches, 212; northern response to, 197–198; and the press, 210–211; and southern churches, 220; and southern college professors, 227; and southern women, 234; of states of the lower South, 22–24; of states of the upper South, 35–38

Second Corps, Army of the Potomac, at Gettysburg, 139

Seddon, James A., 111, 129, 133; and western strategy, 133

Sedgwick, John: at Chancellorsville, 123, 126–127; death of, 179; at Marye's Heights, 124, 126; and Spotsylvania Courthouse, 179; and the Wilderness campaign, 177

Seminole Indians, 38

Semmes, Raphael, 167–168

Seven Days' battles, 72–73. *See also* Richmond campaign

Seven Pines, battle of, 69

Seward, Frederick W., 200–201

Seward, William Henry: and the Compromise of 1850, 4, 8; diplomacy of, 162–163, 165, 169, 171; and election of 1860, 19; efforts to remove from cabinet, 191; and the Emancipation Proclamation, 99; and European war plan, 161; and Fort Sumter, 32, 191; and Great Britain, 161; opposition against, 191; peace talks with Lincoln and Stephens, 245; and the Radical Republicans, 191; and raid on St. Albans, Vermont, 171; and secession, 25; as secretary of state, 32, 88–89, 161; seriously wounded, 253; and the *Trent* incident, 164

Seymour, Horatio, 94

Sharpsburg, battle of, *see* Antietam, battle of

Shenandoah Valley campaign: of 1862, 68–70; of 1864, 182–185

Sheridan, Philip H.: at Appomattox Courthouse, 250; and Army of the Potomac, 174; at battle of Cedar Creek, 185; at battle of Fisher's Hill, 185; at battle of Sayler's Creek, 250; at battle of Winchester, 185; at Five Forks, 249; and Lee's attempt to unite with Johnston, 250; at Petersburg, 249; raiding along the Virginia Central Railroad, 181; and the Shenandoah Valley, 185, 247–248; at Spotsylvania Courthouse, 177; and the Wilderness campaign, 180; at Yellow Tavern, 180

Sherman, Thomas W., 66

Sherman, William Tecumseh: and Atlanta campaign, 174, 186–190, 238; and battle of Bentonville, 248; and battles for Chattanooga, 156; and battle of Nashville, 241–242; and capture of Savannah, 242; and Chattanooga campaign, 155–156; at Chickasaw Bluffs, 131; at Columbia, 242, 248; generalship of, 261; at Goldsboro, 248, 249; and Hood's Tennessee campaign, 238, 241, 242; at Jackson, Mississippi, 147; and Joseph E. Johnston's surrender, 254–255; and Kentucky-Tennessee campaign, 57–58; and the march to the sea, 238–240, 242; in North Carolina, 244; as possible Republican presidential nominee in 1864, 195; president of Louisiana State Seminary and Military Academy, 227; respect for Confederate cavalry, 189; in South Carolina, 242; and strategy of pillaging, 219; tactics in Atlanta campaign, 190; terroristic methods in Mississippi, 239; and Vicksburg campaign, 122, 131, 147–148; warfare against civilians, 238–240

Shields, James, 69

Shiloh, battle of, 60–64, 66, 103, 114; press accounts of, 212

Sibley, Henry H., 64

Sickles, Daniel E.: and battle of Gettysburg, 142–143; at Chancellorsville, 123, 125

Sigel, Franz: at New Market, 180; in the Shenandoah Valley, 176, 180; and Wilderness campaign, 176; at Wilson's Creek, 54

Simms, William Gilmore, 223

Sims, Frederick W., 108

Slave Power conspiracy, 10, 15

Slavery, 1; abolition of, 3, 97, 194, 263; anti-slavery groups, 12; attempts to reopen African slave trade, 17; attitudes concerning, 2–3, 9; colonization efforts, 98–99; conduct of slaves during the war, 229–230, 232–233; and Confederate diplomacy, 160; Confederate seizure of free blacks in Pennsylvania, 136; and Confederate war effort, 90, 104, 106, 114–115, 230; destruction of by the war, 228–229; and emancipation, 83, 97–100; escaped slaves and Sherman's army, 240; expansion of, 11, 14; and fugitive slave law, 5, 9, 17; impact on the Confederacy, 39; possible impact of slave rebellion on the Confederacy, 234; proposed enlistment of slaves in Confederate Army, 246–247; relations

Slavery (*Continued*):
between slave and master, 234; and religion, 3, 220; and Second Confiscation Act, 90; and southern women, 236–237; and Thirteenth Amendment, 98; and Union Army, 233; and Union war effort, 89
Slemmer, Adam J., 30
Slidell, John: biographical sketch of, 164; and James Buchanan, 25; as Confederate emissary to France, 164–166, 169–171, 247; and Erlanger loan, 169–170; and *Trent* incident, 164
Slocum, Henry W.: at battle of Bentonville, 248; at Chancellorsville, 123, 125
Smalls, Robert, 233
Smith, Caleb, 32
Smith, Charles H. ("Bill Arp"), 223
Smith, Edmund Kirby: and battle of Richmond, Kentucky, 84; and battle for Vicksburg, 148; and Chattanooga campaign, 84; commander of Trans-Mississippi Department, 149, 174–175, 255; and invasion of Kentucky, 85
Smith, Richard M., 222
Smith, William A., 247
Smith, William F. "Baldy," at Petersburg, 181, 182
Society of Friends, 208
Soldiers: camp life, 46–49, 95, 107, 109; and charity support of, 206, 207; clothing, 106; death rates, 109; desertion, 48; discipline, 48; *The Life of Billy Yank*, 209; *The Life of Johnny Reb*, 209; malnutrition, 95; medicine, 95; pay of, 217; pillaging by, 219; as prisoners of war, 108–109; religion, 49; training, 47; vote in election of 1864, 196
"Somebody's Darling," 227
Sons of Liberty, 91
South: in the American revolution, 261; attitudes toward the Civil War, 38, 66; attitudes about centralized government, 113; austerity measures of, 217–218; and cotton, 2, 162–163; demoralization of, 247; and emancipation, 97–100; folk music of, 226; food supply, 218; hardships faced during the war, 237; impact of the war upon, 215–237; military-mindedness of, 110; and patriotism, 215; population of, 2, 37, 39, 104; pro-Union sentiments within, 116, 259; racial attitudes, 2; reaction to Davis's policies, 116; and reconstruction, 116, 253; resources of, 40–41, 106, 114; response to Lincoln's death, 253; and slavery, 3, 104, 112, 115, 228–234, 236–237. *See also* Confederacy

South Carolina: and secession, 22, 197; Sherman takes Columbia, 242; University of, 227
South Mountain passes, battle of, 80
Southern Avengers, 216
Southern nationalism, 45, 220; versus state rights, 113–114
Southside Railroad, 183–184
Soviet Union, 261
Spence, James, 160
Spinner, Francis, 204
Spotsylvania Courthouse, battle of, 177–180
Springfield rifle, 47–48
St. Albans, Vermont, 171
Stanton, Edwin M.: biographical sketch of, 94; and black soldiers, 100; and Lincoln's death, 253; and McClellan, 76; and reconstruction, 252; and Richmond campaign, 73–74; as secretary of war, 90, 94–95, 213; and Vicksburg campaign, 129
Stanton, Elizabeth Cady, 205
Star of the West, 30
State rights, 45, 46; and Confederate Army, 113; and Confederate war effort, 104, 113, 218, 257; and conscription, 104; and Nashville Convention, 4, 8; in the North, 94; versus southern nationalism, 113–114
Steele, Frederick: at battle of Poison Spring, 175; and Trans-Mississippi campaign, 174
Stephens, Alexander H.: biographical sketch of, 29; opposes conscription, 104; opposes secession, 23; peace efforts of, 116, 117, 245; vice president of the Confederacy, 27, 45
Stephenson, Nathaniel W., 257
Stevens, Thaddeus, 89
Stevenson, Carter L., 156
Still, William N., with Beringer, Hattaway, and Jones, 113, 257
Stoeckl, Edouard de, 159–160
Stone, Charles P., 90
Stone, Lucy, 205
Stone, Sarah Katherine, 224
Stoneman, George, 123
Stone's River, battle of, 120–121
Stowe, Harriet Beecher, 9–10
Strategy, 41–42; of Albert Sidney Johnston, 56, 58; in Atlanta campaign, 189–190; of attrition by Grant, 181; and battles for Chattanooga, 158; and battle of Shiloh, 63; and battle of Stone's River, 121; Beauregard's western strategy, 129; of Braxton Bragg, 84; of Burnside at Fredericksburg, 118; and Chickamauga, 154; of Clausewitz, 40; Confederate, 44, 78, 114; and

Strategy (*Continued*):
  Confederate counteroffensive of 1862, 78; and Confederate strategy in the West, 129, 133; of Davis after Gettysburg, 152; evaluation of Confederate, 260; of Grant as general in chief, 173–175, 190, 242; of Grant in the Wilderness campaign, 179, 181; and guerrilla warfare, 261; of Hooker at Chancellorsville, 123–124; impact of West Point upon, 44; importance of Gettysburg, 158; of Jomini, 45; and Kentucky campaign, 86; of Lee as general in chief, 72, 79, 129, 133–134, 248; of Lee during the Gettysburg campaign, 135–136; of Lee during the Maryland campaign, 80; of Lee in the Wilderness campaign, 179, 181; of Lee to unite with Johnston, 250; of Lincoln after Gettysburg, 152; of Lincoln regarding Lee's army, 173; of Longstreet at Gettysburg, 139; and Maryland campaign, 83; of McClellan, 79; and Mississippi campaign, 87; and Mississippi River, 120; and northern press, 211; of pillaging by Union armies, 219; and railroads, 84, 121, 183–184, 188, 190; and Richmond campaign, 68–69; and Seven Days' battles, 74; of Sherman's march to the sea, 238; strategic situation after Vicksburg, 152; strategic Union victories in 1863, 158; of the Union, 258; in the West, 120
Stratton, Charles S. ("General" Tom Thumb), 201
Stringham, Silas H., 66
Strikes, 206
Strong, George Templeton, 164, 196–198, 209, 214; and Lincoln assassination, 253; and northern press, 211
Stuart, J. E. B.: at battle of Brandy Station, 136; at Chancellorsville, 124–126; criticisms of, 136; death of, 180; at Fredericksburg, 118; and Gettysburg campaign, 136–137, 144–145, 180; and Maryland campaign, 78; and raid on Carlisle, Pennsylvania, 136; and Richmond campaign, 72; at Yellow Tavern, 180
Studebaker, Clement, 199
Suffolk, battle of, 124
Sumner, Charles: as a Radical Republican, 89; speech on Kansas, 13; and *Trent* incident, 164
Sumner, Edwin V.: at Fredericksburg, 119; at Antietam, 80
Supreme Court, U.S., 31; and Dred Scott decision, 14; *ex Parte Milligan*, 93
Sykes, George, 124

Tactics, 40, 42, 44–45, 47; of Albert Sidney Johnston 52, 60; and Atlanta campaign, 188, 190; and battle of Gettysburg, 140; and battle of Stone's River, 121; of Burnside at Fredericksburg, 118; at Chickamauga, 154; at First Bull Run, 52; of Grant at Petersburg, 184; of Grant at Vicksburg, 149; of Grant in the Wilderness campaign, 179; of Henry Halleck, 60; importance of battle of Nashville, 241; Jomini on, 60; of Lee and Jackson at Chancellorsville, 125; of Lee at Gettysburg, 144, 146; of Lee in the Wilderness campaign, 179; Lee's theories of, 75; of Longstreet at Gettysburg, 139, 144; and Maryland campaign, 80; of McClellan at Antietam, 83; of McClellan during the Maryland campaign, 80; of Meade at Gettysburg, 144; and Mississippi campaign, 87; at Perryville, 86; and Richmond campaign, 68; of Rosecrans during the Chattanooga campaign, 149; of Sherman against civilians, 238–239; of Stonewall Jackson, 68–69. *See also* Srategy
Talleyrand, 161
Taney, Roger, 31; and Dred Scott decision, 14; *ex parte Merryman*, 92; and writ of habeas corpus, 92
Tate, Allen, 215
Taylor, Richard: and battle for Port Hudson, 133; driven from Mobile, 244; on McClellan, 55; at Pleasant Hill, 174; at Sabine Crossroads, 174; surrender of at Citronelle, Alabama, 255; and Trans-Mississippi campaign, 174
Taylor, Zachary, 6, 8
Tennessee: and presidential reconstruction, 193; and secession, 36; and support for the Union, 39
Tennessee, C.S.S., 185
"Tenting on the Old Camp Ground," 209
Texas, secession of, 24, 26
Third Union Corps at Gettysburg, 142
Thirteenth Amendment, 98, 205, 246
Thomas, George H.: at battle of Nashville, 241–242; at battle of Peachtree Creek, 189; and battle of Stone's River, 121; and campaign for Atlanta, 186–190; and Chattanooga campaign, 152–156; at Chickamauga, 153–154; and Hood's Tennessee campaign, 238, 240; and Kentucky campaign, 84; at Logan's Crossroads, 58; and Selma campaign, 244
Thomas, Emory, 103, 136, 220
Thompson, Jacob, 25

Thoreau, Henry David, 18
Thornwell, James H., 3
Thouvenel, Edouard, 161
Tom Thumb, "General" (Charles S. Stratton), 201
Tiger Rifles, 216
Tilghman, Lloyd, 58
Times [London], 160, 163, 166, 200
Timrod, Henry, 222; and southern women, 234–235
Tompkins, Sally L., 235
Toombs, Robert: as Confederate secretary of state, 30, 110–111, 162; Confederate military service, 112; and Fort Sumter, 33–34; and suspension of the writ of habeas corpus, 115; urges secession, 23
"Tramp! Tramp! Tramp!," 210
Trans-Mississippi campaign (Confederate), 174–175
Trans-Mississippi Department, 149, 174–175, 255
Tredegar Iron Works, 106
Trenholm, George, 105
Trent incident, 96, 164
Turner's Gap, 80
Tyler, John, 26
Tyler, Nathaniel, 222

Uncle Tom's Cabin, 9
Union: advantages over the Confederacy, 258; diplomacy of, 160–162, 164, 166–169, 171, 258; explanations for victory, 256–262; leadership of, 258; lives lost, 262–263; military leadership of, 257; population of, 39; strategy of, 242, 258, 261. *See also* North
Union Army: administration of, 93–95; and black soldiers, 39, 100, 102, 233; bounties, 93–94; camp life, 46–47, 95, 201; and censorship of the press, 211; command structure of, 173; and commutation, 93; and conscription, 93; and emancipation, 100; enlistments in, 94; Enrollment Act, 93; equipment, 43, 47; and escaped blacks, 230–232; and immigrant recruits, 161; financing of, 95–97; formation of, 35, 42; Grant appointed general in chief, 172; impact of state rights on, 94; *The Life of Billy Yank*, 209; malnutrition, 95; medical care, 95, 207; nurses, 204, 207; officers, 42; organization of, 94–95; and prisoners of war, 108, 109; recruiting policies, 93–94, 198; and religious activities, 207; supplies, 95, 199; in suppression of labor unrest, 206; training, 47; and volunteer and charity organizations, 206–207; in the West, 78

Union Navy, 242–244; and battle of Hampton Roads, 67–68; and battle of Mobile Bay, 185; black sailors, 100; and blockade, 242–244; and seizure of neutral vessels, 169; and Sherman's march to the sea, 242; and *Trent* incident, 96, 164
Union party, 12; and election of 1864, 191, 193
United Daughters of the Confederacy, 108–109, 237
United States Christian Commission, 207
United States Military Academy, impact on strategy and tactics, 44–45
United States Sanitary Commission, 205, 207, 209
Upton, Emory, 179
Vallandigham, Clement L., 92, 195
Van Dorn, Earl, 61; and battle of Corinth, 78, 86–87; in Holly Springs raid, 122; Mississippi campaign, 86

Vance, Zebulon, 116; and public education, 228; and state rights, 114; and Confederate war effort, 114; reelection as governor of North Carolina, 116
Vandiver, Frank E., 106
Vicksburg campaign, 120, 122, 129–133, 147–149, 158, 172, 192
Victoria, Queen of Great Britain, 159, 163
Vietnam, 261
Virginia: and presidential reconstruction, 193; and secession 32, 35, 37, 45; significance to the Confederacy 35, 37
Virginia, C.S.S., 67–68
Virginia Military Institute, 180
Voegeli, V. Jacque, 194

Wade, Benjamin, 89, 193
Wade-Davis Bill, 193–194
Wadley, William, 108
Walker, Leroy P., 30, 46, 111
Wallace, Lew, 63
Warren, Gouverneur K.: and battle of Gettysburg, 142–143; at Globe Tavern, 184; at Spotsylvania Courthouse, 177; and Wilderness campaign, 176–177
Warren, Lavinia, 201
Washington Chronicle, 210
Washington College, 228
Washington Peace Convention, 26
Washington, Booker T., 234
Washington, D.C.: "Hooker's Division," 202; Lincoln's concern for safety of, 68; threatened by Early's campaign, 183; vulnerability of, 37
Washington, William, 225
Walthall, Edward C., 156

Weaponry, 42, 44; cannon, 48; as cause for
    Confederate defeat, 257; Minié balls,
    47, 257; repeating carbines, 244; rifled
    muskets 47–48, 257; and Union
    campaign for Selma, 244. *See also*
    Munitions
Webster, Daniel, 5–6, 8–9
Webster, H. D. L., 227
Weigley, Russell, 95
Weld, Theodore Dwight, 213
Weldon Railroad, 183–184
Welles, Gideon: on reappointment of
    McClellan, 76; as Union secretary of
    the navy, 32
West Point, *see* United States Military
    Academy
West Virginia, 36, 51
Wheeler, Joseph, 219; and battle of Stone's
    River, 121; and campaign for Atlanta,
    190; and Chattanooga campaign, 154,
    155; and guerrilla warfare, 261; and
    Hood's Tennessee campaign, 238
Whig party, 20; binding North and South, 10;
    collapse of, 12; and election of 1852, 8;
    and election of 1854, 12; and election
    of 1856, 13
Whitman, Walt, 207–208
Whittier, John Greenleaf, 208
Wigfall, Louis T., 117, 247
Wilder, John T., 84
Wilderness, battle of, 176–178
Wiley, Bell I., 198, 201, 209, 234; and causes
    of Confederate defeat, 257; and
    southern individualism, 257; views on
    Davis, 260
Wiley, Calvin, 228
Wilkes, Charles, 164
Williams, T. Harry, 44
Wilmington, North Carolina, Union capture
    of, 244
Wilmot Proviso, 4, 6
Wilson, Charles Reagan, 221

Wilson, Henry, 256
Wilson, James H., 244–245
Wilson's Creek, battle of, 54
Winchester, battle of, 185
Wirz, Henry, 108
Wise, Henry A., 44
Women: and the Confederacy, 215, 224,
    234–236; and emancipation, 205;
    fashions during the war, 201; impact
    of the war upon, 204–205, 236–237;
    and northern war effort, 199, 204–205;
    as nurses, 204–205, 235–236; and
    slavery, 236, 237; wartime employment
    opportunites of, 204; and wartime
    prostitution, 201, 236; and womens'
    rights movement, 205
Women's Loyal League, 205
Wood, Fernando, 198
Woodbury, David B., 212
Woodward, C. Vann, 224
Wright, Horatio G., 179
Writ of habeas corpus: in the North, 37,
    91–92, 116, 191, 193, 211; in the South,
    115

Xerxes, 181

Yale University, 213
Yancey, William L., 162; and African slave
    trade, 17; against secrecy in the
    Confederate government, 115; and
    Jefferson Davis, 28; election of 1860,
    20; and formation of the Confederacy,
    27
Yates, Richard, 94
Yeadon, Richard, 222
"Yellow Rose of Texas, The," 226–227
Yellow Tavern, battle of, 180

Zollicoffer, Felix K.: and Kentucky-Tennessee
    campaign, 56; at Logan's Crossroads,
    58

Roland, Charles Pierce, 1918-
   An American Iliad : the story of the
C   Wa   mp   --
Lexington, KY : University Press of
Kentucky, 1991.
   xii, 289 p. : ill., maps : 24 cm.

   1. United States--History--Civil War,
1861-1865.

-1530-910819   VEHAcc   90-38392